PROBLEMS OF A WORLD MONETARY ORDER

PROBLEMS OF A WORLD MONETARY ORDER

Second Edition

GERALD M. MEIER
Professor of International Economics
Stanford University

New York Oxford
OXFORD UNIVERSITY PRESS
1982

Library of Congress Cataloging in Publication Data

Meier, Gerald M.
Problems of a world monetary order.

Includes bibliographies.
1. International finance. 2. Foreign exchange problem. I. Title.
HG3881.M43 1982 332.4′5 81-9447
ISBN 0-19-503010-9 AACR2

Printing (last digit): 9 8 7 6 5 4 3 2 1

Printed in the United States of America

For Andrew

PREFACE

"Mystery," "maze," and "muddle" are the words that most frequently follow "international monetary." These words became current during the early 1970s when the Bretton Woods system was breaking down. They continue to describe the present regime of managed floating exchange rates. And they also apply to efforts for international monetary reform.

This book attempts to remove some of the mystery by involving the reader in three policy situations relating to the attainment of new international monetary arrangements. In an analytical narrative integrated with source materials, the policy problems carry the reader from the Bretton Woods system to an assessment of the recent experience with managed floating and on to an interpretation of prospects for reform —but one hopes, with an illumination of the maze and a removal of the muddle.

The policy problems unfolded here relate to the search for an international monetary order: the design of an international code of conduct at Bretton Woods and the eventual fall of the Bretton Woods system (Problem I), the management of the floating rate regime after Bretton Woods (Problem II), and the continued quest for monetary order through more formal proposals for a reformed international monetary system (Problem III).

These policy problems are not intended to be a record of events, but a means of highlighting fundamental issues that call for understanding through the application of basic principles of international monetary economics. The particular events are significant only as indicators of the wider and longer-term issues that dominate the shape of a world monetary order: the amount and distribution of international liquidity, the adjustment mechanism, confidence in different reserve assets, and the international harmonization of national policies.

This book, the second of three volumes on problems in international political economy, is designed as both a self-contained study of international monetary policy and a bridge connecting the first volume on trade policy with the third volume on development policy.[1] I have written this book with the same purposes in mind that I expressed in the first volume's introductory words to the student:

From a study of the policy problems in this book I want you to appreciate that economics is still concerned with social betterment; that economic problems cannot be solved in a political vacuum; that qualitative appraisals may be as important as quantitative calculations; and that in public policy formulation, the formal economic principle must usually give way at some point to a value judgment.

These problems do not allow a technocratic approach to policy-making. On the contrary, they emphasize that most policy problems have no natural boundaries and that decision-making is an art as well as a science. Long ago, Keynes observed that economics does not constitute a body of knowledge immediately applicable to policy. Notwithstanding all the advances in the "science" of decision-making, few—if any—economists would yet deny Keynes's dictum. And all who have experienced the complexities of actual decision-making in international economic affairs will appreciate that technical analysis must sooner or later yield to judgment—or to the qualities of imagination and intuition which Keynes believed to be as much a part of economics as logic and fact.

A word on organization. This book begins with a general expository introduction on international monetary affairs that recapitulates some basic principles and provides some perspective of the prob-

1 Volume one is *Problems of Trade Policy* (1973); volume three is *Problems of Cooperation for Development* (1974).

lems that follow. The materials for each policy problem are then set forth in a way that I thought would best reveal the development of events and the execution of policy decisions. I have tried to unfold the "biography" of each policy situation by presenting an analytical narrative and a set of source materials so that you might gain a sense of the crucial issues in each situation, the types of international conflict involved, and the modes of resolution and cooperation effected.

To allow you to discover the major policy issues in the problem, I have tried to use to advantage, documents, reports, and other source materials—while providing continuity with a narrative. Some "seasoning" has been added by giving the observations of the actors, observers, or commentators of the time. Finally, I have provided questions designed to aid you in analyzing and evaluating the specific policy decisions.

This method of presenting policy problems is intended to encourage your own thinking about these problems. Although materials are offered to illuminate the particular policy problem, it is up to you to identify and analyze the major issues. And you must be prepared to adopt and defend your own policy position with respect to the problem's resolution. You need not worry about a "correct" answer to the problem, but you should be very much concerned about the quality of the reasoning behind your own answer—about the "why" of your conclusion. Your specific recommendations are not as important as your understanding of the complexity of the policy problem and your clarity on criteria for judging the merits of alternatives. Each problem has two objectives: to extend your capacity to evaluate the quality of public policy-making and to suggest ways of improving the process in international economic affairs.

In considering each problem, you will therefore have to exercise your own judgment on a set of questions: What were the crucial policy issues in the problem? How were they resolved? Would another course of action have been preferable? What do you now conclude about the desirable future course of action?

I am again indebted to my students at Stanford University for enduring early drafts of these problems; their receptivity was most encouraging. I especially appreciate the help from Margaret Garritsen de Vries, Historian of the IMF; Sir Joseph Gold, Senior Consultant and former General Counsel and Director of the Legal Department of the IMF; Werner Dannemann of the IMF's Bureau of Statistics; and Sterie T. Beza of the IMF who have been generous in their answers to my many questions. I alone remain responsible for errors of omission and commission. The librarians at Her Majesty's Public Record Office and the World Bank-International Monetary Fund Joint Library have provided invaluable assistance. Special acknowledgment must be given for the exceptional services of Anne C. M. Salda and Yvonne G. B. Liem of the Joint Library. Their professionalism was exceeded only by their good cheer and encouragement in leading me through the Library's indispensable collection.

Joanne O'Donohue merits my admiration and gratitude for being all that an author could hope for in keeping track of innumerable revisions and in promptly and efficiently producing several typescripts.

Extracts from published works are reprinted by permission, and gratefully acknowledged.

G.M.M.

Stanford
March 1981

CONTENTS

PROBLEMS OF A WORLD MONETARY ORDER

THE CONTEXT
International Financial Conduct

Our subject is the continuing search for an organized world monetary order. How can the standards of international financial conduct be raised? How can international arrangements provide a more adequate system of monetary decision-making? In seeking answers to these questions, we shall encounter international monetary problems that are as fascinating as they are perplexing combining as they do a rich mixture of technical economics, political repercussions, and even the psychology of symbols and beliefs.

We shall note how policy-making in international affairs proceeds beyond the narrow rigor of economic analysis or the quantification of econometric relationships. Beyond the teachings of technical economics, international currency experience is being continually shaped by the evolution of international institutional arrangements, by the extension of international law into national financial affairs, and by multinational negotiations as well as impersonal economic forces. The art of international financial diplomacy combines with economic analysis to shape the process of collective decision-making in international monetary affairs. As we review international monetary history and contemplate future international monetary reform, we shall attempt to discover ways for improving the quality of this policy-making process—both in its policy objectives and its policy instruments.

We shall examine policy problems that span more than one-half century of international monetary change—from 1925 when Britain returned to the gold standard, through the par-value exchange rate system established in 1944 at the Conference at Bretton Woods, New Hampshire (Problem I), to the present managed floating system (Problem II), and proposals for international monetary reform (Problem III).

At the outset, we should draw a distinction between a monetary *system* and a monetary *order*. As expressed by Professor Robert Mundell, "An *order*, as distinct from a system, represents the framework and setting in which the system operates. It is a framework of laws, conventions, regulations, and mores that establish the setting of the system and the understanding of the environment by the participants in it. A monetary order is to a monetary system somewhat like a constitution is to a political or electoral system. We can think of the monetary system as the *modus operandi* of the monetary order."[1]

Twice during the last one-half century, the passing of hegemony from a center-country and the decline in a key currency marked the culmination of a process of international monetary disintegration and a breakdown in world monetary order. In 1931, Britain abandoned the gold standard: overvaluation of the pound sterling coupled with a deep depression brought the downfall of the pound-centered standard. After years of international currency disintegration, nations finally agreed at Bretton Woods to establish the International Monetary Fund (IMF). The Bretton Woods system, together with the economic hegemony of the United States, provided a remarkable degree of monetary order for some 25 years. But 40 years after the fall of the pound, the dollar-centered standard also went into eclipse as the United States announced on August 15, 1971 the suspension of convertibility of the dollar into gold, and the dollar was devalued in 1971 and again in 1973. With the floating of the major currencies in 1973, the par-value system of exchange rates—the very essence of the Bretton Woods system—ended. The suspension of par-value

1 Robert Mundell, "The Future of the International Financial System" in A.L.K. Acheson et al., *Bretton Woods Revisited* (1972), p. 92.

obligations and the diffusion of economic and political power away from the United States toward the European Community, Japan, and the Organization of the Petroleum Exporting Countries (OPEC), raise questions about exchange-rate policy, as well as concern about more effective remedial policies for adjustment to balance-of-payments problems and attention to what should be the amount and distribution of international liquidity.

These issues run throughout our policy Problems. A similar set of issues concerned participants at Bretton Woods. Of the establishment of the IMF at Bretton Woods, it has been said that "it is difficult even for those familiar with the International Monetary Fund as a working organization to realize what a remarkable achievement its creation was. It came into being as a result of a supreme act of faith—the decision to surrender to an untried and imperfectly visualized international body the supervision of one of the most cherished attributes of national sovereignty, the right to change the rate of exchange. That this surrender was hedged round with safeguards is not surprising; that it was made at all and was accompanied by vesting in the same body an appreciable fraction of the member's international reserves, can be explained only by the coincidence of the hour and the men."[2]

If the task at Bretton Woods was to achieve world monetary order, so too is it now. The comparisons of "the hour and the men" within the institutional environment of recent years and against recent technical developments in analytical economics should be of interest in assessing the progress toward international monetary reform since the Bretton Woods system collapsed.

1. MULTIPLE POLICY OBJECTIVES

The reduction of trade barriers is a frequently avowed policy target for most countries; even more vigorously, national governments affirm their belief in economic expansion—a satisfactory rate of growth in rich countries and the acceleration of development in poor countries. Attainment of these objectives is, however, strongly conditioned by the type of international monetary system that exists. The design of the international monetary system is more than a matter

2 J. Keith Horsefield, *The International Money Fund 1945–1965*, Vol. I (1965), p. 3.

of instituting a technical mechanism: it necessarily involves policy choices that take international monetary affairs into the political arena, affecting the distribution of benefits and costs among nations and often requiring the resolution of conflicting interests.

Since the end of World War II, the overriding international economic policy question for most nations has been whether they can attain simultaneously the multiple objectives of high levels of employment, price stability, economic growth, trade liberalization, and balance-of-payments equilibrium. To the extent that these objectives may be incompatible, some policy trade-offs are necessary. In their efforts to achieve full employment, countries have often moved away from trade liberalization by resorting to import restrictions or to controls on capital movements. Even though international trade theory would label the advocacy of trade restrictions in order to promote full employment as a "nonargument" or as a "third, fourth, or *n*th best" policy measure,[3] governmental policies have in reality often had this neomercantilistic character. The pursuit of full employment also can entail balance-of-payments disequilibrium: as a country undertakes domestic expansion to achieve full employment, its imports may increase or its exports may fall so much that a deficit arises in the country's international payments balance. Some trade-off must then occur between full employment and balance-of-payments equilibrium or between full employment and trade liberalization. Finally, if a balance-of-payments deficit arises, the country will likely attempt to remedy the situation either by undertaking measures that restrict employment and contract income, in order to reduce imports and stimulate exports, or by imposing trade restrictions or controls over capital movements.

When confronted by these policy conflicts, most governments have allowed the objective of full employment to dominate national economic policy even at the cost of a retreat from trade liberalization or pressure on the balance of payments. The central challenge to the operation of an international monetary system, therefore, is how to allow nations to pursue their domestic economic objectives with-

3 Economists refer to the theory of the "second best" as a guide to policy norms. See R. G. Lipsey and K. Lancaster, "The General Theory of Second Best," *Review of Economic Studies*, Vol. 24 (1965), pp. 11 ff. The objective of the "second best" is to minimize costs of market intervention and to avoid an excess burden when the "first best" is unattainable (because it is impossible to have optimum conditions in every sector of the economy).

out having to forgo the gains from trade or to suffer balance-of-payments disequilibrium.

The Bretton Woods conference anticipated these problems. It was believed that establishment of the IMF would allow nations to give primacy to their domestic employment policies over balance-of-payments adjustment. The belief that national policies for full employment could be given priority rested on three assumptions of the Bretton Woods system: first, that the IMF would be a source of international liquidity in sufficient amount to allow a deficit country adequate time for the adjustment of its balance of payments without having to resort to deflationary measures or trade restrictions; second, that although exchange rates were to remain fixed in the short run, they would have some flexibility in the long run as the Fund would approve an alteration of exchange rates when a country experiences "fundamental disequilibrium"; third, that deficit countries would not have to bear the sole responsibility for reequilibrating their balance of payments, since surplus countries would share the responsibility. If a surplus country adopted no remedial action and its currency remained in short supply on foreign exchange markets, then the IMFs "scarce currency" clause allowing discriminatory controls against the "scarce currency" could become operative.

In the late 1960s and early 1970s, the major assumptions of the Bretton Woods system were severely tested. For a perspective on this challenge, we should recognize that any international monetary system can be analyzed in terms of three essential functions: the determination of exchange rates, the adjustment process to a disturbance in the balance of payments, and the provision of international liquidity. Interpretative analysis of these functions is involved in all the Policy Problems in this book. Taken together, these problems relate to the political economy of shaping a new international monetary order.

We shall see that international monetary arrangements are the outcome of history, multinational negotiation, and market forces. The history of money shows a long evolution from commodity money toward the increasing use of credit money. A central issue in international monetary reform is how far this trend can now be extended internationally. Even though it may have economic logic, many would contend that a further extension of international credit money is still politically premature. In the past, negotiations among nations have also resulted in the establishment of such international monetary institutions as the IMF, or more recently, swap arrangements among central banks and the inclusion of Special Drawing Rights in the IMF in accordance with the Rio agreement of 1967.

The impact of market forces on the international monetary system has recently been reflected in the extension of multinational corporations, the increased flow of capital internationally, and the emergence in the later 1960s of the Eurocurrency market. Although the structure or framework of an international monetary system may be determined through the deliberations of finance ministers, central bankers, and economists, the details of international monetary events will depend on the behavior of private actors—as well as public actors—on international commodity and capital markets.

2. THE NEED FOR REMEDIAL POLICY

Under any international monetary system, the most important issues involve decisions about the need for remedial action and the character of this corrective action. For although the accounting of the balance of payments is such that the balance of payments always balances,[4] this does not mean that there is no deficit or surplus in the balance of payments that requires remedial policy.

The crucial consideration is how the balance of payments is brought into balance: What are the "balancing" or "settlement" items? And do they portend the need for remedial policy? If we exclude some transactions—namely, those that act as "settlement" transactions—then the balance of the remaining "ordinary" transactions can be in deficit or surplus. If we refer to "ordinary" or "autonomous" transactions as being "above the line," and consider the "settlement" or "induced" items as being "below the line," then we want to focus on those items below the line that accomplish the financing of any deficit in the ordinary items above the line. Where the line is drawn depends on evaluation of the need for remedial policy—and this is a matter of judgment. Because judgments on a

4 In balance-of-payments accounting there is always an identical equality between credits and debits, insofar as credit items that result from receipts from sales of goods, claims or gold and foreign exchange must be matched by debit items that result from payments for purchases of goods, claims, or gold and foreign exchange. For details of balance-of-payments accounting, see Gerald M. Meier, *International Economics: Theory of Policy* (1980), Chap. 5.

country's need for corrective policies may differ, so too may the interpretations of what is the deficit in the country's balance of payments. In this sense, it has been said that a "balance of payments deficit cannot be measured, it can only be analyzed."[5]

Under the gold exchange standard of the Bretton Woods system (to be explained in Problem I), the changes in gold reserves acted as a balancing item. Monetary gold flow would therefore be placed below the line, and a gold outflow would indicate the size of the deficit or the negative balance above the line. When we consider capital items, however, there can be different interpretations of which capital transactions should be placed above the line and which should be regarded as settlement items below the line. A short-term capital inflow is equivalent to an increase in liabilities to foreigners or a decrease in claims on foreigners. A short-term capital inflow into the United States, for example, is composed of an increase in deposits held by foreigners in American banks, an increase in foreign holdings of United States short-term securities (such as Treasury bills), and a decrease in American-owned deposits in foreign banks. If the increase in liabilities is to foreign official monetary authorities, it is placed below the line. But should an inflow of foreign short-term private capital also be treated as a settlement item in the United States balance of payments in the same way as a gold outflow or inflow of official short-term capital? Or should it be treated as an "autonomous" transaction, primarily in response to market forces, and placed above the line? Analysis of these capital flows will be highly significant in the Problems presented.

Depending on how the question of the foreigner's motivation for holding short-term dollar assets is answered, the private short-term capital inflow can be considered as speculative balances so that the private holdings can switch into the official holdings or, instead, as working balances for ordinary transaction purposes. Accordingly, depending upon whether analysis places foreign private short-term capital above or below the line, there will be different measurements of the balance-of-payments position.

One measure has been the "balance of official reserve transactions." According to this measure, the United States is in deficit if there is an inflow of official short-term capital (an increase in liabili-

5 See C. P. Kindleberger, "Measuring Equilibrium in the Balance of Payments," *Journal of Political Economy* (November–December 1969), p. 873.

ties to foreign monetary authorities), a loss of monetary gold (a decline in an American reserve asset), or an increase in the United States net indebtedness position in the IMF.

Another measure has been the "net liquidity balance." This incorporates the change in reserves plus the net flow of liquid short-term capital. The net liquidity balance exceeds the official reserve transactions balance when there is a net inflow of liquid short-term capital.

Utilizing the official reserve transactions concept, we may say that a country has a balance-of-payments deficit if its reserve assets are declining and/or if the claims of foreign monetary authorities on the country are rising. To the extent that this deficit cannot be continued indefinitely, but must be corrected, we may conclude that the country is suffering from balance-of-payments disequilibrium. There is pressure on the balance of payments, and unless the deficit country can have unlimited access to sources of international liquidity, the country will sooner or later have to undertake some remedial policy measures to re-equilibrate its balance of payments.

It is, of course, equally correct to say that equilibrium in a country's balance of payments is the absence of a surplus as well as absence of a deficit. A country has a balance-of-payments surplus, according to the official reserve transactions concept, if its reserve assets are increasing and/or if the claims of foreign monetary authorities on the country are decreasing. Although the balance of payments of the surplus country is technically in disequilibrium, the surplus country is not compelled to take corrective action—as the deficit country must do eventually. As is often stressed in the Problems, it is desirable that the surplus country also take corrective action along with the deficit country. Whereas competitive devaluations by deficit countries handicapped the adjustment mechanism during the 1930s, the competitive nonrevaluations of surplus countries handicapped the adjustment mechanism during the 1960s and the 1970s (see Problems I and II). From the standpoint of facilitating the adjustment mechanism, it is desirable that the surplus country take appropriate action that complements—rather than competes with—action by the deficit country.

Given a situation of disequilibrium in its balance of payments, a government must institute some remedial policy if it cannot look forward to having an actual deficit in its balance of payments supported through "accommodating" capital imports and depletion of its gold and exchange reserves, or if it is unwilling to sacrifice other policy objectives and endure unemployment or impose direct controls on trade or capital movements in order to avoid a deficit. By what means can balance-of-payments equilibrium then be restored? How rapidly? And with what repercussions to the domestic economy? These questions dominate the Policy Problems below.[6]

The type of remedial policy a country will *want* to adopt will depend upon its interpretation of the sources of its balance-of-payments problem and on its other domestic objectives. The country will want to seek the least costly mechanism of adjusting its balance of payments, without sacrificing domestic economic autonomy. It will also be evident that the policy a country *can* adopt will depend upon the type of international monetary system that exists and the code of international economic conduct that the world monetary order imposes.

3. TYPES OF INTERNATIONAL MONETARY SYSTEMS

At various times, the world economy has been on a gold-bullion standard, an inconvertible paper standard, and a gold-exchange and reserve-currency system. Under the gold-bullion standard, as it existed in the pre-1914 period and from 1925 to the early 1930s, the exchange rates were fixed and the international reserve asset was gold. Under a paper standard, as it existed in the interwar period, the exchange rates were freely floating and the need for reserves was removed, unless the monetary authorities wanted to intervene to hold the exchange rate fluctuations within limits. Under the gold-exchange and reserve-currency standard, as established in the postwar period with the institution of the IMF, and until President Nixon's New Economic Policy of August 15, 1971, exchange rates were fixed, but subject to adjustment under conditions of "fundamental disequilibrium," and reserves consisted of a substitute for gold in the form of drawing rights at the IMF. (Details of this will be examined in Problem I.)

6 For the theory of balance-of-payments policy, see Meier, *International Economics: Theory of Policy* (1980), Chaps. 6–10. Here we concentrate on the empirical, institutional, and applied aspects of balance-of-payments policy. But a background knowledge of the theoretical principles of balance-of-payments policy will make our discussion more meaningful.

Under the various international monetary systems, the sources and amount of international liquidity differ and so does the degree to which the balance of payments exercises discipline on a country. The more it is desired that an international imbalance should exercise discipline on a country's domestic policies, the less access the country should have to international liquidity. The less the country's access to liquidity, the more it must resort either to internal measures to remove its balance-of-payments problem or to external measures. Through a tight monetary policy and budgetary surplus, the internal measures entail deflation if the country is in deficit; to this extent the country loses domestic autonomy over its full employment policies. The external measures constitute the imposition of restrictions on trade and capital movements or a depreciation of the currency; to this extent, the country diminishes its gains from trade or incurs the costs of depreciation.

The internal measures can be viewed as "expenditure-reducing" policies that reduce national income and hence the domestic demand for resources. Since the "absorption" of goods and services is equivalent to the aggregate demand generated by consumption, investment, and government expenditures, the absorption approach to the adjustment mechanism emphasizes disabsorption or expenditure reduction to lower the domestic demand for tradable commodities in order to improve the country's balance of payments position.[7]

The external measures can be viewed as "expenditure-switching" policies. A devaluation or depreciation of the country's currency will raise the price of tradable commodities relative to the price of non-traded domestic goods and, thereby, cause a switch in the pattern of expenditure and production. The allocation of home resources will switch out of the production of non-tradables to the production of tradables. And the pattern of expenditure will switch away from tradables, to non-tradables. Based on these price effects in the mechanism of adjustment, one type of analysis of devaluation or depreciation is the elasticities approach.[8]

Another approach to the adjustment mechanism is the monetarist. In the monetary approach, money is a stock for which the optimal level is related to current output. The actual level can be ad-

7 For an analysis of the absorption approach, see *Ibid.*, Chap. 7.
8 For an analysis of the elasticities approach, see *Ibid.*, Chap. 6.

justed through balance-of-payments surpluses or deficits. If the actual stock of money is not equal to the desired stock, the stock disequilibrium will be removed through reserve flows in the balance of payments. Remedial policies must therefore concentrate on the change in domestic credit creation relative to the demand for money.[9]

With floating exchange rates, it has become common to adopt an asset-market approach to the exchange rate. This focuses more broadly on changes in asset portfolios as the proximate cause of exchange-rate variations in the short run. The capital flows associated with international trade in financial assets can be a part of the adjustment process, as well as a source of pressure on the exchange rate.

If a country has access to sufficient international liquidity it may be able to eschew both internal and external measures and simply cover its imbalance by drawing upon its international reserve assets. Access to sufficient official international liquidity would allow the country to sustain its level of national expenditure: there would be no need for expenditure-reducing or expenditure-switching policies. Resort to international liquidity would be expenditure sustaining, and the balance of payments would exercise no discipline over domestic policies.

The range of policy instruments available to a country that is seeking to adjust its balance of payments can now be summarized by referring to the following Figure 1. The three vertices of the triangle in Figure 1 depict the exclusive use of each of the three broad policy approaches in coping with international imbalances. If a country has to remove a balance-of-payments deficit, it must now select some set of policies within the triangle. The country need not proceed to one vertex or rely exclusively on one type of measure. But the feasible area of the triangle within which the country can operate will be bounded by certain constraints on the country's policy choices.[10] A country will want to retain a certain degree of domestic autonomy in its policy-making and may therefore refuse to endure "internal measures" beyond the boundary line $C'F'$. It may also be

9 For an analysis of the monetary approach, see *Ibid.*, Chap. 8.

10 The following analysis is adopted from R. N. Cooper, "The Relevance of International Liquidity to Developed Countries," *American Economic Review*, LVIII (May 1968), p. 627; Meier, *International Economics: Theory of Policy* (1980), Chap. 10.

Figure 1 The Feasible Policy-Space for Coping with International Imbalance

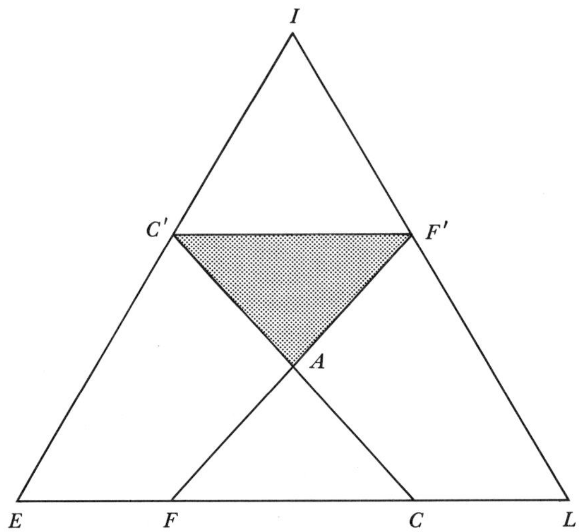

I: Internal measures (expenditure-reducing policies).
E: External measures (expenditure-switching policies).
L: International official liquidity (expenditure-sustaining policies).
EL: Size of *ex ante* deficit.

Shaded triangle represents boundaries of the feasible policy-space. At *A, EF* of the deficit is financed by international liquidity, *LC* of the deficit is removed by external measures, *FC* of the deficit is removed by internal measures.

unwilling to resort to "external measures" beyond the boundary line *CC′*. And the country's access to international official liquidity confines it to the area left of the boundary *FF′*. The shaded area therefore represents the boundaries of the feasible policy-space. These boundaries will be determined by the nature of the international monetary system and the state of the domestic economy.

Suppose that the country selects within the policy-space (the shaded area in Figure 1) a particular policy position at *A*. If the triangle is an equilateral triangle, the size of the *ex ante* deficit will be denoted by the length of a side of the triangle. The deficit is *EL*. Of this total deficit, the portion *CL* is removed by external measures (expenditure-switching policies). Another portion of the deficit, represented by *EF*, is financed by international liquidity. The remaining portion *FC* is removed by internal measures (expenditure-reducing policies).

The shaded policy-space contrasts with policies under the pure gold standard, which operated at the vertex of "internal measures." Or with an international paper standard, which would operate at the vertex of "external measures." Or with the international payments policies pursued during the 1930s and World War II, when countries again relied on "external measures" that controlled imports and capital flows. With the establishment of the IMF and the reliance on reserve currencies for additional liquidity after World War II, the area representing effective policy-making was able to move from the external measures vertex closer to the center of the triangle.

Now the essential question is whether the feasible area of policy-making provides sufficient scope for the adjustment process to operate without requiring a country to remove its balance-of-payments deficit by sacrificing its domestic stability or its gains from trade. Can a government achieve both internal balance and external balance without imposing trade restrictions? The crucial issues confronting the international monetary system are whether the system requires fundamental modification so as to create more liquidity and allow the deficit country to move to the right of the boundary *FF'*, whether the country will be forced to give up more domestic autonomy and endure policies beyond *C'F'*, whether the country will retreat farther from the objective of trade liberalization and undertake policies to the left of *CC'*, or whether the country will not intervene in the exchange market and let its currency depreciate.

4. POLITICAL ECONOMY OF MONETARY REFORM

Beyond their own importance, changes in the international monetary system can also be studied as instructive examples of international economic policy-making. How is an economic theory translated into policy? What is the quality of policy-making? How should nations behave toward each other in international economic affairs?

Answers to these questions call for a return to the older tradition of political economy—to an economics of statecraft that would insist that economics be relevant for policy and that would recognize that the political element combines with economic thought in shaping economic policy.[11]

Proceeding within the tradition of political economy, John Maynard Keynes became the economist who exericsed the most influence on policy in this century—in both national and international economic affairs, as we shall note in Problem I. To Keynes, policy-making was not a pure science; most important were practicality and the scope for implementing a policy. And Keynes emphasized that an apparatus of thought was not identical with an apparatus of action. "Economists," Keynes insisted, "have to try to be very careful to distinguish the two."[12]

But Keynes was also the rationalist. As one reviewer of Keynes' work states, "His whole life was a constant campaign, in his eyes, against "madmen in authority", "lunatics" (a very common word in his vocabulary) and others who acted according to prejudices and rules of thumb rather than reason carefully applied to an evolving situation—whether in making peace treaties, commercial policy proposals, exchange rate decisions or mundane administrative decisions. . . .

"Keynes always believed that "a little clear thinking" or "more lucidity" could solve almost any problem. Throughout his life, he used every means available to encourage it. . . .

"In his attempts at persuasion, Keynes had great faith in rationality. He believed that individuals, both inside and outside, could appreciate the appropriateness of a line of policy. Proper persuasion could wear down prejudice and open previously unexploited areas of choice."[13]

To Keynes, the specifications of a first-class economist were that "He must be purposeful and disinterested in a simultaneous mood; as aloof and incorruptible as an artist yet sometimes as near the earth as a politician."[14]

Keynes believed that "economics is essentially a moral science and not a natural science . . . it employs introspection and judgments of value. . . ."[15]

11 For incisive analyses of the politicization of international economic issues, see Fred Hirsch et al., *Alternatives to Monetary Disorder* (1977); C. Fred Bergsten and Lawrence B. Krause (eds.), *World Politics and International Economics* (1975).
12 D. E. Moggridge (ed.), *Keynes: Aspects of the Man and His Work* (1974), p. 59.
13 *Ibid.*, pp. 65–66.
14 J. M. Keynes, *Essays in Biography* (1933), p. 174.
15 *Collected Writings of John Maynard Keynes*, vol. XIV (1973), pp. 297, 300.

This broad view of economics comes through in Keynes' architecture of a new international organization for managing international monetary affairs after World War II. The organization that eventually emerged from his draft proposal—the IMF—is unique in the history of international political economy. Perhaps no economic measure has been the subject of so much study and negotiation as was the institution of the IMF. For the first one-quarter century of its existence, the IMF deserves to be considered among the most successful multilateral accords ever made.

Nothing less than the modern development of an effective public international law of money stems from the Articles of Agreement of the IMF. As the leading legal authority on the Fund states, "The adoption of these rules is a remarkable development in international relations because it represents massive agreement on the introduction of the rule of law into an area in which previously the discretion of states to act as they wished was almost wholly unlimited. Although this is an immense advance, and although the rules that have been adopted are of the greatest intrinsic importance, the rules are relatively few. They are perhaps only the first great move toward the development of international law in this field. Many of the plans and ideas for the modification or reform of the international monetary system that continue to be debated can be regarded from one aspect as projects to extend the scope of this branch of international law."[16]

In propounding a code of international financial conduct, the IMF has been unprecedented. Its legislative history is a tribute to rationality. But the operation of the Fund has not been without a political element. As a former Managing Director of the Fund, Pierre-Paul Schweitzer, states

> What we call the international monetary system is of course the monetary relationships between those countries which have accepted multinational obligations and responsibilities, which means in fact the members of the International Monetary Fund.
>
> The problems involved are of course of a highly political nature. The balance of payments and exchange rates affect the whole economic and social life of a country. The domestic policies which have to be pursued in order to achieve certain objectives are at the core

16 Joseph Gold, *The International Monetary Fund and International Law*, IMF Pamphlet Series No. 4 (1965), pp. 10–11.

> of each country's political life, and I might add that in my experience there is no field where governments at present attach so much importance to sovereignty as the monetary field, be it only because of its economic and social repercussions. In my opinion, it is easier to belong to NATO and to fulfil one's obligations to NATO than to belong to the IMF and fulfil one's obligations to the IMF, because it affects people much more directly.
>
> Therefore the question is: How can the Fund exercise its jurisdictional and regulatory powers and decide about access to its resources—which is sometimes quite important—without running into insuperable political difficulties? On the other hand, how can countries co-operate within and with the Fund without feeling that they have to give up too many of their sovereign rights?[17]

No matter by how much the development of economics has advanced in technical analysis since Keynes promulgated his draft proposal, any modification of the international monetary system to meet changing needs will still require the settlement of political issues for each of its essential components.

If by "politics" is meant the process by which conflicting visions of a common purpose are agitated or settled, then politics will enter into the determination of exchange rates, the provision of international liquidity, and the adjustment process. These issues have become a matter of "high politics," no longer simply relegated to the silent level of technically soluble "low politics." Determination of exchange rates involves controversial matters of national prestige and political appearance. Devaluation of one's own currency has never held any political attraction; to the contrary, it has frequently meant the fall of the government or the removal of at least the finance minister. The possibility of several currencies pegging to one currency, for example, the dollar bloc, or a common exchange-rate policy for a regime, such as the European Economic Community, or the formation of an optimum currency area—all these regimes of exchange rate determination are intertwined with political implications in allowing, or denying, different countries various policy options and in bestowing different degrees of economic power to various countries.

Questions involving the sources and amount of liquidity may be

17 Pierre-Paul Schweitzer, "Political Aspects of Managing the International Monetary System," *International Affairs* (April 1976), p. 208.

even more political, especially because they raise some new issues with no negotiating precedents. If gold is to be replaced by credit international reserve money, who is to authorize the amount of increase in the credit money? And who is to determine its distribution? The advantage of being able to create international reserve money as "negotiated" reserves may at the same time be offset by the disadvantages involved in the politicization of the process of creating reserves through multilateral negotiation instead of having nations rely simply on their "owned" reserves (such as the nation's own gold stock). If liquidity were now increased, would not countries be able to escape unduly from balance-of-payments discipline? And would not the increase in liquidity impart too great an inflationary bias to the world economy? These reservations were once raised by the United States at the Bretton Woods conference, and other countries raise them again today. The explication of "unduly" and "too great," as expressed in these reservations, is as much a matter of political judgment and social values as economic analysis.

Again, recognizing that the access to an infinite supply of liquidity or the operation of a perfect adjustment mechanism would be perfect policy substitutes for meeting a payments imbalance, we can say that the major task of the international monetary system is to determine the degree of control over this policy trade-off. In doing this, there are bound to be different national positions. In general, surplus countries will seek to minimize liquidity and force deficit countries to adjust. Deficit countries, in contrast, will seek to maximize liquidity and force surplus countries to initiate the adjustment mechanism.

The initiation of the adjustment process may depend not only on the amount and distribution of liquidity, but also on the rules of conduct that can be imposed on countries in deficit or surplus. International coordination is required to ease the adjustment process. The fact of ever-greater international economic interdependence, with the resultant spillover effects of one country's policies on another, also requires evermore coordination of policies. And yet, nations continue to want domestic economic autonomy in the choice of their policies. At what point can national interest be made to be seen as coinciding with the collective interest, and thereby have nations become dependent on multilateral decision-making? It is now a political economy issue of the first order to coordinate policy formation and avoid the competition in policy-making that has plagued international monetary policy in recent years as countries sought to avoid the burdens of the process of adjustment to payments imbalances.

The question of the "appropriate" division of the burden of adjustment among different countries remains as much political as economic. By what criteria are the costs of international adjustment to be distributed? Should the adjustment be through flexibility in exchange rates; restrictive domestic measures in the deficit country; or by some means that compel the surplus country or give it the incentive, to restore equilibrium in its balance of payments? Depending on how these questions are answered, the costs of balance-of-payments adjustment will appear in different countries in varying degrees through the effects of currency depreciation or appreciation, deflation or inflation, trade restrictions or liberalization.

These political economy issues enter into the major themes that proceed through all the Policy Problems in this book. One theme is the need for policy-makers to operate in the realm of international financial crisis management at the same time as they try to achieve longer-run, more fundamental reformation of the international monetary system. A second theme is the way the benefits and costs of different international monetary arrangements are perceived by the policy-makers of different countries, and how through international financial diplomacy, or market operation, or simply ad hoc or de facto action there does result a certain distribution of these benefits and costs. A third theme is how to reconcile nationalist politics and the desire for autonomy in domestic economic policy-making with international economic forces that are making the world economy evermore integrated in real economic terms. Finally, a fourth theme considers what features of a world monetary order must be politicized and what features can be relegated to technical solutions.

Problem I

THE BRETTON WOODS SYSTEM
Designing a Code of Conduct

"What is past is prologue." Some brief monetary history should illuminate current international monetary issues and place the future of international monetary reform in perspective. We should realize how the international monetary disorder of the interwar period shaped the Bretton Woods Conference at the end of World War II and how the central issues considered at Bretton Woods have again come to the fore since the collapse of the Bretton Woods system in 1973.

As in the past, international economic cooperation is still sought to resolve issues of exchange rates, international liquidity, and balance-of-payments adjustment. Should exchange rates be fixed or flexible? If exchange rates float, should intervention by a government's Monetary Authority be allowed? Under what conditions? Should efforts concentrate on the stabilization of the key currencies, such as the dollar, Deutsche mark, and yen? How should the amount of official liquidity be determined? And how should it be distributed among nations? Does the task of adjustment to balance-of-payments disequilibria fall on deficit countries alone? Or should surplus countries also share in the adjustment process? And by what means should adjustment be attained? Are the answers to these questions to be determined by a deliberately planned reform of the system or by an evolutionary approach to monetary reform? Lessons from the past should be instructive as the search for world monetary order again seeks answers to these central questions.

1. INTERWAR MONETARY DISORDER

Before the interwar disorder set in, the pure gold standard (or gold-bullion standard) had given stability to international monetary relations from 1878 to World War I. Each currency was convertible into gold at fixed parities (the national Monetary Authority stood ready to buy and sell gold at a fixed price). Par values were thereby established for each currency, and the exchange rates could not vary beyond the very small range of the gold points (to cover changes by governments and the cost of shipping gold as means of international payment). Each country had a fixed gold value for its currency, and the exchange rates were thus also fixed. For example, \$4.86: £1 was the "mint parity" rate for 35 years before 1914.

1.1 The Decision to Return to Gold

Having placed an embargo on the export of gold during World War I, countries deliberated after the war whether to return to the rules of the gold standard. The central debate occurred in Britain—whether to return to gold at all, and if so, whether it should be at the pre-1914 parity or at a lower exchange rate for the pound. Considering the issue in 1918, the Cunliffe Committee readily concluded that "there was no difference of opinion among the witnesses who appeared before us as to the vital importance of these matters" and that the overriding aim of British economic policy in the postwar period should be to return to the gold standard at the prewar parity.[1]

The virtues of the gold standard had two functions: "to correct unfavorable exchanges and check undue expansion of credit." If Britain's balance of trade went into deficit, it would lose gold reserves. This loss of reserves would then result in a contraction of the money supply and a rise in the Bank of England's bank rate to retain and attract foreign funds. The tight money policy would lead to a

1 *First Interim Report of the Committee on Currency* as reprinted in T. E. Gregory (ed.), *Select Statutes, Documents & Reports Relating to British Banking, 1832–1928* (1929).

decline in investment activity, a release of goods from inventories, and a decline in the domestic price level. The deflation would stimulate Britain's exports and reduce its imports, thereby adjusting the balance of trade. The adjustment mechanism was pictured as automatic and painless, involving quickly adjusting movements in interest rates and prices. The Committee did not recognize that prices might be rigid and inflexible, that there could be foreign repercussions, and above all that monetary deflation would have effects not only on prices, but also on levels of employment and income. Nowhere was it admitted that the automatism of the system—the elimination of the scope for discretionary policies—which the Committee proclaimed as the gold standard's greatest virtue was at the expense of jobs and income.

A return to the pre-war parity also dominated the outlook of the British Treasury and the Bank of England. As Governor of the Bank of England, Montagu Norman was a leading exponent of a return to the gold standard at the prewar rate. "He preferred the discipline of an international gold standard to the exhortation of—or to—Chancellors, as security for a policy which respected the country's external needs."[2]

John Maynard Keynes emerged, however, as a major critic of the official current of economic thought in Britain. Questioning the operation of the gold standard and fearing that the "discipline" of an international gold standard would force Britain to sacrifice the level of employment and standard of living for the sake of maintaining a fixed exchange rate, Keynes thought it folly to return to the prewar gold standard. In his *Tract on Monetary Reform* (1923), Keynes had already posed the choice before British policy-makers in the years ahead as being between deflation and devaluation; between giving priority to stabilization of the internal price level and concentrating on maintenance of the external value of the pound. Given that inflation had left Britain with a higher price level than other major countries, Keynes argued that if Britain were to return to the gold standard it would have to do so at a lower rate than the prewar parity, or else it would have to deflate in order to return to the prewar value. He did not suggest, however, that Britain should return to gold at a lower parity. As a student of the period summarizes Keynes' position:[3]

2 Henry Clay, *Lord Norman*, London (1957), pp. 158, 171.
3 Donald Winch, *Economics and Policy, A Historical Study* (1969), pp. 80–81.

> His main heresy was confined to giving an unorthodox answer to the question: should the aim of monetary policy be the stabilisation of the domestic price level or the stability of the exchange rate? This question merged with another: should an attempt be made to restore the gold standard or should some alternative system be found? While recognising the importance of stable exchanges to a nation reliant on foreign trade, he came down firmly on the side of stabilising the internal purchasing power of currencies where the two aims were in conflict. His final reason for rejecting the policy of a return to the gold standard was that under post-war conditions it would be difficult to achieve domestic stability. His chief contention was that the value of gold itself was no longer the impersonal outcome of a number of independent factors; rather it was subject to the policy decisions of a small number of Central Banks, and to the views of the largest gold-holder, the United States, in particular. There was no question, therefore, of a return to the supposed automatism of the prewar gold standard. The only question at issue was whether there would be sufficient co-operation between Central Banks, and wisdom on the part of the American Federal Reserve Board, to make the workings of the new "managed" gold standard tolerable.
>
> Since Keynes was sceptical on both counts he went on to suggest an alternative to gold. He proposed that the Bank of England should use its control of the monetary mechanism to maintain stability of the domestic price level and employment rather than fix its attention on the sterling-dollar exchange. If the Federal Reserve Board did likewise a firm basis for future co-operation could be established.

The decision whether to return to gold at the prewar parity was ultimately to be made by Winston Churchill as Chancellor of the Exchequer. In 1925, Churchill sided with the dominant official view, and ignoring Keynes' arguments, Churchill announced in his first budget the decision to return to the gold standard at the prewar rate of £1 = $4.86. It was a decision with far-ranging consequences, still debated. Eventually Churchill himself came to believe that the decision was the greatest mistake of his life. But at the time, he was convinced of the realism of his decision. And he maintained that he had been convinced that it was the right decision by the experts at the Bank of England and the Treasury, whose opinions "count more than the clever arguments of academic theorists."[4]

4 *House of Commons Debates*, May 4, 1925, c. 670.

In his speech on the Gold Standard Bill, Churchill put forward what was the core of the case in favor of the change: "We are often told that the gold standard will shackle us to the United States. I will deal with that in a moment. I will tell you what it will shackle us to. It will shackle us to reality. For good or ill, it will shackle us to reality."[5]

After the decision, Keynes' criticism was keen. In a pamphlet entitled *The Economic Consequences of Mr. Churchill,* Keynes explained Churchill's error thus: "Partly, perhaps, because he has no instinctive judgment to prevent him from making mistakes; partly, because, lacking the instinctive judgment, he was defeated by the clamorous voice of conventional finance; and most of all, because he was gravely misled by his experts."[6]

Keynes went on to contend that the decision entailed an overvaluation of sterling vis-à-vis the dollar by 10 to 12 per cent, and that Churchill was thereby committing himself to forcing down money wages and prices, without any idea how it was to be done. In Keynes' words,

> Mr. Churchill asked the Treasury Committee on the Currency to advise him on these matters. He declared in his Budget speech that their Report "contains a reasoned marshalling of the arguments which have convinced His Majesty's Government." Their arguments—if their vague and jejune meditations can be called such—are there for anyone to read. What they ought to have said, but did not say, can be expressed as follows:
>
> "Money-wages, the cost of living, and the prices which we are asking for our exports have not adjusted themselves to the improvement in the exchange, which the expectation of your restoring the Gold Standard, in accordance with your repeated declarations, has already brought about. They are about 10 per cent too high. If, therefore, you fix the exchange at this gold parity, you must either gamble on a rise in gold prices abroad, which will induce foreigners to pay a higher gold price for our exports, or you are committing yourself to a policy of forcing down money wages and the cost of living to the necessary extent.
>
> "We must warn you that this latter policy is not easy. It is certain to involve unemployment and industrial disputes. If, as some people think, real wages were already too high a year ago, that is all

5 Robert Rhodes James, *Churchill: A Study in Failure 1900–1939* (1970), p. 176.
6 John Maynard Keynes, *The Economic Consequences of Mr. Churchill* (1925), p. 10.

the worse, because the amount of the necessary wage reductions in terms of money will be all the greater.

"The gamble on a rise in gold prices abroad may quite likely succeed. But it is by no means certain, and you must be prepared for the other contingency. If you think that the advantages of the Gold Standard are so significant and so urgent that you are prepared to risk great unpopularity and to take stern administrative action in order to secure them, the course of events will probably be as follows.

"To begin with, there will be great depression in the export industries. This, in itself, will be helpful, since it will produce an atmosphere favourable to the reduction of wages. The cost of living will fall somewhat. This will be helpful too, because it will give you a good argument in favour of reducing wages. Nevertheless, the cost of living will not fall sufficiently and, consequently, the export industries will not be able to reduce their prices sufficiently, until wages have fallen in the sheltered industries. Now, wages will not fall in the sheltered industries, merely because there is unemployment in the unsheltered industries. Therefore, you will have to see to it that there is unemployment in the sheltered industries also. The way to do this will be by credit restriction. By means of the restriction of credit by the Bank of England, you can deliberately intensify unemployment to any required degree, until wages *do* fall. When the process is complete the cost of living will have fallen too; and we shall then be, with luck, just where we were before we started.

"We ought to warn you, though perhaps this is going a little outside our proper sphere, that it will not be safe politically to admit that you are intensifying unemployment deliberately in order to reduce wages. Thus you will have to ascribe what is happening to every conceivable cause except the true one. We estimate that about two years may elapse before it will be safe for you to utter in public one single word of truth. By that time you will either be out of office, or the adjustment, somehow or other, will have been carried through."[7]

The Commonwealth followed Britain's return at the prewar parity, and most European nations were also back on the gold standard in the late 1920s. From 1927 to 1931, a brief period of exchange stability emerged, though there was continual pressure on Britain's

7 *Ibid.*, pp. 12–13.

exchange rate. With the Great Depression in the early 1930s, the gold standard was to be abandoned as only a fair-weather craft.

1.2 Abandonment of the Gold Standard

By the dictates of the gold standard, a deficit country had to deflate when it lost gold reserves in settlement of its international deficit. This meant a deflation not only in prices, but also in income through a loss of output and creation of unemployment. The deflation would have to occur regardless of the domestic state of the economy: even though there was already domestic imbalance—less than full employment—the discipline of the balance of payments would nonetheless require a deficit country to remove its deficit by creating even more unemployment in the course of adopting a tight money policy to deflate the economy. Not surprisingly, the gold standard could not maintain its discipline during the Great Depression. With an overvalued pound and high labor unit costs, Britain had already suffered since 1925 a greater degree of unemployment than other countries. The orthodox medicine required a policy of reducing wages and prices. But it was extremely difficult to accomplish this. Instead of flexible wages, the government encountered a General Strike in 1926, sparked by the attempt to drive down miners' wages.

By 1931, when Britain's current account was heavily in deficit, when the unemployment rate was already 12 per cent, when the holdings by foreigners of British Treasury Bills exceeded Britain's stock of gold, and when bank accounts were being converted into gold and withdrawn from London—when so much pressure was being placed on reserves and the exchange rate, the British chose to suspend gold payments and allowed the pound to depreciate relatively to other currencies. Instead of suffering additional unemployment for the sake of maintaining £1 = $4.86, Britain abandoned the gold standard. The freedom to pursue full employment policies became more compelling than the maintenance of fixed exchange rates. The Bank of England therefore no longer entered the foreign exchange market to maintain the exchange rate; the pound was allowed to float and find its own level against other currencies; and in the brief period between September and December 1931, the pound depreciated by 30 per cent relative to the dollar. Following

Britain, the rest of the British Empire, nearly all of Europe, most of South America, and Japan were forced off gold.

An attempt to restore fixed exchange rates came to nought at the World Monetary and Economic Conference held in London during the summer of 1933. Although France was the major proponent of a general and immediate return to the gold standard, President Roosevelt refused to give the dollar a fixed price in terms of gold in case it would make American exports less competitive. The conference broke up in disorder.

The next year (1934) the United States chose to stop converting the dollar into gold for private individuals, and the Treasury devalued the dollar against gold by 60 per cent by raising the buying and selling price from $20.67 to $35.00 per ounce of gold. There the dollar price of gold was to remain until the Nixon shock of August 15, 1971.

One country after another left the gold standard during the deepening depression of the 1930s. By 1936, France and a few other countries constituting the gold bloc were forced to abandon gold. The international financial system collapsed. Countries resorted to direct controls over the use of foreign exchange, to trade restrictions, and to multiple exchange rates (different rates for different categories of international transactions by country and type of transaction). Competitive depreciations ensued as each country tried to offset the competitive gain of another country's depreciation by "cheapening" its currency in relation to others in order to make its exports cheaper in terms of foreign currency.

To stem this disintegration, there was one other attempt at intergovernmental cooperation in 1936 in the form of a Tripartite Agreement between France, Britain, and the United States. The objective of this Agreement was to reduce fluctuations in the sterling-franc-dollar exchange rates by having each country agree to support each other's currencies so long as the currency purchased was repurchased with gold at the end of each trading day. The Tripartite Agreement operated in only a halting fashion from 1936 to 1938.

Summarizing what went wrong in international monetary affairs during the interwar period, one commentator lists the following main features—features that were also to reappear in more recent years:

1. The initial parity imbalance

In 1925, when sterling returned to the gold standard the pound was—for prestige reasons—overvalued against the dollar by around 10 per cent. The French franc was undervalued by about the same amount.

2. Failure to adjust

(*a*) Britain—the overvaluation was realized, but it was thought that it would be possible to get British costs, including wages, down by the necessary amount. The General Strike of 1926 proved this idea wrong.

(*b*) France—the undervaluation resulted in an inflow of gold. But instead of allowing this to increase the credit base, and so push up French costs, this gold was 'sterilized' and hoarded.

3. The dependence on short-term money

In order to maintain the position of sterling Britain was forced to rely on hot money inflows. This money was attracted by holding interest rates in London above those in New York. This worked against the economic needs of both the UK and the US. Britain needed low interest rates to stimulate production; the US high ones to help curb the Wall Street boom. Worse, the hot money on which Britain was depending was to depart rapidly in 1931 forcing sterling to leave the gold standard.

4. The rise of protectionism

Countries, including Britain, resorted to import controls and tariffs to try to reduce imports and so stimulate home production.

5. Export promotion

The other method by which countries tried to stimulate home production was by increasing exports (a mutually defeating process when set against (4) above). This was done in two main ways: by currency manipulation (i.e. competitive devaluations and multiple exchange rates) and by export subsidies.

6. Currency blocs

The rise of protectionism led to the creation of currency blocs (for example, the sterling area).

7. CURRENCY FLUCTUATIONS

The system of floating rates adopted by many countries (after they were forced off gold) made international trade increasingly difficult.

8. FALL IN RESERVE ASSETS

The fact that currencies like sterling were no longer acceptable to the same extent in international trade reduced the volume of assets available. Thus countries were forced to depend even more on gold.[8]

In the midst of this period of international financial disarray, Keynes wrote his classic *General Theory of Employment Interest and Money*—emphasizing the policy objective of full employment. Keynes claimed that the goal of domestic economic stability could be attained by domestic fiscal policy and monetary policy without resorting to the exportation of unemployment through beggar-my-neighbor trade policies or foreign exchange policies. Full employment was to come during the wartime economies of 1939–45. But the need to reconstruct the international monetary system persisted. How could national governments be assured freedom to enjoy domestic economic autonomy in their full employment policies after the war, without beggar-my-neighbor disharmony? How could countries pursue domestic policies for internal balance without sacrificing the gains from trade by having to impose trade restrictions or without suffering external imbalance in international payments?

These questions were very much in mind when President Roosevelt invited delegates from 44 member countries of the United Nations to "a quiet meeting place" at the Mount Washington Hotel in Bretton Woods to devise international arrangements that it was hoped would avoid the monetary problems encountered before the war.

Document 1

UNITED NATIONS MONETARY AND FINANCIAL CONFERENCE

Mount Washington Hotel, Bretton Woods, New Hampshire

8 William M. Clarke and George Pulay, *The World's Money*, 2nd ed. (1972), pp. 116–17.

General Information

Bretton Woods.

Bretton Woods, New Hampshire consists solely of the Mount Washington Hotel and its appendages. The hotel community is surrounded by the scenic White Mountain National Forest, which covers nearly one million acres and is dominated by Mount Washington, highest peak of the Presidential Range.

Hotel Rates.

By special arrangement with the Mount Washington Hotel, persons participating in the Conference in any official capacity will be charged a flat rate of $11.00 per day, American plan (meals included). Persons assigned to superior accommodations will be obliged to pay a surcharge. The eleven-dollar rate applies to double-occupancy rooms with bath or single rooms without bath. Persons occupying single rooms with bath will be charged fifteen dollars or eighteen dollars per day, in accordance with the nature of the accommodations. Ten percent of the daily charge will be added by the hotel to cover gratuities to hotel personnel.

Offices.

Space limitations require that the number of rooms devoted to offices be strictly limited. A flat rate of ten dollars per day will be charged for all rooms furnished as offices situated on the first, second, third, and fourth floors where, it is anticipated, the offices of the delegations will be concentrated. Offices will be furnished with executive desks, stenographic desks or tables, and appropriate chairs.

Recreation.

Participants in the Conference will be permitted the gratuitous use of the tennis courts, swimming pool, and motion picture theater. Other facilities, such as the golf course, riding horses, et cetera, will be available at customary rates.

Religious Services.

An Episcopal Church is located on the hotel grounds, within easy walking distance of the hotel. A Roman Catholic Church is located at Fabyan, a distance of approximately one mile.

Special Transportation to Bretton Woods.

Separate notices are being issued with regard to special arrangements for transportation to the seat of the Conference.

The month after the Allies established the second front on the Normandy beachhead in 1944, the Bretton Woods conference opened. After three weeks of negotiation, and some 600 documents later, the 730 delegates at Bretton Woods had agreed to the creation of the International Monetary Fund and the International Bank for Reconstruction and Development. By the end of 1945, a sufficient number of governments had ratified the Articles of each institution, and in 1946, the first meetings of the IMF and IBRD (now World Bank) were held.

2. NEGOTIATIONS AT BRETTON WOODS

Preparation for the Bretton Woods Conference began as early as 1941 when Keynes circulated his first *Proposals for an International Clearing Union*—a blueprint for a postwar international monetary institution that would resemble an international central bank for national central banks. A redraft in 1942 entitled "The International Clearing Union (Not Utopia, but Europia)" was "to be passed on to the Americans," but was first circulated for criticisms in Whitehall and among a few British economists.[9] The draft called for the establishment of an International Clearing Union, "based on international bank-money, called (let us say) bancor, fixed (but not unalterably) in terms of gold and accepted as equivalent of gold by the members of the Union for the purpose of settling international balances."

After reading Keynes' draft, Oxford's Roy Harrod wrote the Second Secretary of the Treasury: "a really great document worthy of the occasion." And Cambridge's Dennis Robertson wrote Keynes that he had "sat up last night reading your revised 'proposals' with great excitement—and a growing hope that the spirit of Burke and Adam Smith is on earth again to prevent the affairs of a Great Empire from being settled by the little minds of a gang of bank clerks."[10]

At Bretton Woods, two plans dominated the negotiations—the British plan for an International Clearing Union, presented by Keynes, and the American plan for an International Stabilization

9 Quotations in this paragraph are from Lord Keynes' Personal Files, Class T 247, Her Majesty's Public Record Office.

10 Donald Moggridge (ed.), *The Collected Writings of John Maynard Keynes,* vol. XXV (1980), p. 67.

Fund, presented by Harry Dexter White of the United States Treasury.[11] A brief consideration of the objectives of the two plans may provide a useful background to the provisions that were actually included in the Bretton Woods agreement for an International Monetary Fund.

2.1 The Keynes Plan

As early as 1941, Keynes was considering postwar currency policy. His first proposal for an International Clearing Union was prefaced with the following summary of the lessons of history.

> So far from currency laissez-faire having promoted the international division of labour, which is the avowed goal of laissez-faire, it has been a fruitful source of all those clumsy hindrances to trade which suffering communities have devised in their perplexity as being better than nothing in protecting them from the intolerable burdens flowing from currency disorders. Until quite recently, nearly all departures from international laissez-faire have tackled the symptoms instead of the cause.
>
> International currency laissez-faire was breaking down rapidly before the war. During the war it has disappeared completely. This complete break with the past offers us an opportunity. Things are possible to-day which would have been impossible if they involved the prior disestablishment of a settled system.
>
> Moreover in the interval between the wars the world explored

11 Lord Keynes has been the subject of numerous studies: R. F. Harrod, *The Life of John Maynard Keynes* (1951); Milo Keynes (ed.), *Essays on John Maynard Keynes* (1975); D. E. Moggridge, *Keynes* (1976); Elizabeth S. Johnson and Harry G. Johnson, *The Shadow of Keynes* (1978).

Harry Dexter White was also a fascinating and perplexing individual. He received his A.B. and A.M. degrees in economics from Stanford University and his Ph.D. from Harvard where he won the Wells Prize for his dissertation on *The French International Accounts, 1880–1913.* He was Director of the Division of Monetary Research in the United States Treasury and Assistant to the Secretary of the Treasury before Bretton Woods. In 1946, President Truman appointed White to be the first United States Executive Director for the IMF. He resigned in May 1947. In July 1948, Elizabeth Bentley, an ex-Communist courier for Soviet intelligence in the United States, testified before the House of Representatives Committee on Un-American Activities that White had been involved in espionage. White appeared before the House Subcommittee on Un-American Activities and denied the allegations under oath. Three days later White died of a heart attack.

A member of the House Subcommittee was Richard Nixon, who, by his Presidential action in 1971, was to hasten the end of the Bretton Woods system. See Nathan I. White, *Harry Dexter White—Loyal American* (1956); David Rees, *Harry Dexter White: A Study in Paradox* (1973); Herbert Packer, *Ex-Communist Witnesses* (1962).

in rapid succession almost, as it were, in an intensive laboratory experiment all the alternative false approaches to the solution—

(i) the idea that a freely fluctuating exchange would discover for itself a position of equilibrium;

(ii) liberal credit and loan arrangements between the creditor and the debtor countries flowing from the mere fact of an unbalanced creditor–debtor position, on the false analogy of superficially similar nineteenth-century transactions between old-established and newly-developing countries where the loans were self-liquidating because they themselves created new sources of payment;

(iii) the theory that the unlimited free flow of gold would automatically bring about adjustments of price-levels and activity in the recipient country which would reverse the pressure;

(iv) the use of deflation, and still worse of competitive deflations, to force an adjustment of wage- and price-levels which would force or attract trade into new channels;

(v) the use of deliberate exchange depreciation, and still worse of competitive exchange depreciations, to attain the same object;

(vi) the erection of tariffs, preferences, subsidies *et hoc genus omne* to restore the balance of international commerce by restriction and discrimination.[12]

Keynes believed that something new was needed to avoid the mistakes of the past. Accordingly, he proposed an International Clearing Union with features of a super central bank.

PROPOSALS FOR AN INTERNATIONAL CLEARING UNION*

PREFACE

In preparing these proposals care has been taken to regard certain conditions, which the groundwork of an international economic system to be set up after the war should satisfy, if it is to prove durable:

(i) There should be the least possible interference with internal national policies, and the plan should not wander from the international *terrain*. Since such policies may have important repercussions on international relations, they cannot be left out of account.

*Reprinted in J. Keith Horsefield (ed.), *The International Monetary Fund 1945–1965*, vol. III: *Documents* (1969), pp. 19–22. This is the April 1943 draft of the Keynes Plan (Cmd. 6437).

12 Moggridge (ed.), *The Collected Works of John Maynard Keynes*, vol. XXV (1980), pp. 22–23.

Nevertheless in the realm of internal policy the authority of the Governing Board of the proposed Institution should be limited to recommendations, or at the most to imposing conditions for the more extended enjoyment of the facilities which the Institution offers.

(ii) The technique of the plan must be capable of application, irrespective of the type and principle of government and economic policy existing in the prospective member States.

(iii) The management of the Institution must be genuinely international without preponderant power of veto or enforcement to any country or group; and the rights and privileges of the smaller countries must be safeguarded.

(iv) Some qualification of the right to act at pleasure is required by any agreement or treaty between nations. But in order that such arrangements may be fully voluntary so long as they last and terminable when they have become irksome, provision must be made for voiding the obligation at due notice. If many member States were to take advantage of this, the plan would have broken down. But if they are free to escape from its provisions if necessary they may be the more willing to go on accepting them.

(v) The plan must operate not only to the general advantage but also to the individual advantage of each of the participants, and must not require a special economic or financial sacrifice from certain countries. No participant must be asked to do or offer anything which is not to his own true long-term interest.

It must be emphasised that it is not for the Clearing Union to assume the burden of long term lending which is the proper task of some other institution. It is also necessary for it to have means of restraining improvident borrowers. But the Clearing Union must also seek to discourage creditor countries from leaving unused large liquid balances which ought to be devoted to some positive purpose. For excessive credit balances necessarily create excessive debit balances for some other party. In recognising that the creditor as well as the debtor may be responsible for a want of balance, the proposed institution would be breaking new ground.

1. The Objects of the Plan

About the primary objects of an improved system of International Currency there is, to-day, a wide measure of agreement:—

We need an instrument of international currency having general acceptability between nations, so that blocked balances and bilateral clearings are unnecessary; that is to say, an instrument of currency used by each nation in its transactions with other nations, operating through whatever national organ, such as a Treasury or a Central Bank, is most appropriate, private individuals, businesses and banks other than Central Banks, each continuing to use their own national currency as heretofore.

We need an orderly and agreed method of determining the relative exchange values of national currency units, so that unilateral action and competitive exchange depreciations are prevented.

We need a *quantum* of international currency, which is neither determined in an unpredictable and irrelevant manner as, for example, by the technical progress of the gold industry, nor subject to large variations depending on the gold reserve policies of individual countries; but is governed by the actual current requirements of world commerce, and is also capable of deliberate expansion and contraction to offset deflationary and inflationary tendencies in effective world demand.

We need a system possessed of an internal stabilising mechanism, by which pressure is exercised on any country whose balance of payments with the rest of the world is departing from equilibrium *in either direction*, so as to prevent movements which must create for its neighbours an equal but opposite want of balance.

We need an agreed plan for starting off every country after the war with a stock of reserves appropriate to its importance in world commerce, so that without due anxiety it can set its house in order during the transitional period to full peace-time conditions.

We need a central institution, of a purely technical and non-political character, to aid and support other international institutions concerned with the planning and regulation of the world's economic life.

More generally, we need a means of reassurance to a troubled world, by which any country whose own affairs are conducted with due prudence is relieved of anxiety for causes which are not of its own making, concerning its ability to meet its international liabilities; and which will, therefore, make unnecessary those methods of restriction and discrimination which countries have adopted hitherto, not on their merits, but as measures of self-protection from disruptive outside forces.

There is also a growing measure of agreement about the general character of any solution of the problem likely to be successful. The particular proposals set forth below lay no claim to originality. They are an attempt to reduce to practical shape certain general ideas belonging to the contemporary climate of economic opinion, which have been given publicity in recent months by writers of several different nationalities. It is difficult to see how any plan can be successful which does not use these general ideas, which are born of the spirit of the age. The actual details put forward below are offered, with no dogmatic intention, as the basis of discussion for criticism and improvement. For we cannot make progress without embodying the general underlying idea in a frame of actual working, which will bring out the practical and political difficulties to be faced and met if the breath of life is to inform it.

In one respect this particular plan will be found to be more ambitious and yet, at the same time, perhaps more workable than some of the variant versions of the same basic idea, in that it is fully international, being based on one general agreement and not on a multiplicity of bilateral arrangements. Doubtless proposals might be made by which bilateral arrangements could be fitted together so as to obtain some of the advantages of a multilateral scheme. But there will be many difficulties attendant on such adjustments. It may be doubted whether a comprehensive scheme will ever in fact be worked out, unless it can come into existence through a single act of creation made possible by the unity of purpose and energy of hope for better things to come, springing from the victory of the United Nations, when they have attained it, over immediate evil. That these proposals are ambitious is claimed therefore to be not a drawback but an advantage.

The proposal is to establish a Currency Union, here designated an *International Clearing Union*, based on international bank-money, called (let us say) *bancor*, fixed (but not unalterably) in terms of gold and accepted as the equivalent of gold by the British Commonwealth and the United States and all the other members of the Union for the purpose of settling international balances. The Central Banks of all member States (and also of non-members) would keep accounts with the International Clearing Union through which they would be entitled to settle their exchange balances with one another at their par value as defined in terms of bancor. Countries having a favourable balance of payments with the rest of the world as a whole would find themselves in possession of a credit account with the Clearing Union, and those having an unfavourable balance would have a debit account. Measures would be necessary (see below) to prevent the piling up of credit and debit balances without limit, and the system would have failed in the long run if it did not possess sufficient capacity for self-equilibrium to secure this.

The idea underlying such a Union is simple, namely, to generalise the essential principle of banking as it is exhibited within any closed system. This principle is the necessary equality of credits and debits. If no credits can be removed outside the clearing system, but only transferred within it, the Union can never be in any difficulty as regards the honouring of cheques drawn upon it. It can make what advances it wishes to any of its members with the assurance that the proceeds can only be transferred to the clearing account of another member. Its sole task is to see to it that its members keep the rules and that the advances made to each of them are prudent and advisable for the Union as a whole.

2.2 The White Plan

About the same time as Keynes began drafting his proposal, so too did White. In July 1942, Keynes was shown a copy of an American Memo for Post-War Currency Arrangements—the "Harry White Scheme." Keynes' notes on the "Harry White Scheme" contain the following criticisms:

White's Stabilization Fund is not close to the Clearing Union.

White's Stabilization Fund makes no attempt to use the banking principles.

Only helps the countries which already have a gold reserve. "To him that has it is given." No adequate provision is offered for what happens when the resources provided, which in some cases would be exceedingly moderate, have been used up.

The volume of international currency is not adjusted to need, but dependent on the volume of gold mining and policy of those countries which already have large gold reserves.

It is reported that President (Roosevelt) wants a genuine international currency. President would like to call his version of bancor Demos or, perhaps, Victor. No one apparently has suggested Pluto.[13]

The provisions of the White Plan differed from the Keynes Plan on three major points. First, the United States opposed the larger amount of liquidity that would have been provided by the Clearing Union on the ground that it was unnecessary and had potentially unmanageable inflationary effects. A typical reaction was that of the

13 Lord Keynes' Personal Files T 247/123, OF 272/120; Her Majesty's Public Record Office.

National City Bank's *Monthly Economic Letter* of July 1944 which objected that the Keynes Plan "is likely to serve more as a means of credit expansion than of stabilization—in other words, an application of the principle of deficit-financing translated from the domestic to the international scene."[14] (It is interesting to compare how much liquidity would have been created by the Clearing Union with the amount that was subsequently actually provided by the United States in the form of Marshall Aid to Western Europe, foreign aid to developing nations, and the deficit in the United States balance of payments). Instead of Keynes' bancor, the White plan proposed that the Stabilization Fund should operate with the smaller amount of $5 billion in gold and national currencies contributed by member countries, not in bancor that could be created.

Second, the United States did not welcome the possibility of as much flexibility in exchange rates as the Clearing Union envisaged. Instead of flexible rates within a 5 per cent of parity as proposed by Keynes, the Stabilization Fund proposed that rates be fixed by the Fund and changed only with the consent of 80 per cent of the voting power. The third difference was with respect to exerting pressure on a creditor country. The United States wished to limit the liability of the United States as potentially the largest creditor in the postwar world, and the Stabilization Fund had no provision comparable to the payment of interest by a surplus country as in the Clearing Union.

The objectives of the White Plan are outlined in the following excerpt.

PROPOSAL FOR AN INTERNATIONAL STABILIZATION FUND*

The International Stabilization Fund of the United and Associated Nations is proposed as a permanent institution for international monetary cooperation. The resources of this Fund would be available under adequate safeguards to maintain currency stability, while giving member countries time to correct maladjustments in their balance of payments without resorting to extreme measures destructive of international prosperity. The resources of the Fund

*Preliminary Draft Outline, July 10, 1943. Reprinted in J. Keith Horsefield (ed.), *The International Monetary Fund*, vol. III: *Documents* (1969), pp. 85–86.

14 For other objections of this character, see John Blum, *The Morgenthau Diaries*, vol. III (1967), Chap. V.

would not be used to prolong a basically unbalanced international position. On the contrary, the Fund would be influential in inducing countries to pursue policies making for an orderly return to equilibrium.

The Fund would deal only with member governments and their fiscal agents, and would not intrude in the customary channels for conducting international commerce and finance. The Fund is intended to provide supplemental facilities for the successful functioning of the established foreign exchange institutions and to free international commerce from harmful restrictions.

The success of the Fund must ultimately depend upon the willingness of nations to act together on their common problems. International monetary cooperation should not be regarded as a matter of generosity. All countries have a vital interest in the maintenance of international monetary stability, and in the balanced growth of multilateral international trade.

The United Nations and the countries associated with them recognize, as declared in the Atlantic Charter, the need for the fullest cooperation among nations with the object of securing economic advancement and rising standards of living for all. They believe that attainment of these objectives will be facilitated by international monetary cooperation. Therefore, it is proposed that there be established an International Stabilization Fund with the following purposes:

To help stabilize the foreign exchange rates of the currencies of the United Nations and the countries associated with them.

To shorten the periods and lessen the degree of disequilibrium in the international balance of payments of member countries.

To help create conditions under which the smooth flow of foreign trade and of productive capital among the member countries will be fostered.

To facilitate the effective utilization of the blocked foreign balances accumulating in some countries as a consequence of the war situation.

To reduce the use of such foreign exchange restrictions, bilateral clearing arrangements, multiple currency devices, and discriminatory foreign exchange practices as hamper world trade and the international flow of productive capital.

2.3 Establishment of the IMF

After a series of mutual consultations and redrafts of the Keynes and White plans before the Bretton Woods Conference, and after the extensive discussions at the Conference, there was finally approval of the Articles of Agreement for the International Monetary Fund—an institution closer to White's plan than to Keynes'.

The Articles of Agreement stated the purposes of the IMF.

ARTICLES OF AGREEMENT*

ARTICLE I. PURPOSES

The purposes of the International Monetary Fund are:

To promote international monetary cooperation through a permanent institution which provides the machinery for consultation and collaboration on international monetary problems.

To facilitate the expansion and balanced growth of international trade, and to contribute thereby to the promotion and maintenance of high levels of employment and real income and to the development of the productive resources of all members as primary objectives of economic policy:

To promote exchange stability, to maintain orderly exchange arrangements among members, and to avoid competitive exchange depreciation.

To assist in the establishment of a multilateral system of payments in respect of current transactions between members and in the elimination of foreign exchange restrictions which hamper the growth of world trade.

To give confidence to members by making the Fund's resources available to them under adequate safeguards, thus providing them with opportunity to correct maladjustments in their balance of payments without resorting to measures destructive of national or international prosperity.

In accordance with the above, to shorten the duration and lessen the degree of disequilibrium in the international balances of payments of members.

The Fund shall be guided in all its decisions by the purposes set forth in this Article.

The accomplishments at the Bretton Woods conference can be interpreted in terms of the uneasy triangle of how to allow nations to pursue their domestic economic goals without being required to forgo the gains from trade liberalization or to suffer the costs of cor-

*For the Articles of Agreement, as established at Bretton Woods, see Horsefield (ed.), *The International Monetary Fund,* vol. III: *Documents* (1969), pp. 185 ff.

recting balance-of-payments disequilibrium. In the interests of their pledge to full employment, nations would no longer tolerate—as under the pure gold standard—deflation as a means of removing a balance-of-payments deficit. Nor did they want to endure again successive rounds of competitive currency depreciations. To provide domestic autonomy for the pursuit of full employment, there must be the possibility of drawing upon sources of international liquidity other than the limited amount of gold reserves. To avoid the extremes of a freely fluctuating exchange rate, or a fixed exchange rate, there must be initially some fixity of exchange rates, as determined by the IMF, but subsequently some provision for adjustments in the value of a country's currency.

To achieve these objectives, the Fund established a detailed code of international monetary conduct based on four fundamental principles.

First, a country's foreign exchange rate is a matter of international concern; a par value system should be the subject of international scrutiny and endorsement. All member countries of the Fund must establish par values for their currencies, expressed in terms of gold or of the United States dollar of specified gold content, and may not change them without consultation with the Fund. [See Article IV below.] Exchange rates should therefore be fixed (ignoring permitted fluctuations within 1 per cent of either side of the fixed parities). To maintain the stability of its exchange rate, the official monetary authority of a member country should act as the residual buyer or seller on foreign exchange markets, intervening in the market as necessary to keep the currency from rising or falling. The exchange rate may be subject to periodic change—the "adjustable peg" feature of the Fund—but this variation in the exchange rate is allowed by the Fund only to correct a "fundamental disequilibrium" in the member's balance of payments.

The second basic principle of the IMF is that exchange controls on current international payments should be prohibited, except temporarily under certain extraordinary conditions. [Article VIII (2) (a).] Members were also prohibited from engaging in "any discriminatory currency arrangements or multiple currency practices." [Article VIII (3).] There was also the obligation to convert at par balances of a member's currency held by another member. [Article VIII (4).] A country's currency would be "convertible" when it complied with these Article VIII obligations that were designed to establish a system of stable and unitary exchange rates.

Third, national gold and currency reserves must be augmented so that countries need not be forced to meet short-run, balance-of-payments deficits by suffering domestic deflation and unemployment. This should be in the form of prescribed "drawing rights" by a member country on its "quota" at the Fund. [See Article III below.] A member's subscription to the Fund is equal to its quota. The financial resources subscribed to the Fund constitute an international reserve pool of currencies against which members can draw for short-term financial assistance. A member's right to purchase other currencies from the Fund with its own currency is subject to complex rules [Article V]. A member has "drawing rights" up to 125 per cent of its quota, divided into five equal *tranches*. Only the first tranche—originally called the "gold tranche" and now the "reserve tranche"—can be drawn upon automatically and unconditionally to achieve international liquidity. Beyond the reserve tranche, discretionary factors enter into the Fund's decision on whether the member country can exercise its drawing rights and under what conditions. A drawing country must repurchase its own currency from the Fund within three to five years by payment to the Fund in the foreign currency previously acquired or in any other currency acceptable to the Fund. Outstanding drawings are subject to interest charges that increase with the number of credit tranches used and with the time for which the drawing has been outstanding. This temporary access to the Fund's financial resources offers only short-term financing to help ease the adjustment process for short-term, balance-of-payments problems. For "fundamental disequilibrium," a term left undefined in the Articles, the adjustable peg comes into force.

Finally, the IMF adopted the principle that a balance-of-payments disequilibrium is necessarily two sided between deficit and surplus countries; the adjustment obligations are therefore the joint responsibility of both surplus and deficit countries. In recognition of this principle, the Agreement permits the Fund to declare that a particular currency suffers from a "general scarcity" [Article VII]. If this "scarce currency" clause is invoked against a country that runs a large and persistent surplus in its balance of payments, members may impose a temporary limitation on exchange of the scarce currency and can practice discriminatory exchange restrictions against it.

A deficit country is still expected to undertake remedial measures to correct a "fundamental disequilibrium" in its balance of payments. These measures should go beyond the temporary use of the secondary reserves provided by the Fund and fall short of alteration of its exchange rate. Pending the adoption of measures to restore equilibrium in its balance of payments, a deficit country has recourse to the international pool of currencies held by the Fund. But the system does not grant a member country immunity from the "discipline of the balance of payments." A member's access to the Fund's resources is contingent upon the member's undertaking some process of adjustment. Balance-of-payments discipline will ultimately be exercised, though a country may gain some "breathing time" by using its drawing rights at the Fund.

It is illuminating to recall Keynes' report to the British Parliament, explaining the nature and scope of the Fund.

THE INTERNATIONAL MONETARY FUND*

My Lords, it is almost exactly a year since the proposals for a Clearing Union were discussed in your Lordships' House. I hope to persuade your Lordships that the year has not been ill-spent. There were, it is true, certain features of elegance, clarity, and logic in the Clearing Union plan which have disappeared. And this, by me at least, is to be much regretted. As a result, however, there is no longer any need for a new-fangled international monetary unit. Your Lordships will remember how little any of us liked the names proposed—bancor, unitas, dolphin, bezant, daric, and heaven knows what. Some of your Lordships were good enough to join in the search for something better. I recall a story of a country parish in the last century where they were accustomed to give their children Biblical names—Amos, Ezekiel, Obadiah, and so forth. Needing a name for a dog, after a long and vain search of the Scriptures they called the dog "Moreover." We hit on no such happy solution, with the result that it has been the dog that died. The loss of the dog we need not too much regret, though I still think that it was a more thoroughbred animal than what has now come out from a mixed marriage of ideas. Yet, perhaps, as sometimes

*Speech delivered by Lord Keynes before the House of Lords, May 23, 1944.

occurs, this dog of mixed origin is a sturdier and more serviceable animal and will prove not less loyal and faithful to the purposes for which it has been bred.

I commend the new plan to your Lordships as being, in some important respects (to which I will return later), a considerable improvement on either of its parents. I like this new plan and I believe that it will work to our advantage. . . .

What, then, are these major advantages that I hope from the plan to the advantage of this country? First, it is clearly recognized and agreed that, during the post-war transitional period of uncertain duration, we are entitled to retain any of those wartime restrictions, and special arrangements with the sterling area and others which are helpful to us, without being open to the charge of acting contrary to any general engagements into which we have entered. . . .

Second, when this period is over and we are again strong enough to live year by year on our own resources, we can look forward to trading in a world of national currencies which are interconvertible. For a great commercial nation like ourselves, this is indispensable for full prosperity. Sterling itself, in due course, must obviously become, once again, generally convertible. . . .

So far from an international plan endangering the long tradition by which most Empire countries, and many other countries, too, have centred their financial systems in London, the plan is, in my judgment, an indispensable means of maintaining this tradition. With our own resources so greatly impaired and encumbered, it is only if sterling is firmly placed in an international setting that the necessary confidence in it can be sustained. Indeed, even during the transitional period, it will be our policy, I hope, steadily to develop the field within which sterling is freely available as rapidly as we can manage. Now if our own goal is, as it surely must be, the general inter-convertibility of sterling with other currencies, it must obviously be to our trading advantage that the same obtains elsewhere, so that we can sell our exports in one country and freely spend the proceeds in any other. It is a great gain to us in particular, that other countries in the world should agree to refrain from those discriminatory exchange practices which we ourselves have never adopted in times of peace but from which in the recent past our traders have suffered greatly at the hands of others. . . .

Third, the wheels of trade are to be oiled by what is, in effect, a great addition to the world's stock of monetary reserves, distributed, moreover, in a reasonable way. The quotas are not so large as under the Clearing Union. . . . But they are substantial and can be increased subsequently if the need is shown. The aggregate for the world is put provisionally at £2,500,000,000. Our own share of this—for ourselves and the Crown Colonies which, I may mention, are treated for all purposes as a part of the British monetary system (in itself a useful acknowledgment)—is £325,000,000, a sum which may easily double, or more than double, the reserves which we shall otherwise hold at the end of the transitional period. The separate quotas of the rest of the sterling area will make a further large addition to this. Who is so confident of the future that he will wish to throw away so comfortable a supplementary aid in time of trouble? Do the critics think it preferable, if the winds of the trade cycle blow, to diminish our demand for imports by increasing unemployment at home, rather than meet the emergency out of this Fund which will be expressly provided for such temporary purposes?

I emphasize that such is the purpose of the quotas. They are not intended as daily food for us or any other country to live upon during the reconstruction or afterwards. Provision for that belongs to another chapter of international co-operation, upon which we shall embark shortly unless you discourage us unduly about this one. The quotas for drawing on the Fund's resources are an iron ration to tide over temporary emergencies of one kind or another. . . .

There is another advantage to which I would draw your Lordships' special attention. A proper share of responsibility for maintaining equilibrium in the balance of international payments is squarely placed on the creditor countries. This is one of the major improvements in the new plan. The Americans, who are the most likely to be affected by this, have, of their own free will and honest purpose, offered us a far-reaching formula of protection against a recurrence of the main cause of deflation during the inter-war years—namely, the draining of reserves out of the rest of the world to pay a country which was obstinately lending and exporting on a scale immensely greater than it was lending and importing. Under Clause VI of the plan, a country engages itself, in effect, to prevent such a situation from arising again, by promising, should it fail, to release other countries from any obligation to take its exports, or, if taken, to pay for them. I cannot imagine that this sanction would ever be allowed to come into effect. If by no other means than by lending, the creditor country will always have to find a way to square the account on imperative grounds of its own self-interest. For it will no longer be entitled to square the account by squeezing gold out of the rest of us. Here we have a voluntary undertaking, genuinely offered in the spirit both of a good neighbor and, I should add, of enlightened self-interest, not to allow a repetition of a chain of events which between the wars did more than any other single factor to destroy the world's economic balance and to prepare a seed-bed for foul growths. This is a tremendous extension of international co-operation to good ends. I pray your Lordships to pay heed to its importance.

Fifth, the plan sets up an international institution with substantial rights and duties to preserve orderly arrangements in matters such as exchange rates which are two-ended and affect both parties alike, which can also serve as a place of regular discussion between responsible authorities to find ways to escape those many unforeseeable dangers which the future holds.

Here are five advantages of major importance. The proposals go far beyond what, even a short time ago, anyone could have conceived of as a possible basis of general international agreement. What alternative is open to us which gives comparable aid, or better, more hopeful opportunities for the future? I have considerable confidence that something very like this plan will be in fact adopted, if only on account of the plain demerits of the alternative of rejection. You can talk against this plan, so long as it is a matter of talking—saying in the same breath that it goes too far and that it does not go far enough, that it is too rigid to be safe and that it is too loose to be worth anything. But it would require great fool-hardiness to reject it, much more fool-hardiness than is to be found in this wise, intuitive country.

Therefore, for these manifold and substantial benefits I commend the monetary proposals to your Lordships. Nevertheless, before you will give them your confidence, you will wish to consider whether, in return, we are surrendering anything which is vital for the ordering of our domestic affairs in the manner we intend for the future. My Lords, the experience of the years before the war has led most of us, though some of us late in the day, to certain firm conclusions. Three, in particular, are highly relevant to this discussion. We are determined that, in future, the external value of sterling shall conform to its internal value as set by our own domestic policies, and not the other way round. Secondly, we intend to retain control of our domestic rate of interest, so that we can keep it as low as suits our own purposes, without interference from the ebb and flow of international capital movements or flights of hot money. Thirdly, whilst we intend to prevent inflation at home, we will not accept deflation at the dictate of influences from outside. In other words, we abjure the instruments of bank rate and credit contraction operating through the increase of unemployment as a means of forcing our domestic economy into line with external factors.

Have those responsible for the monetary proposals been sufficiently careful to preserve these principles from the possibility of interference? I hope your Lordships will trust me not to have turned my back on all I have fought for. To establish those three principles which I have just stated has been my main task for the last twenty years. Sometimes almost alone, in popular articles in the press, in pamphlets, in dozens of letters to *The Times*, in text books, in enormous and obscure treatises I have spent my strength to persuade my countrymen and the world at large to change their traditional doctrines and, by taking better thought, to remove the curse of unemployment. Was it not I, when many of to-day's iconoclasts were still worshippers of the Calf, who wrote that "Gold is a barbarous relic"? Am I so faithless, so forgetful, so senile that, at the very moment of the triumph of these ideas when, with gathering momentum, governments, parliaments, banks, the press, the public, and even economists, have at last accepted the new doctrines, I go off to help forge new chains to hold us fast in the old dungeon? I trust, my Lords, that you will not believe it. . . .

The question, however, which has recently been given chief prominence is whether we are in any sense returning to the disabilities of the former gold standard, relief from which we have rightly learnt to prize so highly. If I have any authority to pronounce on what is and what is not the essence and meaning of a gold standard, I should say that this plan is the exact opposite of it. The plan in its relation to gold is, indeed, very close to proposals which I advocated in vain as the right alternative when I was bitterly opposing this country's return to gold. The gold standard, as I understand it, means a system under which the external value of a national currency is rigidly tied to a fixed quantity of gold which can only honorably be broken under *force majeure;* and it involves a financial policy which compels the internal value of the domestic currency to conform to this external value as fixed in terms of gold. On the other hand, the use of gold merely as a convenient common denominator by means of which the relative values of national currencies—these being free to change—are expressed from time to time, is obviously quite another matter.

My noble friend Lord Addison asks who fixes the value of gold. If he means, as I assume he does, the sterling value of gold, it is we ourselves who fix it initially in consultation with the Fund; and this value is subject to change at any time on our initiative, changes in excess of 10 per cent requiring the approval of the Fund, which must not withhold approval if our domestic equilibrium requires it. There must be *some* price for gold; and so long as gold is used as a monetary reserve it is most advisable that the current rates of exchange and the relative values of gold in different currencies should correspond. The only alternative to this would be the complete demonetization of gold. I am not aware that anyone has proposed that. For it is only common sense as things are to-day to continue to make use of gold and its prestige as a means of settling international accounts. To demonetize gold would obviously be highly objectionable to the British Commonwealth and to Russia as the main producers, and to the United States and the Western Allies as the main holders of it. Surely no one disputes that? On the other hand, in this country we have already dethroned gold as the fixed standard of value. The plan not merely confirms the dethronement but approves it by expressly providing that it is the duty of the Fund to alter the gold value of any currency if it is shown that this will be serviceable to equilibrium.

In fact, the plan introduces in this respect an epoch-making innovation in an international instrument, the object of which is to lay down sound and orthodox principles. For instead of maintaining the principle that the internal value of a national currency should conform to a prescribed *de jure* external value, it provides that its external value should be altered if necessary so as to conform to whatever *de facto* internal value results from domestic policies, which themselves shall be immune from criticism by the Fund. Indeed, it is made the duty of the Fund to approve changes which will have this effect. That is why I say that these proposals are the exact opposite of the gold standard. They lay down by international agreement the essence of the new doctrine, far removed from the old orthodoxy. If they do so in terms as inoffensive as possible to the former faith, need we complain?

No, my Lords, in recommending these proposals I do not blot a page already written. I am trying to help write a new page. Public opinion is now converted to a new model, and I believe a much improved model, of domestic policy. That battle is all but won. Yet a not less difficult task still remains—namely, to organize an international setting within which the new domestic policies can occupy a comfortable place. Therefore, it is above all as providing an international framework for the new ideas and the new techniques

> associated with the policy of full employment that these proposals are not least to be welcomed. . . .
>
> It is on this note of emphasizing the importance of furthering all genuine efforts directed towards international agreement in the economic field that I should wish to end my contribution to this debate. The proposals which are before your Lordships are the result of the collaboration of many minds and the fruit of the collective wisdom of the experts of many nations. . . .
>
> I affirm that these discussions have been without exception a model of what such gatherings should be—objective, understanding, without waste of time or expense of temper. I dare to speak for the much abused so-called experts. I even venture sometimes to prefer them, without intending any disrespect, to politicians. The common love of truth, bred of a scientific habit of mind, is the closest of bonds between the representatives of diverse nations.

Although the Fund was a compromise, the British had wanted to depart radically from the strictures of the old gold standard, whereas the United States had advocated a system retaining more features of the gold standard. At the same time as the American Congress was being told that the dollar was "defined" in terms of gold and that the Fund would operate much like the gold standard, Keynes was insisting that the domestic supply of money would no longer be regulated by gold flows and that the Fund proposals were the "exact opposite of the gold standard."

Keynes was keen to disabuse the British public from believing that the Fund gave gold a prominent position. To Keynes, gold had been dethroned, if not demonetized. In a letter to the editor of *The Economist*, he corrected a misquotation.

> *To the Editor of* The Economist, *29 July 1944*
>
> Sir,
>
> In your issue of July 15th which has just come to my notice, you report me as having said in a Press conference at Bretton Woods that 'The real purpose of the Monetary Fund is to bring back gold as a fundamental reserve money'. In fact I said nothing of the kind. In case the matter is of any interest, the following is an extract from the report of the Press conference in question, published in *The New York Times:*

> Lord Keynes said the modified form of gold standard being considered here was not inconsistent with his denunciation of the old gold standard in 1933 as 'a barbarous relic'. The old standard was so 'rigid', he explained, that it could not stand the strain of crisis and finally broke. Under the proposed standard, all currencies would have a 'link' with gold, but it would be 'flexible' enough to permit orderly changes in exchange rates when necessary to avert the breakdown of monetary systems, competitive currency depreciation and similar measures of economic warfare. . . .
>
> British sentiment is strongly opposed to a return to the 'rigid' gold standard, he went on, adding that the present 'scheme', as he called it, was 'quite different' in its flexibility. 'It retains the link with gold, but it can be adapted to changing circumstances from time to time', said Lord Keynes. 'It provides the machinery of consultation and agreement by which orderly changes can be made. I have never argued that gold was "a barbarous relic" in this sense. When I was criticising the old gold standard, I made various proposals for retaining the link with gold. I proposed that gold be made a "constitutional monarch", so to speak, which would be subject to the constitution of the people and not able to exercise tyrannical power over the nations of the world.' He said it would be very 'foolish' to propose 'departure from the gold link'. With the United States and certain western European countries holding large quantities of gold, and with the British Commonwealth and Russia producing large quantities of the precious metal every year, he went on, 'no one in his senses would want to make the gold resources of the world useless or throw the gold mines of the world out of employment'.
>
> Yours, etc.
>
> KEYNES

A few months later, President Roosevelt sent his message to Congress urging adoption of the Bretton Woods proposals. He stated:

> It is time for the United States to take the lead in establishing the principle of economic cooperation as the foundation for expanded world trade. We propose to do this, not by setting up a super-government, but by international negotiation and agreement, directed to the improvement of the monetary institutions of the world and of the laws that govern trade. . . .
>
> The United Nations Monetary Conference at Bretton Woods has taken a long step forward on a matter of great practical importance to us all. The Conference submitted a plan to create an International Monetary Fund which will put an end to monetary chaos. The Fund is a financial institution to preserve stability and order in

> the exchange rates between different moneys. It does not create a single money for the world; neither we nor anyone else is ready to do that. There will still be a different money in each country, but with the Fund in operation the value of each currency in international trade will remain comparatively stable. Changes in the value of foreign currencies will be made only after careful consideration by the Fund of the factors involved. Furthermore, and equally important, the Fund Agreement establishes a code of agreed principles for the conduct of exchange and currency affairs.[15]

In a rare display of agreement among economists, approximately 90 per cent of the economists in the American Economic Association who replied to a poll favored adoption of the Bretton Woods proposals.

2.4 The Gold-Exchange Standard

The operation of the IMF and the role played by reserve currencies—dollars and to a much lesser degree, sterling—gave the postwar international monetary system its essential shape until 1971. The system was termed the gold-exchange standard, or more accurately, the gold-exchange and reserve currencies standard. The most important features of this international monetary mechanism were its system of pegged—but adjustable—rates and its provisions for liquidity.

Article IV of the Fund's Articles of Agreement set forth provisions for the par-value exchange rate system.

> ARTICLE IV. PAR VALUES OF CURRENCIES
>
> *Section 1. Expression of par values.* (*a*) The par value of the currency of each member shall be expressed in terms of gold as a common denominator or in terms of the United States dollar of the weight and fineness in effect on July 1, 1944.
>
> (*b*) All computations relating to currencies of members for the purpose of applying the provisions of this Agreement shall be on the basis of their par values.
>
> *Sec. 2. Gold purchases based on par values.* The Fund shall prescribe a margin above and below par value for transactions in gold by members, and no member shall buy gold at a price above par

15 U.S. Treasury, President's Message to Congress, Bretton Woods, Feb. 20, 1945, pp. 6–7.

value plus the prescribed margin, or sell gold at a price below par value minus the prescribed margin.

Sec. 3. Foreign exchange dealings based on parity. The maximum and the minimum rates for exchange transactions between the currencies of members taking place within their territories shall not differ from parity

(i) in the case of spot exchange transactions, by more than one percent; and

(ii) in the case of other exchange transactions, by a margin which exceeds the margin for spot exchange transactions by more than the Fund considers reasonable.

Sec. 4. Obligations regarding exchange stability. (*a*) Each member undertakes to collaborate with the Fund to promote exchange stability, to maintain orderly exchange arrangements with other members, and to avoid competitive exchange alterations.

(*b*) Each member undertakes through appropriate measures consistent with this Agreement, to permit within its territories exchange transactions between its currency and the currencies of other members only within the limits prescribed under Section 3 of this Article. A member whose monetary authorities, for the settlement of international transactions, in fact freely buy and sell gold within the limits prescribed by the Fund under Section 2 of this Article shall be deemed to be fulfilling this undertaking.

Sec. 5. Changes in par values. (*a*) A member shall not propose a change in the par value of its currency except to correct a fundamental disequilibrium.

(*b*) A change in the par value of a member's currency may be made only on the proposal of the member and only after consultation with the Fund.

(*c*) When a change is proposed, the Fund shall first take into account the changes, if any, which have already taken place in the initial par value of the member's currency as determined under Article XX, Section 4. If the proposed change, together with all previous changes, whether increases or decreases,

(i) does not exceed ten percent of the initial par value, the Fund shall raise no objection;

(ii) does not exceed a further ten percent of the initial par value, the Fund may either concur or object, but shall declare its attitude within seventy-two hours if the member so requests;

(iii) is not with (i) or (ii) above, the Fund may either concur or object, but shall be entitled to a longer period in which to declare its attitude.

(*d*) Uniform changes in par values made under Section 7 of this Article shall not be taken into account in determining whether a proposed change falls within (i), (ii), or (iii) of (*c*) above.

(*e*) A member may change the par value of its currency without the concurrence of the Fund if the change does not affect the international transactions of members of the Fund.

(*f*) The Fund shall concur in a proposed change which is within the terms of (c) (ii) or (*c*) (iii) above if it is satisfied that the change is necessary to correct a fundamental disequilibrium. In particular, provided it is so satisfied, it shall not object to a proposed change because of the domestic social or political policies of the member proposing the change.

Sec. 6. Effect of unauthorized changes. If a member changes the par value of its currency despite the objection of the Fund, in cases where the Fund is entitled to object, the member shall be ineligible to use the resources of the Fund unless the Fund otherwise determines; and if, after the expiration of a reasonable period, the difference between the member and the Fund continues, the matter shall be subject to the provisions of Article XV, Section 2 (*b*).

The United States alone chose to maintain the international value of the dollar by making it interconvertible with gold through transactions with official foreign monetary authorities: it agreed to "freely buy and sell gold" within the prescribed limits [Article IV (4) (b)]. Other countries maintained the value of their currencies by using the dollar as the intervention currency, entering the foreign exchange markets to buy or sell dollars as needed to maintain their currencies within 1 per cent on either side of the par values.

Gold entered into the monetary system in two important ways. First, it constituted an official reserve asset and was a means of ultimate settlement in the balance of payments. Second, the value of local currencies was expressed in terms of gold or the dollar, and the dollar was expressed in terms of gold so that par values connected with gold or the United States gold price. "Convertible currencies" were thus convertible into United States dollars, and United States dollars held by monetary authorities of other Fund members were convertible into gold. This is another sense in which gold was referred to as the "final" or "ultimate" asset. It has been observed that if this

delphic reference to gold as the "final" or "ultimate" asset . . . was indeed the theory of the drafters [of the Fund's Articles], they

> probably assumed the continued invulnerability of the United States dollar and the readiness of other members to hold dollars in the quantities that were likely to become available to them. This view of the world and the assumptions on which it rested were not made explicit in the Articles. For example, there is no obligation under the Articles for the United States or any other member to buy and sell gold for its own currency. The Articles recognize the possibility that the monetary authorities of a member may freely buy and sell gold in fact, within the margins of par established by the Fund for gold transactions, for the settlement of international transactions. If a member engages in this practice, it will be maintaining the value of its own currency in direct relation to gold. . . . The United States is the only member which has informed the Fund that it freely buys and sells gold within the meaning of the provision that recognizes that practice.[16]

This practice meant that official monetary authorities could sell gold to the United States Treasury for dollars, and until August 15, 1971, they also had the privilege of converting their holdings of dollars to gold at the United States Treasury.

By being left with these functions, gold was not demonetized under the IMF—even if it was "dethroned" from the central position it had previously occupied under the pure gold standard. The contribution of gold to international liquidity has, however, been limited. By "international liquidity" is meant the aggregate stock of assets held by the national monetary authority that is available unconditionally to settle the country's imbalance in international transactions. At present, official reserve assets consist of official gold holdings, a member country's unconditional drawing rights at the IMF (its reserve tranche), the special drawing rights allocated to a member country of the IMF and official holdings of convertible foreign currencies—mainly the United States dollar as a reserve currency.

Drawing rights at the IMF depend on the size of the member's quota. Quotas were specified as follows.

> ARTICLE III. QUOTAS AND SUBSCRIPTIONS
>
> *Section 1. Quotas.* Each member shall be assigned a quota. The quotas of the members represented at the United Nations Mone-

16 Joseph Gold, "The Code of Conduct," in Horsefield (ed.), *International Monetary Fund 1945–1965*, vol. II (1969), pp. 559–560.

tary and Financial Conference which accept membership before the date specified in Article XX, Section 2 (*e*), shall be those set forth in Schedule A. The quotas of other members shall be determined by the Fund.

Sec. 2. Adjustment of quotas. The Fund shall at intervals of five years review, and if it deems it appropriate propose an adjustment of, the quotas of the members. It may also, if it thinks fit, consider at any other time the adjustment of any particular quota at the request of the member concerned. A four-fifths majority of the total voting power shall be required for any change in quotas and no quota shall be changed without the consent of the member concerned.

Sec. 3. Subscriptions: time, place, and form of payment. (*a*) The subscription of each member shall be equal to its quota and shall be paid in full to the Fund at the appropriate depository on or before the date when the member becomes eligible under Article XX, Section 4 (*c*) or (*d*), to buy currencies from the Fund.

(*b*) Each member shall pay in gold, as a minimum, the smaller of

(i) twenty-five percent of its quota; or

(ii) ten percent of its net official holdings of gold and United States dollars as at the date when the Fund notifies members under Article XX, Section 4 (*a*) that it will shortly be in a position to begin exchange transactions.

It is noteworthy that at the outset the size of the Fund was limited by the United States and that the initial total of quotas in the Fund, about $8.8 billion, was only about one-third the size of resources Keynes wished to make available. The American quota was initially $2.75 billion and the United Kingdom's $1.3 billion. The subsequent growth of the Fund has depended upon the quinquennial review of quotas during which members have agreed to enlarge quotas.

Most notable has been the increasing use of dollars as reserves. This has permitted the amount of international liquidity to increase far beyond that which was provided by only increases in the total gold stock and Fund quotas. Tables I.1 and I.2 indicate the growth in international reserves and the changing sources of international liquidity over the period 1949–71. As will be seen below, the growth in the supply of dollars as reserves has been associated with a "deficit" in the U. S. balance of payments.

Table I.1 Composition of World Monetary Reserves: 1949–71 (in billions of U.S. dollars)

	1949	*1969*	*1970*	*1971*
I. Gold	33.5	39.1	37.2	39.2
II. Special drawing rights	—	—	3.1	6.4
III. Reserves in IMF	1.7	6.7	7.7	6.9
IV. Foreign currencies	10.4	32.4	44.5	77.6
Dollars	3.2	16.0	23.9	50.7
Sterling	6.9	9.0	6.6	7.9
Eurodollars, etc.	0.3	7.4	14.0	19.1
V. Total	45.5	78.2	92.5	130.1
United States	26.0	17.0	14.5	13.2
Other countries	19.5	61.2	78.1	116.9

SOURCE: IMF, *International Financial Statistics.*

3. CURRENCY CRISES OF THE 1960s

By the mid-1960s, both academic and government economists were expressing ever-greater concern about weaknesses that were becoming increasingly evident in the monetary system. Stresses and strains became more pronounced as nations followed independent monetary policies and divergent rates of inflation; exchange rates were pegged—but the peg was adjustable; and both the dollar and gold served as international monies.

3.1 Financial Crisis Management

For some, the most vulnerable aspect of the system was that it had become dollar-centered, but the dollar still had to coexist with the other reserve asset of gold. Professor Robert Triffin repeatedly warned that the persistent deficit and piling up of short-term in-

Table I.2 Gross and Net Reserves of the United States: 1949–71 (in billions of U.S. dollars)

	1949	*1969*	*1970*	*1971*
I. Gross reserves	26.0	17.0	14.5	13.2
of which: gold	24.6	11.9	11.1	11.1
II. External liabilities (−)	− 3.2	−17.0	−25.3	−53.5
to:				
1. IMF and SDR allocat.	—	− 1.0	− 1.4	− 2.8
2. Foreign central banks	− 3.2	−16.0	−23.9	−50.7
III. Net reserves (I + II)	+22.8	− 0.1	−10.8	−40.3

SOURCE: IMF, *International Financial Statistics*.

debtedness of the United States, as a reserve center, were bound to undermine, in the end, the confidence of other countries in the ability of the United States to honor its commitment to redeem dollar holdings in gold. In the early 1960s Triffin was pointing out that "other countries derived from net U.S. reserve losses nearly 60 per cent of their total reserve increases in 1950–57, and 80 per cent in 1958–62, i.e., in these last five years nearly eight times as much as the amount of reserves derived from gold production in the West.

"Nobody can any longer seriously defend such a system—or rather lack of system—as a safe and rational way to regulate the increase of international reserves which must serve as the ultimate basis, particularly under convertibility conditions, for the increases in national money supplies necessary to support growing levels of production and trade in an expanding world economy."[17]

If international liquidity was proving inadequate, there was at the same time a reluctance to rely on the adjustment mechanism of the adjustable peg in exchange rates. In the 1950s, there were few changes in rates, especially for the major currencies in world trade: the United States dollar, pound sterling, French franc, German mark, and Japanese yen. The anticipated political and economic costs, and the realization that their currencies were interdependent, made the major countries consider adjustment of rates to be only a last resort device. It should also be remembered that the Fund was not empowered to propose a change of par value to a member; its voice was only a negative one. And a member's own proposal to change the exchange value of its currency was to be "considered only when essential to the correction of fundamental disequilibrium."

Even with the fundamental disequilibrium provision, however, formal devaluations have turned out to be fewer than anticipated at Bretton Woods, and the Fund found its members reluctant to change their exchange rates even at times when such changes might have been the best solution of their difficulties. The pound sterling was devalued in 1949 and 1967, and the French franc was devalued

17 Robert Triffin, *The Evolution of the International Monetary System: Historical Reappraisal and Future Perspectives*, Princeton Studies in International Finance, No. 12 (1964). Triffin's forecast of forthcoming crises appeared earlier in his *Europe and the Money Muddle* (1957), pp. 296–301; testimony to the Joint Economic Committee on October 28, 1959 [reproduced in his *Gold and the Dollar Crisis* (1960)].

in 1949, 1959, and 1969. Exchange rates of major countries remained fixed between 1956 and 1966 with only three exceptions.

Not until after the mid-1960s did exchange rate variations become more frequent. They were then increasingly associated with the buildup of currency crises. Indeed, by establishing the fundamental disequilibrium criterion for adjusting the peg, the Fund clearly presumed that rates would not be changed for a transitory imbalance and that the imbalance would have to persist. In persisting though, the imbalance tended to grow, and speculation against the currency intensified when the adjustment was delayed and could only result in eventually large changes in the rates.

And yet if there was criticism of the system in the 1960s, there was also defense—especially by the Fund:

> the official views of the Fund and also of practically all central banks continued to favor—strongly—fixed exchange rates. Accordingly, when the Group of Ten agreed in August 1964 to study proposals for the reform of the international monetary system, changes in the exchange rate system were explicitly ruled out.
>
> Reluctance to tamper with the par value system reflected at least in part the experience of the Fund and its members during the previous twenty years. . . . [T]here were other arguments in favor of fixed exchange rates—that they put national monetary authorities under pressure to integrate their policies; that they have to be defended by anti-inflationary measures; that they eliminate the danger of competitive depreciation. In addition to these arguments in favor of fixed exchange rates, the Fund had yet another reason for preferring the par value system: in the Fund's view an alternative exchange rate system would make the process of international collaboration more difficult.
>
> As the year 1965 drew to a close, the debates over exchange rates were continuing and becoming more heated. [And currency crises were to become more frequent.][18]

In the latter-1960s, there were several currency crises in the sense of a severe disequilibrium that threatened the maintenance of value of the currency under attack and the preservation of the international monetary structure. Between 1967 and 1973 conditions in

18 Margaret Garritsen de Vries, "The Par Value System. An Overview," in Horsefield (ed.), *International Monetary Fund 1945–1965*, vol. II (1969), p. 50.

the exchange markets became so disorderly that on 11 occasions one or more of the G-10 countries (the ten leading industrial countries) had to close exchange markets at least for one day and sometimes longer. And the volume of official intervention grew. In Germany, for example, the Bundesbank had to purchase $4 billion between May 1 and May 10, 1969 in order to hold the mark:dollar rate.

The speculative flights from a currency under pressure to stronger currencies called for financial crisis management. When a country was losing international reserve assets at a serious rate—and it was not willing to take remedial measures in the form of deflation or devaluation—it had to manage the crisis by other national measures, in the form of direct exchange controls or trade controls, or else seek international financial assistance. As will be seen in the currency crises examined below, the international assistance can come through a formal system of providing additional liquidity (as in the IMF), or a less formal ad hoc arrangement to meet short-run speculative attacks (as when several central banks co-operate to support a currency under pressure). The imposition of conditions under which this international monetary relief is granted can be highly significant to the recipient country that is trying to manage its economy so as to achieve internal as well as external balance.

As the recounting of the currency crises below indicates, there is a need to avoid the buildup of the crisis and the need to lessen the cost of crisis management. Short-run management—and provision of "crisis liquidity"—is required to finance or contain the immediate deficit. Beyond that is the longer-term question of monetary reform and provision of "trend liquidity" or other policy action to make the adjustment mechanism more effective.

3.2 Anatomy of a Devaluation Crisis: Britain (1967)

Within 24 hours of taking office in October 1964, the new Labor Government made a decision not to devalue the pound sterling. Of that first day, the ex-Prime Minister Harold Wilson recalls that a decision was needed immediately on the three courses that the Treasury had worked out in detail and presented to the new government: devaluation of sterling; quantitative restrictions on imports; or a surcharge on a wide range of imports.

Wilson acknowledges that it was "politically tempting" to devalue at once, "when we could have put all the responsibility on our

Conservative predecessors." But he was convinced that "to devalue could have the most dangerous consequences."[19]

Instead of devaluing, the Government imposed a 15 per cent import surcharge on most imports. A tight money policy was also followed. But there was still heavy pressure on sterling. Wilson recalls that there was daily a heavy drain on reserves, sometimes amounting to more than £50 million in a day, while "our total gold and convertible currency reserves barely totalled £1000 millions. . . . The pound was at its support level. Rumours were reaching feverish proportions."[20]

Compounding the Government's dilemma was the insistence by the Governor of the Bank of England (Lord Cromer) that the government should submit to all-round cuts in expenditure in order to "restore confidence" in the pound. But this would have meant sacrifices in the Government's social and economic priorities. Wilson states that his government

> had to listen night after night to demands that there should be immediate cuts in Government expenditure, and particularly in those parts of Government expenditure which related to social services. I said that we had now reached the situation where a newly-elected Government with a mandate from the people was being told, not so much by the Governor of the Bank of England but by international speculators, that the policies on which we had fought the election could not be implemented; that the Government was to be forced into the adoption of Tory policies to which it was fundamentally opposed.[21]

Wilson then threatened "to go back to the electorate for a mandate" giving him full powers to handle the crisis and to let the pound float in the meanwhile. Lord Cromer pointed out that the election would occupy about four weeks, the run on sterling would intensify, and "our reserves, which had already fallen considerably, would have run out long before polling day." Wilson, in turn, indicated that the international financial community would be the last to want Britain to float the pound or to be forced by speculation into devaluing. He asked Lord Cromer to ask "his central banking col-

19 Harold Wilson, *The Labour Government 1964–1970, A Personal Record* (1971), pp. 6–7.
20 *Ibid.*, p. 35.
21 *Ibid.*, pp. 34, 37.

leagues [who] had a vested interest in exchange stability and the strength of sterling" what they were prepared to do to avert a crisis. The next day Wilson received a message that the Governor had successfully raised $3 billion from the central bankers. "He had done a magnificent job," Wilson acknowledged. "Sterling was safe—for a time."[22]

The Bank of England had arranged with the Federal Reserve Bank of New York, the Bank for International Settlements, and the central banks of eight European countries, Canada, and Japan, for facilities to borrow up to $3 billion in various currencies during the next three to six months. In the following interview, Charles Coombs, Vice-President in charge of the Foreign Department, Federal Reserve Bank of New York, recalls how the support for sterling was arranged.[23]

> The chronology of the $3 billions package of sterling in November 1964 is, to the best of my recollection, roughly as follows: On November 23, the Bank of England raised its discount rate from 5 to 7 per cent. Perversely enough, market reaction to such forceful use of monetary policy by the Labour Government quickly degenerated into fears that the threat to sterling must have reached a truly crisis stage. Whether these reactions might have been averted by earlier bank rate action, more particularly on the usual Thursday date for bank rate announcements, may be debated for some time to come. In any event, the sterling market situation assumed increasingly grave significance on the London afternoon—on the New York morning of Tuesday, November 24—when a virtual avalanche of selling developed. If sterling were to be rescued, it quickly became clear that a major package of international credit assistance would be required, and I so advised President Hayes [of the Federal Reserve Bank of New York] shortly before 10 o'clock that morning. President Hayes immediately telephoned Chairman Martin and U.S. Treasury officials and found that their thinking was moving along the same lines.
>
> On the afternoon of the 24th, the Federal Open Market Committee—meeting through a telephone conference—approved the Special Manager's recommendation of an increase in the Federal Reserve/Bank of England swap line from $500 to $750 millions, on condition that credit assistance on a roughly corresponding scale

22 *Ibid.*, p. 38.
23 "Interview with Charles Coombs," *The Banker* (November 1966), pp. 746–747.

> could be secured from other central banks. That evening the Export-Import Bank gave assurance of a $250 millions standby facility while two foreign central banks informally indicated a sympathetic attitude. Beginning early on the morning of November 25, President Hayes and I joined forces with Lord Cromer in explaining by telephone to the governors of other major central banks the magnitude of the danger and the urgency of immediate defensive action in the form of a massive credit package. After roughly ten hours of almost continuous telephone communication, it was announced at 2 P.M., New York time, that a $3 billion credit package provided by 11 countries and the BIS was at the disposal of the Bank of England. Interest in the mechanics of how the money was raised through such teamwork has unfortunately tended to obscure the more fundamental point that each central bank's decision to lend was squarely based on the character and integrity of the Bank of England and its Governor.

During the next three years, the government attempted to contain an underlying crisis of confidence in the pound. As Table I.3 indicates, the actual current account balance showed a large deficit only in 1964, 1967, and 1968. But it has been estimated that the deficit would have been much larger every year between 1961 and 1967 if the domestic economy had been allowed to grow at a higher rate of 3 or 4 per cent instead of being held below its full capacity for balance-of-payments reasons. Not only was the government forced to follow "stop-go" policies of restraint on employment, but there were also voluntary and mandatory wage freezes, reduced overseas government expenditure, and tariff surcharges.

Nonetheless, the belief persisted that sterling was overvalued, and confidence in the government's ability to maintain sterling parity was diminished as short-term liabilities to foreigners in sterling exceeded greatly the country's gold and convertible currency reserves. There were frequent speculative runs against sterling. Although these speculative attacks were resisted by large short-term government borrowings, a financial crisis of serious dimensions developed in the fall of 1967, aggravated by a Middle East crisis, closure of the Suez Canal, and a series of strikes in Britain. Finally, the government was forced to announce a 14.3 per cent devaluation of the pound on November 18, 1967.

Table I.3 Summary Balance of Payments, United Kingdom (£ million)

	1961	*1962*	*1963*	*1964*	*1965*	*1966*	*1967*	*1968*	*1969*	*1970*	*1971*
Current account											
Visible trade	−152	−102	− 80	−519	−237	− 73	−557	− 648	−143	+ 12	+ 299
Invisibles	+158	+224	+204	+137	+188	+157	+242	+ 377	+587	+ 669	+ 741
CURRENT BALANCE	+ 6	+122	+124	−382	− 49	+ 84	−315	− 271	+444	+ 681	+1,040
Currency flow and official financing											
Current balance	+ 6	+122	+124	−382	− 49	+ 84	−315	− 271	+444	+ 681	+1,040
Investment and other capital flows	−316	− 3	− 99	−305	−332	−574	−600	−1,007	−106	+ 547	+1,839
Balancing item	− 29	+ 73	− 83	− 8	+ 28	− 57	+244	− 132	+405	+ 59	+ 349
TOTAL CURRENCY FLOW	−339	+192	− 58	−695	−353	−547	−671	−1,410	+743	+1,287	+3,228
Allocation of Special Drawing Rights (+)	—	—	—	—	—	—	—	—	—	+ 171	+ 125
Gold subscription to IMF (−)	—	—	—	—	—	− 44	—	—	—	− 38	—
Total	−339	+192	− 58	−695	−353	−591	−671	−1,410	+743	+1,420	+3,353
Financed as follows											
Net transactions with overseas monetary authorities	+370	−375	+ 5	+573	+599	+625	+556	+1,296	−699	−1,295	−1,817
Official reserves (drawings on +/ additions to −)	− 31	+183	+ 53	+122	−246	− 34	+115	+ 114	− 44	− 125	−1,536

SOURCE: Central Statistical Office, *United Kingdom Balance of Payments 1972,* H.M.S.O. (1972), p. 5.

D—FOR DEVALUATION—DAY*

Sir Leslie O'Brien, governor of the Bank of England, woke this morning in his London flat near St. Paul's Cathedral, a five-minute walk from the bank on Threadneedle Street. Most Friday nights he quits London to spend the weekend at his suburban home in Wimbledon.

In Paris, President de Gaulle met in the forenoon at his office in the Élyseés Palace with his Premier, Georges Pompidou, Foreign Minister Maurice Couve de Murville, and Finance Minister Michel Debré.

There have been reports that the Élyseés meeting was "stormy". If so, the argument was more likely over what aid France might or might not give Britain rather than over whether to devalue. The only certainty is that the decision was against devaluation and in favor of giving some assistance.

One-half hour later, Britain's Ambassadors, having received their final cables from London, personally and simultaneously called on the relevant officials of the governments to which they were assigned, to give them official notice. Some knew already.

At 4 in the afternoon, the Monetary Committee of the six Common Market countries met in Brussels at the Cortenburg, a downtown building of concrete slabs and brick that houses Common Market offices. It was the first time that they had been able to hold a meaningful meeting all week.

In London, at the same moment, Prime Minister Wilson had a teatime rendezvous with a delegation of eight women from the Stretford and Urmston Labor party. They did not discuss devaluation. "He was very relaxed," one of the visitors said afterward, "as though he didn't have a thought on his mind."

The public announcement was set for 9:30 that night, London time—10:30 Continental time, 4:30 in New York. But a Japanese journalist scooped the world by 90 minutes, evidently informed by someone at or close to the International Monetary Fund in Washington.

Unperturbed, the British Treasury made its announcement on schedule. The announcement also revealed that the bank rate would be raised to 8 per cent, corporation taxes would be increased, Government spending cut, Britain's export rebate repealed, and that $3-billion of external aid was being arranged—

New York Times (December 17, 1967). © 1967 by the New York Times Company. Reprinted by permission.

> $1.4-billion from the I.M.F. and $1.6-billion directly from other countries.
>
> The BBC was showing a Doris Day movie. Shaw's "Heartbreak House" was playing at the Lyric, where the manager called out an American who had asked to be notified if the news came during the show. "That does it", said the manager, "I'm emigrating."
>
> As the sun set on the British Empire, the reverberations were already beginning to show.
>
> In Washington the White House announced that President Johnson "unequivocally" reaffirmed the United States commitment "to buy and sell gold at the existing price of $35 an ounce"—that is, not to devalue the dollar. The Federal Reserve Board met in an extraordinary Saturday night session to approve an increase in the discount rate of 4½ per cent, one-half as a counteraction to London's new 8 per cent bank rate, and one-half as symbolic notice to the world that the United States was ready to act fast.
>
> The Common Market countries—West Germany, Italy, France, Belgium, the Netherlands and Luxembourg—and Canada, Japan, Norway, Finland, and South Africa announced that they would not devalue, either. Denmark, Ireland and Israel announced that they would.
>
> In Bonn, a special "devaluation team" spent the weekend in the Economics Ministry, assaying developments and nourishing itself on what one member called "English" whisky.

An account by the Deputy Managing Director of the IMF discloses the IMF's role in the sterling crisis:[24]

> Over the weekend of November 11–12, the discussions in the IMF made it clear that U.K. officials considered that $3 billion would be needed if the par value was to be defended. A standby arrangement of that size would bring U.K. use of Fund resources to 266 per cent of quota, which was not a practical possibility. Schweitzer informed Evan Maude, the U.K. Executive Director, that he would be prepared to recommend to the Executive Board a standby arrangement in the amount of $1.4 billion, to be coupled with a sterling devaluation and an adequate domestic program. . . . Schweitzer and the staff believed that, while there would be a substantial number of devaluations by other countries, parity changes among Common Market countries could be avoided.

24 Frank A. Southard, Jr., *The Evolution of the International Monetary Fund*, Princeton Essays in International Finance, No. 135 (December 1979), pp. 30–32. Copyright © 1979. Reprinted by permission of the International Finance Section of Princeton University.

While these discussions continued from Monday through Friday, November 13–17, selling pressure on sterling was intense and the United Kingdom was drawing heavily on swap lines and reserves. The market was clearly expecting a devaluation.

It was the view of Schweitzer and, it became clear as the discussions continued, of U.K. officials that the proposed $1.4 billion standby would be effective only if it was coupled with an adequate program and a devaluation. At the same time, it also became clear that other support to raise the fund to $3 billion was not going to be available.

Finally, at midday on November 17, Maude gave Schweitzer a memorandum from Chancellor of the Exchequer James Callaghan notifying the Fund of a change in the par value from $2.80 to $2.40 per pound sterling, and of the U.K. Government's intention to request a standby arrangement in the amount of $1.4 billion. Schweitzer sent a mission to London on November 18 to discuss the terms of the proposed standby. It was agreed that the Board would be alerted at 8 A.M. on Saturday, November 18, and provided with a staff paper at 9 for a meeting at 10.

During the day on Saturday, Schweitzer and senior staff members conferred by phone with financial officials of a number of countries in an effort to hold down the range of other devaluations. In the event, between November 18 and 27, fourteen countries devalued their currencies, ten of which were closely linked to sterling. No Common Market country devalued, and Australia and Japan in the end decided not to.

The remaining task was to negotiate the standby arrangement, including the elements that Schweitzer and the staff wanted to have included in the U.K. program of corrective action. The negotiation was completed in record time and the Executive Board approved the standby arrangement on November 29. The discussion between the U.K. authorities and the mission had focused chiefly on the issue of a reduction in public expenditure and a limit on Treasury borrowing. The standby in the amount of $1.4 billion brought U.K. access to Fund resources close to 200 per cent of quota. No use was made of the standby until June 1968, when the entire amount was drawn.

The U.K. program did not include quantitative limits on public expenditures or credit, nor was there any phasing of drawings: the United Kingdom could draw any amount at any time. As Schweitzer had anticipated, Executive Directors, especially those representing less-developed countries, were quick to point to the less onerous terms imposed on the United Kingdom, although they agreed that a standby arrangement in support of a major convertible currency need not include any phasing of drawings. As a result, there was an extensive review of standard terms for standby agreements later in 1968, with the aim of assuring uniform treatment of all Fund members. The next U.K. standby arrangement, in 1969, conformed to those terms.

This involved and difficult U.K. case was illuminating in several respects. First, it demonstrated that the Managing Director, by setting the terms on which he would be prepared to recommend use of Fund resources, could influence a country to devalue. Of course, if the country's currency was important, he would want to know that the financial officials of other leading countries agreed that continued support of the existing par value was not likely to be successful. Second, it demonstrated that a negotiation could be carried out without a breach of confidence and without Executive Directors' insisting on being kept informed, although the countries in G-10 (the Group of Ten—the industrialized countries associated with the General Arrangements to Borrow) did at least in general know what was going on. Third, it demonstrated that any treatment for one country markedly more lenient than that accorded to others would be quickly called into question; while Executive Directors would approve that case, they would demand a review of policy.

3.3 French Franc, Deutsche Mark, and Canadian Dollar

The primary interest of the Executive Directors of the IMF was to prevent a chain reaction to the devaluation of sterling. They praised the U.K. authorities for proposing a degree of devaluation that would avoid major disruptive effects on the majority of other countries and that should not set off many other devaluations. The U.S. authorities were especially eager to prevent devaluations that might worsen the U.S. balance-of-payments deficits. The U.S. Director said that this was a historic moment of testing whether the system of par-value exchange rates under the Fund's Agreement could withstand strain and adversity. He emphasized that the United States did not want other members to respond automatically to the devaluation of sterling by devaluing their own currencies: such devaluations should be limited to those necessary for correcting fundamental disequilibria.

The British devaluation, in fact, did not precipitate a round of other devaluations, except in those countries closely tied to the pound. A year after the British devaluation, however, the West German mark and the French franc were subject to large speculative capital flows, based on expectations of a revaluation of the mark and a devaluation of the franc. In the three days November 16–19, 1968, the Deutsche Bundesbank (German central bank) acquired approximately $1.8 billion in efforts to hold the mark at its ceiling—an inflow unprecedented in the history of the Federal Republic. Much of the massive inflow was in the form of French francs. On November 8, 1968, the French Premier Maurice Couve de Murville addressed a nationwide television audience and laid the immediate blame for the current monetary crisis on the "frenzied—I would say phenomenal" speculation in the mark. He did not mention speculation in the franc, but took the extraordinary step of advocating change in another country's currency parity: the mark must be revalued.

Just before his address, the French had refused to accept an emergency loan of $1 billion from the Basel group of central bankers of eleven major industrial nations. This refusal was designed to put another form of pressure on West Germany and to indicate a position of strength on the part of France. It was true that French reserves were still more than $4 billion, but they had declined by $3 billion since the national strikes during May and June 1968, and some action would eventually be necessary to stop the flow of "hot money" from France to West Germany. At a Group of 10 meeting in Bonn on November 20, 1968, a West German spokesman said that any reversal of its decision not to revalue the Deutsche mark was "out of the question." The only action taken by the German government was to impose a 3 per cent tax on exports and rebate on imports—a measure equivalent to a small fiscal revaluation of the mark.

By the following March, however, the belief was intensifying that France could no longer refuse to devalue. New wage negotiations were being undertaken, and unions had called a national strike to back up wage demands the Government considered inflationary. There had been continual deficits in the French balance of payments, and reserves were only one-half what they had been a year previously. Nonetheless, international credit facilities available to France were still sizable, with approximately $4 billion available from these sources: $3 billion of short-term central bank credits and $1 billion of conditional credits (one-half of which would be almost automatically available from the IMF).

In April, General de Gaulle resigned. The new post-de Gaulle government reversed de Gaulle's stand and finally bowed in August to the pressure of massive reserve losses, a continuing trade deficit, and inflationary pressures: it was decided to devalue the franc by 12.5 per cent.

Two months after the franc devaluation, the German mark was revalued. Revaluation had been a major issue in the political campaign of September 1969, and when the Social Democrats were elected they allowed the mark to float in exchange markets. The free-floating mark was achieved by the government's directive to the Bundesbank to stop selling marks every time a wave of buying sent the price more than 1 per cent over the fixed rate of 3.98 marks to the dollar.

Commending the action as a "float for freedom," *The Economist* stated:

> All the world should welcome last Monday's floating of the D-mark. It is another sign that, in the very last resort, even international economic problems do now tend to be handled with a saving common sense. It is a pity that solemn assurances had had to be given that this will not last for long, so that the International Monetary Fund has been promised that "Germany will resume maintenance of the limits around par at the earliest opportunity." But, even in the very brief interval during which this floating of a major currency has been allowed, one can dare to hope that a process of economic education has been set afoot, which is likely to lead towards wider and wiser use of more flexible exchange rates in the future. . . . Britain, with its pretensions to running the less-favoured of the two big international currencies, has suffered particularly from the pains inflicted by the fixed rate system. That is why there has for some time been a strong argument that Britain should act first to break the nexus by moving sterling to a more flexible exchange rate. But since the British Government would not move, and the Americans could not move (although some of President Nixon's advisers are eager for reform), it had also become clear that the second best country to break the ice would be Germany.[25]

The annual meeting of the IMF coincided with Germany's action. At this meeting, Dr. Otmar Emminger, Deputy Governor of the Bundesbank said, "A system of fixed exchange rates can only be

25 *The Economist* (October 4, 1969), p. 14.

maintained if the major countries of the world are prepared to coordinate their monetary and fiscal policies. But this they have dismally failed to do, with the common market countries among the worst offenders." This led Dr. Emminger to question whether there is not a better alternative to the present jumpy and costly method of occasional, large, ad hoc parity changes.

The question became how long Germany would allow the mark to float and at what value it would repeg. This was of especial concern to the EEC countries. Within two weeks, the government decided to establish a new par value for the mark at 9.29 per cent above the previously established par.

The float of the Deutsche mark was followed shortly by the floating of the Canadian dollar in June 1970. This was the second time Canada floated its currency. The earlier decision in 1950 to adopt a floating rate for the Canadian dollar was taken under conditions similar to the German float in 1969. The Canadian dollar was undervalued in the face of a heavy inflow of foreign investment, and the expectation of a revaluation stimulated speculation on a scale that the Canadian monetary authorities could not control. The inflow of capital was adding to the money supply, and tending to lower interest rates, thus augmenting inflationary forces. The Canadian authorities therefore obtained the approval of the IMF to float, but the floating rate was intended as a temporary device to determine what the market would establish as a new parity rate. Although the Fund requested the re-establishment of an effective par value as soon as circumstances warranted, the Canadian dollar actually continued to float until 1962. The Fund's ultimate objective was to create the conditions for the restoration of a stable and unified exchange rate, and the fluctuating rate was regarded only as a temporary means to an end. In effect, Canada's exchange rate fluctuated by only 3 to 5 per cent, and for practical purposes the benefits commonly associated with exchange rate stability were not lost.

Again, in June 1970, Canada decided to float under conditions broadly similar to those of 1950—a general belief that the Canadian dollar was undervalued, a massive inflow of short-term funds, and a desire to pursue domestic anti-inflationary policies. The speculative inflows made it extremely difficult for the Bank of Canada to avoid an inappropriately expansive monetary policy. In order to free domestic monetary policy from the balance-of-payments situation, the government abandoned the fixed parity of United States 92.5 cents.

At the time of the float, the IMF merely noted "the current situation in Canada" before going on to emphasize the responsibility that rests on all members to promote exchange stability and maintain orderly exchange arrangements with one another. A *New York Times* editorial was, however, commendatory:

> Canada's move should have important educational value for other countries with undervalued currencies. For instance, Japan's trade problems vis-à-vis the United States and Western Europe could be greatly eased if the Japanese also permitted their currency to find its true market value. An appreciated Japanese yen could help to forestall the imposition of rigid quotas or other artificial barriers to trade.
>
> In fact, a more flexible exchange rate system adopted by all nations could prevent the growing wave of protectionism from wrecking the international market for goods and capital which took so long to rebuild after the Depression and World War II.
>
> The world's finance ministers and central bankers, a notoriously conservative group, would be extremely ill-advised to try to persuade the Canadians to abort an experiment with so much educational value to other nations in terms of both domestic and international economic policy. The longer the Canadian experiment lasts, the better.[26]

The Canadian action did not receive such support, however, from the Managing Director of the IMF and his staff. An account of the negotiations between the IMF and Canadian authorities states

> On May 27 the Canadian Executive Director, Robert Johnstone, described the developing situation to Schweitzer (Managing Director of the IMF) and informed him that Canadian officials were considering possible lines of action and did not rule out letting the Canadian dollar float. Johnstone was flying to Ottawa the next day and asked for Schweitzer's views. Later that day, after discussion with the staff, Schweitzer reviewed the Canadian situation with Johnstone, arguing that the current-account surplus was of recent origin, that it was premature to conclude that there was a fundamental disequilibrium, and that there were other ways the Canadian authorities could offset the impact of capital inflow if that was the main problem. He strongly advised against allowing the cur-

26 Editorial, *New York Times* (June 3, 1970).

> rency to float. . . . In a telephone conversation with Louis Rasminsky, Governor of the Bank of Canada, Schweitzer summarized his reasons for urging that the par value be maintained at least until there was a longer span of experience with the developing payments position. Rasminsky repeated the analysis and arguments that Johnstone had already presented. . . .
>
> The Canadian action was particularly unwelcome, since the Executive Directors were well advanced in considering the 1970 report, *The Role of Exchange Rates in the Adjustment of International Payments*, which would give a ringing endorsement of the par-value system.[27]

From the outset of the float, the Canadian authorities had stated they did not intend to let the exchange rate adjust completely to market forces, but reserved the right to intervene on exchange markets to keep the Canadian dollar from rising too rapidly and to stabilize the rate. Thus, the Governor of the Bank of Canada stated

> The exchange rate is a very important price in a country that trades with the outside world on the scale that Canada does: changes in it have important effects on the level and nature of economic activity in Canada, particularly on the position of industries that export and that compete with imports. It is not therefore possible to ignore it, even when it floats. Public financial management must continue to be concerned that the exchange rate is broadly suitable to the development of Canada's international trade, and compatible with the desired structure of our balance of payments, in particular the size of the balance on current account. . . . If the exchange rate moves or threatens to move outside that range it will be prudent to review the mix of financial policy in Canada to see if some other mix would be more appropriate. Whether it will be monetary policy or fiscal policy or both that will need to be changed will depend on the circumstances.

In following a policy of first keeping the rate down and then stabilizing it, Canada's Exchange Fund Account intervened to purchase U.S. or Canadian dollars as needed "to maintain orderly conditions in the market." Canadian foreign exchange reserves increased by approximately $850 million in 1971, indicating that the

27 Southard, *The Evolution of the International Monetary Fund*, pp. 34–36.

float was not "clean," but subject to intervention by the Canadian authorities to keep their dollar from rising above the United States dollar.

4. THE DOLLAR PROBLEM

The dominant factor shaping international financial diplomacy since the end of World War II has been the evolution from "dollar shortage" in the immediate postwar years to "dollar glut" since the mid-1950s. Many economists have believed that while the dollar was undervalued until the mid-1950s, it then became overvalued until the devaluations of August 1971 and February 1973. Of all the postwar currency crises, the dollar crisis of August 1971 has had the most far-reaching implications—making the need for reform of the international monetary system obvious. But there has been a wide range of opinion among government officials, the international financial community, and academic economists as to the causes and the cures for the dollar "deficit."

As one authority summarized the period since the war:

> On August 15, 1971, the United States placed the world on a virtually pure dollar standard by suspending indefinitely the convertibility of the dollar into U.S. reserve assets. . . . The postwar monetary system is now in its third phase. The first phase lasted through 1958, when only the dollar among major currencies was convertible into other currencies and into the reserve assets of the issuing country. The second phase lasted from 1959 until August 1971, when the currencies of all major countries were convertible both into one another and into their own reserves. The third phase began in August 1971, when the dollar alone among those major currencies became inconvertible into the reserves of its issuing country—though through the actions of the private markets and other countries, it remained convertible into other currencies. So the dollar has moved from being the only *convertible* major currency to being, at least in part, the only *inconvertible* major currency.[28]

28 C. Fred Bergsten, *Reforming the Dollar: An International Monetary Policy for the United States* (1972), pp. 5–6.

Certain features stand out in the international monetary history of the past quarter century:

(i) From 1950 to the 1971 crisis there was a persistent "deficit" in the U.S. balance of payments (except for a single surplus in 1957).

(ii) The foreign holdings of dollar assets rose markedly throughout the period, and the U.S. gold stock diminished from $23 billion in 1957 to less than $11 billion at the time of the gold crisis in March 1968.

(iii) But while the "deficit" in the U.S. balance of payments served to provide additional liquidity to the international monetary system, the very creation of the "deficit" also undermined confidence in the future exchange-rate stability of the dollar.

(iv) Nonetheless, the dollar—possessing some functions of international money—retained a unique position in the gold-and-dollar reserve system.

(v) For the United States, however, there was no readily available mechanism of adjustment to balance-of-payments disequilibrium.

Considering the political economy of the U.S. balance-of-payments deficit, one student of the problem has observed:

> Two of the most sensitive areas of sovereign power are defense and money. The former determines a nation's security, and the latter influences its allocation of material resources. When seen in this light, it is not coincidental that, given the absence of an over-all political consensus, major problems confronting the Atlantic community have to do with the control of nuclear weapons and international liquidity.
>
> [T]he clear-cut U.S. superiority in military technology persists, a fact which effectively keeps European fingers off the alliance's nuclear button. But the similarity in the Atlantic problems ends as soon as the U.S. nuclear stockpile is compared with its gold stockpile. The former has grown bigger and better in the 1960's, while the latter has been decimated. The European offensive for authority in monetary affairs and the U.S. reaction have understandably reflected the fact that this country's international economic performance has not been as successful as its military performance. Nuclear warheads have been produced in greater quantities than gold bullion. . . .

> To say that the U.S. balance-of-payments deficit is extraordinary is a classic understatement. Its causes, severity, duration, method of financing, impact on other countries, and means of elimination are all without comparison in international monetary history.[29]

The emphasis on control of nuclear weapons and international liquidity is not purely rhetorical. In the early 1960s these were precisely the problems that were of major concern to the Kennedy Administration. It has been reported that

> The balance of payments remained a constant worry to Kennedy. Of all the problems he faced as President, one had the impression that he felt least at home with this one. He used to tell his advisers that the two things which scared him most were nuclear war and the payments deficit. Once he half-humorously derided the notion that nuclear weapons were essential to international prestige. "What really matters," he said, "is the strength of the currency. It is this, not the *force de frappe,* which makes France a factor. Britain has nuclear weapons, but the pound is weak, so everyone pushes it around. Why are people so nice to Spain today? Not because Spain has nuclear weapons but because of all those lovely gold reserves." He had acquired somewhere, perhaps from his father, the belief that a nation was only as strong as the value of its currency; and he feared that, if he pushed things too far, "loss of confidence" would descend and there would be a run on gold. But he was determined not to be stampeded into restrictive domestic measures, and he brought steady pressures for remedies which would not block expansion at home. The problem perhaps constrained him more in foreign affairs. He thought, for example, that the continuing payments deficit gave France, with its claims on American gold, a dangerous international advantage; and at times he even briefly considered doing things which would otherwise run athwart his policy, like selling submarines to South Africa, in the hope of relieving the strain on the balance of payments.[30]

To reach an understanding of the causes of the dollar "deficit" and to appraise the significance of the accumulation of foreign holdings of dollars and the gold outflow, we must first appreciate the special position of the dollar in the world monetary system.

29 Stephen D. Cohen, *International Monetary Reform, 1964–69* (1970), pp. 19–20.
30 Arthur M. Schlesinger, Jr., *A Thousand Days: John F. Kennedy in the White House* (1965), pp. 654–655.

4.1 The Dollar as an International Currency

Whatever passes as "money" is supposed to meet three basic needs: a unit of account, a medium of exchange, and a store of value. These needs relate just as much to international money as they do to domestic currency. It is important to recognize the extent to which the dollar, by fulfilling certain functions, has acquired the characteristics of an international currency.

Under the Bretton Woods system, the dollar came to fulfill several functions more effectively than any other currency, being essentially a world currency. The dollar is widely used as a transactions or "vehicle" currency. A large portion of world trade is invoiced and transacted in dollars, and the dollar has had a dominant medium-of-exchange function in international transactions.

The dollar has also been central to the IMF system because the United States was the sole country to peg its currency to gold, and other countries pegged their currencies in relation to the gold value of the dollar. The dollar thereby became a *unit-of-account currency,* in the sense that exchange rate parities were initially expressed in terms of the dollar as the unit of account.

Another major role of the dollar is as an *intervention currency.* It will be recalled that the original IMF agreement obligated governments to maintain their exchange rates "within the limits of plus or minus 1% of the defined parities of the currencies." To keep their currencies pegged within this narrow band, governments bought and sold in the dollar exchange market to offset discrepancies between demand and supply of their own currencies. When intervening as residual buyers or sellers, governments use the dollar as the intervention currency.

Most important, the dollar has also been the primary "*reserve currency*" insofar as the dollar has been useful for a store-of-value purpose in official reserve assets. Convertible currencies, under the Fund Agreement, are convertible into dollars; and dollars held by official monetary authorities were convertible into gold at a known price until the crisis of August 1971.

Given the special roles of the dollar, the international monetary policy of the United States has differed from that of other countries in an important respect. Until August 1971, the United States maintained its exchange rates within the parity band by freely buying and selling gold against dollars offered by foreign monetary authorities at a fixed price of $35 per ounce [under Article IV, sec. 4(b) of the IMF Agreement]. The United States was the only government committed to selling gold at a fixed price. Because other countries used the dollar as a unit of account and an intervention currency, U.S. monetary authorities were technically unable to change the relationship between the dollar and other major currencies. It was the *other* currency that had to be devalued or revalued—or maintained within the set margins of parity—vis-à-vis the dollar. Other countries had to change the price at which *they* bought and sold dollars to bring about a change in the exchange rate of the dollar.

In analyzing U.S. balance-of-payments policy, many economists have emphasized the international asymmetry in the adjustment of balance-of-payments disequilibria as between the United States and the rest of the world. A strong statement of this follows:

> At the moment . . . it is a dollar world, just as 1913 was a sterling world. In the view of some American economists . . . , this produces certain asymmetries in financial relationships which are an inherent part of the present system. Put baldly and with some exaggeration, these are:
>
> (i) The dollar is the world medium of exchange, unit of account, store of value, standard of deferred payment. It is the vehicle currency through which French francs are transferred into Deutschmarks, for example, and lire into Danish kroner. No other currency performs a similar role on a similar scale.
>
> (ii) If the dollar is a world money, the United States is a bank and not a firm as other countries are. The difference between a firm and a bank, of course, is that the liabilities of the former are expected to be paid off at regular intervals, while those of the latter are passed from hand to hand as money, and tend to be permanent in fact, despite being "demand" in form. . . . To the extent that a country is a bank and not a firm, its balance of payments must be viewed from a different perspective, with equilibrium, deficits and surplus measured on a different basis.
>
> (iii) The dollar is a money's money, a *numéraire* for foreign exchanges, and cannot be regarded as other currencies. It cannot float, except as other currencies float against it, and its value is the reciprocal of the value of all other currencies, not its price in one.
>
> (iv) The United States can change the value of gold, but not the

price of the dollar. Other countries can readily change the value of their currencies against the dollar, but not the price of gold.[31]

The extent to which these asymmetries actually existed and were controlling in the formation of balance-of-payments policy is a fundamental question throughout this Problem. In differing degrees, many American economists would have regarded the statement of these asymmetries as objective statements of fact, but many European economists would view them merely as subjective claims by the United States to preferred treatment. In opposing these claims, it is difficult to sort out how much of the negative reaction in Europe is objection to the economic analysis and how much objection to the political dependence of Europe implicit in the asymmetrical or hierarchical relationship.

In acquiring functions of an international currency, the dollar reaps some benefits, but also some costs. The major benefit is that when foreigners are willing to accumulate dollars, the United States is able to sustain a larger balance-of-payments deficit than would otherwise be possible. Instead of losing gold, the United States can finance its deficit through voluntary accumulations of dollar liabilities held by foreigners. As long as confidence is retained in the dollar, this allows the United States to run a larger cumulative deficit over time than it otherwise could. It has been said that by financing its deficit through its own creation of international money, the United States obtains a kind of "free" command over real resources, which can be used to enlarge its purchases of foreign goods, services, and assets (including interest-paying reserves). This benefit is sometimes likened to the gain from "seignorage"—the reference being to an earlier period when the state treasury gained the difference between the circulating value of a coin and the cost of bullion and its minting. By running a cumulative deficit in its balance of payments, the United States can create internationally held dollars in a costless fashion and gain an increase in real national expenditure relative to national income.

On the other side, however, the major cost of being a reserve currency country is the opportunity cost in policy-making—the pol-

31 C. P. Kindleberger and Andrew Shonfield (eds.), *North American and Western European Economic Policies* (1971), pp. xiii–xiv.

icies that the country must forgo in order to prevent the withdrawal of past foreign accumulations of its money. To the extent that there is an "overhang" of dollar liabilities, the United States may have to forgo the use of expansionary monetary and fiscal policies that would otherwise be undertaken for domestic economic objectives, but which if undertaken might lessen the foreigners' confidence in the United States government's ability or willingness to maintain dollar convertibility at a fixed rate of exchange.

An appraisal of the benefits and costs of having some functions of international money is in the background of U.S. international monetary policy. When the benefits become less than the costs, it might be expected that the United States would recognize that reform of the international monetary system is essential to remove pressure on the dollar and allow greater freedom in domestic policy formation.

4.2 Analyzing the Deficit

Table I.4 summarizes the international liquidity position of the United States in the period 1961–70. It can be noted that external liquid liabilities increased from $23 billion in 1961 to almost $47 billion in 1970 (line 11, Table I.4); of this total in 1970, official holdings amounted to approximately $24 billion and private holdings to approximately $22 billion, but the gold stock was only $11 billion.

Trends in the net liquidity balance and the official settlements balance are shown in Figure I.1. The surplus in the official settlements balance in 1968 and 1969 is explained by the large inflow of short-term funds when U.S. interest rates were higher than foreign rates. In 1970, United States interest rates were below foreign rates, and the outward flow of short-term capital funds was so large that the official settlements deficit was nearly $10 billion.

When announcing the new presentation of balance-of-payments data, the Commerce Department stated that "it isn't possible to define a single balance which can adequately represent the underlying position of the United States . . . and equilibrium in the external position of the United States cannot be equated with zero in any of the possible balances, in either the short run or long run."[32] The accountant's measurement of the "deficit" is no substitute for the

32 *Wall Street Journal* (July 7, 1971), p. 6.

Table I.4 International Liquidity Position of the United States

International liquidity	*1961*	*1962*	*1963*	*1964*	*1965*	*1966*	*1967*	*1968*	*1969*	*1970*	*1971*	*1972*
Monetary authorities reserves	18.75	17.22	16.84	16.67	15.45	14.88	14.83	15.71	16.96	14.49	13.19	13.15
Gold	16.95	16.06	15.60	15.47	14.06	13.23	12.07	10.89	11.86	11.07	11.08	10.49
SDRs	1.69	1.06	1.04	.77	.60	.33	—	—	—	.85	1.19	1.96
Reserve position in the fund	.12	.10	.21	.43	.78	1.32	.42	1.29	2.32	1.94	.63	.46
Foreign exchange	—	—	—	—	—	—	2.35	3.53	2.78	.63	.28	.24
Fund position												
Credit tranche position: stand-by	4.12	4.12	4.12	4.12	4.12	5.16	—	—	—	—	—	—
Credit tranche position: other	5.81	5.19	5.16	4.89	4.73	5.49	5.16	5.16	5.16	6.70	7.27	7.27
Net draw./fund sales (−) to date	−.64	−.03	−.02	.23	.38	.91	.79	—	−1.05	−.30	1.17	1.38
Quota	4.12	4.12	4.12	4.12	4.12	5.16	5.16	5.16	5.16	6.70	7.27	7.27
External liabilities	22.94	24.07	26.32	29.00	29.12	29.78	35.67	38.47	45.91	46.96	67.81	82.90
Central banks & governments	11.83	12.71	14.35	15.42	15.37	13.66	18.19	17.34	16.00	23.78	50.65	61.50
Canada	2.48	3.11	1.79	1.61	1.53	1.19	1.31	1.87	1.62	2.95	3.98	4.28
Western Europe	9.56	9.27	8.44	9.22	8.61	7.49	10.32	8.06	7.07	13.62	30.13	34.20
Latin America	1.20	1.20	1.06	1.24	1.50	1.13	1.58	1.87	1.91	1.68	1.43	1.72
Asia	2.84	3.29	2.73	3.02	3.30	3.34	4.43	5.00	4.55	4.71	13.82	17.57
Africa	.34	.43	.15	.16	.19	.28	.25	.25	.55	.41	.42	.78
Other			.18	.18	.24	.23	.30	.30	.29	.41	.87	2.96
Other banks & other foreigners	8.36	8.36	9.20	11.06	11.48	14.21	15.76	19.38	28.23	21.77	15.09	19.77
of which: short-term to banks	5.38	5.25	5.71	7.22	7.36	9.86	11.08	14.47	23.64	17.17	10.95	14.82
International agencies	2.75	3.00	2.76	2.52	2.26	1.92	1.71	1.75	1.68	1.41	2.07	1.63
By type: short-term	19.48	21.16	22.14	24.72	24.75	26.79	29.91	30.95	39.45	41.39	55.19	60.95
Marketable	2.65	2.11	2.68	2.40	2.33	1.71	1.47	.93	.87	.86	2.40	5.66
Nonmarketable convert.	—	—	.70	1.08	1.20	.26	.71	.70	.56	.43	6.09	12.11
Fund gold deps. & invest.	.80	.80	.80	.80	.83	1.01	1.03	1.03	1.02	.57	.54	—
Nonliquid liabilities	—	.26	.25	.35	.48	1.31	2.55	4.86	4.02	3.72	3.59	4.18
External claims	6.85	7.32	9.00	12.24	12.25	12.02	12.53	12.28	12.92	13.88	16.94	20.45
Short-term	4.82	5.16	5.98	7.96	7.74	7.84	8.61	8.71	9.67	10.80	13.28	15.54
Long-term	2.03	2.16	3.03	4.28	4.52	4.18	3.92	3.57	3.25	3.08	3.66	4.91

SOURCE: IMF, *International Financial Statistics*, 1972 Supplement.

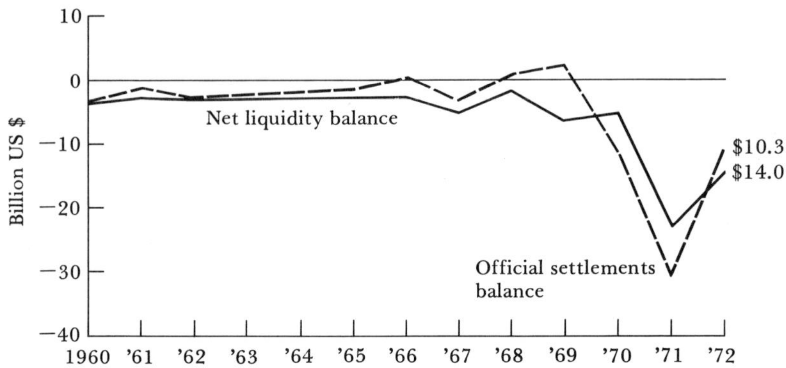

Figure I.1 United States Net Liquidity and Official Settlements Balance

economist's analysis of the "deficit." The accountant's measurement is of transactions ex post; the economist's analysis involves the more difficult attempt to identify the motives of the transactors. The economist tries to analyze the ex ante disequilibrium in "autonomous" transactions (as contrasted with the "induced" or "accommodating" transactions that finance the deficit). Analysis of the deficit requires interpretation of cause and effect relationships within the accounts, and the determination of whether remedial policy measures are required—and if so, what measures are desirable and feasible. This analysis is complex and has an inescapable judgmental quality.

As we turn to the specific issues involved in the problem of the dollar deficit, we should respond to the economist's task of analysis by keeping in mind some fundamental analytical, as well as the political, questions:

Does a deficit necessarily represent a disequilibrium among currencies? If we define an equilibrium situation as a constellation of forces that can be maintained, can we argue that the U.S. balance of payments can be in equilibrium even though there is a deficit in one of the measures of the balance?

Even if we do contend that there can be an economic equilibrium with a deficit, is this also a political equilibrium—or do political forces require some adjustment process?

If remedial policies are required, should they be in the form of changes in the level of national income and expenditure or price changes or exchange rate variations? And should the adjustment be forced through unilateral actions or negotiated through international consultations?

If in the postwar period economists narrowed their differences on domestic stability policy, the same could not be said for international monetary policy. In the case of the U.S. balance of payments, the range of views was exceptionally wide. Since 1959, American officials introduced a series of measures to meet the U.S. balance-of-payments problem. But among economists, there were differences in determining whether the United States really had to adjust to a balance-of-payments disequilibrium; whether the essential problem was one of "adjustment" or "liquidity"; whether the dollar could—or should—be made the preferred asset to gold or other reserve assets. There was also wide diversity in diagnosis—and prescription—among the international business and financial community, central bankers, and government officials.

In 1966, a celebrated article presented "a minority view" on the U.S. balance of payments and world liquidity.[33] Exception was taken to the consensus in Europe and the United States that the U.S. deficits were no longer available as a generator of liquidity because the accumulation of dollars had gone so far that it had undermined confidence in the dollar, and that to forestall headlong flight from the dollar, it is necessary above all else to correct the U.S. deficit. In opposition, the minority view focused on the role of the United States as a financial intermediary as an explanation of the "deficit." Financial intermediation could give rise to a "deficit" that is compatible with equilibrium. Thus, it was stated:

> While the United States has provided the world with liquid dollar assets in the postwar period by capital outflow and aid exceeding its current account surplus, in most years this excess has not reflected a deficit in a sense representing disequilibrium. The outflow of U.S. capital and aid has filled not one but two needs. First, it has supplied goods and services to the rest of the world. But secondly, to the extent that its loans to foreigners are offset by foreigners putting their own money into liquid dollar assets, the U.S.

33 Emile Despres, C. P. Kindleberger, and Walter S. Salant, "The Dollar and World Liquidity: A Minority View," *The Economist* (February 5, 1966), pp. 526–29. A later elaboration is presented by Salant, "Financial Intermediation as an Explanation of Enduring 'Deficits' in the Balance of Payments," in *International Mobility and Movement of Capital*, Fritz Machlup et al. (eds.) (1972), pp. 607–659. See also C. P. Kindleberger, *International Money* (1981).

> has not overinvested but has supplied financial intermediary services. The "deficit" has reflected largely the second process, in which the United States has been lending, mostly at long and intermediate term, and borrowing short. This financial intermediation, in turn, performs two functions: it supplies loans and investment funds to foreign enterprises which have to pay more domestically to borrow long-term money and which cannot get the amounts they want at any price; and it supplies liquidity to foreign asset-holders, who receive less for placing their short-term deposits at home. Essentially, this is a trade in liquidity, which is profitable to both sides. . . . Such lack of confidence in the dollar as now exists has been generated by the attitudes of government officials, central bankers, academic economists, and journalists, and reflects their failure to understand the implications of this intermediary function. Despite some contagion from these sources, the private market retains confidence in the dollar, as increases in private holdings of liquid dollar assets show. Private speculation in gold is simply the result of the known attitudes and actions of government officials and central bankers.[34]

This view diminishes the emphasis placed on the liquidity deficit, and it also indicates that the adjustment problem involves not only the current account, but also the capital account. Attempts to correct the "deficit" by deflation or direct controls on trade and capital movements are likely to make the cure of the balance-of-payments policy worse than the disease of balance-of-payments deficit. The more appropriate policy, it was argued, would be to deny foreign holders of dollars the option of switching from dollars to gold to dollars. The dollar would then become the preferred asset. And unlike any new internationally created reserve asset, which would meet only the need for external liquidity, an increase in the liquid liabilities of the United States in response to a growing total "stock demand" would meet the needs of savers for internal liquidity and of borrowers in the same country for long-term funds. It was therefore concluded that

> Mutual recognition of the role of dollar holdings would provide the most desirable solution, but if, nevertheless, Europe unwisely chooses to convert dollars into gold, the United States could re-

34 *Ibid.*, p. 608.

store a reserve-currency system, even without European cooperation in reinterpreting deficits and lifting capital restrictions. The decision would call for cool heads in the United States. The real problem is to build a strong international monetary mechanism resting on credit, with gold occupying, at most, a subordinate position. Because the dollar is in a special position as a world currency, the United States can bring about this change through its own action. Several ways in which it can do so have been proposed, including widening the margin around parity at which it buys and sells gold, reducing the price at which it buys gold, and otherwise depriving gold of its present unlimited convertibility into dollars.[35]

The minority view, however, had few adherents in official circles. Perhaps Secretary of the United States Treasury Fowler came close to it when on March 17, 1967, before a meeting of the American Bankers Association at Pebble Beach, California, Secretary Fowler chose to issue a statement that was interpreted as an ultimatum to the Group of 10 to create a substitute for the dollar in the form of a new international reserve or else face the prospect of a reconsideration of U.S. commitment to its current gold policy. Secretary Fowler declared that the United States feels impelled to find more ways to "neutralize" the threat of a gold loss, and he warned that lack of enough reserves to support growing world trade would mean "retreat into stale and timid and destructive restrictionism."

A substitute reserve asset—eventually in the form of Special Drawing Rights (SDRs)—was not to be actually created for another two years. And although the supply of gold remained insufficient to serve as the only external reserve, the dollar confronted a confidence problem as questions were raised how long the dollar could continue to be the major source of liquidity and endure a rising ratio of official liabilities-to-gold-reserves without endangering the foreign exchange value of the dollar. In this situation, the world's monetary authorities would have to choose—sooner or later—among three courses of action: (i) to raise the price of gold and thereby increase the value of gold as a reserve asset in the system; (ii) to demonetize gold in favor of the reserve currency as the fundamental reserve money in the system; (iii) to create through international negotiation a new international reserve money to substitute for both gold and the dollar.

35 *Ibid.*, p. 658.

In contrast to official action, a few economists continued to advocate that the United States should stop buying gold and allow exchange rate flexibility. The following letter again expresses this view.

STRONG DOLLAR SEEN IN FREE MARKETS*

To the Editor:

A few days ago the pound was devalued by the arbitrary margin of 14.3 per cent. This happened after long-drawn-out and wasteful efforts to maintain a sterling rate that was clearly incompatible with the requirements of economic equilibrium. The abrupt devaluation that occurred on Nov. 18 is apt to cause substantial dislocations. These could have been avoided if sterling, instead of having been pegged, had all along been allowed to find its true equilibrium level by gradual adjustments in the market.

Will other countries, including the United States, continue to make costly efforts to maintain an administratively determined exchange-rate structure many elements of which are wholly arbitrary by market criteria?

These efforts would involve senseless sacrifices at the expense of significant economic objectives. Furthermore, it is highly questionable whether the administrative controls that would be needed to preserve this artificial structure would be effective even by their own standards. The obvious objective of these controls is to suppress the forces of the market, and this is neither a laudable nor a promising objective.

FLEXIBLE EXCHANGE RATE

As is well known, many economists have favored exchange rate flexibility in free markets for a long time. Recent events have further strengthened our own conviction that policy makers at home and abroad should put flexible exchange rates promptly into effect, with allowance for the probable desire of some countries to form larger currency areas.

As for the United States, we favor letting the market determine the dollar rates without pegging operations of any sort. For a specified final period the American monetary authorities should continue to offer conversion into gold at $35 an ounce for such foreign official dollar holdings as were acquired prior to Nov. 18. Our pres-

*_New York Times_ (November 26, 1967).

ent standing offer to buy gold should stop at once. Thus we should make the dollar independent of gold and should cease to link our currency to foreign currencies at rates that do not satisfy the conditions of international equilibrium.

The United States has the most widely used currency in the world. The strength of the dollar has been obscured by the administrative restrictions of recent years, but it would express itself very clearly in free, unmanipulated markets, unless we should adopt irresponsible monetary and fiscal policies for an extended period of time. There is no reason whatever why we should have to pursue such policies, but if we should nevertheless do so, then the present artificial and wasteful pegging arrangements would collapse anyway.

WILLIAM FELLNER
MILTON FRIEDMAN
HARRY G. JOHNSON
FRITZ MACHLUP

New Haven, Nov. 22, 1967

The writers are professors of economics at universities here and abroad.

In the last quarter of 1967, gold losses from the United States mounted to more than $1 billion and to more than $1.5 billion in January and February 1968. Countries in the gold pool found it increasingly difficult to support the London gold price. By mid-March, the gold drain reached crisis proportions.

GOLD POOL MEETING*

The frenzied London gold market was ordered closed today as top international financial officials were summoned into an urgent weekend meeting in hopes of keeping the monetary crisis from toppling the Free World into economic disaster.

Almost simultaneously with last night's announcements, the Senate in Washington acceded to intense Administration entreaties and sent to the White House the "gold cover" repeal bill making clear that none of the U.S. gold stock need be tied up as "backing" for domestic currency.

**Wall Street Journal* (March 15, 1968).

When President Johnson signs the bill, the historic link will be broken and the $11.4 billion of gold that's left, as of last count, in the U.S. stocks will all be unquestionably available for dollar-propping sale to foreign governments and central banks.

In announcing the exceptional assembly of finance officials from the seven countries active in the London "gold pool," the Treasury said the "temporary closing of the London market doesn't affect the U.S. undertaking to buy and sell gold in transactions with monetary authorities at the official price of $35 an ounce."

While the wording assured that the governmental gold dealings that are the underpinning of world currency stability aren't to be disturbed—at least for now—it pointedly stopped short of assuring that the seven nations would continue pouring gold into hands of private speculators and hoarders through the pool. Whether to continue incurring the immense drain this policy has caused in recent days undoubtedly is the key question before the meeting.

Last night's moves came after a furious day of gold buying in London and European markets sent volume to avalanche proportions, surpassing by well over 100% the record turnover of Wednesday.

And, after the closing of the London gold and securities markets was announced, a bank holiday in Britain was declared. From London, however, the Associated Press said that British banks would be supplying domestic customers with their normal cash requirements in sterling; but that only.

In Washington, a U.S. Treasury spokesman made clear the closing of the gold exchange was at "the suggestion of the U.S." because the London gold market "had become disorganized and didn't permit the handling of business in a reasonably orderly fashion."

Invitations From Fowler, Martin

Treasury Secretary Fowler and Federal Reserve Board Chairman William McChesney Martin jointly invited the European banking officials "to consult with us on coordinated measures to insure orderly conditions in the exchange markets and to support the present pattern of exchange rates based on the fixed price of $35 an ounce of gold."

Close Vote in Senate

The Senate vote to remove the 25% gold backing of domestic currency was a dramatically close 39 to 37.

> The bill removing the gold cover, passed earlier in identical form by the House, would make the Treasury's entire $11.4 billion gold stock available to support the dollar's international value. The Senate approved the bill without amendment under the lash of Administration arguments that putting up the entire gold supply for potential international sale at $35 an ounce could help calm speculative gold-buying fever in Europe.
>
> The rule requiring a $1 gold reserve for every $4 in Federal Reserve currency in circulation has tied up about $10.4 billion of gold, leaving a rapidly dwindling cushion of "free" metal for sale to foreign central banks and governments, and to meet the U.S. contribution to the London gold pool.

After the emergency meeting of the Gold Pool countries, it was decided to terminate gold sales to the private market, and establish a two-tier gold price arrangement by maintaining the official price of $35 for transfers of gold among official monetary authorities while allowing the private market to find its own level without any government dealings with private holders of gold.

With this action, the world's monetary authorities had taken a major step towards the demonetization of gold. The result of this decision could be interpreted as putting the world de facto on an international dollar standard, since it was obvious that the United States could also at any time refuse to convert dollars into gold for official holders of dollars. The action of the Gold Pool also left ambiguous the future role of gold and made its price uncertain.

4.3 Creation of SDRs

After the mid-1960s, there was increasing concern over the adequacy of world reserves. The rate of growth of world reserves slowed down in 1965 and 1966, and the reserves of the industrial countries, taken as a group, declined in 1967. Not only were there actual declines in world reserves, but there were also significant changes in the composition of reserves. Although, in 1966, gold continued to be the largest component of world reserves, constituting $41 billion or about 57 per cent of the total of $72 billion, the percentage had been falling for many years. Moreover, the additions of gold to official monetary reserves ended after 1964, so that at the end of 1966 the gold holdings of national monetary authorities were no higher than they had been in 1964. As private demand for gold increased in anticipation of a price rise, hoarding of gold became intense, and the gold holdings of national monetary authorities declined in 1968 to some $37 billion, the lowest level in a decade.

With these movements in reserves and shifts in reserve policies by various countries, a number of officials feared that a constant reserve supply could not meet the needs of a rapidly expanding world economy. A shortage of official international liquidity could lead to trade restrictions and a slowing down of domestic growth rates to protect the balance of payments. Consequently, the subject of reserve creation became the main focus of Fund meetings in 1967. The 1967 IMF meeting in Rio de Janeiro was historic for approving the outline agreement of "a facility based on special drawing rights in the fund." The new special drawing rights (SDRs) were to be simply entries in the IMF ledgers that allow deficit countries to settle part of their payments imbalances with allotments of SDRs.

At the time of the Rio agreement, the Managing Director of the Fund explained SDRs as follows:

> These special drawing rights, created, as it were, by a stroke of the pen, will be essentially entries in the books of the Fund. Their use will be confined to national monetary authorities, and perhaps one or two international bodies, including the General Account of the Fund itself. Some people like to think of them as money, others as a form of credit. As Dr. Emminger, the former Chairman of the Deputies of the Group of Ten, has aptly put it, they are a sort of zebra which can with equal accuracy be described as a white animal with black stripes or a black animal with white stripes. The material point is not how they are named but what can be done with them. Their value will derive essentially from the fact that participants will be obliged to accept them when properly transferred and to provide in exchange convertible currency or gold, up to a point where they are holding three times as many special drawing rights as have been allocated to them by the Fund. The acceptance limit was set at this level in order to ensure that, on any reasonable view, the scheme would be endowed with a sufficient margin of liquidity.[36]

The Rio agreement is significant because it involved international negotiation among many countries to determine the required

36 Pierre-Paul Schweitzer, *The New Arrangements to Supplement World Reserves and Their Implications for the Developing Countries* (1967), p. 11.

decisions on the basic period for, the timing of, and the amount and distribution of the new reserve asset. The Fund's Historian has assessed the significance of the new asset in these words:

> The significance of an arrangement whereby the Fund could create reserves was commented upon by President Johnson in mid-1968 when he signed into law the U.S. Special Drawing Rights Act: "For the first time in the world's financial history, nations will be able to create international reserves by deliberate and joint decision—and in amounts needed to support sound growth in world trade and payments."
>
> To bring the idea into reality had required an intensive period of study, negotiation, and, finally, legislation. The process had seemed long and drawn out to the watching public and to the financial markets, as well as to those intimately involved. That the negotiations were so prolonged—they had taken longer than those that had preceded the birth of the Fund itself in 1944—and that substantial compromise was required of all parties reflected the nearly equal financial strength of the major industrial countries. Unlike the situation toward the close of World War II, one or two economically dominant countries could not, in the second half of the 1960 decade, draw up an international monetary arrangement to which other countries could be expected to adhere.
>
> To most the effort seemed worthwhile. The Managing Director, for example, said that "given the novelty, the complexity, and the responsibility of the task, I am convinced that the time invested in building a sound structure, and in developing the understanding necessary for the proper use of that structure, has been well justified."
>
> The new drawing rights were certainly novel, and were unlike any other reserve asset or money. Their uniqueness has been described by the General Counsel of the Fund in these words:
>
> "The characteristics of special drawing rights are not the result of any single approach. They are the distillation of a chemistry—some might say an alchemy—in which many theories and many compromises, economic, legal, and political, went into the alembic. The product cannot be classified according to such familiar categories as legal tender, money, or credit. Special drawing rights are *sui generis*."
>
> It seemed that the Fund could create reserves, as it were, out of nothing; it did not need to hold a corresponding amount of financial resources. Just how revolutionary the introduction of SDRs was may be noted by recalling some of the views prevalent at the time

of the Bretton Woods Conference. A document issued by the U.S. Treasury in June 1944, for example, explained that the International Monetary Fund then being proposed would not have any means of creating, holding, or transferring currencies or deposits that did not originate with the member countries themselves. It was explicitly noted that the creation of credit was to remain exclusively a function of the monetary authorities of member countries. Among the reasons cited for preferring this arrangement to one permitting the Fund to create some new or special monetary unit was the following: ". . . The financial strength and stability will be greater in the case of a Fund which possesses a substantial amount of tangible resources for carrying on its operations than in the case of an international institution which has no resources other than an agreement on the part of member countries to accept the credits created by that institution in exchange for real goods and services."

By coincidence, the date on which the amendment to the Articles became effective, July 28, 1969, was 25 years almost to the week after the date, July 22, 1944, on which the original Articles were adopted at the Bretton Woods Conference. The advance made in that interval was that the Fund was at last to be given the power to create reserves that it had not received at Bretton Woods.[37]

THE AGREEMENT*

INTRODUCTION

The facility described in this Outline is intended to meet the need, as and when it arises, for a supplement to existing reserve assets. It is to be established within the framework of the Fund and, therefore, by an Amendment of the Fund's Articles.

I. ESTABLISHMENT OF A SPECIAL DRAWING ACCOUNT IN THE FUND

A. An Amendment to the Articles will establish a Special Drawing Account through which all the operations relating to special drawing rights will be carried out. The purposes of the facility will be set forth in the introductory section of the Amendment.

B. The operations of and resources available under the Special Drawing Account will be separate from the operation of the present Fund which will be referred to as the General Account.

II. PARTICIPANTS AND OTHER HOLDERS

1. Participants. Participation in the Special Drawing Account will be

*J. Keith Horsefield (ed.), *The International Monetary Fund*, vol. III *Documents* (1969).

37 Margaret Garritsen de Vries, *The International Monetary Fund, 1966–1971* (1976), pp. 187–188.

open to any member of the Fund that undertakes the obligations of the Amendment. A member's quota in the Fund will be the same for the purposes of both the General and the Special Drawing Accounts of the Fund.

2. *Holding by General Account.* The General Account will be authorized to hold and use special drawing rights.

III. Allocation of Special Drawing Rights

1. *Principles for decisions.* The Special Drawing Account will allocate special drawing rights in accordance with the provisions of the Amendment. . . .

2. *Basic period and rate of allocation.* The following provisions will apply to any decision to allocate special drawing rights.

(i) The decision will prescribe a basic period during which special drawing rights will be allocated at specific intervals. The period will normally be five years in length, but the Fund may decide that any basic period will be of different duration. The first basic period will begin on the effective date of the first decision to allocate special drawing rights.

(ii) The decision will also prescribe the rate or rates at which special drawing rights will be allocated during the basic period. Rates will be expressed as a percentage, uniform for all participants, of quotas on the date specified in the decision. . . .

V. Use of Special Drawing Rights

1. *Right to use special drawing rights.*

A. A participant will be entitled, in accordance with the provisions of V, to use special drawing rights to acquire an equivalent amount of a currency convertible in fact. A participant which thus provides currency will receive an equivalent amount of special drawing rights.

B. Within the framework of such rules and regulations as the Fund may adopt, a participant may obtain the currencies referred to in A either directly from another participant or through the Special Drawing Account.

C. Except as indicated in V.3.C., a participant will be expected to use its special drawing rights only for balance of payments needs or in the light of developments in its total reserves and not for the sole purpose of changing the composition of its reserves.

D. The use of special drawing rights will not be subject to prior challenge on the basis of this expectation, but the Fund may make representations to any participant which, in the Fund's judgment, has failed to observe the expectation, and may direct drawings to such participant to the extent of such failure.

2. *Provisions of currency.* A participant's obligation to provide currency will not extend beyond a point at which its holdings of special drawing rights in excess of the net cumulative amount of such rights allocated to it are equal to twice that amount. However, a participant may provide currency, or agree with the Fund to provide currency, in excess of this limit.

3. *Selection of participants to be drawn upon.* The Fund's rules and

instructions relating to the participants from which currencies should be acquired by users of special drawing rights will be based on the following main general principles, supplemented by such principles as the Fund may find desirable from time to time:

A. Normally, currencies will be acquired from participants that have a sufficiently strong balance of payments and reserve position, but this will not preclude the possibility that currency will be acquired from participants with strong reserve positions even though they have moderate balance of payments deficits.

B. The Fund's primary criterion will be to seek to approach over time equality, among the participants indicated from time to time by the criteria in A above, in the ratios of their holdings of special drawing rights, or such holdings in excess of net cumulative allocations thereof, to total reserves.

C. In addition, the Fund will, in its rules and instructions, provide for such use of special drawing rights, either directly between participants or through the intermediary of the Special Drawing Account, as will promote voluntary reconstitution and reconstitution under V.4.

D. Subject to the provisions of V.1.C, a participant may use its special drawing rights to purchase balances of its currency held by another participant, with the agreement of the latter.

4. Reconstitution.

A. Members that use their special drawing rights will incur an obligation to reconstitute their position in accordance with principles which will take account of the amount and the duration of the use. These principles will be laid down in rules and regulations of the Fund.

B. The rules for reconstitution of drawings made during the first basic period will be based on the following principles:

i. The average net use, taking into account both use below and holdings above its net cumulative allocation, made by a participant of its special drawing rights calculated on the basis of the preceding five years, shall not exceed 70 percent of its average net cumulative allocation during this period. Reconstitution under this subparagraph i will be brought about through the mechanism of transfers, by the Fund directing drawings correspondingly. . . .

VI. INTEREST AND MAINTENANCE OF GOLD VALUE

A. *Interest.* A moderate rate of interest will be paid in special drawing rights on holdings of special drawing rights. The cost of this interest will be assessed against all participants in proportion to net cumulative allocations of special drawing rights to them.

B. *Maintenance of gold value.* The unit of value for expressing special drawing rights will be equal to 0.888671 grams of fine gold. The rights and obligations of participants and of the Special Drawing Account will be subject to an absolute maintenance of gold value or to provisions similar to Article IV, Section 8 of the Fund's Articles.

By mid-1969, a sufficient number of Fund members had ratified the agreement to allow it to take effect. The allocation of a specific amount of SDRs was then in order. The Group of 10—the leading industrial nations—finally reached a mutually agreeable formula for a three-year allocation of SDRs, with a total of $3.5 billion to be allocated for 1970 and $3 billion in each of the two succeeding years. After this initial three-year period, the SDR operation was to be reassessed. The initial allocation was according to each country's size of quota in the IMF—so that the United States received more than 25 per cent of the total, the Group of 10 approximately 60 per cent, and all the less-developed countries only 25 per cent.

Some hailed SDRs as a "landmark in monetary evolution." And it could certainly be claimed that the securing of official agreement to the international negotiation of a new reserve asset was the most notable accomplishment in international monetary cooperation since Bretton Woods. Nonetheless, some economists called attention to the opportunity cost of the SDR agreement. To those who believed that the adjustment process remained the fundamental problem of the international monetary system, the limited increase in liquidity was merely a diversionary tactic. A few others regarded the agreement "as positively harmful . . . [because] it would distract attention from the more fundamental problems facing the world system and . . . while its long-run potential for good or bad was substantial, the major hurdle was to get beyond the immediate short run. Solution of the short-run problem would involve substantial changes in the structure of the system and the long-run creation of a new international money should be integrated into or evolve out of this short-run reconstruction of the system."[38]

As to the crucial question of whether SDRs would become, in fact, an effective supplement to the present international monetary system, Professor Johnson replied, "time alone will tell. Some authors still hark back to the idea of returning to gold as the basic international monetary reserve, by means of a general increase in its monetary price. Others are convinced that gold has been superseded by the new invention of SDRs. Still others argue that the dollar, as a "natural" outcome of the evolution of the world economy since World War II, will dominate the SDRs and prevent any

38 Robert Mundell, "Toward a Better International Monetary System," *Journal of Money, Credit, and Banking* (August 1969), p. 626.

return to gold at a higher monetary price. My own view is that gold has had its day and that the problem for the future lies between the dollar and the Special Drawing Rights."[39]

For the first time in monetary history, there had been the creation of an owned reserve asset by international negotiation—and simply by means of a computer entry by an international organization. But the creation was to constitute only a small percentage of reserves. Indeed, although $9.3 billion of SDRs were to be created in 1970–72, international reserves in the form of U.S. dollar liabilities were to expand by $45.5 billion during the same period.

5. MAKING OF THE DOLLAR CRISIS

At the same time as the United States was supporting negotiation for creation of the Special Drawing Account in the IMF, the Administration began stressing the need for balance-of-payments discipline and emphasized the connection between "domestic economic management" and the country's external payments position. But although the Administration vowed that the dollar would remain strong and secure, the U.S. deficit continued to increase, and the Eurodollar market continued to grow.

5.1 The Eurodollar Slop

The Eurocurrency market deals mainly in time deposits denominated in U.S. dollars on deposit with banks—so-called Eurobanks—outside the United States. The dollars may be transferred by American residents or foreigners from American banks to offshore centers.

In considering the interaction of political and economic factors, causes and responses during the events of 1971, one analyst has said:

> The underlying source of trouble in the winter of 1970–71 was what some journalist graphically described as "the Eurodollar slop," the large and ever-expanding pool of expatriate credit funds which, though free to move around the globe, tended mostly to slosh back and forth across the Atlantic. This was partly because most Eurocurrencies were dollars and partly because the major

39 Harry G. Johnson, *Efficiency in Domestic and International Money Supply*, International Economics Series, No. 3, University of Surrey (1970), p. 15.

dealers in the market were the foreign branches of American banks, and their parent banks in the United States could easily raise or lower their total liabilities to them. Clearly, the Eurodollar slop made it increasingly difficult for the United States both to manage its domestic economy, whether by promoting growth or restraining inflation and, at the same time, to avoid sudden explosive increases in its external deficit.[40]

EURODOLLAR TRANSMISSION BELT*

The Eurodollar market acts as an efficient transmission belt linking the U.S. and European money markets. Interest rates in the Eurodollar market respond almost immediately to changes in U.S. interest rates, while short-term funds move out of European countries and into Eurodollars, and back again, on the basis of small interest-rate differentials.

In the last two years, changes in the volume of Eurodollars used by banks in the United States have played a crucial role in the transmission of U.S. monetary influence to Europe. When the Federal Reserve adopted a highly restrictive policy, banks in the United States increased their takings of Eurodollars by $7 billion. Eurodollar rates rose steeply and funds flowed out of the European banking systems into the Eurodollar market. In Britain, France and Germany, the outflow contributed to a slowdown in monetary expansion, the effect of which has been felt on business activity this year.

The decline of U.S. short-term interest rates this year and the backflow of Eurodollars released by U.S. banks as domestic monetary conditions have eased have pushed Eurodollar rates down, creating a strong incentive for firms in Germany and other European countries to borrow Eurodollars. For domestic interest rates in Europe this year have been generally higher and credit tighter than in the United States. The resulting inflow of funds has hampered European, especially German, monetary authorities in their struggle with inflation.

If the Eurodollar market did not exist, changes in U.S. monetary policy probably would not be felt as strongly in Continental Europe. The effects would be transmitted through more traditional channels, such as international lending by banks and the U.S. se-

***Monthly Economic Letter*, First National City Bank (November 1970).

40 Susan Strange, "The Dollar Crisis," *International Affairs* (April 1972), p. 198.

> curities markets. These channels are neither as efficient international movers of short-term funds nor as free of regulation as the Eurodollar market—which, of course, is why the Eurodollar market came into existence.
>
> European central banks could doubtless reduce the consequences of dollar ebbs and flows through more effective open-market operations or by changes in the reserves required to be maintained by commercial banks. Yet, given the size of the movements of funds into and out of European currencies relative to the size of bank reserves in these countries, such measures would often be difficult to apply with sufficient vigor and foresight to prevent large changes in local monetary conditions, when conditions in U.S. money markets were changing rapidly.
>
> In any event, the more fundamental political issue remains. Sovereign nations are likely to find irksome, and some of them may in time find unacceptable, a relationship in which their money supplies are partly determined by the vagaries of U.S. monetary policy. . . .
>
> Europe's malaise about the dollar has been greatly intensified by the experience of the last five years. The excessive expansion of the U.S. money supply in the 1965–68 period and its inflationary impact in Europe made Europeans much more aware than they had been previously of the transatlantic monetary leverage of a U.S. payments deficit. The impact of the Federal Reserve's restrictive monetary policy in 1969 on European interest rates and central bank reserves was another sharp reminder of monetary interdependence.

During the decade of the 1960s, the Eurodollar market had increased from some $3 billion to an estimated $50 billion. Although national capital markets were regulated, the growth in the unregulated Eurodollar market was viewed by many as a source of potential trouble.

5.2 *Dollar Outflow*

Although stating that he did not want to engage in "malignant preoccupation" (the opposite to "benign neglect"), Nobel Laureate Paul A. Samuelson nonetheless chose to call attention to the "shakey dollar" in his *Newsweek* column in April 1971. Samuelson wrote that "by every rational test the dollar has been an overvalued currency for almost fifteen years now," and that the situation is not improving.[41]

Capital outflows during the latter part of 1970 had begun to put additional pressure on the dollar. To promote more investment and expansion in the American economy, the United States undertook an easing of monetary policy in the autumn of 1970. But tight monetary conditions in France, Italy, the United Kingdom, and most particularly, Germany encouraged large capital inflows from the United States to these nations. By late 1970, Germany's foreign exchange reserves had risen to $13.5 billion—a larger amount than before the 1969 revaluation of the mark and almost twice what they had been earlier in the year.

A calm view of the international monetary "flurry" was taken by both the chairman of the President's Council of Economic Advisers, Paul W. McCracken, and the Under Secretary of the Treasury for Monetary Affairs, Paul A. Volcker. Addressing the International Economics Forum in Chicago on May 3, Mr. McCracken said there were "heartening signs that the worst may be over" in the outflow of short-term capital, and that "both logic and the facts of experience" suggest that the overall United States balance of international payments will get better, not worse, with an expanding domestic economy. At the same meeting, Mr. Volcker said that "national views converge" on the proposition that the short-term capital problem should be handled "by cooperative arrangements within the basic framework of the convertible currency system at stable exchange rates." Both Mr. McCracken and Mr. Volcker put the "basic" deficit at about $2.5 billion in 1970. Citing the $2.5 billion figure, Mr. Volcker said this was equal to "about 3 per cent of our total trade and less than 2 per cent of our total international transactions. A deficit of that magnitude should certainly be manageable for a time, whether viewed from the standpoint of its effect on our international liquidity position or its impact on flows of funds to other countries. The size is not so great as to appear prohibitive in terms of achieving adjustment over a reasonable period."[42]

41 *Newsweek* (April 19, 1971).
42 *New York Times* (May 4, 1971).

5.3 *The Balance-of-Payments Mess*

Only a few weeks later, however, the Joint Economic Committee was conducting hearings on what it chose to call "The Balance-of-Payments Mess."

OPENING STATEMENT OF CHAIRMAN REUSS*

CHAIRMAN REUSS. Good morning.

The Subcommittee on International Exchange and Payments will be in order for the first of several hearings on the balance-of-payments mess. Spokesmen for the Treasury, the Council of Economic Advisers, and the Federal Reserve System have been denying for a decade that the U.S. external payments situation is a mess; instead they have been maintaining that one more regulation or a minor adjustment in interest rates would buy the time required until a fundamental recovery took hold. Now, however, the time has come to candidly acknowledge the extent of our problem.

Despite all the ad hoc measures, U.S. balance-of-payments deficits are larger than ever and massive international flows of short-term dollar assets have grown into a new problem provoking widespread concern. The Treasury now admits that the United States has a chronic basic payments deficit of $2 to $3 billion annually. The true figure is undoubtedly somewhat larger, since the controls and measures introduced over the last decade tend to mask its proper dimensions. It would certainly seem that the time has come to lay aside palliatives and to consider fundamental adjustment mechanisms to correct the U.S. balance of payments. The role of the dollar as the chief reserve currency in the international monetary system makes decisive corrective action especially urgent.

Earlier this week Mr. Jelle Ziljlstra, chairman of the board of directors and president of the Bank for International Settlements, said in a speech, "The dollar cannot remain the basic currency of the system if the United States does not participate fully in the adjustment process." The purpose of these hearings is to determine whether the United States has participated in the adjustment process as fully as it should. In addition, we will apply the same question to the actions of other nations—in particular to the amount of payments by Germany for the maintenance of U.S. troops in Eu-

The Balance-of-Payments Mess, Hearings before the Subcommittee on International Exchange and Payments of the Joint Economic Committee, 92nd Congress, 1st Session, June 16, 1971, pp. 1–2, 316–324, 382–385, 409–416.

rope and to the external value of the yen as maintained by Japanese monetary authorities.

Senator Javits has suggested, and I concur, that these issues should be discussed and I would hope resolved in an international monetary conference. Unfortunately, the administration seems to be opposed to the idea of such a conference. In addition, I have suggested that if no conference is held, the United States should formally sever the link between the dollar and gold and permit the dollar to temporarily float in exchange markets until an appropriate realignment of rates has occurred, upon which time we would continue to support the parity value of the dollar through exchange operations. These proposals by Senator Javits and myself will also undoubtedly come up for discussion during the course of these hearings.

SENATOR JAVITS. Thank you very much, Mr. Chairman.

CHAIRMAN REUSS. I will now ask Mr. Bergsten, Mr. Halm, and Mr. Willett to come forward.

Gentlemen, we thank you for coming. We now would like to ask each of you to proceed either to summarize or to read your prepared statements.

We will start out first with Mr. Bergsten.

STATEMENT OF C. FRED BERGSTEN

Visiting Fellow, Council on Foreign Relations, and Guest Scholar, The Brookings Institution

The fundamental international monetary issue to any particular country is the degree of control which it can exercise over the liquidity-adjustment tradeoff in the system as a whole. Liquidity and adjustment are perfect substitutes. An infinite supply of liquidity obviates any need for adjustment, and a perfect adjustment process obviates any need for liquidity. Deficit countries usually seek to maximize liquidity and force surplus countries to initiate the process of adjustment. Surplus countries usually seek to minimize liquidity and force deficit countries to initiate adjustment. Both seek to impose their own economic and foreign policy preferences on the other in the process. This essentially political question underlies all of the issues raised for the present hearings.

The adjustment mechanism in the present international monetary system is weak. Countries increasingly orient their domestic economic policies to their domestic needs, which frequently conflict with the needs of external equilibrium. Exchange rate changes are traumatic, psychologically and politically and even in real economic terms, as the recent events remind us once more—although these events also remind us that exchange rates in fact will change. Controls over international transactions are thus the path of least resistance, and hence the most likely response to payments imbalances. Yet these controls vitiate the basic objective of the fixed exchange rate system—to maximize the freedom of international trade and capital movements; are usually inefficient in achieving their objective and therefore tend to proliferate rapidly; and, at this point in history, could easily tip the scales toward protectionist trade policies in the United States and elsewhere, with disastrous economic and international political consequences.

Countries thus wish to avoid adjustment of their imbalances, and none is sufficiently powerful to force adjustment on others. In addition, most want to run continual surpluses to build their reserves as protection against future deficits. The result is that the international monetary system needs lots of liquidity.

Gold now provides very little new liquidity, and will soon provide none since production is stagnant and industrial demand is rising rapidly. Special drawing rights were, of course, created to meet this very need, and are adding about $2 billion yearly to "owned" reserves—the 70 percent of gross allocations which need never be "reconstituted." Under the present international monetary system, the only other major source of additional reserves is the dollar.

The U.S. balance-of-payments position must be seen in this context. I agree with the official calculation that there is a basic deficit of about $2.5–$3 billion annually in the U.S. balance of payments, and has been for many years. The underlying deficit may be a bit larger, in fact, since some U.S. capital outflows have been suppressed by the existing control programs. This deficit long preceded the Vietnam war. It not only preceded our present inflationary excesses, but coexisted with our remarkable price stability of the early 1960's. It has been a permanent feature of the postwar world, through all combinations of cyclical situations and despite dramatic structural changes in the world economy. The basic issue is whether it represents a disequilibrium in any meaningful economic or political sense.

It is impossible to provide a quantitative answer with precision. However, I believe that any U.S. disequilibrium, in the framework of the present international monetary system, is small if indeed it exists at all. Private foreigners clearly want to add to their dollar holdings by at least $1 billion annually, in view of the dollar's unchallenged use as the world's chief transactions currency and the steady growth of the need for such a currency. The revealed desires of foreign monetary authorities to accumulate reserves clearly "justify" additions of at least $1.5 to $2.5 billion annually to world reserves in dollar form, beyond the present level of SDR allocations, as recognized in the IMF analysis of world reserve needs on which the first SDR allocation was based. An underlying U.S. payments imbalance of $2.5 to $3 billion thus appears reasonably close to equilibrium, defined in global economic terms.

The same conclusion holds if we ask the more proper question in assessing the situation of the dollar: Are any major foreign countries in disequilibrium on the surplus side? Switzerland and Austria have just revalued. Canada, Germany, and the Netherlands are floating and will probably eventually repeg at revalued levels, although the very small appreciation of the floating mark—especially prior to Bundesbank intervention—the guilder, and the Belgian "financial franc" raise doubts over the degree of disequilibrium which exist even there. Japan is the only major country with a clearly undervalued exchange rate at this time. Any U.S. disequilibrium on the deficit side is thus matched by disequilibrium on the surplus side only by Japan, and perhaps a few less important countries where exchange rate changes would not have much effect anyway.

Finally, the U.S. balance-of-payments "problem" has never been a direct function of our own balance-of-payments deficits. A real "problem" has occurred for the United States only when surpluses accrued to countries unwilling to hold their reserve increments in dollar form. We could be in surplus on any accounting definition yet have a "problem" if unwilling dollar holders were also in surplus. Fortunately, only a few major countries are consistently unwilling to add to their dollar balances and their persistent surpluses are relatively small even in relation to our sharply reduced stock of reserve assets. Over time, there easily appear to be enough willing dollar holders to maintain the equilibrium situation outlined above: underlying U.S. deficits averaging $2.5 billion annually.

The United States should therefore adopt no new unilateral measures in an effort to reduce its balance-of-payments deficit. In fact, recent econometric studies indicate that our balance of payments could gain well over $1 billion from the recent exchange rate moves, assuming that the Canadian dollar eventually settles near its present level and that the mark and guilder settle 5 percent above their present parities. The additional improvement we would get from an adequate revaluation of the Japanese yen would seem to nail down beyond much doubt the absence of any U.S. balance-of-payments disequilibrium.

I strongly oppose the proposal for a unilateral U.S. effort to change our exchange rate by unpegging the dollar from gold. Such a move is certainly unnecessary at this time. It would be extremely disruptive politically, at home, and especially abroad. It might not even result in any exchange rate changes, since other countries could simply maintain their present dollar intervention points. It would provide no lasting improvements in the adjustment process, even if we were never to repeg to gold but at some point assumed instead the obligations of "current account convertibility" under the Articles of Agreement of the IMF, and it would drastically hurt our efforts to achieve such improvement. U.S. action of this type would clearly be seen as an effort to build our trade balance and hence alter the structure of our balance of payments, which would be all too reminiscent of the competitive devaluations of the 1930's and thus hurt badly, rather than help, the crucial effort to combat protectionism around the world. . . .

CHAIRMAN REUSS. Thank you very much, Mr. Bergsten. . . .
We will now finally hear from Mr. Willett.

STATEMENT OF THOMAS D. WILLETT
Associate Professor of Economics and Public Affairs, Cornell University

MR. WILLETT.

I am particularly happy to be here today because I think these hearings are quite important. I think the international monetary system is at an important crossroads because we no longer have an international monetary system, I think, in the sense of a coherent set of principles such as those laid out at Bretton Woods, which are adhered to by the major participants of the system. The Bretton Woods system in the last few years has finally proved unworkable and is currently on its last legs, if it is not its ghost that we are currently observing.

Clearly the gold exchange portion of the Bretton Woods system is by sheer numbers no longer working. The dollar liabilities outstanding greatly exceed our gold supply and the idea of a gold exchange standard is no longer workable. Likewise, the exchange rate mechanism of adjustable pegs envisioned in the Bretton Woods system is under serious doubt both from the action of member countries and from academic arguments.

It is most appropriate that we do consider what directions the future international monetary system will go. I think it is entirely possible that the present system will continue to muddle on for quite awhile. This would be an undesirable result in which we would keep getting current financial crises that we have seen too frequently in recent years.

In looking at the alternatives for possible directions in which the international monetary system might go, it would be helpful to begin with the question of basic objectives of the system, at least what would be a major objective with which we would want the system to be consistent. For the most important objective we suggest the freedom of macroeconomic policy to be geared to the dictates of domestic economy.

The major cause of tensions and problems in the present international monetary system is where you get deficits resulting from supply side phenomena emanating from the United States. It would be hard to argue that all of the U.S. measured deficit in recent years was a result of the increase in foreign countries' demand for dollars. Certainly it in part was a reflection of the Vietnam war and the concomitant inflation and serious deterioration in the trade balance. This was clearly a case in which we forced a dilemma on other countries, either they had to accept unwanted dollars or take measures to correct deficits themselves or the United States would have to take measures.

I think that this will be less of a problem in the future as countries begin to use greater exchange rate flexibility. If we go that route with other countries we are back to a monetary system in which we treat the dollar like all other currencies. And I might add this point, this doesn't make a lot of economic sense because there are very real economic reasons why the dollar reached the position it did. It was really a result of private entrepreneurs' actions in response to this, not some political scheme on the part of the United States, that put the dollar in its present position. But if we say largely for political reasons we don't want a system in which the United States is an inconvertible center of the system, we want to rely on special drawing rights or an international Federal Reserve System to manage international liquidity, then we are going to have to find some way to restore effective exchange rate adjustment for the United States. . . .

Now, what I am arguing is that there are only two reasonable types of international monetary systems. One would be a system in which we have some sort of a full passive U.S. balance-of-payments policy and we tell everybody else to adjust or finance deficits. The other one is one in which we are treated like every other country, we have the same adjustment responsibilities as other countries but we have to also be given the same adjustment techniques. If you are looking at the criteria for flexible exchange rates, the criteria for ranking countries as better or worse candidates for using exchange rate adjustments to correct their balance of payments, the United States is the leading candidate. It would not really in any sense be reasonable to try to run an international monetary system in which the United States does have adjustment responsibility but doesn't have necessary techniques to carry it out.

Now, the problem is that these are sort of two polar systems and, as you well know, in politics you tend to muddle around in the middle. In the last few years we have moved first in one direction, a little bit toward a dollar standard, and then moved a little bit toward a SDR standard, and you have the tremendous problem of having a case which tends to combine the worse features of the two prototype systems rather than the best features. Now, between the two systems, these two polar systems which I think are the most reasonable, I don't think it makes a great deal of difference to the United States which system was chosen.

I think the major U.S. interest could be secured in either way. We would not have to worry about the balance of payments as a severe constraint on domestic economic policies or need to resort to controls to correct our balance of payments. We get out of this problem under either system and in fact the sort of differences in the two systems are probably much more important for our European neighbors than they are for us because a major part of the choice concerns how useful is the dollar to others as an international transaction currency and how repugnant to the Europeans are the political implications of the use of the dollar. Really the decision between the two polar positions is a question that we could well leave to the international community to decide. But what the United States does need to do is to force a decision because otherwise we will just continue to muddle through. Hopefully, some increase in exchange rate flexibility and the SDR creation will be a distinct improvement over the way the system has been running in the last few years, but still I think a very much second-best solution.

5.4 Other Disturbing Events

The outlook for the dollar remained precarious even after the revaluations of the European currencies. The United States Treasury's gold stock was diminished by conversions of dollars into gold by France and Belgium in mid-May, and the *Wall Street Journal* disclosed that these purchases of gold reduced the Treasury's gold stock "to what is probably its lowest level since the end of World War II. Unless offset by undisclosed U.S. purchases of gold from other countries, the sales . . . would leave the U.S. gold stock at about $10.6 billion."[43] Speculation in gold intensified, and by mid-May the price of gold in private bullion markets reached the highest level since October 1969.

Few economists (outside of South Africa and France) advocated a rise in the price of gold. A notable exception was Sir Roy Harrod, biographer of John Maynard Keynes. Although Keynes had earlier denigrated gold as a "barbaric relic" and had sought its demonetization at Bretton Woods, Harrod's view was now quite different.

TRIPLE THE DOLLAR PRICE OF GOLD*

To the Editor:

The gyrations of the world currency crisis of the last few days have been formidable. We may expect further crises in the future, unless something is done about it.

There is a very simple solution, which would, I feel quite confident, free us from crises of this kind for a few decades ahead. The Americans, by agreement with the International Monetary Fund, should raise the dollar price of gold.

We are supposed to be, but for some years have not in fact been, living under the Bretton Woods system. This has two parts. One is that countries have to maintain exchange rates within fixed limits within their own territories. For this purpose they have been using the dollar as "the currency of intervention"; this is a convenient system, which has, however, no official sanction. The other part is that each country is obliged to pay gold in exchange for accumulations of its currency in the hands of other members. This obligation applies to all member currencies and not, as is sometimes asserted,

*Letters to the Editor, *New York Times* (May 18, 1971).

43 *Wall Street Journal* (May 13, 1971).

to the dollar only. (Article VII, 4a of Articles of Agreement of I.M.F.)

In recent years some countries have refrained from asking the Americans for gold in exchange for unwanted dollars, sometimes perhaps out of consideration for the Americans, sometimes perhaps under political pressure and recently because it was evident that there was not enough gold in Fort Knox to enable the Americans to honor their obligations.

Thus the Bretton Woods system has ceased to function. It will take many years for the Special Drawing Rights to become a sufficient substitute.

For some twenty years I have advocated a doubling of the dollar price of gold. But as the average of the dollar prices of goods has gone up about three times since President Roosevelt fixed the existing dollar price of gold, a trebling would seem to be appropriate ($105 = one ounce of gold). This would make the gold stock in Fort Knox worth about $36 billion.

And then a remarkable thing would happen. Much of the desire by other central banks to convert dollars into gold would fall right away. Recently there has been restiveness about holding dollars because of what is called "a credibility gap"; but with $36 billion of gold in Fort Knox this would end.

And then the dollar could indeed become the world's currency for practical purposes, which it certainly is not at present. Nothing could be more wrong-headed than to see gold as a sort of rival to the dollar. On the contrary it is via gold that the dollar could achieve its maximum usefulness in the world.

Some Americans have told me that owing to statements by Presidents Kennedy, Johnson and Nixon they feel bound in honor to maintain the dollar at $35 = one ounce of gold. There is no sense in this when the rest of the world does not want them to do so. It is as though a father promised an infant son a horse when he attained the age of twelve. When the boy does so, it turns out that he is entirely unathletic, would not go near a horse, still less ride on it. But the father says, "I have promised my son a horse and a horse he shall have." Further to this, the Americans have not been making the dollar de facto gold convertible at will. They have only provided a painted, wooden horse.

There might be some question of compensation. The sums involved would not be large in relation to the new situation.

Nothing said above is inconsistent with the idea of having more flexible exchange rates, which I have not discussed.

ROY HARROD

Reports of the United States balance of trade were certainly underscoring the difficulties of the U.S. trading position, particularly vis-à-vis Japan. In April, May, June, and July, imports exceeded exports, and the balance of trade threatened to show an annual deficit for the first time since 1893.

Finally, Rep. Henry S. Reuss gave the authority of his Joint Economic subcommittee to demands for altering the exchange value of the dollar. On June 3, 1971, Reuss introduced a "sense of Congress" resolution in the House of Representatives that would formally end the United States commitment to sell gold to foreign central banks at $35 an ounce and would eventually have the Federal Reserve System support the exchange value of the dollar, as other countries do, by operations in the foreign exchange market. Reuss proposed an interim period during which the dollar would float, with the aim of removing present "disequilibrium" in exchange rates, particularly against the Japanese yen. He stated: "The United States under the present monetary system unnecessarily cripples itself by its inability to alter its exchange rate with other countries. . . . Only by closing the gold window and letting the dollar find a newer and sounder relationship with the yen can we avoid the deterioration of our trading position and a return to trade autarky."[44]

A spokesman for the Treasury, however, was quick to state that the Reuss plan was "certainly not the position of the United States Government." He pointed to a statement by Treasury Secretary Connally the previous week in Munich that "we are not going to devalue the dollar."

Again, on August 6, Representative Reuss' subcommittee reported that based on hearings held by the subcommittee in June, the subcommittee came to the "inescapable conclusion" that the dollar is "overvalued" in relation to most other currencies, and that a "new external value for the dollar" had to be found. The United States should urge the IMF to pressure other countries to revalue their currencies upward, the subcommittee said, but warned that if the IMF continues to fail to take such strong actions, "the U.S. may have no choice but to take unilateral action to go off gold and establish new dollar parities." The report said that the United States could announce that it will no longer be the only country stabilizing its currency by dealing in gold and will intervene by dealing in for-

44 *New York Times* (June 4, 1971).

eign currencies as other countries do. The subcommittee also suggested that the United States might resort to a "transitional float or a controlled rate of depreciation until the reestablishment of an appropriate U.S. balance-of-payments position."[45]

In response to this report, the Treasury once again insisted that the "limited hearings" did not reflect or develop any wide body of congressional opinion in support of the views expressed earlier by Representative Reuss. The Treasury reaffirmed its position: "No discussions are planned or anticipated with respect to exchange-rate realignments at the IMF or elsewhere."[46]

On the same day—August 6—that Representative Reuss' subcommittee recommended exchange-rate realignment to eliminate the U.S. deficit, the United States Treasury reported a loss of gold and other reserve assets totaling more than $1 billion. Over the following week, the flight from the dollar sharply accelerated as $3.7 billion moved across the exchanges and into central bank hands.[47]

At the close of the week, on August 14, an editorial in *The Financial Times* (London) was headlined "The $ Under Pressure."

> The troubles of the dollar have become a permanent part of the international scene, but its difficulties during the past week have been worse than ever. It has been weak in relation to all the main European currencies, and the steady pressure has been so strong at times, that central banks, including the Bank of England, have offered support in the market. The D-Mark has floated upwards to a premium of more than 8 per cent above its original dollar parity. . . . When the Swiss authorities, the sternest custodians of the fixed exchange system, limit dollar convertbility, as they did briefly at one point in the week, it may be assumed that uncertainty is unusually great. . . .
>
> The American symptoms are familiar by this time—a continuing deterioration of the trade balance, a steady outflow of the capital account and a dwindling gold reserve. This last problem has become particularly ominous during the last few months as the gold reserve shrunk towards the magic $10,000 million figure which the

45 *Action Now to Strengthen the Dollar,* Report of the Subcommittee on International Exchange and Payments of the Joint Economic Committee, 92nd Congress, 1st Session (August 1971).
46 *Wall Street Journal* (August 9, 1971).
47 Charles A. Coombs, "Treasury and Federal Reserve Foreign Exchange Operations," *Monthly Review of Federal Reserve Bank of New York* (October 1971), p. 215.

> authorities have traditionally regarded as the minimum safety level. The reluctance of other countries to accept further accumulations of dollar holdings is once again becoming acute. . . . In the light of all this there is a general disposition to agree with the Reuss Committee's diagnosis that the dollar is overvalued.
>
> No one doubts that the objective must be to produce a more realistic exchange relationship between the dollar and the currencies of America's chief economic partners. The difficulty is to find a way of achieving this which does not meet apparently insuperable political objections.[48]

The next day the *New York Times'* economics analyst wrote:

> There is one overriding feature of the present situation of monetary turmoil that must be reported: Nobody really knows what to do. . . . In this kind of situation, what happens is that each government must react on a very short-term basis to the events that threaten its own situation—its economy's internal liquidity, the competitiveness of its export industries, its rate of inflation, the problem of imports. . . . [It is] a time when very good minds are groping and when nations sometimes find themselves forced into actions by the pressure of events rather than collective judgment.
>
> It is not, as far as can be seen now, the kind of time when a meeting of the "Group of Ten" big financial powers can settle everything, or even anything. It is a time, perhaps, when events are in control and when no predictions are worth very much.[49]

That night—Sunday, August 15, 1971—President Nixon announced on television his New Economic Program of domestic and international economic measures. The private and public pressure to convert the dollar into other assets—foreign currencies and ultimately reserve assets or their equivalent—had become overwhelming. Action was being forced by "the pressure of events rather than collective judgment": market pressures across the international exchanges—not the collective judgment of another Bretton Woods conference—were dictating policy reactions.

48 *Financial Times* (August 14, 1971).
49 Edwin L. Dale, Jr., "Monetary Strife: No One Wants It, But . . ." *New York Times* (August 15, 1971).

5.5 Action of August 15, 1971

On August 15, 1971, President Nixon suspended convertibility of the dollar into gold. The United States Treasury ceased selling gold to other governments at $35 an ounce in order to bring about depreciation of the dollar by allowing the dollar to float. Other measures were also announced to protect the nation's trade and payments position: a temporary surcharge of generally 10 per cent on goods imported into the United States; a 10 per cent cut in foreign aid; and a request to other nations "to bear their fair share of the burden of defending freedom around the world." Coupled with the international measures were a freeze on wages and prices and some changes in domestic taxes.

The President called his range of actions "the most comprehensive new economic policy to be undertaken in this nation in four decades."

The Governor of the Federal Reserve System Arthur Burns had protested that the Treasury recommendation to close the gold window was premature—but he carried no weight in the decision that had been reached at the Camp David meeting. Alfred Hayes, President of the Federal Reserve Bank of New York, had not been consulted or even informed of the decision. Budget Director George Shultz and others in the Camp David meeting favored a floating dollar, whereas [Secretary of the Treasury] "Connally's advice was usually to take the chance, to press the luck, to go for broke."[50] The dollar was therefore cast adrift.

Neither had the IMF been consulted. A former U.S. Executive Director and Deputy Managing Director of the Fund reviews events of this period as follows:[51]

> The year 1971 was by all odds the most dramatic since the beginning of the Fund. It was marked by the appointment of a new U.S. Secretary of the Treasury, John Connally, who would play a leading role; the abandonment of support of the dollar par value in August; and a series of G-10 ministerial meetings culminating in the agreement reached at the Smithsonian Conference which, in a moment

50 William Safire, *Before the Fall* (1975), pp. 506, 513–514. See also Charles A. Coombs, *The Arena of International Finance* (1976), pp. 217–220.

51 Southard, *The Evolution of the International Monetary Fund*, pp. 36–39. Copyright © 1979. Reprinted by permission of the International Finance Section of Princeton University.

of exuberance, President Nixon labeled the greatest in monetary history.

There is space here to recount only the main events that led to the U.S. decision on August 15, 1971. In 1970 the persisting erosion of the U.S. payments position worsened. Although there was a trade surplus of $2.2 billion, the over-all payments deficit was $10 billion. By the first half of 1971, the payments deficit was running at an annual rate of $20 billion, and the prospect was for an even larger deficit in July and August. With the increase in liquid funds in the international money market, the point had been reached when as much as a billion dollars could cross the exchanges in a single day, and in early August that happened.

Schweitzer and staff economists were watching developments with concern in the spring months. In the first days of May, the flow of funds out of dollars into European countries surged, and on May 5 European exchange markets were closed. Schweitzer guided the Executive Board through two informal reviews. On the basis of Article XVI, he proposed a substantial widening of margins beyond the 1 per cent authorized by Article IV, which would have been an innovation. On May 6 he explored this proposal in private meetings with groups of Executive Directors. For a few days, this effort appeared to be promising. The German Executive Director, Schleiminger, considered that what was happening was in effect the beginning of the devaluation of the dollar and agreed that wider margins would enable countries to retain their par values. But several important countries (notably the United Kingdom and Japan) instructed their Executive Directors to oppose the use of Article XVI, arguing that it would open the door to widespread legalized floating.

That initiative failed. On Sunday, May 9, Germany and the Netherlands notified the Fund that on reopening their exchange markets they would cease to maintain the margins, and Belgium adjusted its dual-market regulations. In contrast, Austria and Switzerland revalued their currencies, setting new par values. This floating of important European currencies was to continue until the actions taken by the United States in August. The floating of the Canadian dollar the preceding year was passed off as a special case, but there was a growing awareness that these new abandonments of par values were a sign of a deep malaise in the international monetary system. A major eroding of the par-value system was occurring, notwithstanding continuing brave supporting declarations. The Managing Director's effort to speed up the examination of the question of exchange flexibility though meriting better marks than

King Canute's reported efforts to roll back the tide, in the end had no better success.

With the coming into office of Secretary Connally, relations between the Secretary of the Treasury and the Managing Director of the Fund, which had always been close, ceased to be so. Nevertheless, anticipating the international banking conference that was to convene in Munich late in the month, Schweitzer and I, accompanied by Economic Counsellor Jacques Polak, spent an hour and a half with Secretary Connally and Under Secretary Volcker on May 17 to review current developments. It was a wide-ranging discussion, covering various possibilities, including dual rates and capital controls. Secretary Connally emphasized the need for a reduction of trade barriers and insisted that there was no *financial* solution to persistent U.S. payments deficits. He said he would welcome revaluations, especially by Germany, Japan, and Canada, which he felt were the main problem, but these revaluations would have to be more substantial than 5 per cent. At one point, he asserted that the dollar was not overvalued and that the United States was not going to devalue. When Schweitzer argued that broader parity changes would be needed if there was to be an effective adjustment of payments imbalances, the Secretary repeated that such changes would not solve the problem and that the United States would have to review its various overseas commitments and seek reductions in trade barriers, especially in Canada and Japan.

Following that one exchange of views with Secretary Connally, Schweitzer's working contacts with U.S. financial officials were chiefly with Under Secretary Volcker. Secretary Connally made it obvious that he personally did not intend to continue a consultative relationship with the IMF.

As summer approached, Schweitzer and his staff were fully aware that a crisis was in the making. But there was no indication whatever that U.S. authorities were contemplating major action. In a meeting with Schweitzer not long before a secret high-level conclave at Camp David, Volcker, quite plainly deeply worried, said only that various possible domestic measures were being studied.

On August 15, at about 7:30 P.M., U.S. Executive Director Dale telephoned Schweitzer to ask him to come to the Treasury Department at 8:30, thirty minutes before a scheduled television broadcast by President Nixon in the White House. Schweitzer and I met Volcker and Dale in Secretary Connally's office; the Secretary was at the White House. In the few minutes remaining before the broadcast, Volcker informed Schweitzer what measures would be announced: cessation of official gold sales, no intervention to maintain exchange-rate margins, the imposition of a temporary 10 per cent surcharge on most dutiable imports, and wage and price controls. United States officials expected a realignment of exchange rates and wanted it to be adequate, but even though he was leaving at once to meet with European financial officials, Volcker would have no proposals to make and would not be negotiating. He also said that no one outside the government except Schweitzer had been given advance notice.

There was a brief discussion of some aspects. Volcker mentioned G-10 or a special committee of IMF Governors as the vehicle for negotiation and made it clear that the Executive Board of the Fund would not in his view be the focus. When Schweitzer said the Fund staff had done some work on relative exchange rates, and that some parities should be appreciated and others left unchanged or depreciated, Volcker interjected that the United States had no intention of changing the gold price. This position was maintained by U.S. officials until the eve of the Smithsonian Conference in December, adding greatly both to the difficulty and to the emotional content of the negotiations. Schweitzer's assertion (which I echoed in a speech at the National Foreign Trade Conference in November) that the United States should expect to participate in the prospective realignment did not improve his and the Fund's relations with Secretaries Connally and Volcker.

At the end of the broadcast, which we watched on television, Schweitzer and Volcker had a brief interchange, the main points being that cessation of gold payments by the United States was essential to allow for negotiation, that any basic reform of the system (which had been mentioned by President Nixon) would take time, and that in the meantime a viable rate structure was needed. Secretary Connally entered the room for a few minutes but did not discuss matters with Schweitzer before he and I left. Thereafter, Schweitzer met until midnight with a staff team to prepare for an Executive Board meeting the following morning and to plan a meeting with the staffs of all area departments of the Fund to get them started on a study of appropriate rate adjustments.

For a full week after August 15, 1971, the major European governments kept their exchange markets closed as they sought to develop some joint policy response to Nixon's closure of the gold window. These negotiating efforts failed, and the European governments had no alternative but to reopen their exchange markets on an uncoordinated basis. And, although Japan kept money markets open, the Bank of Japan had to continue massive dollar purchases to keep the yen's dollar value from rising.

The type of exchange rate system that would come remained unclear. But it was obvious that one of the foundation stones of the international monetary system as it had operated under the Bretton Woods agreements—the convertibility of officially held dollar balances into gold—had crumbled. Following the President's actions, the par-value system of exchange rates was also at an end. Other members of the Fund now had to decide whether to continue to accumulate dollars or to let their exchange rates fluctuate. And there was the immediate question, of considerable interest to the readers of the *Wall Street Journal:* "would there be widely varying degrees of intervention and controls that resulted in 'dirty floats' instead of allowing free floating according to the objective, impersonal forces of the market place?" Beyond that, there was the more inclusive question of whether an international code of financial conduct would be restored and the authority of the IMF regained?

QUESTIONS

1. a. What do you think should be the norms or standards of an international monetary order?

b. During its first 25 years, did the Bretton Woods system contribute to the attainment of these norms?

c. How strict a code of international monetary conduct did the IMF impose upon its members? Has this code served its purposes?

2. a. Do you think the Articles of the IMF were drafted according to economic logic alone without political considerations? What would it mean to say that the IMF should be "politically neutral?" Could it be?

b. At the inaugural meeting of the Boards of Governors of the Fund and the Bank in 1946, Keynes delivered a reflective speech in which he evoked the assistance of the good fairies to watch over the newborn Bretton Woods twins. But at the end he hoped that no malicious fairy, no Carabosse, had been forgotten at Bretton Woods, lest coming uninvited she should curse the children. "You two brats," he visualized her saying, "shall grow up politicians; your every thought and act shall have an *arrière-pensée;* everything you determine shall not be for its own sake or on its own merits but because of something else." [The full speech is reproduced in R. F. Harrod, *Life of John Maynard Keynes* (1951), pp. 631–632.]

Do you think the Fund has grown up more politician than economist? Have the practices of the Fund retained the confidence of the international community? Should international monetary reform proceed through the Fund, or should the Fund be liquidated?

3. What were the principles of adjustment implicit in the Bretton Woods system? Did these prove adequate up to the early 1960s? Why were there more difficulties in the adjustment experience after the mid-1960s?

4. Why has the IMF's scarce currency clause [Article VII (3)] never been invoked? Could other sanctions have been imposed on surplus countries to share some of the burden of adjustment?

5. How did the IMF relate to the promotion of development? What political power did the less-developed countries have at the Bretton Woods conference? Should the Fund have made more provision for development finance, or should this have been left solely to the International Bank for Reconstruction and Development?

6. a. Recall that some of the original provisions of Keynes's plan for a Clearing Union were the creation of bancor as an international currency, the inconvertibility of bancor into gold, interest charges on the accumulation of credit balances by surplus members, and the right of a member to change the par value of its currency by 5 per cent a year without consent of the Governing Board of the Clearing Union.

Would the adoption of these provisions at Bretton Woods have avoided the international currency crises of the 1960s? Would you have argued for their adoption at Bretton Woods? Why were they not adopted?

b. Do you think the international currency crises since the mid-1960s indicate that there has been insufficient international liquidity to make the pegged exchange-rate system viable? Insufficient harmonization of national policies?

7. In reviewing Canada's experience with a floating rate, Deputy Governor Lawson of the Bank of Canada said that

> the most important question for a government in respect of exchange policy is not should the exchange rate be "fixed" or should it float, but what should the exchange rate be? . . . I am aware that some people seem to believe that if the exchange rate is determined in a free market without direct official intervention it will inevitably be the right rate, but this view seems to me to be a considerable oversimplification. A floating rate may be influenced

> indirectly in a variety of ways to make it float freely at quite different levels. A decision to float does not therefore offer an escape from the fundamental question—what should the exchange rate be? . . . Good exchange rate policy is thus a blend of economics and politics; it requires analysis of the costs and benefits of the exchange rates that are possible in the circumstances, and then a choice between them.

Would you agree with this view? If you were Governor of the Bank of Canada, under what conditions would you recommend that the Bank intervene in the foreign exchange market to contain the limits within which the Canadian dollar might float? Why not rely simply on the law of supply and demand in foreign exchange markets? What other norms may there be for exchange-rate adjustment?

8. a. If the U.S. balance of payments had not been in deficit during the 1960s, do you think there would have been sufficient international liquidity? Is it helpful in answering this question to distinguish between trend liquidity, market liquidity, and crisis liquidity?

b. If foreign official monetary authorities had refused to accumulate dollar reserve balances during the 1960s, what difference would it have made for United States military expenditures in Vietnam? For American direct foreign investment in France? For United States restrictions on imports? For United States foreign aid? For the unemployment rate in the United States?

9. a. President Nixon's action on August 15, 1971, stopped the convertibility of dollars into gold. Would it have been better for the United States to restrict its purchases of gold against dollars, while continuing to sell gold for dollars at the then $35 an ounce price?

b. On what grounds can it be argued that the use of the dollar as a reserve asset, together with the use of gold as a reserve asset, must mean that sooner or later the monetary price of gold must be raised or else gold must be demonetized? Do the events of March 1968 and August 1971 support this argument?

c. Should foreign official dollar holdings again be made convertible into gold? Or into some other "ultimate" international reserve asset? Or remain inconvertible?

10. A student of international law has said: "Whether reform would come more easily as the result of the 'Nixon shock' (as it was called in Japan), or by working within the existing system of exchanges and consultations was perceived not only by the United States, but by its principal

adversaries, as a question of strategy, not really as a question of law. President Nixon and Secretary Connally succeeded, in short, in having their financial crisis viewed in the way major crises of war and peace are commonly viewed—as occasions when considerations of law inevitably occupy a subordinate place."

Do you think the action of President Nixon on August 15, 1971 was subject to criticism under international monetary law? Do you agree with the approach taken?

11. What were the various policy options that the Nixon administration could have considered on August 14, 1971? Which policy would you have recommended at that time?

READINGS

1. *On the gold standard:*

   Brown, W. A., *The International Gold Standard Reinterpreted, 1914–1934* (1970).

   Chandler, Lester V., *Benjamin Strong* (1958).

   Clay, Henry, *Lord Norman* (1959).

   Harrod, R. F., *Life of John Maynard Keynes* (1951), pp. 331–370.

   Moggridge, Donald, *Return to Gold 1925* (1969).

   Winch, Donald, *Economic Analysis and Policy* (1969), Chap. 5.

2. *On international currency disintegration of the 1930s:*

   Drummond, Ian, *The Floating Pound and the Sterling Area 1931–1939* (1981).

   Kindleberger, C. P., *The World in Depression 1929–1939* (1973).

   Nurkse, Ragnar, *International Currency Experience* (1944).

3. *On the Bretton Woods Conference:*

   Acheson, Dean, *Present at the Creation* (1969).

   Eckes, Alfred E. Jr., *A Search for Solvency* (1975).

   Gardner, Richard, *Sterling-Dollar Diplomacy*, 3rd ed. (1980).

   Moggridge, Donald (ed.), *The Collected Writings of John Maynard Keynes: vol. XXV: Activities 1940–1944: Shaping the Post-War World: The Clearing Union* (1980); *vol. XXVI: Bretton Woods and Reparations* (1980).

   Oliver, Robert W., *International Economic Cooperation and the World Bank* (1975).

   Samuelson, Paul A., "Bretton Woods, Pro and Con," *The New Republic* (April 9, 1945), pp. 467–469.

U.S., Department of State, *Postwar Foreign Policy Preparation, 1939–45* (1949).

Van Dormael, Armand, *Bretton Woods: Birth of a Monetary System* (1978).

4. *On the Bretton Woods system and currency crises:*

Acheson, A. L. K. et al., *Bretton Woods Revisited* (1972).

Coombs, Charles A., *Arena of International Finance* (1976).

Cooper, Richard N., *The Economics of Interdependence* (1968).

de Vries, Margaret Garritsen, *The International Monetary Fund 1966–1971: The System under Stress*, vol. I, *Narrative;* vol. II, *Documents* (1977).

Hirsch, Fred, *Money International* (1969).

Horsefield, J. Keith (ed.), *The International Monetary Fund, 1945–65*, vol. I *Chronicle;* vol. II, *Analysis* (1969).

IMF Staff Papers, extensive bibliographies on the IMF appear in issues dated April 1951, April 1953, August 1955, Nov. 1958, Nov. 1962, Nov. 1965, March 1968, March 1972, July 1974, March 1978, June 1979.

Johnson, Brian, *The Politics of Money* (1970).

Lowenfeld, Andreas F., *The International Monetary System* (1977).

Solomon, Robert, *The International Monetary System, 1945–1976* (1977).

Strange, Susan, *International Monetary Relations* (1976).

Strange, Susan, *Sterling and British Policy* (1971).

Tew, Brian, *International Monetary Cooperation 1945–70* (1970).

Thirwall, A. P. (ed.), *Keynes & International Monetary Relations* (1976).

Triffin, Robert, *The Fate of the Pound* (1969).

Triffin, Robert, *Our International Monetary System* (1968).

Triffin, Robert, *World Monetary Maze* (1966).

Yeager, L. B. *International Monetary Relations* (1966).

5. *On the dollar problem:*

Aliber, Robert Z., *Choices for the Dollar* (1969).

Cooper, Richard N., "The Dollar and the World Economy," in Kermit Gordon (ed.), *Agenda for the Nation* (1968).

Fellner, W., "The Dollar's Place in the International System," *Journal of Economic Literature* (September 1972).

Haberler, Gottfried, "The U.S. Balance of Payments: Freedom or Controls," *Banca Nazionale del Lavoro* (March 1970).

Hearings before the Subcommittee on International Exchange and Payments of the Joint Economic Committee, annual.

IMF, *International Financial Statistics*, monthly.

Kenen, Peter B., "The International Position of the Dollar in a Changing World," *International Organization* (Summer 1969).

Kindleberger, Charles P., *Europe and the Dollar* (1966).

Kindleberger, Charles P., *International Money* (1981).

Krause, Lawrence B., "A Passive Balance of Payments Strategy for the U.S." *Brookings Papers on Economic Activity*, No. 3 (1970).

Lary, Hal, *Problems of the United States as World Trader and Banker* (1963).

Machlup, Fritz, *Plans for Reform of the International Monetary System* (Princeton International Finance Section) (1964).

Mikesell, R. F., *U.S. Balance of Payments and International Role of the Dollar* (1970).

Shultz, George P. and Dam, Kenneth W., *Economic Policy Beyond the Headlines* (1977), Chap. 6.

Triffin, Robert, *The Evolution of the International Monetary System: Historical Reappraisal and Future Perspectives* Princeton Studies in International Finance, No. 12 (1964).

Triffin, Robert, *Gold and the Dollar Crisis: The Future of Convertibility* (1960).

Problem II

FLOATING EXCHANGE RATES
Assessing the New Regime

With the United States' action of August 15, 1971, two foundations of the IMF's Articles of Agreement were removed—the par-value system and the gold convertibility of the dollar. The ministers and central bank governors of the Group of 10 then attempted to reach agreement on the realignment of their currencies. But no basic measures of international monetary reform were acceptable to the negotiating parties.

Even though nations have been unable to design another Bretton Woods agreement, the international monetary situation has continued to evolve through market developments and some new institutional arrangements. Since 1973, a regime of floating rates has emerged, but with the notable feature of repeated interventions by central banks in the foreign exchange markets to limit the degree of floating. The Eurocurrency market has also become more prominent. After 1974, the recycling of petrodollars and the lending by commercial banks to developing countries became a problem of ever-increasing severity. Further, the European Monetary System emerged as an important regional arrangement, and the upsurge in gold prices became a source of speculation to some and a cause of concern to many. Through these developments, the international monetary regime has become far different from the old Bretton Woods system.

1. DEMISE OF BRETTON WOODS

When foreign exchange markets opened a week after August 15, 1971, the situation was described as follows.

WIDELY DIFFERING MONETARY POLICIES*

LONDON—The world appeared little, if any, closer to a new monetary system after a week's closedown of major foreign exchange markets and a hasty round of conferences and discussions among major nations.

Instead, world money markets will reopen today under an "every man for himself" basis of widely differing national monetary policies. There will be controlled floats, fixed parities with wider bands on each side of the rigid figure, two-tier systems and, in one case, the worst action from the standpoint of the U.S. balance of payments: an outright devaluation against the dollar. Israel cut the dollar value of its pound 20%.

Not one major industrial nation has yet accepted the course of action which President Nixon recommended a week ago when, cutting the dollar's tie to gold, he urged foreign nations with strong currencies to raise the stated value of their currencies against the dollar.

The U.S. would like such increases in the parities of strong currencies since politically this would be the easiest way to, in effect, devalue the sick dollar. Such currency revision would improve the U.S. trade balance by raising the cost of imports into the U.S. while cutting the price of America's goods on the world marketplace.

This outcome may be difficult to arrange. Common Market nations still are split after their abortive attempt to devise a joint monetary policy. Japan welcomes Europe's disunity, using it to stall its own monetary decisions. Cautious Switzerland is so worried that it may keep its money markets closed all today until money trends become evident.

While European moneymen generally favor a return to fixed parities as soon as it can be arranged, nobody is very hopeful about

***Wall Street Journal* (August 23, 1971).

quick return after seeing the way Common Market nations split in Brussels. Some American government sources have expressed the belief that it may take until the end of this year or into 1972 before money markets sort themselves out and a new monetary system can be introduced.

Some sources in Europe, however, think the world may stumble along a lot longer before finding a solution, and even then it may be only a jerry-built affair. "We have missed an important opportunity," says Sicco Mansholt, vice president of the Common Market governing body, speaking about the Brussels meeting that saw the six nations attempt to work out a joint policy flounder on division between France and Germany.

France insisted on sticking to a two-tier system that, if it works, effectively would cancel out any trade advantage America had hoped to gain by floating its dollar. Germany sought a joint float of all Common Market currencies against the dollar and tight parities within the bloc.

New developments aren't expected on the Common Market front until the next meeting of the group's finance ministers Sept. 13 in Brussels. "It isn't unreasonable to give oneself a certain delay for reflections," comments Valery Giscard d'Estaing, France's finance minister.

That nonchalant attitude causes many to believe that France, along with Japan, will be the biggest footdraggers when it comes to reform of the monetary system. France wants gold to play an important role in any such reform and would like to downgrade the dollar. . . .

In capsule form, here is how major nations will be handling foreign exchange when markets reopen today:

Britain—Pound sterling will float from a base of $2.38 to the pound, a base which will be protected by the Bank of England.

West German—Deutschmark will continue the float that was in effect when markets closed Aug. 13.

France—A two-tier market is being introduced, with the official franc parity of 5.55415 to the dollar being maintained for commercial transactions. The rate for financial, tourist and other transactions will float.

Italy—The market will open with the lire at its old official parity of 625 to the dollar. As the Bank of Italy says it won't intervene in the market, however, the dollar will float. But Italy will hold the tourist dollar at 618.5 lire at least through Monday evening.

Switzerland—Money markets won't open this morning although they might in the afternoon if the monetary situation is clarified.

Netherlands—The guilder will continue to float against other currencies as it had been doing up to closing of markets Aug. 13. However, Belgium, Holland, and Luxembourg will seek to maintain pre-crisis rates among themselves, thus creating a two-tier system, but one far different from France's.

Belgium—Francs will float with the central bank expected to intervene to control that float and to maintain intra-Benelux parities.

Norway—The krone will be revalued when the exchange market opens today. The new exchange rates are expected to be announced before noon.

Japan—Money markets, open all last week, again will open with yen parity unchanged. The Bank of Japan, however, probably will have to continue massive dollar purchases to keep the yen's dollar value from rising. (Such purchases have already boosted Japan's holdings of gold and foreign exchange, mostly dollars, $3.7 billion since Aug. 1 to a total of some $11.6 billion, United Press International reports.)

It's evident in Europe that Japan welcomes the Common Market's inability to formulate a joint monetary policy. "We can't act until Europe does something," says Japanese official observer of the Brussels meeting. He explains that if West European nations raise their parities, Japan could go along, confident that it could retain its European markets. But if Japan alone raised the value of its yen, it would lose European as well as American markets.

During the six weeks between the announcement of August 15 and the annual meeting of the IMF at the end of September, there was considerable sparring between the United States and the other members of the Group of 10—the other leading industrial nations of the world, notably the EEC countries and Japan.

The EEC countries could not agree on a united position after the announcement of August 15. The French preferred a two-tier exchange market, and agreement on a joint float among Common Market currencies was impossible. A correspondent for *The Times* (London) philosophized:

"What went wrong? After the best part of 15 hours discussion together of how to respond to the dollar crisis, the Common Market countries ended up where they started, with no common position. When the exchange markets open on Monday, every country—including Britain—is going to go its own way.

Yet here was an opportunity—literally a golden opportunity,

> since the American decision to break the dollar's link with gold was what the crisis was all about—for the Six to hammer out a European approach. . . .
>
> After all, the idea of European nations coming together to deal on equal terms with the United States is part of the rationale of the European Community. The crisis meeting was a chance to do so, not for theoretical reasons, but because there was a clear and urgent need for combined action. . . .
>
> The truth is the meeting went wrong for the simple reason that the French and the Germans did not agree, and national positions, whether right or wrong in logic, prevailed as they usually do over Community theory.[1]

Recognizing the serious implications for the future of the IMF, Mr. Pierre-Paul Schweitzer, Managing Director of the IMF, responded quickly to the announcement of President Nixon's new economic policy. In a cable sent to the 118 governors of the IMF, he said,

> The recent developments which have overtaken the international monetary system give great cause for concern but at the same time create the opportunity for strengthening the system.
>
> Unless prompt action is taken, the prospect before us is one of disorder and discrimination in currency and trade relationships which will seriously disrupt trade and undermine the system which has served the world well and has been the basis for effective collaboration for a quarter of a century. We must not sacrifice the efforts and achievements of the postwar period, which I fear are in jeopardy.
>
> Piecemeal approaches to change are not likely to yield beneficial results even for a single or a few countries, and much less for the whole community of countries represented in the fund. In my view, it is vitally important to take prompt collective and collaborative action in the interest of the prosperity of all members.[2]

At the opening of the IMF's annual meeting, Schweitzer again argued that it would "be desirable" if "all the major countries involved were to make a contribution to the realignment of currencies." He also declared that "real dangers are inherent in a prolon-

1 *The Times*, London (August 20, 1971).
2 *The Times*, London (August 20, 1971).

gation of the present impasse," citing especially the possibilities of "serious disarray" in currency and trade affairs and "an abandonment of rules of law providing for orderly and just international economic relations."

I.1. Smithsonian Agreement

In December 1971, the G-10 held meetings at the Smithsonian Institution in Washington "to resolve fundamental and interrelated issues of monetary reform." From these meetings, there emerged agreement on realignments of the world's major currencies, a widening of the margins of exchange rate fluctuation to 2.25 per cent above and below the new "central rates," and an increase in the monetary price of gold to $38 per ounce—thereby devaluing the dollar by 8.57 per cent.

President Nixon hailed the Smithsonian agreement as "the most significant monetary achievement in the history of the world." It is true that this agreement was the first time in world monetary history that several nations had negotiated their exchange rates around a conference table. But the Smithsonian agreement was to disintegrate after only 14 months. The agreement had responded to the immediate situation, but the major questions of a new world monetary order had not been answered. Sources of potential instability remained. The dollar was still inconvertible. No new reserve asset was created; indeed, when the initial Rio allocation of SDRs was exhausted in 1972, there had been no decision about whether another allocation should be made. And instead of greater rate flexibility, the EEC countries actually established in April 1972 a plan whereby intra-EEC rates were to be kept within one-half the range allowed by the Smithsonian agreement—the "snake" within the "tunnel."

The dollar's inconvertibility remained a major concern. Some authorities continued to urge a joint float by EEC countries against the dollar. The deputy Governor of the Bank of Italy, Rinaldo Ossola, said in a speech in London that "As long as the dollar remains inconvertible—that is, probably during most of the 1970s—the problem of adjustment between the United States and the European Economic Community should be solved through the free fluctuation of the dollar vis-à-vis the EEC currencies as a whole, these latter's reciprocal relations being based on relatively fixed parities."

The Bank of International Settlements also warned in its annual report, that rather than accept inconvertible dollars or increase the value of their currencies, other countries are likely to impose controls on dollar flows and that this could split the world into restrictive monetary blocs.

The annual meeting of the IMF also ended with no consensus—let alone action—on monetary reform. Secretary of the Treasury Shultz outlined the United States proposals for a reformed system, and the new "Committee of 20" high-level government officials, representing all the member countries of the Fund, held its first session to consider a report on the problems of international monetary reform and possible solutions, prepared by the Executive Directors of the Fund. It was clear that the process of negotiation would be complex and prolonged.

The Economist stated in its issue of February 10, "What remains of the Smithsonian exchange parities should get a decent burial. The end looks near." This was scarcely prediction, but simply observation: the outflow of dollars was again threatening the values of the mark and the guilder; the Canadian dollar, British pound, and Swiss franc were already floating outside the Smithsonian band; and the French franc, Belgian franc, and Italian lira were operating on two-tier financial markets that observed Smithsonian rules for only some transactions.

The pressure on foreign currencies had become so great that over the weekend it was decided to close the foreign exchange markets in Europe and Japan. And late Monday evening—February 12, 1973—the United States announced another devaluation of the dollar.

Considering the energetic efforts that Treasury Under Secretary Volcker had devoted to altering exchange rates in 1973, it is ironical to recall an editorial in the *New York Times* almost exactly four years earlier.

STRICTLY ACADEMIC*

Paul A. Volcker, the new Under Secretary of the Treasury for Monetary Affairs, minced few words in dismissing the notion that the international monetary mechanism would work better if ex-

**New York Times* (February 17, 1969).

> change rates were free to fluctuate more widely. He told a Paris news conference that there has been much discussion of such ideas "in academic circles, and that's where they can stay."
>
> Mr. Volcker, a bank economist, served in the Treasury in the Kennedy and Johnson Administrations; his defense of rigidly fixed exchange rates—sardonic though it is—comes as no surprise. But winds of change are at work. The idea of floating the pound sterling—cutting it loose from parity and permitting it to find its own levels in the foreign exchange markets—is now openly deliberated in respectable British circles. The farewell report of the Johnson Council of Economic Advisers acknowledged that the flexibility concept was achieving serious analysis in many areas as a possible safeguard against breakdowns of the monetary system. So what is strictly academic today might well be tomorrow's reality.

In Japan, the day after the dollar devaluation marked near-record levels of trading volume on the foreign exchange market as the yen was floated. The yen appreciated 14 per cent, at which point the Bank of Japan intervened to prevent the price of the dollar from falling further (the rate had fallen from 301 yen: $1 to 270 yen:$1). The repercussions again extended to Parliament where the opposition demanded the resignation of the Premier and his cabinet. But Premier Tanaka promptly denied any responsibility for the move, placing the blame directly on the United States and pleading ignorance of predevaluation conversations between his Finance Minister and Mr. Volcker.

Many leading Europeans also expressed anxiety over the durability of the latest monetary settlement. The Finance Minister of West Germany and the Common Market's monetary chief both pointed out that the currency realignment following the dollar devaluation was fragile and that there was an urgent need for progress in monetary reform to resolve the problem of excess dollars.

Speculators in gold also showed little confidence in the new rates. The price of gold began to climb steadily, and only 10 days after its devaluation, new speculation broke out against the dollar as speculative buying of gold reached new heights. On February 22, the price of gold touched $90, rising in London by almost $10 above the previous day's closing quotation.

The outflow of dollars to Germany accelerated, and by February 23 the dollar had again fallen to its floor against the mark. On March

1 the West Germans closed their official foreign exchange market after having to buy $2.7 billion in one day. Other members of the EEC followed suit, and in an unprecedented move the nine members decided on March 4 to close their foreign exchange markets for two weeks while they sought to establish a European defense system in the latest currency crisis.

The EEC countries announced they had decided to float their currencies against the dollar in three separate groups. Six countries would float together: West Germany, France, Belgium, Holland, Luxembourg, and Denmark. Their currencies would be locked within a 2.25 per cent margin of each other, while floating as a unit against the dollar. Britain and Ireland would float together separately from the others, and Italy would float alone. But these other countries were to study ways to bring their currencies into line with the joint float of the six in the future. And a European monetary fund was to be established by mid-year, representing a large fund of pooled reserves of the six in the joint float.

No sooner was the joint float announced than *The Economist* predicted a "breakdown" and "another currency crisis. . . . An attempt to maintain fixed exchange rates today is like an order to walk upon the water. Proponents of a joint float somehow think that it will be safer if some of us join hands while doing so." By March 1973, there was a generalized adoption of floating rates.

I.2 Role of the IMF

Reviewing the role of the IMF during this historic period, a former Deputy Managing Director of the Fund has stated:[3]

> Shaken to its roots by the collapse of the Bretton Woods par-value system in 1971–73, the Fund displayed a capacity for survival and adaptation which gainsaid the funeral orations preached over its casket at that time. . . .
>
> The events of 1971–73—the collapse of the par-value system and the resort to floating rates by all major industrial countries—led to a general belief that the Fund could no longer be an effective institution. There was much reason for this. The Fund had no legal basis for approving fluctuating rates. It was thought that its finan-

3 Frank A. Southard, Jr., *The Evolution of the International Monetary Fund,* Princeton Essays in International Finance No. 135 (December 1979), pp. 1, 42–43. Copyright © 1979. Reprinted by permission of the International Finance Section of Princeton University.

cial operations would be crippled by the exchange-risk uncertainties inherent in drawings and the use of SDRs. It was also thought that with fluctuating rates there would be little need for official intervention in exchange markets and hence little occasion to use Fund resources.

For a number of reasons, the prediction of collapse in Fund usefulness was not borne out by events: (1) The long exercise on the reform of the international monetary system was carried out under the auspices of the Fund and soon centered on finding ways to recast the system within the framework of an amended Articles of Agreement. (2) Notwithstanding the floating of important currencies, most countries continued to peg their currencies to the dollar or some other major currency and had the same need for Fund technical and financial assistance as before. (3) The huge increase in oil prices at the end of 1973 confronted even the floaters with a need for Fund resources, and the Fund's prompt action to establish the oil facility made a good impression. (4) Probably most important was a renewed realization that international financial collaboration was essential, that the floating-rate system needed management (as time passed, large-scale intervention reemerged), and that there was no alternative to the IMF as a global authority. This was emphasized by the amended Article IV. However permissive it is in allowing countries to choose any exchange system they wish, it requires them to collaborate, and it gives the Fund a mandate to oversee the international monetary system and the compliance of each member with its obligations, and to exercise "firm surveillance" over the exchange-rate policies of members.

2. MANAGED FLOATING

After the par-value system ended, a new era of managed floating came into being. There was no single decision to install a new exchange-rate system. Some currencies floated jointly, some floated independently, and some were pegged to other currencies or the SDR. Table II.1 shows the various exchange arrangements of member countries of the IMF.

A number of countries maintain margins for their exchange rates against the U.S. dollar, a few against sterling, and some against the French franc. Others peg against the SDR, or some weighted basket of currencies, and European Economic Community countries maintain narrow margins for the movement of their exchange rates

Table II.1 Exchange Arrangements

(*As of March 31, 1981*)

Currency pegged to							
US Dollar	*French Franc*	*Other currency*	*SDR*	*Other currency composite* [a]	*Exchange rate adjusted according to a set of indicators* [b]	*Cooperative exchange arrangements* [c]	*Other* [d]
Bahamas	Benin	Equatorial Guinea (Spanish Peseta)	Burma	Algeria	Brazil	Belgium	Afghanistan
Barbados	Cameroon	Gambia, The (Pound Sterling)	Guinea	Austria	Colombia	Denmark	Argentina
Burundi	C. African Rep.	Lesotho (South African Rand)	Guinea-Bissau	Bangladesh	Peru	France	Australia
Chile	Chad	Swaziland (South African Rand)	Iran	Botswana	Portugal	Germany	Bahrain
Costa Rica	Comoros		Jordan	Cape Verde		Ireland	Bolivia
Djibouti	Congo		Kenya	China, P. R.		Italy	Canada
Dominica	Gabon		Malawi	Cyprus		Luxembourg	Ghana
Dominican Rep.	Ivory Coast		Mauritius	Fiji		Netherlands	Greece
Ecuador	Madagascar		São Tomé and Principe	Finland			Iceland
Egypt	Mali		Seychelles	Kuwait			India
El Salvador	Niger		Sierra Leone	Malaysia			Indonesia
Ethiopia	Senegal		Uganda	Malta			Israel
Grenada	Togo		Viet Nam	Mauritania			Japan
Guatemala	Upper Volta		Zaïre	Norway			Korea
Guyana			Zambia	Papua New Guinea			Lebanon
Haiti				Singapore			Maldives
Honduras				Solomon Islands			Mexico
Iraq				Sweden			Morocco
Jamaica				Tanzania			New Zealand
Lao P.D. Rep.				Thailand			Nigeria

Liberia		Philippines
Libya	Tunisia	Qatar
Nepal	Zimbabwe	Saudi Arabia
Nicaragua		South Africa
Oman		Spain
Pakistan		Sri Lanka
Panama		Turkey
Paraguay		U. Arab Emirates
Romania		United Kingdom
Rwanda		United States
Somalia		Uruguay
St. Lucia		Yugoslavia
St. Vincent		Western Samoa
Sudan		
Suriname		
Syrian Arab Rep.		
Trinidad & Tobago		
Venezuela		
Yemen Arab Rep.		
Yemen, P.D. Rep.		

[a]Comprises currencies, which are pegged to various "baskets" of currencies of the members' own choice, as distinct from the SDR basket.
[b]Includes exchange arrangements under which the exchange rate is adjusted at relatively frequent intervals, on the basis of indicators determined by the respective member countries.
[c]Refers to the cooperative arrangement maintained under the European Monetary System.
[d]Covers a heterogeneous group of exchange arrangements, including those of members whose currencies may be deemed to be floating independently and those that cannot be properly classified under other categories.

against one another. Within each of these blocs, rates are pegged, but across the blocs, rates are not maintained, and there is flexibility in rates between the blocs. Moreover, those countries that do not maintain their currencies within specified margins are the world's largest trading nations. Some six-sevenths of world trade is therefore transacted under flexible exchange rates.

Since the onset of floating rates, however, governments have had to determine the degree to which the determination of exchange rates should be left to the free play of market forces. For a number of reasons, the "management" of floating rates has become common as governments have been reluctant to allow freely floating rates. This management has occurred through interventions on the foreign exchange markets by central banks and monetary authorities in the form of official purchases and sales of foreign currencies out of owned or borrowed reserves or through swap arrangements. Direct interventions by official purchases or sales in the foreign exchange markets have been undertaken to limit or slow movements of the exchange rates.

2.1 Exchange Rate Movements

There follows a summary by the IMF of the variability of exchange rates and official efforts to influence the exchange markets in recent years.

VARIABILITY OF EXCHANGE RATES AMONG MAJOR CURRENCIES*

In assessing the impact of more active official intervention and increased orientation of monetary policies toward exchange rate objectives, it is worthwhile to compare recent exchange rate movements with those in previous years. These movements result from closely related developments in underlying economic factors, official policies designed to influence exchange markets, and shifts in expectations in those markets. In some respects, exchange markets tend to behave like other financial markets: at times, they go through periods of unusual volatility, and it is not always evident, even with the benefit of hindsight, which economic forces have induced the increased volatility. For these reasons, shorter-term fluctuations—i.e., movements that reverse themselves within a

*IMF, *Annual Report 1980*, pp. 47–48.

Table II.2 Average Monthly Variability of Effective Exchange Rates, April 1973–December 1979[a] (In per cent)

	1973–76[b]	*1977*	*1978*	*1979*
Industrial countries	1.41	1.13	1.44	0.96
Canada	0.87	1.14	1.40	1.21
France	1.62	0.50	1.61	0.64
Germany, Fed. Rep. of	1.82	0.98	1.33	0.64
Italy	1.98	0.60	0.73	0.68
Japan	1.36	1.68	3.13	2.03
Switzerland	1.42	1.73	3.38	0.91
United Kingdom	1.45	0.97	1.61	2.16
United States	0.74	0.42	0.94	0.60
Other industrial countries	1.41	1.21	1.22	0.87
Developing countries[c]	1.60	0.98	1.67	1.48
Pegged to U.S. dollar	1.47	0.56	1.57	1.53
Pegged to SDR	1.93	0.63	1.99	2.58
Pegged to French franc	0.81	0.25	0.70	0.37
Other developing countries	1.87	1.63	1.99	1.53

[a] Monthly import-weighted effective exchange rates are used in these calculations. Variability is defined here as the standard deviation of monthly percentage changes in the effective exchange rate about the average percentage change during each year. Figures for groups of countries are unweighted averages of those for the countries in each group.
[b] Annual average, with the period April–December used for 1973.
[c] Countries are classified according to their exchange arrangements as of June 30, 1980.

day, a week, or a month—cannot always be distinguished, at the time of their occurrence, from the longer-term movements of exchange rates spanning several quarters or perhaps years. A large irreversible shift in the exchange rate may occur within a short period of time, and long-term readjustments are often accompanied by large short-term fluctuations.

A useful measure of short-term variability of exchange rates is the average divergence of the monthly percentage change in the effective exchange rate from the average of monthly changes during the period examined. This measure of variability suggests that for the industrial countries exchange rates were substantially more stable during 1979 than during 1978 and the average of the years 1973–77 [Table II.2]. For developing countries, the reduction in the variability of the effective exchange rate in 1979 paralleled that in the industrial countries, but was less marked.

The experience of individual industrial countries confirms the general increase in exchange rate stability already noted [Table II.2]. France, the Federal Republic of Germany, Japan, Switzerland, and the United States, as well as the group of "other indus-

Chart II.1 Eight Industrial Countries: Indices of Effective Exchange Rates, January 1975–June 1980 (monthly average of daily rates, 1975 = 100[a])

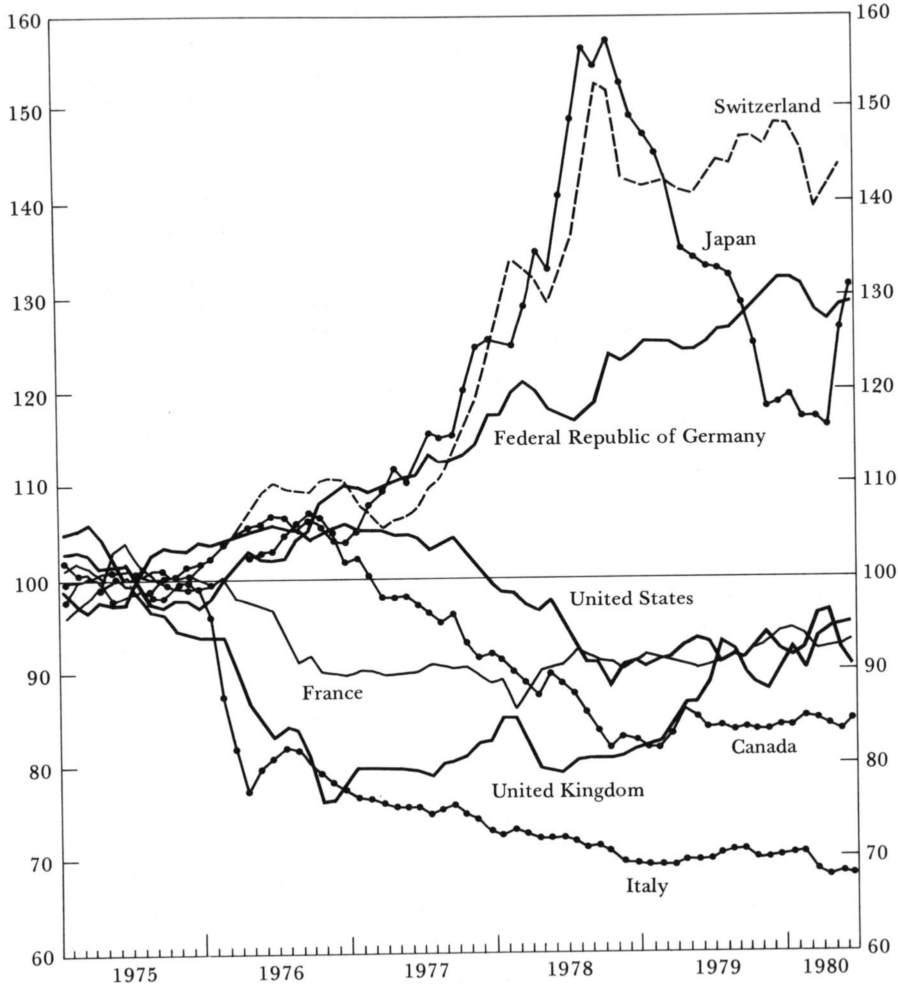

[a] The weights for calculating effective exchange rates, derived from the Fund's multilateral exchange rate model, take into account the relative importance of a country's trading partners.

trial countries," all show a sharp reduction in the variability of exchange rates in 1979 compared with both 1978 and the earlier years of floating. The reduction from 1978 to 1979 was more moderate for Canada and Italy than it was for the other countries. Italy has maintained a remarkably steady and low level of effective exchange rate variability for the lira for the past three years, in contrast to the earlier years of floating. The variability of the effective exchange rate of the pound sterling declined during 1978, but increased again in 1979 to a level above the average for the floating period as a whole. [Chart II.1]

While the authorities in industrial countries have taken measures to limit excessive exchange rate fluctuations, the private sector has increasingly sought to reduce the impact of exchange rate variability by diversifying exchange risk in the forward exchange markets, which have become wider and more differentiated in recent years, and also in the financial markets, e.g., by hedging through trade credits in the invoice currency. In addition, there seemed at times to have been large portfolio shifts between financial and commodity markets. For example, there were occasions when sharp exchange rate movements were reflected in gold prices, as funds shifted out of one currency were placed not only in other currencies but also in nonfinancial assets, including gold.

2.2 *Managing the Rates*

The Fund's report also notes that official efforts to influence developments in exchange markets have intensified in recent years because of large disruptive exchange rate movements, the growing realization that the market cannot always be relied upon to perform the function of dampening fluctuations in exchange rates, and perceptions regarding the harmful effects of excessive fluctuations. The report analyzes these interventions as follows.

OFFICIAL INTERVENTIONS*

The policy of smoothing such fluctuations involves measures aimed at both maintaining orderly conditions in exchange markets and counteracting the tendency for exchange rates to overshoot the mark in moving to new equilibrium levels. Such measures are complicated by the need for the authorities to judge whether market-determined movement in the exchange rate signals a longer-run

*IMF, *Annual Report 1980,* pp. 49–50.

change justified by underlying economic conditions rather than a temporary fluctuation based on ephemeral causes. Hence, while official intervention can assist the process of adjustment by preventing exchange rate movements unjustified by underlying factors, it may also at times prevent movements in rates that would have fostered adjustment.

Moreover, the adverse effects of excessive exchange rate fluctuations must be seen in proper perspective. In particular, they need to be compared with the harmful consequences of protracted deviations of exchange rates from their medium-term equilibrium levels. The policies pursued by different countries reflect their perceptions regarding the balance between the economic costs of excessive exchange rate fluctuations, on the one hand, and those of protracted deviations from equilibrium rates, on the other. While the consequences of such deviations are well known, the effects of excessive fluctuations are less clear and bear some discussion.

A principal reason for taking measures to stabilize exchange rates is the fear that exchange rate variations apparently unrelated to underlying economic conditions would have perverse effects on patterns of trade and production, thereby impeding desired adjustments in current accounts. After some years of experience with floating rates, the private sector might be expected to be more aware of the often temporary nature of changes in price competitiveness induced by exchange rate fluctuations and accordingly respond only to those changes in relative wages and employment opportunities that are regarded as permanent. There may nevertheless be good reason for concern that overshooting of exchange rates could lead to unnecessarily large fluctuations in prices, wages, and employment, because the initial changes in exchange rates may induce reactions in prices and wages that are subsequently not easily reversed.

Another reason for official actions to dampen exchange rate fluctuations has been the belief that such fluctuations in exchange rates have been damaging to the growth of foreign trade and investment. Although statistical studies and business surveys have yet to show clear evidence on this point, it is admittedly difficult to come to a judgment on this question. Such a judgment implies a comparison with more stable exchange rates, but greater stability might not have been achievable during this period without at times suppressing rate movements that were justified by underlying economic developments, and this in turn could have discouraged foreign trade and investment. Moreover, in view of the various contemporaneous developments that have had adverse effects on both economic growth and price stability since 1973, there is some question whether the occasional tendency toward excessive fluctuations of exchange rates has been one of the symptoms of these developments or an additional cause of slow growth and inflation.

A further reason for official actions to influence exchange markets is that market-determined movements in exchange rates may, at times, hamper anti-inflationary policies. It has, moreover, been argued that the more freely floating are exchange rates, the weaker is the political support for anti-inflationary policies. There is indeed some evidence that under the par value system the contractionary demand-management measures taken by countries with balance of payments deficits tended to be stronger than the expansionary measures taken by countries with surpluses of comparable magnitude. While this tendency alone would have produced a marked deflationary bias in the world economy, there were also many instances during that period when countries with higher than average inflation rates resorted to an increased use of exchange restrictions or exchange rate action rather than to anti-inflationary monetary and fiscal policies. The effect of floating exchange rates in this respect would appear to be a neutral one. To be sure, floating rates permit countries to maintain inflation rates above the world average without changes in the price competitiveness of their traded-goods sectors. Equally, however, market-determined exchange rates assist countries with relatively low rates of inflation in insulating their economies from the impact of higher rates of inflation in the rest of the world. Whether, under market-determined exchange rates, there is any systematic tendency for low-inflation or high-inflation countries to adjust to the average is uncertain: while low-inflation countries may at times resist appreciation of their currencies in order to avoid harming their export sectors, there is also pressure on the authorities of high-inflation countries to avoid inflation, since the depreciation of their currencies tends to reinforce domestic price increases by raising import prices. On balance, the resistance of a government to inflationary pressures appears to have much less to do with the extent of exchange rate management than with the country's past history of inflation and unemployment, its industrial and labor union structure, and the effectiveness with which policies can be implemented through its monetary and fiscal institutions.

A related concern is that some countries might be drawn into a vicious circle of inflation and currency depreciation, based on the feedback effects of movements in exchange rates on import prices, money wages, domestic prices, and export prices, and the fact that the effects on prices and wages are more rapid than the corrective effects on the current account. The extent to which exchange rate changes lead to a vicious or virtuous circle depends on the characteristics of an economy, such as its size and openness as well as the degree of wage and price indexation that is present. There is evidence for the industrial countries suggesting that the smaller and more open is a country, the greater is the extent to which domestic price effects of a depreciation are apt eventually to offset much, if not all, of the competitive advantage gained by the depreciation. The authorities of these economies face especially great difficulties in resisting the inflationary pressures generated by a depreciation of their currencies. Nevertheless, exchange rate depreciation and domestic inflation both typically reflect an excessive rate of money expansion, and the domestic currency cannot depreciate indefinitely unless accompanied by an accommodating monetary policy that is excessively expansionary relative to that of other countries.

A further reason why large, frequent fluctuations in exchange rates may raise rates of inflation above what they would otherwise be has to do with the supposition that effective depreciation of a country's currency tends to accelerate the domestic rate of inflation while an appreciation does not have a corresponding dampening effect on inflation because of the downward inflexibility of wages and prices. Empirical evidence shows that import prices do fall after exchange rate appreciations and that domestic prices do not seem to react in a significantly different manner to positive and negative changes in import prices. Nevertheless, money wages tend in general to be highly rigid in a downward direction. There is thus some basis for concluding that wage and price effects of depreciations and appreciations are somewhat asymmetrical. There is also an additional worry for the authorities in countries with deeply embedded inflationary expectations that those expectations would be immediately exacerbated by a depreciation of the domestic currency while they may respond more sluggishly to an appreciation.

While there are often good reasons for active official intervention in exchange markets and other policy measures to influence exchange rates, such actions can at times be at the expense of attaining domestic monetary targets. This is true both of intervention, to the extent that its monetary impact cannot readily be offset by other monetary measures, and of monetary policies employed to influence exchange rates. The benefits of measures to stabilize exchange rates must be weighed against their domestic monetary impact.

The balance between fostering orderly market conditions and allowing appropriate exchange rates to be established in the market is important, not only for the industrial countries involved but also for the rest of the world. Large exchange rate fluctuations for the major currencies unfavorably affect the conditions under which most of world trade is transacted. It is, however, in the interest of all members to allow those exchange rate movements to take place that foster international adjustment, and this concern must continue to be a prime consideration in framing exchange rate policies.

Illustrative of the scope of official interventions by the United States is the following summary[4] of Federal Reserve exchange operations during the six-month period February–July 1980.

In the context of unsettled exchange market conditions and volatility of exchange rates, the United States authorities intervened frequently during the six-month period, operating on both sides of the market. In the early phase through early April when the dollar was in demand, the United States authorities were able to acquire sufficient currencies in the market and from correspondents to repay earlier debt and to build up balances, buying German marks, Swiss francs, and Japanese yen. By late March–early April, the Trading Desk intervened on several occasions openly as a buyer of currencies to counter disorderly conditions in the market. Subsequently, when the dollar came under bursts of heavy selling pressure, the United States authorities intervened in size, selling German marks, Swiss francs, and French francs. By the end of July, the United States authorities were again accumulating currencies to repay swap debt and rebuild balances.

For the period as a whole, total intervention sales of currencies amounted to \$3,982.7 million equivalent, of which \$3,530.6 million was in German marks, \$291.4 million was in Swiss francs, and \$160.7 million in French francs. Total acquisition of currencies amounted to \$6,266.9 million, of which \$1,476.2 million was in the market and \$4,790.7 million was from correspondents; by currency, the acquisitions were \$5,691.1 million of German marks, \$357.8 million of Swiss francs, \$216.8 million of Japanese yen, and \$1.2

4 *Federal Reserve Bank of New York Quarterly Review* (Autumn, 1980), p. 20.

million of French francs. As of July 31, the Federal Reserve's swap debt to the German Bundesbank was $879.7 million equivalent and to the Bank of France was $166.3 million equivalent. Also during the period, the Federal Reserve's reciprocal swap arrangement with the Bank of Sweden was increased by $200 million to $500 million.

3. INTERNATIONAL RESERVES AND LIQUIDITY

The global stock of official monetary reserves is influenced by developments in the exchange markets and by the response of monetary authorities to international imbalances. By intervening in the same direction, the authorities of many countries may increase or reduce their aggregate holdings of the principal reserve currency. A change in the SDR prices of reserve currencies will also cause a change in the value of foreign exchange reserves measured in SDRs. Movements in interest rates among countries will also affect the expected earnings on short-term investments in reserve currencies and hence the growth of these currency holdings.

The period 1969–72 was phenomenal in translating the large and mounting deficits in the United States' balance of payments into a doubling of world reserves—increasing reserves in these three years by as much as in all previous centuries in recorded history! This can be seen in entry II of Table II.3. International monetary reserves doubled again in the following five years. Most of this increase was in foreign exchange holdings, mainly dollars and Eurodollars. The first allocation of SDRs was in the amount of SDR 9.5 billion over a three-year period beginning in 1970 and allocated in accordance with a percentage of each member's quota. The IMF allocated another SDR 4 billion to Fund members in each of the three years 1979, 1980, and 1981. SDR allocations, however, have accounted for only a negligible percentage of the creation in reserves. Most of the increase has come from central banks' accumulation of dollars and Eurodollars and from the rise of gold market prices measured in SDRs and from the rise of the SDR itself vis-à-vis the dollar.

Table II.4 summarizes developments in international liquidity over recent years, whereas Table II.5 indicates the distribution of reserves among categories of countries.

Table II.3 The Inflationary Explosion of International Liquidity (in billions of U.S. dollars)

	End 1969	*End 1972*	*End 1977*	*Mid-1978*	*Mid-1978 % of 1969*
I. Foreign Dollar Claims	78	146	363	373	478
A. On U.S. Government and Banks	49	85	210	221	451
B. On Foreign Branches of U.S. Banks	29	61	153	152	524
II. International Monetary Reserves	79	159	319	330	418
A. Foreign Exchange	33	104	244	256	776
1. Dollars & Eurodollars	20	81	197		985
2. Other Currencies	7	15	27		386
3. Other	7	8	22		314
B. Other: World Monetary Gold, SDR Allocations and IMF Loans and Investments	46	55	75	75	163
III. Commercial Banks Foreign Liabilities in:	121	217	658	700	579
A. Dollars and Eurodollars	94	157	481		512
B. Other Currencies	27	60	177		656

SOURCE: Robert Triffin, "The International Role and Fate of the Dollar," *Foreign Affairs* (1979), p. 270.

The phenomenal increase in international liquidity raises the question of the extent to which this has contributed to the world-wide phenomenon of inflation. A particularly strong stance on this issue is taken by Professor Robert Triffin who argues as follows.

THE MAIN MONETARY SOURCE OF THE WORLD INFLATION*

Admittedly, the root causes of the world inflation in which we are now engulfed lie outside the monetary policies and institutions, national or international. . . . (N)on-monetary factors are the basic roots of the world inflation. They have brought within our horizon increasing scarcities of essential foods and raw materials, and environmental problems, which can be overcome only by huge investments and rising costs of production. These latter are further accelerated by collective bargaining and pressure groups, and spread from the scarce sectors to the others.

*Robert Triffin, "The Future of the International Monetary System," *Banca Nazionale del Lavoro* (March 1978), pp. 30–32.

Table II.4 Official Holdings of Reserve Assets, End of Years 1973–79 and End of May 1980 (in billions of SDRs)

	1973	*1974*	*1975*	*1976*	*1977*	*1978*	*1979*	*May 1980*
All countries								
Total reserves minus gold								
Fund-related assets								
Reserve position in the Fund	6.2	8.8	12.6	17.7	18.1	14.8	11.8	12.1
Special drawing rights	8.8	8.9	8.8	8.7	8.1	8.1	12.5	16.2
Subtotal, Fund-related assets	15.0	17.7	21.4	26.4	26.2	22.9	24.2	28.3
Foreign exchange	101.6	126.5	137.3	160.3	200.3	221.1	246.0	258.7
Total reserves excluding gold	116.6	144.2	158.7	186.7	226.5	244.1	270.2	287.0
Gold								
Quantity (*millions of ounces*)	1,020	1,018	1,017	1,013	1,015	1,022	930	934
Value at London market price	94.9	155.1	121.9	117.4	137.8	177.3	361.4	381.5
Industrial countries								
Total reserves minus gold								
Fund-related assets								
Reserve positions in the Fund	4.9	6.2	7.7	11.8	12.2	9.6	7.7	7.8
Special drawing rights	7.1	7.2	7.2	7.2	6.7	6.5	9.3	11.9
Subtotal, Fund-related assets	12.0	13.3	14.9	19.1	18.9	16.0	17.1	19.6
Foreign exchange	65.7	64.9	68.7	73.7	100.0	127.2	135.9	143.3
Total reserves excluding gold	77.7	78.3	83.7	92.7	118.9	143.1	153.0	162.9
Gold								
Quantity (*millions of ounces*)	874	874	872	872	881	884	789	789
Value at London market price	81.3	133.1	104.5	101.2	119.6	153.4	306.7	322.1
Oil exporting countries								
Total reserves minus gold								
Fund-related assets								
Reserve positions in the Fund	0.3	1.9	4.3	5.4	5.4	4.4	3.0	3.1
Special drawing rights	0.3	0.3	0.3	0.3	0.4	0.5	1.0	1.5
Subtotal, Fund-related assets	0.6	2.2	4.6	5.8	5.7	4.9	4.0	4.6
Foreign exchange	10.2	35.0	42.4	49.1	55.2	40.1	51.0	57.6
Total reserves excluding gold	10.8	37.2	47.1	54.9	61.0	45.0	55.0	62.2
Gold								
Quantity (*millions of ounces*)	34	34	35	37	34	36	37	39
Value at London market price	3.1	5.2	4.2	4.3	4.7	6.3	14.2	15.8
Non-oil developing countries								
Total reserves minus gold								
Fund-related assets								
Reserve positions in the Fund	0.9	0.7	0.6	0.5	0.5	0.9	1.0	1.2
Special drawing rights	1.4	1.4	1.2	1.1	1.1	1.2	2.1	2.8
Subtotal, Fund-related assets	2.3	2.1	1.8	1.6	1.6	2.1	3.1	4.0
Foreign exchange	24.9	25.7	25.3	36.2	44.0	52.8	58.1	56.8
Total reserves excluding gold	27.2	27.8	27.1	37.8	45.6	54.9	61.2	60.8
Gold								
Quantity (*millions of ounces*)	110	108	108	101	98	99	102	104
Value at London market price	10.2	16.5	12.9	11.7	13.2	17.2	39.6	42.6

Table II.5 International Reserves (U.S. $ millions, end of period)

Indicator	1975	1976	1977	1978	1979
			Annual data		
All developing countries					
Gold	19.5	17.8	21.2	29.4	68.2
Foreign exchange and other	53.3	66.0	79.1	95.2	114.6
Total	72.8	83.8	100.3	124.6	182.8
Ratio to imports (%)	31.5	33.9	35.0	38.3	—
Capital Surplus Oil Exporters					
Gold	2.5	2.7	2.8	4.2	9.5
Foreign exchange and other	39.4	47.2	57.9	46.5	53.4
Total	41.9	49.9	60.7	50.7	62.9
Ratio to imports (%)	81.3	75.4	77.0	62.5	—
Industrialized Countries					
Gold	120.3	115.6	142.9	196.5	396.5
Foreign exchange and other	92.4	103.0	138.4	176.4	188.3
Total	212.7	218.6	281.2	372.9	584.8
Ratio to imports (%)	29.9	27.1	30.6	52.2	—

It is at this point that monetary policies enter the inflationary process. They may accommodate it by expanding bank credit to the official and private sectors of the economy, thus financing increases in wage, costs, and prices; or they may refuse such financing, but at the risk of slowing down not only inflation, but economic activity itself, at least temporarily.

The evolution of the national monetary systems and of the international monetary system itself has tended, over the years, to eliminate former constraints on the inflationary proclivities to be expected from both the public and the private sectors of the economy. This, I believe, is the crucial issue in the acceleration of national and international inflation since the first and the second world wars, and particularly at the present juncture. Obvious as it may be, it deserves more emphasis from the economic profession.

Gold was traditionally the major constraint on such proclivities, but its beneficial role in this respect has been vastly exaggerated by the enthusiasts of the gold standard. Credit money—i.e. bank currency and deposits—played an overwhelming part in sustaining feasible rates of economic growth in the century before the first world war. By 1913 already, credit money accounted for about 85 per cent of estimated—or "guesstimated"—world money supply, and its widespread use did not prove incompatible with a closer approach to non-inflationary rates of monetary expansion than in the previous gold and silver money regimes, subject to repeated debasements of the coinage. Any country determined to fight inflation would be better advised to try legal, or constitutional, ceilings on money creation (*x* per cent a year, for instance, *à la* Milton Friedman) than to tie money creation to gold. I shall abstain from pursuing this suggestion any further, and turn instead to my main topic, *i.e.* the *international* monetary system.

The major development here is, without question, the generalization after the first, and particularly after the second, world war of the so-called gold exchange standard, under which all but one or a few countries accumulated their international monetary reserves not only in gold, but more and more in one or a few *national*, so-called "reserve currencies"—primarily sterling at first, and later the U.S. dollar—legally convertible into gold upon simple request by their holders. I pointed out long ago that the inflationary proclivities of such a system made its breakdown inevitable. The gold convertibility of the sterling standard had had to be suspended in 1931, and that of the mightier dollar standard collapsed similarly in 1971.

Most of the academic and official debates concerning the recent evolution of our international monetary system have unfortunately centered on two secondary issues, rather than on the most crucial one:

1) The explosion of oil prices, which occurred only in the last months of 1973, and cannot therefore be blamed for the suspension of the dollar convertibility in 1971, nor for the doubling of world reserves over the years 1970–1972.

2) The merits and demerits of floating *vs* stable (but adjustable) exchange rates. Interesting as it is, this debate obscures the fact that world reserves have grown, under both systems, at a wildly inflationary rate incompatible with the proper functioning of either.

3) Far more significant is the inflationary proclivity of any reserve-currency standard—convertible as well as inconvertible—enabling the reserve-currency center to finance huge and persistent deficits—internal as well as external—by the flooding of world reserves with its own *IOU's*.

4. USE OF THE IMFs RESOURCES

Of especial interest is the extent to which IMF members may draw on the Fund's financial resources to meet their balance-of-payments needs. Members' quotas in the Fund determine their subscription to the Fund, their drawing rights on the Fund under both regular and special facilities, and their share of any allocation of SDRs. Reviews of the quotas of Fund members are held at intervals of not more than five years to determine whether quotas should be increased to take into account growth of the world economy and different rates of development among members. Quotas under the Seventh General Review came into effect in 1980, with total quotas rising to SDR 60.6 billion. In addition to the use of the tranches, there are three permanent facilities for specific purposes—the facility for compensatory financing of export fluctuations, the buffer stock financing facility, and the extended facility.

TRANCHES, SPECIAL FACILITIES*

Tranche Policies.

If the Fund's holdings of a member's currency are less than its quota, the difference is called the reserve tranche. Purchases in the reserve tranche are not subject to prior challenge. Further purchases are made in four credit tranches each of 25 per cent of the member's quota. Normally, the total of purchases under credit tranche policies is confined to an amount that raises the Fund's holdings of the member's currency to 200 per cent of its quota. However, in exceptional circumstances the Fund may decide to allow a member to purchase larger amounts.

A member's indebtedness to the Fund (i.e., the obligation to repurchase) begins when Fund holdings of its currency exceed 100 per cent of the member's quota. A member is expected normally to repurchase as its balance of payments and reserve position improves, and the Fund may convert this expectation into an obligation.

For any drawing, a member is required to represent to the Fund that the desired purchase is needed because of its balance of payments or reserve position or developments in its reserves. Since July 1969, when the Articles of Agreement were first amended, a reserve tranche purchase (known as a gold tranche drawing prior to the entry into force of the Second Amendment of the Articles of Agreement on April 1, 1978) by a member has been legally automatic and the Fund can challenge only *ex post* the member's representation of need.

All requests for the use of the Fund's resources other than use of the reserve tranche are examined by the Fund to determine whether the proposed use would be consistent with the provisions of the Articles and with Fund policies. Under credit tranche poli-

**IMF Survey* (September 1979), pp. 7–10.

cies, use must be in support of economic measures designed to overcome a member's balance of payments difficulties. Prior to submission to the Fund of a request to purchase, a member discusses with Fund staff its financial stabilization program, including fiscal, monetary, exchange rate, and trade and payments policies for the program period, which is usually the next 12 months. However, the Fund has recognized that there are situations which call for adjustment efforts to be spread over a longer period. The criteria used by the Fund in determining whether its assistance should be made available are more liberal when the request is in the first credit tranche (Fund holdings of a member currency rising from 100 per cent but not above 125 per cent of the member's quota) than when it is in the higher credit tranches (that is, when the Fund's holdings resulting from the drawing would exceed 125 per cent of quota).

In the case of a request for a first credit tranche drawing, the member is expected to show that it is making reasonable effort to overcome its difficulties. In practice this criterion has often meant that, when differences of judgment arise, the member receives the benefit of the doubt. Use of the first credit tranche may be requested either in the form of a direct purchase or under a stand-by arrangement. A member requesting a direct purchase expects to draw the full amount after approval of the request; under a stand-by arrangement, a member may request drawings from time to time during the period of the stand-by arrangement.

Requests for purchases in the higher credit tranches require substantial justification and are virtually always made under stand-by arrangements or extended arrangements. The stabilization program presented by a member requesting assistance in an upper tranche is comprehensive. The policies described in a program depend on the cause of the balance of payments difficulties and their expected duration, given the institutional arrangements of the member. The amount available under a stand-by arrangement in the upper credit tranches is phased to be available at specified intervals during the stand-by period, and the member's right to draw is always subject to the performance of certain key policy indicators described in the program or to a further review of the situation. The indicators, also called performance criteria, cover credit policy and policy on trade and payments restrictions; they may also extend to the financing requirements of the government, contracting of short-term and medium-term foreign debt, and maintenance of external reserves. Performance criteria allow both the member and the Fund to assess progress in the implementation of policies during the stand-by arrangement. Failure to meet the criteria signals the need to examine whether further measures are necessary to achieve the objectives of the program. In this case, the member consults with the Fund in order to reach further understanding on needed changes in its program before requesting further purchases.

Stand-by arrangements are usually for one year, but more recently several stand-by arrangements in upper credit tranches have been for longer periods.

COMPENSATORY FINANCING.

The compensatory financing facility is designed to extend the Fund's financial balance of payments support to member countries—particularly primary producing countries—encountering payments difficulties produced by temporary export shortfalls. Members having a balance of payments need may draw on the Fund under this facility in compensation for export shortfalls, if the Fund is satisfied that the problem which caused the shortfall is a short-term one and is largely attributable to circumstances beyond the control of the member and that the member will cooperate with the Fund in an effort to solve its balance of payments difficulties. The export shortfall for the latest 12-month period preceding a drawing request is established against an estimate of the medium-term trend of the member's exports, which is centered on the shortfall period and based on statistical calculation and a judgmental forecast of export prospects. The Fund is prepared to authorize drawings up to 100 per cent of a member's quota. Requests for drawings beyond 50 per cent of quota are met only if the Fund is satisfied that the member has been cooperating in an effort to solve its balance of payments problems. Export shortfalls may include, at the option of the member, receipts from travel and workers' remittances, if adequate data are available.

Drawings under the compensatory financing facility—as well as those under the buffer stock financing and oil facilities—are additional to those to which members are entitled under tranche policies. An effect of this treatment is that the reserve tranche is retained as a reserve asset that can be mobilized by the member with minimum delay. This treatment also means that the member may use the Fund's resources in an amount that could increase the Fund's holdings of its currency beyond 200 per cent of quota, subject to a waiver of that limit. The provisions for repurchases applying to drawings under the compensatory financing facility are generally the same as those applying to drawings under tranche policies.

BUFFER STOCK FINANCING.

The purpose of the buffer stock financing facility is to assist in the financing of members' contributions to international buffer stocks of primary products when members having balance of payments difficulties participate in such arrangements under commodity agreements that meet appropriate criteria, such as the principles laid down by the United Nations in regard to international commodity agreements.

Drawings for buffer stock financing may be made up to the equivalent of 50 per cent of quota. As under the compensatory financing facility, the Fund is prepared to waive the 200 per cent limit on Fund holdings of the member's currency. The member is also expected to cooperate with the Fund in an effort to solve its balance of payments difficulties. The Fund has, to date, authorized the use of Fund resources in connection with tin, cocoa, and sugar buffer stocks, but drawings have been made only with respect to tin. Repurchase provisions are broadly the same as for purchases in the credit tranches.

EXTENDED FACILITY.

Under the extended facility, the Fund may provide assistance to members to meet their balance of payments deficits for longer periods and in amounts larger in relation to quotas than under the normal credit tranche policies. For example, a member might apply for assistance under the facility if it has serious payments imbalances relating to structural maladjustments in production, trade, and prices and if it intends to implement a comprehensive set of corrective policies for two or three years. Or, use of the facility might be indicated by an inherently weak balance of payments position that prevents the pursuit of an active development policy.

A request for an extended arrangement is met only if the Fund is satisfied that the solution to the member's balance of payments problem will require a longer period than is provided for use of resources of the Fund that are available under existing tranche policies. In addition, the member is expected to present a program setting forth the objectives and policies for the whole period of the extended arrangement, as well as a detailed statement of the policies and measures that it will follow in each 12-month period to meet the objectives of the program. Purchases are phased and made subject to performance clauses relating to implementation of key policy measures. Drawings under extended arrangements may take place over periods of up to three years. Purchases outstanding under the extended facility may normally not exceed 140 per cent of the member's quota (nor raise Fund holdings of a member's currency above 265 per cent of the member's quota, excluding holdings relating to compensatory financing, buffer stock financing, and the oil facility). Purchases under the extended facility are additional to those a member can make under credit tranche policies. Repurchases of amounts made available under the extended facility must be made within four to eight years after each purchase in 16 equal installments.

SUPPLEMENTARY FINANCING FACILITY.

The purpose of this facility is to enable the Fund to provide supplementary financing in conjunction with the use of the Fund's ordinary resources to all members of the Fund facing serious payments imbalances that are large in relation to their quotas. The supplementary financing facility will be used only in support of economic programs under stand-by arrangements reaching into the upper credit tranches or under extended arrangements. Such drawings will be subject to the relevant policies of the Fund, including those on conditionality, phasing, and performance criteria. The period of such stand-by arrangements will normally exceed one year and may extend up to three years in appropriate cases. Supplementary financing under stand-by arrangements will enable members to make the necessary adjustment over a somewhat longer period than is normal in connection with the use of the Fund's ordinary resources.

FINANCIAL FACILITIES OF THE FUND AND THEIR CONDITIONALITY

TRANCHE POLICIES

Reserve tranche

Condition—balance of payments need.

First credit tranche

Program representing reasonable efforts to overcome balance of payments difficulties; performance criteria and installments not used.

Higher credit tranches

Program giving substantial justification of member's efforts to overcome balance of payments difficulties; resources normally provided in the form of stand-by arrangements which include performance criteria and drawings in installments.

EXTENDED FACILITY

Medium-term program for up to three years to overcome structural balance of payments maladjustments; detailed statement of policies and measures for first and subsequent 12-month periods; resources provided in the form of extended arrangements which include performance criteria and drawings in installments.

COMPENSATORY FINANCING FACILITY

Existence of temporary export shortfall for reasons beyond the member's control; member cooperates with Fund in an effort to find appropriate solutions for any balance of payments difficulties.

BUFFER STOCK FINANCING FACILITY

Existence of an international buffer stock accepted as suitable by Fund; member expected to cooperate with Fund as in the case of compensatory financing.

SUPPLEMENTARY FINANCING FACILITY/ENLARGED ACCESS POLICY

For use in support of programs under stand-by arrangements reaching into the upper credit tranche or beyond, or under extended arrangements, subject to relevant policies on conditionality, phasing, and performance criteria.

In 1980, the IMF increased, under its enlarged access policy, the maximum amount of borrowing permissible for member countries to 600 per cent of a country's quota (up to 200 per cent each year for a

Possible Cumulative Purchases from the Fund
(per cent of quota)

	Tranche policy	*Extended facility*
Reserve tranche	25.0	25.0
Credit tranches		
4 × 25	100.0	—
1 × 25	—	25.0
Extended facility	—	140.0
Supplementary financing		
1 × 12.5 plus 2 × 30	102.5	—
With extended facility	—	140.0
Subtotal	227.5	330.0
Compensatory financing	100.0	100.0
Buffer stock financing	50.0	50.0
Cumulative total	377.5	480.0

Table II.6 New Loan Commitments and Other Use of Fund Resources (billion SDRs)

	Calendar year								*January–March*	
	1973	*1974*	*1975*	*1976*	*1977*	*1978*	*1979*	*1980*	*1980*	*1981*
1a. New loan commitments under stand-by and extended arrangements in period (including supplementary financing where applicable)	**0.4**	**1.4**	**1.2**	**0.9**	**5.2**	**1.9**	**2.2**	**7.2**	**1.2**	**4.3**
Industrial countries	—	1.0	0.8	—	3.8	0.1	—	—	—	—
Developing countries	0.4	0.4	0.4	0.9	1.4	1.8	2.2	7.2	1.2	4.3
1b. Purchases[a]	**0.2**	**1.9**	**3.6**	**4.6**	**0.3**	**0.7**	**0.7**	**1.0**	**0.4**	**0.1**
Industrial countries	—	0.8	1.5	1.7	—	0.1	—	—	—	—
Developing countries	0.2	1.1	2.1	2.9	0.3	0.6	0.7	1.0	0.4	0.1
2. Trust Fund loans disbursed (developing countries only)	—	—	—	—	**0.2**	**0.7**	**0.5**	**1.3**	**0.3**	**0.4**
Total (1 + 2)[b]	**0.6**	**3.3**	**4.8**	**5.5**	**5.7**	**3.3**	**3.4**	**9.5**	**1.9**	**4.8**

DATA: IMF Treasurer's Department.

[a]Other than purchases under stand-by and extended arrangements (i.e., credit tranche and compensatory financing, buffer stock, and oil facilities).

[b]A broad measure combining commitments made in the period to lend over the ensuing 1–3 years amounts subject to balance of payments need and performance criteria in individual country programs with balance of payments assistance provided in the period outside such arrangements with members.

Note: Components may not add to totals because of rounding.

maximum of three years) exclusive of any drawings made under the compensatory financing and buffer stock facilities. This compares with a previous maximum of 260 per cent of quota, taking into account normal credit tranches, supplementary financing facility and the extended Fund facility. Under the enlarged access policy, different guidelines may be adopted by the Fund from time to time.

Tables II.6 and II.7 summarize Fund transactions in recent years.

5. CONDITIONALITY: IMF VERSUS JAMAICA

At the same time as nations have had to resort to use of the Fund's resources, there has been increasing attention to the "conditionality" aspects of financial stabilization programs imposed by the Fund on members who use the higher credit tranches or the extended

Table II.7 Fund Assistance to Members: Disbursements and Repurchases (billion SDRs)

	Calendar year								January–March	
	1973	*1974*	*1975*	*1976*	*1977*	*1978*	*1979*	*1980*	*1980*	*1981*
1. Purchases under all Fund facilities plus Trust Fund loan disbursements[a]	**0.3**	**3.1**	**4.0**	**6.0**	**3.5**	**1.9**	**2.2**	**4.6**	**1.0**	**1.7**
Industrial countries	—	1.5	1.8	2.4	2.3	0.1	—	—	—	—
Developing countries	0.3	1.6	2.2	3.6	1.2	1.8	2.2	4.6	1.0	1.7
Trust Fund loan disbursements	—	—	—	—	*0.2*	*0.7*	*0.5*	*1.3*	*0.3*	*0.4*
2. Repurchases[b]	**0.6**	**0.6**	**0.4**	**1.3**	**2.9**	**4.8**	**4.2**	**3.3**	**0.7**	**0.6**
Industrial countries	—	0.1	—	0.4	1.6	2.8	2.6	1.4	0.4	0.1
Developing countries	0.6	0.5	0.4	0.9	1.4	2.0	1.6	1.9	0.3	0.5
3. Net purchases (+) and net repurchases (−) (all members)	**−0.3**	**2.5**	**3.6**	**4.7**	**0.6**	**−2.9**	**−2.0**	**1.3**	**0.3**	**1.1**
Repaid to lenders	—	—	—	*0.2*	*0.3*	*2.6*	*2.8*	*0.9*	*0.2*	*0.2*
Industrial countries	—	1.4	1.8	2.0	0.8	−2.7	−2.4	−1.4	−0.4	−0.1
Developing countries	−0.3	1.2	1.8	2.8	−0.2	−0.3	0.5	2.7	0.7	1.2

DATA: IMF Treasurer's Department.
[a] Excludes reserve tranche purchases.
[b] The first Trust Fund loan repayments are not due until July 1982.
Note: Components may not add to totals because of rounding.

facility. Nothing relating to the term "conditionality" appears in the Fund's Articles of Agreement. But the Fund's annual report of 1964 offered something in the nature of a definition: "Drawings beyond the gold tranche . . . are conditional, in greater or lesser degree, on the adoption by the drawing countries of policies designed to ensure the temporary character of their payments problem, and designed also to eliminate or reduce the member's reliance on exchange restrictions or certain other exchange practices." Again, the annual report for 1965 contained the following statement about what it called conditional liquidity: ". . . the credit tranches . . . which are made available on condition that the drawing country maintains or adopts policies calculated to correct in due time the payments deficit in question, constitute 'conditional' liquidity."

A former General Counsel of the Fund states that the word "conditionality" refers to the policies that the Fund wishes to see a member follow in order that it can use the Fund's resources in accordance with the purposes and provisions of the Articles. In various degrees, these policies should help a member to overcome its balance-of-payments problem, avoid the temptation to resort to measures detrimental to itself or to the general welfare, and help it to achieve and maintain a sustainable balance-of-payments position over a reasonable period ahead. A sustainable position does not necessarily involve the elimination of a current account deficit if there is adequate capital inflow. Conditionality must be regarded also as a safeguard that the Fund is required to employ to protect its resources, because the policies that a member follows in accordance with conditionality should enable it to terminate its use of the Fund's resources within a temporary period.

There is no absolute standard of conditionality. The Articles give no express guidance on what policies the Fund should encourage members to follow under its policies of conditionality. The Fund has considered it desirable to maintain a relationship between the resources it makes available unconditionally, or on the basis of mild conditionality, and resources for which it applies stronger conditionality. The Fund's objective is to see that members will have a measure of ease in pursuing their policies, but without inducing them to ignore adjustment.[4]

Prior to a stand-by arrangement, the Fund in consultation with the drawing country will establish certain performance criteria that will be used to monitor the conditional access to additional installments. The objective is to bring about adjustment to the country's payments position. The specifics of such programs will naturally vary according to the causes and severity of the payments problem and the structure and institutional framework of the country's economy. But for any country, the Fund seeks adjustment through means other than tightening restrictions on foreign trade or payments. A common feature of conditionality has been the imposition of a stabilization program designed to limit national overspending through limits on domestic credit, money supply expansion, and limits on government deficit spending. The program usually relates to the broadest possible economic aggregates that would suffice for the achievement of the objective of payments adjustment. The Fund states that it avoids taking a view on the appropriate distribution of the burden of adjustment as between various sections of society.

4 Sir Joseph Gold, *Conditionality*, IMF Pamphlet Series No. 31 (1975).

Table II.8 Fund Members, Quotas with Seventh Review Increases (million SDRs)

Member (currency)	*Quota*	*Member (currency)*	*Quota*
Afghanistan (afghani)	67.5	Grenada (East Caribbean dollar)	4.5
Algeria (dinar)	427.5	Guatemala (quetzal)	76.5
Argentina (peso)	802.5	Guinea (syli)	45.0
Australia (dollar)	1,185.0	Guinea-Bissau (peso)	5.9
Austria (schilling)	495.0	Guyana (dollar)	37.5
Bahamas (dollar)	49.5	Haiti (gourde)	34.5
Bahrain (dinar)	30.0	Honduras (lempira)	51.0
Bangladesh (taka)	228.0	Iceland (krona)	43.5
Barbados (dollar)	25.5	India (rupee)	1,717.5
Belgium (franc)	1,335.0	Indonesia (rupiah)	720.0
Benin (franc)	24.0	Iran (rial)	660.0
Bolivia (peso)	67.5	Iraq (dinar)	234.1
Botswana (pula)	13.5	Ireland (pound)	232.5
Brazil (cruzeiro)	997.5	Israel (pound)	307.5
Burma (kyat)	109.5	Italy (lira)	1,860.0
Burundi (franc)	34.5	Ivory Coast (franc)	114.0
Cameroon (franc)	67.5	Jamaica (dollar)	111.0
Canada (dollar)	2,035.5	Japan (yen)	2,488.5
Central African Republic (franc)	24.0	Jordan (dinar)	45.0
Chad (franc)	24.0	Kenya (shilling)	103.5
Chile (peso)	325.5	Korea (won)	255.9
China, People's Republic (renminbi)	1,800.0	Kuwait (dinar)	393.3
Colombia (peso)	289.5	Lao People's Dem. Rep. (kip)	24.0
Comoros (franc)	3.5	Lebanon (pound)	27.9
Congo, People's Republic (franc)	25.5	Lesotho (rand)	10.5
Costa Rica (colon)	61.5	Liberia (dollar)	55.5
Cyprus (pound)	51.0	Libya (dinar)	298.4
Denmark (krone)	465.0	Luxembourg (franc)	46.5
Dijibouti (franc)	5.7	Madagascar (franc)	51.0
Dominica (East Caribbean dollar)	2.7	Malawi (kwacha)	28.5
Dominican Republic (peso)	82.5	Malaysia (ringgit)	379.5
Ecuador (sucre)	105.0	Maldives (rupee)	1.4
Egypt (pound)	342.0	Mali (franc)	40.5
El Salvador (colon)	64.5	Malta (pound)	30.0
Equatorial Guinea (ekuele)	15.0	Mauritania (ouguiya)	25.5
Ethiopia (birr)	54.0	Mauritius (rupee)	40.5
Fiji (dollar)	27.0	Mexico (peso)	802.5
Finland (markka)	393.0	Morocco (dirham)	225.0
France (franc)	2,878.5	Nepal (rupee)	28.5
Gabon (franc)	45.0	Netherlands (guilder)	1,422.0
Gambia, The (dalasi)	13.5	New Zealand (dollar)	348.0
Germany, Federal Rep. (Deutsche mark)	3,234.0	Nicaragua (córdoba)	51.0
Ghana (cedi)	159.0	Niger (franc)	24.0
Greece (drachma)	277.5	Nigeria (naira)	540.0
		Norway (krone)	442.5
		Oman (rial Omani)	30.0

Table II.8 Fund Members, Quotas with Seventh Review Increases (million SDRs) (*continued*)

Member (currency)	*Quota*
Pakistan (rupee)	427.5
Panama (balboa)	67.5
Papua New Guinea (kina)	45.0
Paraguay (guarani)	34.5
Peru (sol)	246.0
Philippines (peso)	315.0
Portugal (escudo)	258.0
Qatar (riyal)	66.2
Romania (leu)	367.5
Rwanda (franc)	34.5
São Tomé and Principe (dobra)	3.0
Saudi Arabia (riyal)	2,100.0
Senegal (franc)	63.0
Seychelles (rupee)	2.0
Sierra Leone (leone)	46.5
Singapore (dollar)	92.4
Solomon Islands (dollar)	3.2
Somalia (shilling)	34.5
South Africa (rand)	636.0
Spain (peseta)	835.5
Sri Lanka (rupee)	178.5
Sudan (pound)	132.0
Suriname (guilder)	37.5
Swaziland (lilangeni)	18.0
Sweden (krona)	675.0
Syrian Arab Republic (pound)	94.5
Tanzania (shilling)	82.5
Thailand (baht)	271.5
Togo (franc)	28.5
Trinidad and Tobago (dollar)	123.0
Tunisia (dinar)	94.5
Turkey (lira)	300.0
Uganda (shilling)	75.0
United Arab Emirate (dirham)	202.6
United Kingdom (pound)	4,387.5
United States (dollar)	12,607.5
Upper Volta (franc)	24.0
Uruguay (new peso)	126.0
Venezuela (bolivar)	990.0
Viet Nam (dong)	135.0
Western Samoa (tala)	4.5
Yemen Arab Republic (rial)	19.5
Yemen, People's Dem. Rep. (dinar)	61.5
Yugoslavia (dinar)	415.5
Zaïre (zaïre)	228.0
Zambia (kwacha)	211.5
Zimbabwe (dollar)	150.0

Thus, if an improvement in the government budgetary position is an ingredient of the stabilization program, the performance criterion usually applied relates to the extension of bank credit to the government, rather than to specific measures to increase revenue or to cut expenditures. Similarly, performance criteria do not relate to specific prices for individual commodities, but where needed, apply to prices fundamentally influencing the structure of production, such as exchange rates and interest rates.

Controversy surrounding conditionality has increased in intensity in recent years. Inflation and balance-of-payments problems are both reflections of the attempt of a society to absorb more resources than it can currently generate. If the country then has to draw at the Fund and confronts the restraints of conditionality, which involve cutting back on real incomes and the use of resources, there is likely to be strong resistance when each section of society fears that it may have to bear a disproportionate share of the burden of cutting real income. As more of the developing countries turned to the Fund in the 1970s, the Fund came to be viewed as excessively orthodox, conservative, and monetarist in its terms of conditionality. Its programs became widely viewed as being excessively onerous for the developing countries, often requiring unreasonably heavy deflation or massive devaluation, and insensitive to the income distribution and internal social and political effects that the stabilization policies produce.

5.1 New Guidelines

To blunt some of these criticisms, the Fund reviewed its guidelines on conditionality in 1979.[5]

The new guidelines emphasize that the Fund will intensify its efforts to encourage countries to adopt corrective measures that could be supported by the use of the Fund's general resources at an early stage of their balance-of-payments difficulties. They also recognize that for countries facing serious balance-of-payments problems, often of a structural nature, the period of adjustment should extend beyond the norm of one year. Stand-by arrangements may extend up to three years in appropriate cases in order to moderate the impact of the corrective measures on real incomes and to contribute to a distribution of the burden of adjustment within the economy that is socially and politically more acceptable. Longer adjustment periods have been specifically provided for in the extended Fund facility, which supports programs for up to three years, and also in the supplementary financing facility. Adjustment measures frequently encompass sensitive areas of fiscal, credit, incomes, and exchange rate policies, as well as policies on trade and payments restrictions, and governments are rightly concerned about the compatibility of these policies with their domestic social and political objectives and their economic priorities. The new guidelines have made it clear that, in helping countries to devise adjustment programs, the Fund will pay due regard to these concerns and to the circumstances of members, including the causes of their balance-of-payments problems. Moreover, performance criteria will normally

5 The text of the guidelines is printed in the *IMF Survey* (March 19, 1979), pp. 82–83.

be confined to (i) macroeconomic variables, and (ii) those criteria necessary to implement specific provisions of the Articles or policies adopted under them. Performance criteria may relate to other variables only in exceptional cases when they are essential for the effectiveness of the member's program because of their macroeconomic impact.

The new guidelines recognized that countries are often hesitant to initiate corrective measures at an early stage of their balance-of-payments difficulties. In recent years, many countries have turned to the Fund only after their financial situation had already suffered extreme deterioration. In these cases, the stabilization programs have had to be more stringent than they would have been if corrective measures had been adopted earlier.

5.2 IMF and Jamaica

A dramatic illustration of the practice of conditionality and the controversy to which it can give rise is represented by relations between the IMF and Jamaica during the difficult years 1977–80. Jamaica became the largest drawer on the Fund in terms of per cent of quota drawn, with first a stand-by arrangement in 1977 and then extended arrangements in 1978–80.

During the period 1972–76, the Jamaican government embarked upon expansionary policies that resulted in a rise in the central government deficit from 4 per cent to 19 per cent of GDP. Substantial increases in wages also occurred. As a consequence of strong domestic demand pressures, the deficits in the current account of the balance of payments averaged 10 per cent of GDP in 1975–76. Extensive foreign official borrowing, especially from foreign commercial banks, became the major source of external finance. In 1976, with the curtailment of external commercial lending to Jamaica, international reserves were drawn down to cover the current account deficit. As a result of these actions, Jamaica's external public debt quadrupled between end-1972 and end-1976 to about $830 million, and net official reserves fell by about $350 million to minus $230 million.

The composition of aggregate demand also changed, with consumption rising from 78 per cent of GDP in 1972 to over 90 per cent in 1976, while investment declined from 31 per cent to less than 19 per cent. A high rate of inflation also contributed to a deteriorating export performance, and exports became a diminishing proportion of GDP. Aggregate economic activity stagnated and then declined, with real GDP declining by 1 per cent in 1974, 3 per cent in 1975, and 8 per cent in 1976.

The balance of payments deteriorated sharply in 1976, with the decline in international commodity prices and tourism, combined with capital flight associated with large-scale emigration. But the more persistent pressures of excess demand, coupled with declines in export volume, were basic causes of the trade deficit. By 1976, the current account deficit of more than $300 million was equivalent to more than 10 per cent of GDP. By year-end, gross foreign exchange reserves were virtually exhausted, and in December the foreign-exchange market was closed, only to be reopened in early 1977 with extensive new exchange control regulations. The Jamaican authorities then negotiated a two-year stand-by arrangement with the Fund for about $75 million, or 121 per cent of its quota, in support of a program to stabilize the economy. The following year, Jamaica again went to the Fund to draw upon a three-year extended facility arrangement. The Jamaican government's letter of intent follows:

Kingston, Jamaica
May 11, 1978

Mr. H. Johannes Witteveen
Managing Director
International Monetary Fund
Washington, D.C. 20431

Dear Mr. Witteveen:

1. On August 11, 1977 the Fund approved a two-year stand-by arrangement for an amount equivalent to SDR 64 million in support of a Government's comprehensive program to stabilize the economy. In October 1977 Jamaica purchased SDR 19.2 million, an amount equivalent to Jamaica's (enlarged) first credit tranche. Jamaica, however, could not effect subsequent purchases because of breaches of performance criteria due primarily to shortfalls in budget revenues and in receipt of foreign assistance for budget and balance of payments support.

2. In these circumstances, the Government of Jamaica has de-

cided to recast its economic program into a medium-term framework, designed to reverse the economic decline of recent years and restore equilibrium in the balance of payments. In support of this new program, the Government of Jamaica requests the use of Fund resources under the extended Fund facility and for a period of three years in an amount equivalent to SDR 200 million. Before making any purchases under the extended arrangement, the Government of Jamaica will consult the Managing Director of the Fund on the currencies to be purchased from the Fund. The Government also requests that the current stand-by arrangement with the Fund be terminated when the requested extended arrangement is approved.

3. The three-year program is described in the annexed memorandum [not reproduced] which also presents the understandings which form performance criteria for disbursements under the requested extended arrangement during the first year of the program. The Jamaican authorities understand that the intermediate targets will form the basis for their annual reviews, jointly with the International Monetary Fund, of the progress made in the implementation of the program in support of which use of Fund resources is being requested.

4. (a) During any period until June 30, 1979, in respect of which (1) the net bank credit to the public sector exceeded the ceiling specified in Table 2 of the annexed memorandum for the end of the preceding calendar quarter; (2) the net domestic assets of the Bank of Jamaica exceeded the ceiling specified in the same table for the end of the preceding calendar quarter; (3) the net foreign assets of the Bank of Jamaica did not reach the targets specified in the same table for the end of the preceding calendar quarter; (4) arrears subject to the ceilings specified in the same table have exceeded the ceiling for the end of the preceding calendar quarter; (5) the intentions stated in the annexed memorandum in respect of arrears not subject to quarterly ceilings and in respect of multiple currency practices and other restrictions are not being observed; or (6) the limits on the authorization of new foreign indebtedness specified in the annexed memorandum are not being observed, Jamaica will not request any purchase under the extended arrangement until after reaching understandings with the Fund regarding the circumstances in which such purchases may be resumed.

(b) Jamaica will not request any purchase under the extended arrangement after September 30, 1978, except after reviewing performance under the program and after reaching understandings with the Fund on the terms under which Jamaica may make further purchases under the arrangement.

(c) During any period of the extended arrangement after June 30, 1979 and June 30, 1980 in which understandings on performance clauses for the second and third years, respectively, are not reached or understandings thus reached are not observed, Jamaica will not request any purchase under the extended arrangement except after reaching understandings with the Fund regarding the circumstances in which such purchase may be made.

5. The Government of Jamaica believes that the policies set out in the annexed memorandum are adequate to achieve the objectives of its program, but will take any further measures that may become appropriate for this purpose. The Jamaican authorities will periodically review with the Managing Director of the Fund the progress being made in the implementation of the program referred to above, and will make all pertinent information available to the staff of the Fund to enable it to monitor performance under this program. In any event, they will consult the Fund in order to reach understandings with the Fund before September 30, 1978 on the terms under which Jamaica may make further purchases under the arrangement until June 30, 1979; and before June 30, 1979 and June 30, 1980, on their policy intentions and on performance clauses related to the implementation of these policies for subsequent 12-month periods. During the period of the extended arrangement they will also consult the Fund concerning the adoption of any measures that may be appropriate, either at their initiative or whenever the Managing Director of the Fund requests consultation because any of the criteria referred to in paragraph 4 above are not being observed, or because he considers that consultation on the program is desirable. In addition, after the period of the extended arrangement and while the Fund's holdings of Jamaica's currency include holdings resulting from purchases under this arrangement, the Jamaican authorities will consult the Fund from time to time concerning Jamaica's balance of payments policies, either at their initiative or at the request of the Managing Director of the Fund.

Yours sincerely,

/s/
Herbert Walker
Governor, Bank of
Jamaica

/s/
Eric Bell
Minister of Finance

A structural adjustment program was negotiated, which sought to revive economic growth and reverse the substantial fall in investment by allocating additional resources to stimulate production, while gradually replacing reliance on foreign savings with greater domestic savings. The Fund agreed in June 1978 to support Jamaica's adjustment efforts with an unprecedented level of Fund resources—270 per cent of Jamaica's quota, or $460 million over three years. These resources were supplemented by drawings of $20 million under the compensatory financing facility.

5.3 Breakdown of Negotiations

The IMF has recently reviewed its experience with the extended arrangement of 1978–80. A summary follows.[6]

> By end-1976, after years of extensive official external borrowing to finance substantial current account deficits of the balance of payments, Jamaica's foreign reserves and access to foreign commercial banks were virtually exhausted. After three years of declining economic activity, which resulted in a cumulative decline of 11 per cent in GDP (or nearly one fifth in per capita terms), Jamaica was confronted with the need for swiftly adjusting its living standards to accommodate the severe constraint imposed by the reduced inflows of foreign resources. At this point, Jamaica turned to the Fund with an economic and financial program designed to secure a balance between aggregate supply and demand at the highest possible income level through economic policies that would stimulate investment and output while restraining domestic consumption demand.
>
> Given Jamaica's extreme dependence on imported materials, every program sought an expansion of imports in order to achieve the program's goals. To finance greater imports during the period 1977–79, the Fund agreed to provide access to its resources in unprecedented amounts (about $516 million, or 537 per cent of quota). Actual Fund assistance was greatest in the two years of the extended arrangement, when purchases were over $260 million (about 270 per cent of the quota) and the Fund helped to mobilize additional balance of payments support (about $193 million), as well as supporting a medium-term refinancing loan for the bulk of amortization payments due commercial banks ($141 million), along with an increase in short-term commitments of $39 million. Re-

6 *IMF Survey* (December 15, 1980), pp. 378–382.

sources of this magnitude—totaling about $630 million, or about 12.25 per cent of GDP a year during 1978–79—could only be provided on a temporary basis in the expectation that they would be used to build an economic base which would make further massive assistance unnecessary. The prolonged stagnation of fixed capital formation indicates that the emergency balance of payments support, mobilized on a temporary basis, had resulted in financing consumption.

The Fund's contribution to assistance on this scale was to be of limited duration, with repayments beginning three to four years after each purchase. Nevertheless, during the period 1977–79 the Fund was by far the largest single source of external resources. In fact, the level of Jamaica's purchases from the Fund increased from 0.8 per cent of GDP in 1977 to 7.5 per cent of GDP in 1979, reaching a peak equivalent to 10.4 per cent of GDP in the second half of 1979. . . .

The results of the first year of the extended arrangement were mixed. Progress was made, but not to the extent envisaged. Domestic demand was brought into better balance with supply, and Jamaica's international competitiveness improved. However, production continued to decline, although at a slower pace, and investment activity remained weak. The sluggish production partially reflected the limited availability of imported raw materials, in spite of an expansion of imports that produced a widening in the current account deficit of the balance of payments to about 5.5 per cent of GDP in 1978 from about 2.5 per cent the year before. Production and investment activity were also adversely affected by continuing differences among business, labor, and Government. Labor was concerned that its sacrifices were in vain, as investment, production and employment increases were lacking and as capital flight continued. The business community pointed to the inability to secure import licenses for necessary supplies and blamed strikes and other job actions for hampering economic activity.

Equally worrisome were the deviations in fiscal policy from the program target. The overall central government deficit exceeded the target of 11.0 per cent of GDP by 2.3 per cent. This slippage was almost entirely due to a less than expected improvement in the recurrent balance, as government dissaving was equivalent to about 2.4 per cent of GDP rather than the target of 0.5 per cent. Jamaica continued to rely on foreign resources to finance its current budgetary expenditures, a situation that was not sustainable. On the external side, the continued existence of arrears on international payments prevented the return of private external capital flows (even trade credits), hampering Jamaica's productive effort and intensifying its requirements for balance of payments assistance.

For the second year of the extended arrangement, the Jamaican authorities proposed, and the Fund agreed to, a change in the mix of economic policies and a revision of the program targets set in June 1978 in order to respond to the growing social tensions and in an effort to stimulate a more rapid recovery of the economy. The adopted policies included suspension of the monthly currency depreciations, combined with greater moderation in wage demands and in price adjustments in order to diminish the upward pressure on prices, and no increase in taxes. Revisions in the program targets included higher recurrent and overall fiscal deficits and a greater current account deficit of the balance of payments so as to permit a further expansion of imports and promote economic growth.

With emphasis on export-led growth, further efforts were made to mobilize additional resources for investment in export and export-related industries, and a strategy was developed to encourage local banks to extend credit on a priority basis to such industries. Moreover, to help alleviate the foreign-exchange scarcity and promote the expansion of nontraditional exports, qualified exporters were given priority access to import licenses and a guaranteed source of foreign exchange for their imports of raw materials and spare parts.

The fiscal policy stance decided on was to bring the current budget into balance and reduce the overall deficit to about 9 per cent of GDP. The absence of new revenue measures implied a decline in government revenue relative to GDP and placed the burden of adjustment wholly on expenditures. Imports were targeted to continue their expansion relative to GDP, and the external position was to remain in deficit in the full realization that this would be possible only if official assistance to Jamaica was increased. Toward obtaining the necessary external financing, the Fund supported this economic program by doubling its resource commitment over the remaining two years to about $340 million with use of the supplementary financing facility. Total use of Fund resources under the new two-year extended arrangement would, if fully disbursed, rise to about $475 million, with Fund holdings of Jamaica's currency reaching nearly 600 per cent of its quota.

As in the previous year, the Fund joined the Jamaican authorities in seeking additional external assistance. Foreign commercial banks, by continuing their refinancing of debt, were expected to provide $65 million in fiscal year 1979/80. The World Bank committed a program loan of $31.5 million to create an export promotion scheme, while donor countries pledged assistance of about $59 million. For the program year (June 1979 to June 1980), the Fund made available $170 million, or about 6.5 per cent of GDP, and in an attempt to clear up international payments arrears and stimulate imports, made $80 million of this amount available in the first two months of the program. In October, drawings under the compensatory financing and buffer stock facilities of about $43 million increased use of Fund resources during the period June to December 1979 to about $153 million, equivalent to about 10.5 per cent of the corresponding GDP. In 1979, even more than in 1978, the Fund was the largest source of external assistance, providing more than three times the net resources from commercial banks, governments, and international organizations combined.

In 1979, Jamaica, like the rest of the world, was buffeted by higher oil prices and rising interest rates. The country also experienced severe floods in mid-year, which damaged export crops and entitled Jamaica to purchases under the compensatory financing facility already cited. While these external shocks jeopardized the program's objectives, major difficulties in the management of economic policies, particularly fiscal policy, resulted in the nonfulfillment of the quantitative criteria employed to monitor progress.

Greater than agreed wage increases granted to public sector employees and an inability to contain other expenditures resulted in a government recurrent budget deficit of 5.3 per cent, instead of a balance, and contributed to an expansion of the overall deficit to 15.1 per cent of GDP, compared with the target of 8.9 per cent. This deficit was financed primarily by domestic credit expansion, with banking system credit to the Government growing by three and a half times the amount envisaged in the financial program. Excess demand pressures led to a widening of the current account deficit of the balance of payments to 6.8 per cent of GDP, an increase in the overall external deficit, and a doubling of international payments arrears from their mid-year level. These divergencies from program targets led to an interruption in Jamica's right to make purchases under the extended arrangement, pending a review of the conditions under which access to the Fund's resources would be restored.

The greater expansion of domestic credit contributed to higher consumer prices, which created further demands for wage increases and additional labor strife. Labor unrest resulted in interruptions of railroad service, bauxite production, electricity, telecommunications, airline travel, and even the Central Bank's activities. The loss of production through work stoppage then combined with shortages of imported inputs and the effects of the floods to depress economic activity.

In September 1979, when the slippages were recognized, attempts were made to develop new policies to return the economy to the agreed path. Moreover, the Fund was willing to modify the program's ceilings relating to purchases in order to accommodate the changes arising from unforeseen and exogenous developments, just as it had done under the 1978 program. However, a consensus on economic policies did not emerge quickly. During this period of discussion from September 1979 to February 1980, the loss of policy momentum resulted in such departures from the program's targets that the original objectives were clearly unattainable. Moreover, weakening social and political cohesion further complicated development of economic policy.

By the end of the second year of the extended facility, it was evident that Jamaica could not fulfill the conditions for continued access to Fund resources. The IMF had stipulated that the budget deficit should be reduced and that the foreign exchange reserves shortfall should not exceed $370 million at end-1979, but the shortfall was nearly $500 million. For further access to Fund resources, the Fund set the condition of a $150 million reduction in the government deficit in 1980. Prime Minister Michael Manley and the ruling Peoples National Party took strong exception to this condition. The question of continued negotiation with the IMF became a political issue.

The Jamican government first sought a waiver of the conditions, so that it could draw on a further credit tranche. In a television broadcast, Prime Minister Manley explained the impasse.

WHAT THE P.M. SAID TO THE NATION*

For some weeks now the Government has been in very intensive negotiations with a team representing the International Monetary

***The Daily Gleaner* (February 4, 1980).

Fund. This became necessary because last December we failed the Foreign Assets Test which was part of the economic programme agreed with the I.M.F. As a result it was necessary to apply for what is known as a waiver.

This means that you examine the reasons why the economy failed to meet the target which was set in the Test and decide what action has to be taken to correct the problem. The action would have to be consistent with a new programme and sufficient corrective action would have to be taken now to ensure that the economy is getting on track. If agreement is reached on the waiver with the Directors of the I.M.F. foreign exchange payments of $80 million, which were due last month, will be paid to the Bank of Jamaica.

It would then be necessary to work out the details of a new programme with the I.M.F. in which new targets are set and further foreign exchange is made available. So far, the negotiations have not been dealing with the second stage, in which the details of a basic agreement is negotiated. I should make it clear, however, that the first stage of the negotiations, which is the application for the waiver, requires that we settle the basic outlines of a new programme and that we now take corrective action to bring the economy on track and in line with the new programme. The details of this new programme will be negotiated in the second stage, but about 50% of the action required for the new programme would have to be taken now.

There has been a lot of argument in the country about the I.M.F. and the application for the waiver. I want simply to say that the reason why the Government has been dealing with the matter is because the foreign exchange which was not paid in January and which will be paid in early March, if our application is successful, is important to help to buy drugs, food, spare parts, fertilizer and the raw materials to keep our factories going. In addition, the obtaining of a waiver ensures that the country is not in legal default in certain contractual obligations and it may assist in keeping some of our trade credits in place.

After weeks of negotiation, including a trip by Ministers Bell and Small and myself to the Headquarters of the I.M.F. in Washington, it is my duty to tell you tonight that the Government of Jamaica and the team of officials representing the I.M.F. have not been able to reach agreement on the terms of the application for the waiver. Let me repeat, we have not been able to reach agreement . . .

. . . Every Jamaican knows that the country is in very serious economic difficulties. Because of this, we have to be extremely careful with our money and cannot afford to finance many things that we might wish to do. In any case, there are certain things to do with the management of our resources which would be necessary even if we had struck oil and had all the money that we could use.

Therefore, I would like to ask you to come with me through three stages:

First of all, let's examine those sacrifices we have to make and would have to make even if (we) had all the money in the world;

Secondly, those things which we cannot do, even though we would like to, because there is a crisis and money is tight;

Thirdly, those things which would have been a consequence of further reductions of expenditure in order to secure agreement with the Technical Team of the I.M.F.

It is obvious that there have been deficiencies in the area of expenditure control and management generally. We have worked out new systems of financial control and these are being put in place as a part of a general restructuring exercise aimed at more efficient government and better management of resources. We have also looked at production plans and worked out strategies which are aimed at improving performance in agriculture, industry, tourism and the other areas of production.

We have to face the reality that the Budget cannot be used to subsidise many industries and enterprises and, in some cases, the consuming public. This is sometimes for good policy reasons or because money is tight, or both. You will remember that recently we had to increase very substantially the price of sugar and of all petroleum products . . .

. . . All these things which I have just spoken about would be necessary if there were no I.M.F. and no I.M.F. team in Jamaica. However, we have had a difference with the I.M.F. team which relates to the recurrent side of the Budget.

Their opinion is that the 1980/81 Recurrent Budget, if it is developed as a natural continuation of the 1979/80 Budget with due allowances for inflation, etc. would result in a deficit which we would have to reduce by about $150 million. That is the view of the I.M.F. team. The question of the precise items to be cut and whether there should be a combination of less cuts and additional taxes is not the responsibility of the Fund Team but they took the view that they should insist upon a reduction of about $150 million. And they insist that the reductions be done in ways which they regard as lasting and certain so as to ensure that the full effects of the cuts are certain to be felt in the 1980/81 Budget.

Together with our experts, we looked at the economic aspects of things and weighed this against the social aspects in terms of what all these cuts would mean to people: to parents, to children, to workers, to farmers, to students, to the sick, to everybody. We came to the conclusion that it was not possible or advisable through cuts, new taxes or by whatever means to reduce the deficit by more than $100 million. It is this difference of $50 million that has caused the disagreement.

Let me tell you what was involved. One way of saving the additional 50 million would have been to lay off nearly 11,000 workers. In our judgment, this would represent a social disaster and would also represent an administrative disaster because there are whole areas of the Government which simply could not run if you had to axe 11,000 people out of the system.

Another way of saving the further $50 million would be to do a combination of things including removing all subsidies from food, from J.O.S., from fertilizers; bringing the JAMAL programme to an end; making, say, all students at U.W.I., CAST, J.S.A. and other tertiary educational institutions pay full tuition fees. And in addition, thousands of workers would still have to be laid off including some Special Employment workers.

We are firmly of the view, therefore, that it would be wrong to cut an additional $50 million . . .

In the meantime, we call on all Jamaicans who do not believe that there should be a wanton sacrifice of human needs, because of this crisis, to support our application for the waiver on our terms, terms that have been worked out by our leadership and by our technicians and our economists. We all believe that our proposals are reasonable and just, while taking full account of the serious financial difficulties of the present time.

Although demonstrations on the streets of Kingston were directed against the IMF, the IMF refused to grant a waiver of its conditions. Consequently, in March 1980, the Jamaican cabinet announced that it had concluded that the IMF's loan program would involve Jamaicans in more hardship than necessary without resulting in the development of a viable economy. It said Jamaica had devalued its currency, cut subsidies on some basic foods, and slashed social services spending as part of the IMF's conditions. The officials had concluded that the IMF's prescriptions for Third World economies with foreign-exchange problems were unsuitable.

Further, to settle the question of future economic strategy, the government decided to proceed to a new election in October 1980. Whether to oppose the IMF or not was the central issue. The opposition party, led by Edward Seaga, a former Finance Minister, campaigned on a platform that accused Manley of economic mismanagement and of preparing for "Cuban-style society," and that predicted economic collapse unless the conditions of the IMF were fulfilled. In the graffiti on Kingston walls, "IMF" also meant, in Jamaican argot, "Is Manley Fault." But in a message to the Arusha Conference on the International Monetary System and the New International Order, Prime Minister Manley reiterated his conviction[7] that

> IMF prescriptions are designed by and for developed capitalist economies and are inappropriate for developing economies of any kind; the severe suffering imposed on a developing society through IMF conditionality is endured without any real prospect of a favorable economic outcome and without an adequate foundation of social welfare provisions to mitigate the hardships experienced by the people; the notion that with IMF approval international commercial banking institutions will supplement the funds made available by the IMF is a fallacy; the punitive withholding of tranches of foreign exchange as a consequence of the failure to meet periodic IMF tests condemns the defaulting country to a worsening of the foreign exchange situation which the IMF involvement itself is aimed at improving.

Just before the general election, at the annual meeting of the IMF and World Bank, the Jamaican Minister of Finance also defended his government's actions:

> It has been asserted that in per capita terms Jamaica was among one of the highest recipients of IMF lending through the extended Fund facility of 1978, which was augmented in 1979. But one should always remember that in small, open island economies such as those in the Caribbean, there is a much higher ratio of foreign trade and external payments to the size of the economy and the

7 *Development Dialogue* (1980:2), p. 5.

population of the country than in other countries. In per capita terms, the external payments gap is correspondingly much greater, as is the quantum of external finance which is needed to fill that gap. Let us review the "adjustment" that the Jamaican economy and the Jamaican people undertook in 1978 and 1979. In addition to steep devaluation, domestic prices were substantially liberalized to improve the incentives for savings, investment, and production. There were large increases in indirect taxes, and reductions in subsidies, in order to reduce the fiscal deficit. Major new programs to provide credit for private sector exports were introduced. The result of all this was that the average real wage in Jamaica is estimated to have fallen by 35 per cent in 1978 and a further 10 percent in 1979. According to a distinguished report prepared by the UNCTAD Secretariat for the Group of Twenty-Four, such a reduction in real wages would be "unthinkable" in the developed industrial democracies. Which of the developed countries that are the leading members of the Fund and the Bank could contemplate a reduction in real wages of nearly 50 per cent over a period of two years?

In addition to all this, my Government inevitably had to cut back on a number of social programs which had been introduced to correct the social and economic inequities of the past and to make provision for the basic needs of our people. These are programs which are precisely of the type which are being vigorously promoted by the World Bank and the international community as being necessary for the alleviation of poverty and the improvement of the human condition, which are the ultimate objectives of development.

By the end of 1979, Jamaica was unable to meet some of the performance criteria under the second year of the External Facility Program. This was due largely to factors outside the country's control—especially the unanticipated severity of international inflation and rising interest rates, the rising costs of imported energy, and the inadequate level of capital inflows—all related to problems of a worldwide nature which have occupied most of the time of these Annual Meetings. However, at one stage we were told that the further "adjustment" required of our country should take the form of a reduction of about J$300 million—approximately 16 per cent of our fiscal budget; and that this should include the laying off of about 11,000 public sector employees at a time when our rate of unemployment had increased to over 30 per cent. According to our calculations, if the United States was asked to make an "adjustment" of this relative magnitude, it would need to reduce the federal budget for 1980–81 by some US$103 billion. There would also have to be retrenchment of some 1,700,000 employees from the federal and state administrations. We cannot think of any better way to dramatize the *asymmetry of adjustment* and the problem of *conditionality* as it affects the developing countries, in real human terms.

That is why Jamaica has associated itself with a recent statement known as the Arusha Initiative—which calls for the establishment of a new international monetary system. Such a system should be universal in character and participation, democratic in decision-making, and capable of accommodating to the needs of different social and economic systems and alternative paths of development. Above all, it should be able to respond to the evident need for the transfer of resources to developing countries on a stable long-term basis, and within that context to secure real symmetry and equitableness in the process of adjustment to payments imbalances.

Jamaica places special emphasis on certain transitional measures which are needed as steps toward such a system. We emphasize particularly the critical importance of the positions taken by the Ministers of the Group of Twenty-Four in relation to (1) increasing the share of developing countries in the total quota of the Fund from approximately 33 per cent to 45 per cent, in order to increase their weight in the decision-making process; (2) lending at low conditionality the increases in the resources of the Fund secured through quota increases and additional borrowing; (3) the establishment of a medium-term balance of payments facility carrying minimum conditionality and providing support that is significant in relation to the present levels of deficits. We record our regret that these proposals have not been agreed to at this meeting.[8]

The result of the Jamaican election—or the first "IMF election"—was a landslide victory for Mr. Seaga's opposition party. The defeated Prime Minister told his party supporters that "What we did wrong was to challenge the power of the Western economic structure. I will remain unrepentant and unreconstructed." The new Prime Minister said his election marked the end of "ideological adventurism," and he announced that he would seek an early resump-

8 Statement by the Hon. R. H. P. Small, Minister of Finance and Governor of the Fund and Bank for Jamaica, at the Joint Annual Discussion (October 1980).

tion of negotiations with the IMF in the hope of reaching an agreement on a three-year extended facility drawing.

By April 1981, the Fund agreed to the use of Fund resources by Jamaica totaling the equivalent of SDR 536.5 million under various decisions. First, the Fund approved a new extended arrangement authorizing purchases up to the equivalent of SDR 477.7 million over the three years 1981–1984. Of the purchases under the new arrangement, SDR 87.1 million are financed from the Fund's ordinary resources, and SDR 149.3 million are financed from the supplementary financing facility. Second, the Fund agreed to a purchase equivalent to SDR 37 million by Jamaica under the compensatory financing facility because of a shortfall in receipts from exports and tourism in 1980. Third, the Fund approved Jamaica's request to purchase the balance of its first credit tranche, equivalent to SDR 21.8 million. This purchase and the purchases authorized under the new extended arrangement are equivalent to 450 per cent of Jamaica's Fund quota of SDR 111 million.

In addition, eight major international banks agreed to refinance $103 million in existing bank debt, and to establish a new $70 million credit to Jamaica. Of the $103 million in debt, $55 million was scheduled for repayment in 1981. Instead, the entire $103 million was converted into a new six-year loan, of which no payments are due until the fourth year.

Prime Minister Seaga said that this was the beginning of a new period and that "the productive sector should now so organize its efforts as to convert these loan funds into investments, and investments into growth in which the country at large could share. . . . What is being concluded is not the solution, it is only the means to the solution."[9]

6. THE EUROCURRENCY MARKET

Another major development during the 1960s and 1970s was the rapid growth of deposits in the Eurocurrency market, creating an international money market and structure of international interest rates. A Eurocurrency deposit is simply a foreign currency deposit—

9 *The Jamaican Gleaner* (April 6, 1981).

a deposit with a bank in a currency other than that of the country in which the bank is located. The market began with deposits of U.S. dollars in European banks—the Eurodollar market. The Eurodollar market is the largest of Eurocurrency markets, but there are also other deposits in expatriate funds, and "Euro" may include other offshore banks (in Singapore, the Bahamas, Bahrain) besides European banks.

When the United States ran large deficits in its balance of payments, foreign banks and companies accumulated short-term dollar deposits that became the basis for the development of the Eurodollar market. Or, if a central bank sells its currency on the market to prevent an appreciation of its currency, it acquires dollars. The central bank may then choose to deposit the dollars at a non-U.S. bank, which can then on-lend them to a customer. In the 1970s, the amount of officially held Eurodollars increased even faster, mainly by the investment of the oil revenues of OPEC countries. A prime attraction has been the high interest rates offered on time deposits, made possible because the Eurocurrency market is a wholesale market, with large transactions and low margins, and because Eurocurrency accounts are free of mandatory reserve requirements and interest rate ceilings. Multinational corporations also enjoy the convenience value of banking in major trading centers outside the United States.

The growth of the Eurocurrency market is indicated in Table II.9. The rapid growth has had significant effects on the international monetary system—through the sizable amount of Eurodollar deposits held in official reserves and through the enormous amount of public sector borrowing in the Eurodollar market by government entities in both developed and less developed countries.

The Eurodollar money market consists predominantly of short-term deposits, which are lent out through a system of bank credits. Transactions are usually in amounts of $1 million or more, and over one-half of all Eurocurrency transactions are between banks. Banks commonly lend their excess Eurocurrency deposits to other banks for short periods as a means of adjusting their liquidity position or in expectation of movements in interest or exchange rates. The interest charged on these interbank loans is known as the London Interbank Offered Rate (LIBOR). This rate has become the basic rate for many of the transactions on the market, with different

Table II.9 Growth of Eurocurrency Market, 1964–79

	Size[a] *(End of period billion U.S. dollars)*	*Annual growth rate (percent)*
1964	11.6	—
1965	14.5	25.0
1966	17.4	20.0
1967	20.8	19.5
1968	29.7	42.8
1969	44.0	48.1
1970	57.0	29.5
1971	71.0	24.6
1972	92.0	29.6
1973	132.0	43.5
1974	177.0	34.1
1975	205.0	15.8
1976	247.0	20.5
1977	300.0	21.4
1978, First Qtr.	375.0	25.0
1978, Second Qtr.	377.0	—
1979	475.0	26.0

SOURCE: Bank for International Settlements.
[a]Eurocurrency assets or liabilities of banks in Belgium, France, the Federal Republic of Germany, Italy, Luxembourg, the Netherlands, Sweden, Switzerland, and the United Kingdom, net of Eurocurrency holdings of these banks vis-à-vis each other.

spreads above LIBOR to different borrowers according to their credit ratings.

The average deposit from outside the market passes through several banks before being lent to a non-bank borrower. The pyramiding of bank lending means that no single bank can be sure of where the credit it extends will end up. By making loans, and accepting deposits, a Eurodollar bank can create Eurodollars in an amount greater than the deposits held by Eurodollar banks in American banks. The pyramiding need stop only if a loan from a Eurobank is not redeposited in a Eurobank, but is paid to a firm that deposits in a United States bank. Because the Eurocurrency deposits are primarily of an interbank character, however, relatively little *net* liquidity is created. The liabilities of the Eurobanks are about as liquid as the claims.

A special feature of the Eurocurrency market has been the heavy reliance by non-oil developing countries on borrowing from the market ever since the oil crisis of 1975. Through syndicated loans in which several banks participate, the Eurocurrency market has become an international conduit for channelling short- and medium-term funds from surplus countries to deficit countries. The problem of recycling petrodollars is discussed in the next section.

7. RECYCLING NEEDS AND THE CAPITAL MARKETS

Soon after the adoption of floating rates, the rise in oil prices from $1.80 per barrel in June 1973 to $9.50 per barrel in June 1974 placed increasing strain on international payments. In 1974, OPEC's current account surplus was $70 billion and by 1980, $120 billion. Table II.10 shows OPEC surpluses and their disposition.

The large import deficits of the oil-importing countries could not be removed simply by exchange rate fluctuations. Nor was it desirable to allow the deficits to intensify domestic deflation. The resources of the IMF were expanded specifically to deal with the immediate impact of the oil price increase by the creation of the Special Oil Facility in 1974, which provided medium-term financing of $8 billion. The IMF also recommended that deficit countries finance their deficits by external borrowing, preferably from the OPEC countries. But to the extent that the surplus OPEC countries did not lend to the oil-importing countries, the petrodollars had to be recycled through the Eurocurrency market in which OPEC countries did invest.

Instead of coming to the IMF for stand-by arrangements and thereby becoming subject to the conditionality restraints that would

Table II.10 Estimated Disposition of OPEC Surpluses (billions of dollars)

	1974	*1975*	*1976*	*1977*	*1978*	*1979*[a]
Estimated Current Account Surplus	70	31	37	30	7	65
Investments						
In the United States	12	10	12	9	1	7
In the United Kingdom	8	—[b]	−1	1	—[b]	2
In the eurocurrency market	22	8	13	12	3	38
In international financial institutions	4	4	2	—[b]	—[b]	−1
Subtotal	46	22	26	22	4	46
Unidentified investments (net)	24	9	11	8	3	19

[a] Estimate.
[b] Less than $0.5 billion.

Chart II.2 Non-Oil Developing Countries: Financing through International Capital Markets, 1971–79

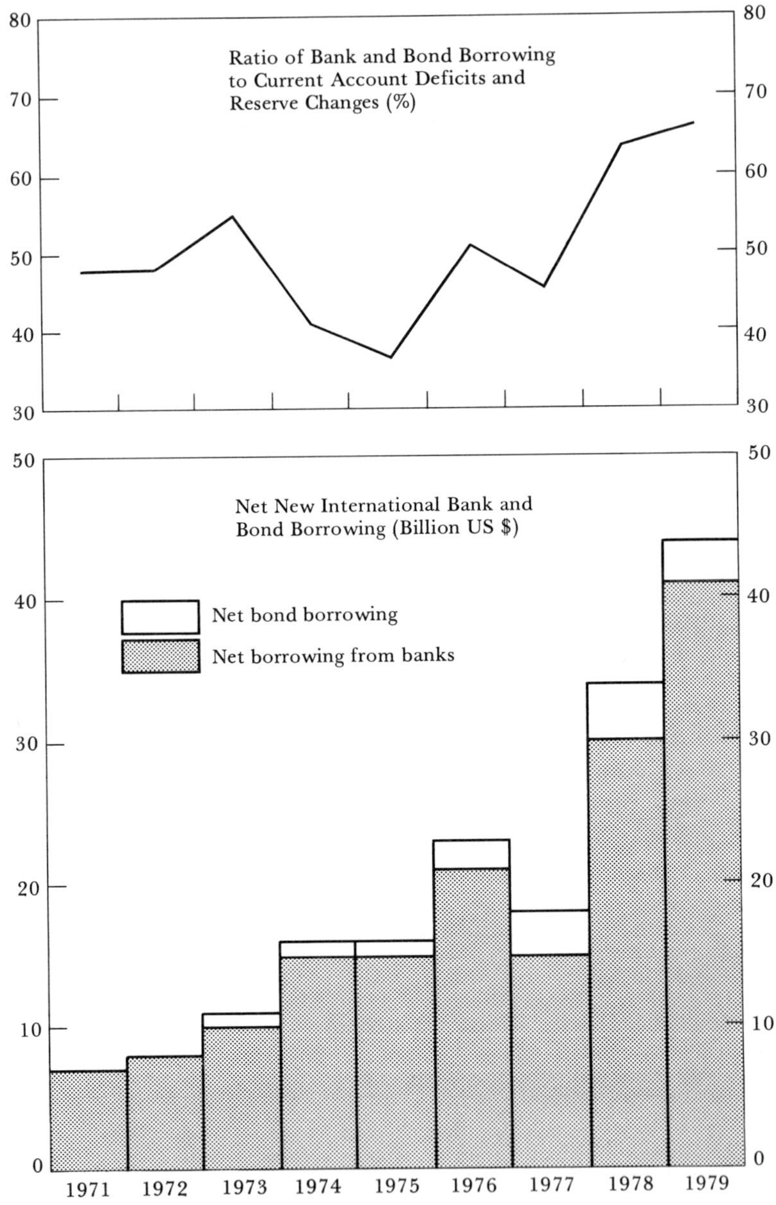

SOURCE: IMF, *International Capital Markets, Occasional Paper 1* (September 1980), p. 3.

be imposed by the Fund, many of the oil-deficit countries turned to borrowing from commercial banks in the Eurocurrency market. Although Eurocurrency loans bore a higher rate of interest, the Eurocurrency market became the dominant financial intermediary between oil importers and OPEC. Total bank claims on non-oil developing countries rose from $44 billion at the end of 1974 to $150 billion at the end of 1979. Chart II.2 shows the extent to which non-oil developing countries have financed their current account deficits through international capital markets.

The growth in these Eurocurrency loans has raised questions about the creditworthiness of the borrowing countries and their capacity to service the debt. Several countries have had to reschedule their debt. But in spite of the adverse experiences of such countries as Zaire, Peru, Turkey, and Jamaica, there has been no general international financial crisis sparked by the default of some borrower. Instead, the floating rate regime and the Eurocurrency market have allowed the recycling problem to be met more effectively than few economists thought possible at the time of the oil price increases of 1973–74.

Now, however, concerns about country risk, the unsettled international environment, and a worldwide economic slowdown may lead to a more critical restraint on financial flows to oil importers. As the IMF warns, if oil surpluses persist, new steps will have to be taken to assist the traditional mechanisms in carrying out the recycling function. The Managing Director of the IMF has suggested that the Fund must, if need be, be prepared to engage directly in recycling activities proper, i.e., borrow funds from countries in a position to lend. In 1980, he estimated that some SDR 6 to 7 billion would have to be borrowed in 1981, with additional sums required in 1982 and 1983. Considering the dimensions of market recycling and the Fund's future role, the Managing Director has said:

> In view of the scale of the imbalances compared with members' quotas in the Fund, we need to be able to provide, when necessary, larger amounts in relation to quotas than has been our practice in the past. This is not to say that the Fund has any desire to supplant the banks in the recycling process. Far from that. But in some cases the Fund's ability to advocate adjustment policies effectively and convincingly is enhanced by the capacity to make substantial resources available to the member. Thus members of the

Fund pursuing sound policies are now able, when necessary, to obtain amounts of assistance from the Fund two to three times greater than constituted normal practice in the past: a guideline of 600 per cent of a member's quota in the Fund over a three-year period has now been generally agreed.

This provision of larger amounts of financing and the stretching of adjustment over longer periods should enable members to undertake the kind of structural measures required in current conditions, phased in a way that is compatible with their particular circumstances.

For many countries, new financing is needed not to bridge a short-term adverse swing in their external balance but to allow time for structural adjustment in their economies to take place. Borrowing countries need to divert resources from consumption to investment and to address urgently the problems of conserving energy and of diversifying their energy sources.[10]

The chairman of the Board of Governors of the Federal Reserve System, Paul Volcker,[11] has also stated:

(The) strengthening of the financial resources of the Fund is an essential element in preparing for the strains that may come in the years immediately ahead. The role of the Fund is important not only because that institution has sizable financial resources, but mainly because through the good offices of the IMF there is a better chance to achieve the right mix between adjustment and financing.

Although there is still some leeway, it seems to me, for reasonable increases in bank lending to these countries, one potential danger in the recycling process that we must avoid as far as possible is the overloading of the commercial banking system . . . (P)roblem cases exist now and will no doubt continue to show up. This is where I see the IMF as a most helpful participant in the recycling process.

What is desirable is that when authorities in borrowing countries see trouble ahead they consult with the IMF promptly to develop a program that will maintain their status as creditworthy borrowers.

10 *IMF Survey* (November 10, 1980), p. 350.

11 Paul A. Volcker, Remarks before the Graduate School of Business Administration, New York University, March 1, 1980.

Chart II.3 Market Prices of Gold Bars in U.S. Dollars (solid line) and Swiss Francs (dashed line), 1968–79 (end-of-month, per fine ounce)

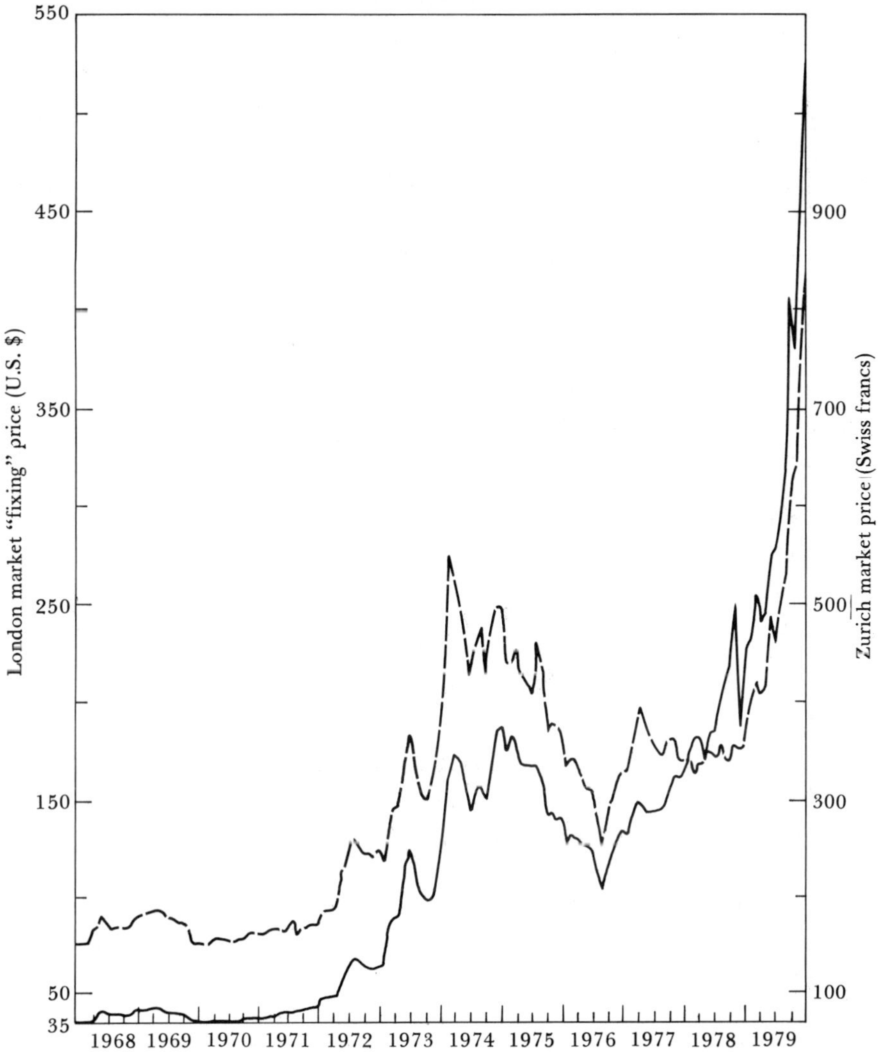

Moreover, it would be helpful if commercial banks, when they recognize that a liquidity problem is developing, would urge the country concerned to seek the advice of the Fund, as well as the Fund's assistance in working out a smooth transition to a more viable rate of external financing. The commercial banks should also structure their lending policies so as to support the Fund's role in the adjustment process.

8. GOLD

During the 1970s, there were also strong speculative forces in the gold market. The official gold price of $35 per ounce disappeared soon after the events of August 15, 1971, and the private market price of gold continued to rise until it passed the $250 mark in February 1979 and reached $850 by January 1980. Chart II.3 shows the large movements in the market price of gold. The rise in oil prices, exchange-rate uncertainties, and concern about inflation all contributed to a rising demand for gold. But the private market is thin and highly speculative, with volatile price movements.

Gold remains a major element in global reserves. The monetary authorities of countries outside the Communist bloc are estimated to hold between them more than 1 billion ounces of gold, of which about 85 per cent belongs to the United States, Canada, Japan, and Western Europe. Although the United States has sold some gold in recent years, no other country has been willing to do so.

At present, however, gold has no well-defined monetary role. To regain such a role, monetary authorities would have to repeg their currencies to gold and then buy and sell gold among themselves. As long as inflation continues and the gold market remains dominated by speculation and price volatility, this "return to gold" is inconceivable—let alone without the support of the United States and the IMF. Moreover, several important features of gold's former role in the monetary system have been eliminated—its use as a common denominator and unit of account, gold convertibility, and its central role in the IMF. Nonetheless, as some selections in the next Problem indicate, a return to gold still has its proponents, especially among a group of monetarists concerned about inflation.

9. ASSESSMENT OF FLOATING RATE EXPERIENCE

Against the background of the Eurocurrency market, recycling needs, and gold speculation, the debate over fixed versus floating exchange rates continues. But now we have several years of experience with the managed floating regime, and actual performance allows a more balanced appraisal between the positive and negative hyperboles of the proponents and opponents of floating rates. The most general assessment is that the regime has not provided a panacea for international monetary problems, nor has it been a disaster.

On the positive side, we should recognize certain achievements. Crises in the foreign-exchange market have not occurred with the frequency of the 1960s, and the world economy has been able to weather the major dislocation of the oil crisis. Adjustment has been made to disparate monetary policies among nations. Trade and capital movements have not been adversely affected by exchange rate movements.

On the negative side, however, movements in exchange rates have reflected more than "underlying changes" in money supply, prices, and costs. On numerous occasions, the rates have moved too rapidly and too far, relative to conditions of comparative advantage and efficient resource allocation. In large part, this has been because financial asset markets have dominated goods markets. The foreign-exchange market can be viewed as an asset market, and the exchange rate between two currencies can be analyzed as a relative asset price that moves with changes in the demand and supply for assets denominated in those currencies. Instability of expectations in financial asset markets has contributed therefore to a greater instability in exchange rates than would have resulted from conditions in only the goods markets. The large overhang of the dollar has also intensified expectations with respect to movements in the dollar rate. And the slow speed of adjustment in the goods markets has contributed to more rate volatility.

Although exchange rate movements have depoliticized the adjustment process and have produced more change in relative prices through rate movements than through changes in aggregate demand, the adjustment process has tended to be slow and in some cases ineffective. There has been the "J-curve" phenomenon—a country's trade balance continues to deteriorate after a depreciation of its currency, taking two years or more before the depreciation translates into greater export revenue.

A major argument for flexible rates is that exchange rate movements should allow a government to forgo deflation or direct controls on trade as alternative adjustment mechanisms. But experience has shown that demand management is still necessary to make depreciation effective. The price changes alone have not provided sufficient disabsorption to improve the trade balance. Only when coupled with demand restraint does the adjustment mechanism operate effectively. It has become increasingly evident that changes in exchange rates can equilibrate payments imbalances only if they are reinforced by appropriate domestic monetary and fiscal policies in both deficit and surplus countries.

As one reviewer of recent experience states:[12]

> It was evident by 1976 that the floating of exchange rates would not by itself restore balance-of-payments equilibrium among the major trading countries. The fragmentation into "weak" and "strong" currency blocs was rooted in a failure of these countries to use domestic macroeconomic policies to support exchange rate policy. Countries with balance-of-payments surpluses, like Germany and Japan, did not take steps to expand domestic demand rapidly enough to offset the deflationary effects of their appreciating currencies on their domestic economies. As a result, they found themselves in a sequence of sluggish domestic growth, reduced price and wage advances, continued current-account surpluses, and a steadily rising exchange rate. Only when the higher exchange rate was supported by an expansion in domestic spending could one expect the restructuring of the local economy away from export sales to be speeded up and prompt adjustment in the balance of payments to become a realistic expectation.
>
> The need for appropriate domestic measures to support changes in the exchange rate has been even more evident in the case of deficit countries with downward-floating currencies. The inflationary effects of a depreciating currency on domestic prices, wages, and expectations have become more rapid and more pervasive since 1973 than they had been a decade earlier. As a result, deficit countries that did not—or simply *could* not—introduce appropriate

12 Samuel I. Katz, Book review, *Journal of Economic Literature* (December 1978), pp. 1472–73.

domestic restraints often found that the downward drifting value of the currency would speed up increases in local prices and wages sufficient to make a further fall in the exchange rate unavoidable.

In short, it is as necessary for balance-of-payments adjustment under managed floating as it had been under pegged rates for demand-management policy to be integrated with exchange rate policy. The adoption of the Fund's Second Amendment underlines a recognition that exchange rate stability now primarily depends not upon pegging commitments nor upon agreements about the reserve-supply mechanism—but upon domestic economic policies, which foster orderly growth with reasonable price stability. The restoration of effective macroeconomic management may not be a sufficient, but it is unquestionably a necessary, condition for any progress toward world monetary order.

Experience has also questioned the contention that floating rates would allow a country more domestic economic autonomy in its policy-making. Many believed that flexible rates would free the authorities from any balance-of-payments constraint and allow them to use policy instruments for reaching only domestic targets. In reality, however, countries have become less insular because of more international trade in commodities and especially the internationalization of capital markets. Capital movements have become extremely significant in affecting exchange rates. And instead of simply allowing exchange rates to adjust to internal policies, governments have undertaken internal policies in order to affect the exchange rates. Exchange rate movements have been especially sensitive to monetary policy, and governments have recognized this effect in determining their domestic policies.

Finally, many would submit that experience with floating rates has shown the inflationary tendencies of such a regime. Flexible rates may lessen the balance-of-payments discipline over monetary and fiscal policies. Depreciation in itself is inflationary as import prices rise and exports increase. Real wage rates tend to be inflexible downwards, and demand management policies have only too often accommodated competing demands with too large a money supply and too large a government deficit, resulting in a vicious circle of inflation, depreciation, and further inflation and depreciation.

These points are elaborated more fully in the following selections that assess the experience with managed floating. First a review of the period 1973–79 by a former Under Secretary for Economic Affairs:

EXPERIENCE WITH FLEXIBLE EXCHANGE RATES*

When we look at the entire 6 years of flexible exchange rates, we find that the broad movement of exchange rates has not been surprising. Nor has it been as great as the newspapers have led us to believe. From the viewpoint of balance-of-payments adjustment, what is important is the movement of each country's currency against some average of the currencies of its trading partners, not its movement against another single currency. When the currencies of all industrial countries are weighted by their importance in U.S. trade (which implies for example that the Canadian dollar is given a weight of about one-fifth), the U.S. dollar is virtually unchanged today from March 1973, when major currencies were allowed to float against one another.

Moreover, the year-to-year movements during those 6½ years have been relatively modest and have followed a pattern which textbook theory would lead us to expect: the dollar appreciated when U.S. economic activity increased less rapidly than elsewhere (or declined), and the dollar depreciated when U.S. economic activity was more vigorous than that elsewhere. The actual percentage changes in the U.S.-trade weighted value of the dollar relative to other OECD [Organization for Economic Cooperation and Development] currencies were as follows: March 20, 1973 to Dec. 31, 1973, +1.5 percent; 1974, −1.4 percent; 1975, +4.9; 1976, +0.7; 1977, −3.5; 1978, −5.4; 1979 through Oct. 26, +3.1; or, for the total period March 1973 to October 1979, +0.4.

Neither have the movements in exchange rates been surprising if we adopt a perspective across countries. If we had forecast accurately in December 1976, for example, the current account imbalances which in fact emerged, we would also have forecast quite accurately the changes in exchange rates which have taken place. At least we would have forecast accurately the rank ordering of exchange rate changes; we might have been off on the exact magnitude, which is a more complicated question. . . .

This pattern of observations is exactly what we would expect of exchange rates if they are to function as a key element in the external adjustment process. Deficits lead to depreciation and surpluses lead to appreciation. I should also note, however, that it is

*Richard N. Cooper, "Flexible Exchange Rates after 6 Years' Experience," U.S. Department of State, *Current Policy No. 114* (November 1979), pp. 1–4.

not only actual current account balances which cause changes in exchange rates. When a country's economic policies are judged to be inadequate to correct expected current account imbalances, an expectation about future exchange rates is created. As often happens in any financial market, these expectations about future prices have an effect on present prices as well. Also, long-term capital flows must be entered into the calculation.

If my judgment that the pattern of exchange rate changes is what we would expect if they are to function as a key element in the adjustment process seems at variance with the popular impression of an unstable exchange rate system, the difference is due to the fact that the financial press exaggerates the economic importance of changes in exchange rates by typically reporting the widest movements in bilateral rates. What is relevant from the point of view of the adjustment process is a trade-weighted average movement in exchange rates for each country's currency. As I noted above, these movements have been very much less than press reports would lead us to believe. For example, Germany is Switzerland's largest trading partner, so movements in the Swiss franc-U.S. dollar rate greatly exaggerate the effective movement of the Swiss franc. Similarly, Canada is the largest trading partner of the United States, so movements between the dollar and the German mark do not capture adequately the effective movement of the U.S. dollar.

Of course, if movements in exchange rates are to be a key element in the adjustment process, trade and service flows must respond to these movements in exchange rates. I have argued that exchange rates moved in response to imbalances in goods and services. But will trade and service flows in turn respond to movements in exchange rates? I think the answer is affirmative, provided it is clear that we are talking about real, rather than nominal, exchange rates changes and that we are talking about the long-run effect rather than the short-run effect. Those who take the view that flexible exchange rates do not work have mistakenly focused on nominal exchange rate changes or have, against all evidence, expected a quick response in current account positions.

The changes in exchange rates that we have observed between major currencies have been influenced by differential rates of inflation between countries. A country's competitive price position is, of course, not affected to the extent that movements in nominal exchange rates only compensate for differential movements in price levels. The movements in exchange rates we have seen in the last 6 years can be only partially explained by differential rates of inflation among the industrial countries. They are therefore largely "real" and may be presumed to account for some part of the shifts in current accounts we are now seeing.

In judging the efficacy of the flexible exchange rate system, it is also important that we look at the long-run effect rather than the short-run effect. Formal studies generally show that price elasticities of demand in virtually all industrial countries are statistically significant and reasonably large over the long run, defined as 2 years or more, but are much smaller in the short run. If one looks only at the short-run effects of exchange rate changes, it would be possible to conclude that the adjustment process does not work. In the short run, import prices (in domestic currency) increase more rapidly than import volume decreases, resulting in a worsening of a country's trade balance. In the long run, however, this trend is reversed, producing the J-curve effect, and the trade balance improves. Changes in real income also have an important impact, and macroeconomic policy must be used to reinforce changes in exchange rates.

When we adopt a long-run perspective, we find that trade flows seem to be responding to the changes in real exchange rates which have taken place. . . .

I mentioned earlier that changes in exchange rates are caused not only by emerging current account imbalances but also by expected imbalances. I want to return briefly to the role of expectations before concluding this discussion of our experience with flexible exchange rates, because the fragility of exchange rate expectations is one of the most disturbing features of our experience during the last 6 years. As I have indicated, the broad direction and magnitude of exchange rate changes are fully explicable by underlying movements of payments positions. Yet there were clearly several occasions, briefly in the fall of 1977 and more notably in October 1978, when exchange rates moved too far too rapidly. It is difficult to explain the developments in October 1978 in terms of the underlying economic developments I have been emphasizing. Contrary to what was asserted at the time, differential inflation rates, actual or reasonably expected, can only go a small distance toward explaining the exchange rate movements during this period. I think, therefore, that we have a problem with highly fragile, easily moved expectations in exchange markets. As a result, governments must be prepared to intervene heavily as stabilizing speculators even in a system of floating exchange rates.

Ten years ago, Federal Reserve Governor Henry Wallich divided mankind—or at least international financial specialists—into four categories: those who advocate fixed exchange rates; those who advocate freely floating exchange rates; those who prefer fixed rates but are nervous about it; and those who prefer floating rates but are nervous about it. I am a nervous floater. We have a floating, or flexible, exchange rate system which works reasonably well. The experience of the last 6 years indicates that exchange rates will change in response to external imbalances, that changes in relative prices—caused by changes in real exchange rates—have a strong influence on the volume of both exports and imports, and that, therefore, flexible exchange rates can make a significant contribution to the external adjustment process. We must remember, however, in judging the flexible exchange rate system that the short-run impact is not the same as the long-run impact, that exchange rates are not the only determinant of a country's external balance, and that exchange rate changes themselves can be caused by expectations as well as by actual economic developments. For these reasons, we have to be patient for the equilibrating results of exchange rate changes. From time to time, monetary authorities will have to intervene heavily in exchange markets in order to break bandwagon movements which develop because of the fragility of expectations and the ease with which they are moved around.

Now let me turn from the recent past to the more distant future. I believe that the U.S. dollar will be the world's leading currency for a long time to come. Very likely the Japanese yen and German mark, and perhaps other currencies, will grow in relative importance; and diversification out of the dollar into other currencies by both private and official holders will take place. Moreover, the diversification will probably not take place smoothly but in fits and starts that create periodic turbulence in exchange markets. Despite these developments, the U.S. dollar will remain the most important currency used internationally.

I can imagine, however, that by the first or second decade of the next century the international role now played by the dollar could be assumed to a great extent by a different asset. Gradually over the next 30 years, the economic dominance of the United States will continue to decline, as it has done during the past 30 years. The U.S. share both of world production and of world trade has fallen, (e.g., from 16% of world exports in 1960 to 10% in 1978), and it will continue to fall—not because the United States is doing badly but because other countries of the world are doing well. Incomes in many other countries will rise relative to incomes in the United States. Over time, this will reduce the relative attractiveness of the dollar as an international currency. No other national currency will offer a clearly preferable substitute. We should, therefore, begin to explore the possibility of developing an effective alternative.

The next selection considers some other issues based on recent experience.

EXCHANGE RATE POLICY*

Aggregate price indices for various groups of countries show that the exchange rate system has been operating in recent years in the context of high and variable inflation. . . . (T)he period 1974–78 has also been one where rates of inflation, growth of real output, and monetary expansion have differed substantially from country to country. It is the intercountry differentials in these variables, rather than their behavior within each national economy alone, that are fundamental in determining exchange rate and reserve changes . . . The dispersion of inflation among the major industrial countries has been much larger (by a factor of about three) in the period of floating rates than during the period 1960–73. The experience of the years since 1973 also suggests that intervals of high average rates of inflation, which are also likely to be periods of large inflation differentials, carry a greater probability of large changes in the structure of exchange rates.

The structure of exchange rates was expected to alter in response to the dispersion of inflation rates, but some exchange rate changes in the recent period have been very abrupt, reversible, and difficult to relate to underlying economic conditions.

The influences operating on exchange markets are too numerous and diverse to permit a single explanation for recent exchange rate variability. It is possible, however to identify some causal factors. For countries with well-developed money and capital markets, conditions in the financial markets are probably more important than those in the goods markets for determining short run exchange rate movements. As with other assets, current rates of return, risk factors, and expected future rates of return are important in determining the current price, and when the factors affecting these returns and risks fluctuate substantially, so too does the current price, that is, the exchange rate. In other words, periods of rapidly shifting interest rate differentials, sudden imposition or relaxation of capital and exchange controls, and changing exchange rate expectations

*Morris Goldstein and John H. Young, "Exchange Rate Policy: Some Current Issues," *Finance & Development* (March 1979), pp. 7–9.

are apt to be periods of large short-term exchange rate variability, even when relative prices move only slowly.

The influence of exchange rate expectations or, more correctly, changes in exchange rate expectations are perhaps worthy of special note because of the many factors influencing these expectations, and because the factors themselves are subject to frequent change, especially in an environment of high inflation and irregular economic growth. While the factors affecting exchange rate expectations are not directly observable, it is known that they include, inter alia, monetary and fiscal policies, relative cyclical positions, current account and trade account imbalances, inflation differentials and relative competitive positions, political uncertainties, official intervention in the exchange market, and, of course, the change in the exchange rate itself. The reason changes in expectations are particularly important for exchange rate variability is that the current exchange rate may already fully reflect all publicly available information. Hence, it is only new and unexpected information that will cause market participants to change their evaluation of the future exchange rate, and thus the present exchange rate as well.

The short-run fluctuations in exchange rates in recent years have caused problems for the less developed countries, despite the fact that most of them continue to peg their exchange rates. For those countries that peg to a single currency—and most of the less developed countries are in this category—greater exchange rate variability between the intervention currency and other currencies is likely to result in increased variability in both the country's effective exchange rate and in the local currency price of its imports and exports. Increased short-run fluctuations among the major currencies also may mean that a less developed country's exchange rate (vis-à-vis countries with which it conducts an important part of its trade) responds to factors more closely associated with the external position of the country issuing its intervention currency than to its own domestic or balance of payments needs.

Some less developed countries have attempted to minimize these problems by switching from a unitary peg to a peg based on a basket of currencies, but many countries find this solution administratively inconvenient, particularly when there is a single dominant currency used in trade and exchange transactions. In addition, a pegged rate is regarded in some less developed countries as providing, in their case, a viable framework for encouraging price stability, for fostering confidence in the authorities' financial policies, for helping their planning process, and for promoting investment.

> In brief, the choice of an appropriate peg has become a difficult one for less developed countries in today's exchange rate environment.
>
> The increase in exchange rate fluctuations has also caused problems of portfolio management for the less developed countries, most of which hold nearly all of their foreign exchange reserves in a single currency. While the fluctuations in exchange rates have diminished the store-of-value function of some of the major currencies, the rise and variability in import costs have led to a demand for higher and more assured levels of reserves. Those less developed countries that peg to a single currency whose future value is uncertain may therefore face the dilemma that they need to hold larger working balances in that currency, yet they may also wish to diversify their reserves.

Regarding the experience of less developed countries with the floating rate regime, Noble Laureate Arthur Lewis[13] has emphasized "four powerful reasons" why the less developed countries (LDCs) should be advised to maintain stable rates even though the more developed countries (MDCs) float:

> In the first place there are forward markets for MDC currencies but not for LDC currencies. This is a particular nuisance for LDCs trading with each other and is one of the obstacles to regional integration and, more generally, to the expansion of inter-LDC trade. (It applies also to LDC trade with MDCs, but the behavior of other LDC currencies is perhaps somewhat less predictable.)
>
> Secondly, fear of devaluation inhibits investment—not portfolio investment denominated in external currencies, but direct investment, whether of foreign or of domestic capital, since there is no certainty that capital values will rise by as much as the currency depreciates.
>
> Thirdly, frequent changes in the value of an LDC currency add to the uncertainty of holding it and increase its instability. If the government is known to be ready to let the currency depreciate whenever it runs into balance of payments problems, nobody is willing to hold it, since the prospect of depreciation is always on people's minds. The onset of every minor difficulty then leads to a

[13] Sir Arthur Lewis, "The LDCs and Stable Exchange Rates," The 1977 Per Jacobsson Lecture, International Monetary Fund (September 25, 1977).

rush to sell and an exhaustion of the country's foreign exchange reserves.

Fourthly, the instruments of monetary control are perhaps more fragile in LDCs than in MDCs. When an LDC devalues, forces are set in motion that it may not so easily control. Our theories of these matters were framed in the eighteenth century, when food was a small proportion of imports, and when trade unions had not yet acquired the power to keep real wages rising in all situations. An economy with weak control over its internal prices is likely to find itself on a treadmill, where devaluation raises domestic money incomes and prices, so setting off further devaluation, *ad infinitum.* Firm control over the level of money incomes is a precondition for successful floating.

For such reasons it is easy to understand why the representatives of LDCs at IMF meetings have always expressed their preference for stability of currencies, and also why LDC central banks have shown so much reluctance to devalue over the past thirty years, even in situations where there was clearly no other viable alternative.

An assessment of the experience with floating rates should also consider its effects on international trade. At issue are questions regarding the effects of floating rates on the level and pattern of international trade and the economic costs imposed by excessive exchange rate fluctuations on individual countries and on the world as a whole. A recent study by two GATT economists addressed these questions. Their answers are summarized below.

DO EXCHANGE RATE CHANGES AFFECT TRADE FLOWS?*

The economic value of trade liberalization is not affected by increased variability of nominal exchange rates. There are no points of legitimate comparison between the two. Whatever the ultimate effect of an exchange rate change, it is uniform across all exports and imports of a country, whereas trade barriers are typically selective, differentiating between industries and product groups. Exchange rate changes are the external reflection of macroeconomic policy, which aims to stabilize at the maximum sustainable level the activity of the economy as a whole, thus also the level of trade.

*R. Blackhurst and J. Tumlir, *Trade Relations under Flexible Exchange Rates*, GATT Studies (September 1980), pp. 3–5, 8–9.

Trade policy is microeconomic policy dealing with particular *obstacles to trade*, thus affecting *the pattern* of production, more fundamentally the pattern of investment, and ultimately the speed of shifts in global location of industry.

A frequent complaint is that the additional cost which exchange rate uncertainty represents for traders, acts as a deterrent to the expansion of trade in general. Although this sounds plausible, with issues of this kind it is always necessary to specify the alternative to be compared with the situation we are analyzing. Flexible exchange rates as against what? Given the large and variable differences in national inflation rates, it is clear that an attempt to maintain fixed exchange rates in the 1970s would have had little chance of succeeding without extensive direct controls on trade as well as capital flows. These, however, would have impeded not only trade expansion but also general economic growth much more than did the additional uncertainty created by floating exchange rates. Compared, on the other hand, with a situation of general price level stability or even price level stability in only a few of the main trading countries, it is true that both GNP growth and trade expansion would have been more rapid than they actually were in the 1970s when inflation became generalized. The fact that even in the 1970s trade continued to expand more rapidly than production (the ratio of trade to production increments remaining essentially unchanged) suggests that there was no direct adverse effect of exchange rate variability on the level of international trade, which remained influenced mainly by the underlying GNP growth.

With these two side issues out of the way, the theoretical core of the first question can be addressed. How does a change in the exchange rate of a particular currency affect that country's trade?

A depreciation which does no more than offset domestic inflation maintains the same conditions of trade as would obtain under a stable price level with a stable exchange rate. We may say that, in this sense, it has no influence on trade. Thus the first step is to distinguish between changes in inflation-adjusted 'real' exchange rates and changes in nominal exchange rates which merely offset relative changes in domestic price levels. It is technically very difficult to measure such changes in real exchange rates as actually occur in a flexible rate system in which all or most countries are inflating at different and variable rates. Measurements that have been made by the various methods available indicate that such real exchange rate changes as have actually occurred were generally moderate, of short duration, and for the most part well within the margin of error which must be posited for exercises of this kind. In short, changes in nominal exchange rates have served in most instances to maintain, not alter, the pattern of international competitiveness.

The second step involves determining whether estimated changes in real exchange rates have had an impact on trade balances. Empirical evidence calculated for eight major countries for the 1970s indicates that the response of trade balances to such real exchange rate changes has been hardly significant, manifest if at all only over periods of such length that the relationship is highly tenuous, many other changes having intervened in the meantime. On the other hand, the relationship between trade balance changes and relative rates of GNP growth—the more rapidly growing country tending to develop a deficit and *vice versa*—is shown to hold much more closely. Researchers working with statistics for other countries and time periods, have reported similar empirical findings.

In short, the evidence tends to confirm what economic theory has long presumed, namely that at the macroeconomic level income effects tend to prevail over the price (elasticity) effects in international trade. It had been taught already in the 1950s that an exchange rate change alone, without a supporting change in macroeconomic policy, cannot attain the intended change in the trade balance. Developments in the 1970s indicate that this proposition continues to hold in the flexible exchange rate system as well. It seems, furthermore, that the transition to the flexible exchange rate system has weakened the impact of exchange rate changes on foreign trade. Since the relative price change caused by an exchange rate movement is now considered to be less certain or durable, the reaction time of trading firms to such price changes has lengthened.

The theoretical analysis of balance-of-payments adjustment evolved from an extreme emphasis on price elasticities of import demand and export supply in the 1930s and 1940s to the so-called absorption approach, introduced in the early 1950s. Both approaches focussed almost exclusively on the relation between the current account and exchange rate changes. While these theories held sway, a massive change was proceeding in the world economy. The volume of capital movements across national boundaries towards opportunities offering the highest (risk-adjusted) rate of return grew rapidly. The large increase in volume led to the development of new capital market techniques and instruments, to the emergence of new financial centres, and to their integration into one world-wide, sensitively interconnected, nearly perfect capital market. The picture of the world offered by the current account approach to exchange rate determination became increasingly at odds with observed developments in the 1970s. In the integrated, informationally efficient contemporary world it is often the case that more foreign exchange transactions are made for investment purposes than for trade purposes.

The more recent monetary view of the balance of payments, paying more attention to changes and adjustments in asset markets, reflects these changing realities. It proceeds from the insight that in a world characterized by a high degree of capital mobility, national currencies must be treated like any other financial asset. The behaviour of the foreign exchange market is seen to resemble that of a stock or securities exchange, rather than being an adjunct of the international goods market. Exchange rate changes are assigned only a small role, if any, in the correction of current account imbalances. Domestic monetary policy has come to be viewed as the most efficient instrument towards this objective. . . .

The fear of a country being injured by excessive exchange rate changes has been immanent in the history of international commercial relations, and has been growing again in the last two decades in the form of concern about the "symmetry of adjustment," and "sharing or shifting the burden of adjustment." It thus deserves closer analysis which, moreover, flows easily from that already presented.

The balance-of-payments adjustment process necessarily implies structural changes within the adjusting economies. Firms producing home-market goods in the deficit country, and tradeable goods in the surplus country will experience a decline, relative or absolute, in their scale of operations. The theoretically correct definition of an objectionable adjustment burden, or injury, was given more than 25 years ago by Friedman. It would occur through overadjustment, involving unnecessary shifts of resources back and forth between sectors, a shrinkage of an industry followed by an expansion when the trade situation normalized again.

The contrast between tight monetary policies in the surplus countries and relative monetary ease in the deficit ones suffices to explain the large variations in exchange rates in the 1970s. Empirical research undertaken for this study, as well as that reported by other economists, suggests strongly that domestic macroeconomic policies have more influence on the trade balance of a country than a change in its exchange rate. Given that the monetary policy of the surplus countries, concerned primarily with domestic price stability, continued to be restrictive, while that of the deficit countries, concerned primarily with employment, was permissive to the extent of being inflationary, the whole adjustment pressure converged on the exchange rates. It is not surprising that at times exchange rates attained what were clearly unrealistic levels from the purchasing-power-parity view, nor that they did not bring about a prompt adjustment. When the really effective policy instruments remain frozen on a contradictory course, the last free element, the exchange rate, will be pushed to large amplitudes but show little effect.

From the viewpoint of individual firms in the export and import-competing industries in the countries whose real exchange rates appreciated, the exchange rate changes did cause real difficulties. However, this should not be confused with injury resulting from "mercantilist" competition for market shares by such means as aggressive dumping. Retrenchment of activity in the tradeable goods sector is a necessary part of the balance-of-payments adjustment process in countries with unsustainable current account surpluses. And, because firms react only slowly to exchange rate changes whose duration is uncertain, it is unlikely that there was serious injury in the form of over-adjustment which would have to be reversed later on. It is true that all economies involved suffered costs from the economic turbulence in the late 1970s, but it must be emphasized that these were unintended costs, caused ultimately by the delayed reactions of national monetary policies.

These events led to a revival of the concern, widely debated under the fixed rate system, about the need for symmetry in adjustment. This argument involved two distinct misunderstandings. It was already shown that the process of balance-of-payments adjustment implies, indeed is accomplished by, certain structural changes in the adjusting economies. For this reason it is impossible for any country to 'shift the real burden of adjustment' onto its trading partners. The simplest way of showing this is to say that in a two-country world, once the deficit or the surplus country adjusts, the other has adjusted.

Insofar as the symmetry argument demanded a better coordination of macroeconomic policies in the deficit and surplus countries, it reflected the belief, prevalent in the 1960s and early 1970s, in the possibility of a permanent trade-off between inflation and unemployment. On the basis of this belief it was argued that the surplus countries should assume a part of the burden of adjustment by following a more expansionary monetary policy at home, thereby reducing the extent of monetary tightening required in the deficit countries. It should be obvious that this practice, if consistently followed, could not but impart an inflationary bias to the international monetary system.

A Governor of the Federal Reserve System, Henry Wallich, offers the following review of the international financial system.

THE INTERNATIONAL MONETARY SITUATION*

The floating exchange rate system has helped us to overcome a period of great difficulties characterized by the oil crisis, a world recession, and high rates of inflation. But there seems to be a widespread sense of uneasiness about the working of this system and where it may take us. There also seems to be a broad-based belief that the exchange rate fluctuations that have occurred within the floating system have been excessive and that we should act to reduce them. Evidence of these beliefs is the creation of the European Monetary System and the policies initiated in the United States in 1978.

I would like to examine the sources of this dissatisfaction with the floating rate system. It is easy enough to point to its defects. But these defects must be evaluated relative to some feasible alternative. There is no doubt that if we could have fixed rates while continuing to enjoy free movement of goods and of capital as we do, that would be preferable. But that is not the option. Worldwide fixed rates could be achieved today, if at all, only by a system of tight trade and exchange controls. That is not an acceptable alternative. We must ask ourselves, therefore, what we do not like about the floating system and how its defects could be remedied.

It is fair to say that the floating system, when it was imposed on the world by *force majeure*, was oversold and overadvertised. It was thought that the system would allow each country to pursue the domestic policies of its choice, unimpeded by balance-of-payments constraints. It was also thought that the system would insulate national economies against international disturbances. We have seen that this did not happen. While individual country experience naturally differs, countries generally found their domestic policy choices constrained, because efforts, for instance, to stimulate the domestic economy quickly led to depreciating exchange rates and consequent domestic inflation. Efforts to curb inflation

*Remarks by Henry C. Wallich at a meeting sponsored by the Landeszentralbank in Berlin, June 18, 1979.

created the risk of making a currency too attractive, leading to excessive exchange rate appreciation or the need for exchange market intervention that threatened to undermine price stability by excessive increases in the money supply.

The promise of speedy adjustment of payments imbalances through exchange rate movements has remained unfulfilled, perhaps because the very ease with which exchange rates could move has diminished political pressure to adopt appropriate fiscal and monetary policies.

The ups and downs of exchange rates have tended to accelerate world inflation because prices rose rapidly where currencies declined but remained sticky where currencies appreciated.

Vicious circles seem to have developed in which exchange rate depreciation feeds inflation and accelerating inflation, in turn, feeds back upon the exchange rate. Countries with appreciating currencies have found themselves caught up in virtuous circles, with cheaper imports reducing inflation and reduced inflation further strengthening the currency. These vicious and virtuous circles have threatened to polarize the world into countries with strong and weak currencies which has come uncomfortably close to splitting the world into strong and weak countries.

It is not surprising, therefore, that the evolution of the world's monetary system has brought us to a phase in which exchange market considerations have become a major priority. Both in Europe and in the United States, this new orientation has led to new forms or at least a new scale of exchange market intervention. It is important to be clear, however, what exchange market intervention can accomplish and what it cannot. Exchange-market intervention can deal with movements which are overly rapid and clearly excessive, of the sort that plainly seem to have occurred. We have lost the earlier faith, if ever we had it, that the market would at all times set exchange rates at the right level. Intervention that counteracts market disorder and helps fundamental factors to assert their influence over exchange rates is promising. Not only does it hold out hope of minimizing the cost of excessive fluctuations, it can also contribute to greater stability of prices, trade, and economic activity generally and thus, again, to greater exchange rate stability. A pre-condition of such intervention is recognition when exchange-rate movements require correction. Nobody can say with any assurance what is the "right" exchange rate. But it should not be impossible to recognize market disorder which is producing rates that are clearly wrong. . . .

A more active intervention policy, relative to market conditions, requires consideration of the currency or currencies in which intervention is to be conducted and reserves are to be held. In the past, the dollar was the world's principal, and for most countries sole, reserve and intervention currency. The United States, meanwhile, relied principally on swap arrangements with foreign central banks to obtain the means of intervention. In execution of the policies initiated in 1978, the United States has become a country holding foreign currency reserves of some magnitude, through actions such as borrowings by the Treasury in D-marks and Swiss francs, sales of SDRs, and drawings on the International Monetary Fund. As a result, the United States now holds reserves in D-marks, Swiss francs, and Japanese yen. This allows somewhat greater freedom of action than sole reliance on swap facilities.

Numerous other countries meanwhile have also added D-marks, Swiss francs, yen, and other currencies to their reserves. This is a change from past practice, when the dollar was regarded as the obvious intervention medium because of its wide international usability, the ease with which investments of reserves balances could be made and liquidated in the U.S. money market, and the economies in transactions costs that resulted from these circumstances. Recently, some holders of international balances have taken a portfolio approach to the investment of their reserves, seeking to reduce risk and stabilize return by diversification. These activities probably have contributed in some degree to exchange market instability, although they have not as of now, impeded the recovery of the dollar from the low levels of October 1978.

In this way, the D-mark, the Swiss franc, and the yen have moved further along the road to being reserve currencies while only sterling has dropped out. The world as a whole has moved a step further along the road to a multi-reserve currency system. The brief experience of the United States in holding foreign currencies for intervention has revealed some relatively minor technical problems that nevertheless deserve to be examined among the pros and cons of a multi-reserve-currency system. Investments in the currencies acquired cannot be made with the same ease with which investments can be made in dollar assets. This is partly the result of controls on capital inflows of some of the incipient reserve-currency countries. More broadly, however, it reflects the relative narrowness of their financial markets and the fact that large-scale operations in these currencies, both for investment and for intervention, have consequences for the monetary, foreign exchange, and capital market policies of these countries. Countries holding dollars as reserves have rarely found it necessary to engage in negotiation or even consultation with the United States when they needed to invest or mobilize funds or intervene in exchange markets to buy or sell dollars. The natural breadth of U.S. financial markets has been assisted in achieving this result by special investment facilities offered by the U.S. Treasury through nonmarketable issues of U.S. Government obligations. This has resulted in a very flexible use of the U.S. dollar by foreign monetary authorities. Given the different structure of the financial markets of the incipient reserve currency countries, the question arises whether it is possible or advisable for them to offer the same kind of facilities.

The German and Swiss authorities have made it clear that they do not welcome the advancement of their currencies to reserve currency status. The Japanese authorities appear to be taking a neutral attitude, neither favoring nor inhibiting the development of the yen as a reserve currency. The German and Swiss authorities seem to be concerned about both the exchange rate and the financial market implications of large international flows in their currencies. Past experience indicates that these movements can indeed cause serious disturbances for monetary and foreign exchange rate policies.

Perhaps the principal burden of being a reserve currency country comes from the softening of balance-of-payments discipline that such a country experiences. It may be helpful from time to time not to have to take unpalatable fiscal or monetary policy measures to restore balance-of-payments equilibrium. But that is a benefit often dearly bought at the price of trouble later. The countries that today are candidates for reserve currency status do not need and would not benefit from the balance-of-payments support that this role can bring. Neither did the United States in the days after World War II when the dollar became the world's reserve currency. It seems to be the nature of the process by which the market elevates particular currencies to reserve currency status that the market first singles out currencies precisely because they are strong, and that performance of the reserve role subsequently weakens discipline and weakens the currencies. Being placed in the passive role of an "*n*-th currency" whose exchange rate is determined by the exchange rates decisions of the "*n* -1" contributes to this weakening. Weakening of discipline and the passive role of an "*n*-th currency" have been the experience, in my view, of, first Britain, and then, the United States. It is difficult not to have sympathy for the reluctance of some countries to take the risk of moving along that road.

The Managing Director of the IMF has also appraised the working of the flexible rate system, emphasizing that flexible rates do not insulate economies in an open world and that they do not lessen the need for basic policy adjustments.

EXCHANGE RATES AND THE ADJUSTMENT PROCESS*

FLEXIBLE RATES DO NOT INSULATE ECONOMIES IN AN OPEN WORLD. It is a matter of observation that, in today's world, a high degree of economic interdependence continues in spite of widespread floating. To some extent this is because the floating is not "clean": central bank intervention results in the transmission of monetary flows from one economy to another. This is an important and growing practice. But, even in the absence of intervention, there are three fundamental reasons why flexible rates cannot fully insulate a domestic economy from external influences.

The first is that real activity in an economy will react to exchange rate changes only to the extent that relative costs adjust, and after the time lag that it takes for demand to respond to changes in these relative costs. It has long been recognized, of course, that exchange rate changes can only be effective if they lead to shifts in the costs of producing goods in one country as compared with others. To the extent, however, that devaluations set off movements in wages and prices that lead to offsetting increases in costs, while appreciations act in the direction of reducing costs, the effects of exchange rate changes can be limited in both time and amount. In a large number of cases changes in nominal rates have been offset by inflation differentials, and thus real exchange movements have often been small. The risk of such feedback is increased by the fact that, for many goods and services, trade volume only responds to relative cost changes over a fairly extended period. This varies from one country to another, from one time to another, and from one type of product to another. Nevertheless, for most devaluing or appreciating currencies it is generally a year or more before a noticeable change occurs in the country's real balance of trade, and a substantial additional period may be required to realize something approaching the full result of the change in the exchange rate. If during this period the relative cost improvement in devaluing countries is eroded by domestic inflation, while the relative cost deterioration in appreciating countries is dampened by reduced

*J. de Larosière, "Exchange Rates and the Adjustment Process," *IMF Survey* (October 19, 1979), pp. 337–338.

rates of inflation, then the full effects of the exchange rate changes will not come through, and the need for adjustment will remain. Adoption of a realistic exchange rate is thus a necessary but not a sufficient condition for adjustment of a country's external accounts.

The second reason why flexible exchange rates cannot entirely insulate economies lies in the high level of external trade in relation to domestic production in many countries. Exchange rate changes cannot, especially given the lags I have mentioned, prevent the level of economic activity in one country from being affected directly by the demand for its products in its principal trading partners. In this important respect, therefore, the flexible rate system has a good deal of similarity to a pegged rate system, and those responsible for economic policy need to continue to take a close interest in economic developments in other countries.

The third aspect of interdependence which is important concerns those countries whose currencies are widely used for international trade and held by other countries in their international reserves. The domestic monetary policies of these major countries are naturally reflected in the external value of their currencies, and if these policies result in sharp fluctuations or in widespread shifts in confidence, then the functioning of the world's markets and the economies of other countries are invariably and directly affected.

These, then, are three reasons for the continuing interdependence of national economies, even under a regime of freely floating rates. Let me now turn to examine the type of exchange rate fluctuations we have seen in practice over the last few years, the factors which have led to the widespread adoption of "managed" floating, and the reasons why these developments, in my view, do not diminish the need for prompt adjustment of general economic policies compared with the position under the previous par value system.

FLEXIBLE EXCHANGE RATES DO NOT LESSEN THE NEED FOR BASIC POLICY ADJUSTMENTS.

During the later years of the par value system, when balance of payments crises were receiving a good deal of attention, there were those who held that the introduction of flexible rates would banish stories about international payments and exchange rates to the back pages of the newspapers. Unfortunately, this has not turned out to be the case, and in recent years developments in exchange markets have often provided the lead stories for the media throughout the world. . . .

Looked at retrospectively, three kinds of exchange rate changes can be identified in the recent experience; firstly, very short-term fluctuations of the day-to-day month-to-month variety; secondly, intermediate-term fluctuations in which a change in one direction of six months to a year is subsequently reversed; and thirdly, long-term structural changes in the pattern of rates.

It has long been held that the authorities should do what they can to smooth out very short-term fluctuations, although on occasion they may have to vary their intervention tactics to avoid being made a target by the market. There is similarly wide agreement that little can be usefully done by intervention alone to resist long-term structural rate changes.

It is, however, in the area of intermediate-term fluctuations that the test of principles becomes clearest, and here there have recently been substantial developments. Following the events of last year all countries are prepared to take a view on whether a movement in the value of their currencies is appropriate, and are prepared to use intervention and other policies to resist a potential intermediate-term change which they regard as undesirable. This is an important change in attitude, and when the commitment to the management of exchange rates reaches this level, the distinction between a flexible rate system and an adjustable peg system has narrowed substantially.

The chief reasons for this adoption of "managed" floating are perhaps as follows. Firstly, it has been accepted that exchange rates alone could not take the full strain of the severe external shocks to which economies have been subjected during the last few years. Secondly, governments have come to recognize that, because of the factors I described earlier, exchange rate movements cannot by themselves, or in the very short term, bring about adjustment between economies. This, in itself, implies that, while the management of exchange rates can make a contribution to stability, adjustment policies must go beyond intervention in exchange markets and also embrace general economic policies to tackle inflationary disorders directly. It is in the underlying economic conditions and policies that the key to exchange stability is to be found.

Finally, there follows an assessment of the extent to which the managed floating rate system represents an improvement over the "adjustable-peg, dollar-standard" (APDS) system of the 1960s.

CURRENT ACCOUNT TARGETS AND MANAGED FLOATING*

Given the potential dangers of the current system, the question remains: how much better is the current system than the old APDS? The answer has three parts. The current system is really a continuation of the former system: countries have not abandoned their policy concerns with respect to the exchange rate and the size and composition of their balance of payments. What has changed has been the size of dollar holdings by foreigners and the consequent ability of central banks to withstand private speculative flows. The likely direction of movement of an exchange rate is no longer a one-sided bet, and private funds are less able to force changes in rates.

Second, the fact that rates are not pegged implies that it requires a conscious decision to intervene in the foreign exchange market. As such, market forces can absorb a much higher fraction of the burden of adjustment than under the APDS system. To the extent that governments were previously forced to take painful decisions before allowing markets to operate, the removal of that pressure is an improvement. Further, the burden of proof is now upon those wishing to intervene, again a step in the right direction.

Thus, in day-to-day operations, the current system represents a distinct improvement over the old APDS. Indeed, it is possible, and perhaps even probable, that market forces can absorb any inconsistencies in targets. However, the possibility of inconsistencies leads to the third part of the answer: the need for international consultation and negotiation is not as apparent as it was under the APDS. Under the old system, mounting dollar balances in European central banks and/or private speculative capital flows signalled the need for international co-operation; it was painfully evident that an alternative to a co-operative solution was a breakdown of the system. Under the current system, it is not obvious that a signal as readily interpretable as huge capital flows will be visible and that the need for negotiations to reconcile divergent interests will be apparent.

The danger, therefore, is that inconsistent targets can lead to mutually contradictory interventions with consequent instability for the system. The way out must be through an agreement upon a mechanism for designation of target current accounts (including,

*Anne O. Krueger, "Current Account Targets and Managed Floating," in Robert Z. Aliber (ed.), *The Political Economy of Monetary Reform* (1979), pp. 39–41.

possibly, levels of transfer of resources to the developing countries). There are three alternatives: (1) rules or criteria and/or intervention can be agreed upon; (2) intervention can be totally eschewed; and (3) continuing diplomacy can monitor current developments as they occur.

Clean floating would be preferable, in that it would approximate the neat flexible-exchange-rates world of the blackboard; but it would require extensive consultation on what does or does not constitute currency intervention. The objections to the Shultz–Volcker plan about incentives to "cheat" would apply to a clean float. The impossibility of setting down rules for currency intervention is also apparent: all the objections about 'cheating' still apply.

That leaves the task to central bankers, finance ministers, and foreign ministers. There is considerable evidence that consultations are already proceeding: agreements that the OECD countries would refrain from imposing additional barriers to imports for one year, and on other matters, have already been announced. In a sense, academic inputs to the discussion will be much more difficult with dirty floating than they were under the APDS system. Government and central bank decisions were clearly visible in that balance of payments figures generally indicated the extent to which market forces were being bucked, while international swap agreements, devaluations and other consultations were fully reported.

Under the new system, international economic interdependence is as great as ever, but the decisions made will be less visible and less easily assessed by those outside government. Evaluation of those decisions will be more difficult as the whole range of issues pertaining to relative bargaining power, *quid pro quos* unrelated to the payments balance, and other non-visible aspects of diplomatic stances will become relevant to a judgment of the efficacy of policy. Sensible academic discussion must surely start with the recognition that the present dirty floating is not the nice classroom abstraction of flexible exchange rates, and that international co-operation and consultation are vital to the stability of the system. Whether academic economists can contribute further remains to be seen.

Experience with a floating exchange rate system has clearly altered the economists' thinking about how such a regime would operate. The hopes of what flexible rates would accomplish have been modified and so have the fears of what might happen. Few would now maintain that price changes alone can equilibrate the balance of payments or that flexible rates insulate an economy from external disturbances or that flexible rates allow a country to maintain some "optimal rate of inflation" by pursuing the mixture of unemployment and price trend objectives that it prefers. On the other hand, at the same time as the advantages of flexible rates have fallen short of expectations by its advocates, the shortcomings have not been as damaging as opponents had anticipated. The existing regime may be most significant in allowing a less costly form of adjustment than did the fixed-rate, discrete-alterations system of the 1960s. Nonetheless, there are still suggestions for improvement, and the debate over international monetary reform remains lively—as will be evident in the next Problem.

QUESTIONS

1. a. In reviewing international monetary developments after August 1971, can you distinguish different objectives in an "American solution," a "European solution," and an "international solution?"

b. How do the international monetary developments since 1971 illustrate the need for harmonization of domestic economic policies as a prerequisite to the maintenance of a system of stable and orderly exchange rates?

2. Have floating exchange rates fulfilled the predictions of the proponents of flexible rates? If not, why not?

3. Has the regime of managed floating allowed countries to exercise domestic economic autonomy without beggar-my-neighbor disharmony?

4. Do you think that the interaction of financial markets and capital flows are now determining the exchange rate more than is the current account outlook?

5. a. Do you think that exchange-rate variability allows countries to pursue their macroeconomic policies free from international constraints and in accordance with only internal economic developments?

b. How is "domestic" monetary policy affected under conditions of international financial integration and financial interdependence?

6. What now remains of the historic monetary role of gold?

7. Do you think the liquidity issue is now one of excess liquidity, not of a potential deficiency, as many believed from 1958 on?

8. There is disagreement among economists as to whether the Euromarkets contribute to inflation. What conceptual issues would you raise in analyzing this question? What data would you want to examine to determine if the Euromarket is an engine of inflation?

9. Why has the large payments disequilibrium that followed the 1974 oil price increase remained largely immune from the effects of exchange-rate changes or other traditional adjustment mechanisms?

10. Do you think that the less-developed countries' criticisms of IMF conditionality are valid?

11. Do you think there should be more official control of Eurocurrency lending? What measures, if any, would you propose?

12. a. What does the experience of the 1970s show about the ability of countries to use the exchange rate as an instrument of national policy?

b. What does the experience show about the efficacy of the exchange rate as an equilibrating factor for the balance of payments?

13. Does the experience of the 1970s suggest any measures of international monetary reform during the 1980s?

READINGS

1. *On general aspects of the floating rate regime:*

Atlantic Council, *The Floating Rate System* (1978).

Black, Stanley W., *Floating Exchange Rates and National Economic Policy* (1977).

Black, Stanley W., *Exchange Policies for Less Developed Countries in a World of Floating Rates*, Princeton Essays in International Finance, No. 119 (1976).

Coombs, Charles, *The Arena of International Finance* (1976).

Crockett, Andrew, *International Money* (1977).

Dufey, Gunther and Ian Giddy, *The International Money Market* (1978).

Dunn, Robert M., *Exchange Rates, Payments Adjustment, and OPEC: Why Oil Deficits Persist,* Princeton Essays in International Finance, No. 137 (December 1979).

Kolhagen, S. W., *The Behavior of Foreign Exchange Markets,* New York University Monograph Series in Finance, (1978).

Mundell, R. A. and Jacques J. Polak (eds.), *The New International Monetary System* (1977).

Murphy, J. Carter, *The International Monetary System* (1979).
Scammell, W. M., *The International Economy since 1945* (1980).
Solomon, Robert, *The International Monetary System 1945–1976* (1977).
Southard, Frank A., *The Evolution of the International Monetary Fund*, Princeton Essays in International Finance, No. 135 (1979).
Willett, Thomas D., *Floating Exchange Rates and International Monetary Reform* (1977).
Williamson, John H., *The Failure of World Monetary Reform 1971–74* (1977).

2. *On the Eurodollar markets:*
Einzig, Paul and Brian Quinn, *The Euro-Dollar System*, 6th ed. (1977).
Gilbert, Milton, *Quest for World Monetary Order* (1980).
McKinnon, Ronald I., *The Eurocurrency Market*, Princeton Essays in International Finance, No. 125 (1977).

3. *On developing countries and conditionality:*
Cohen, Benjamin, *Banks and the Balance of Payments* (1981).
Development Dialogue, Special Issue on "The International Monetary System and The New International Economic Order" (1980:2).
Gold, Sir Joseph, *Conditionality*, IMF Pamphlet Series No. 31, (1980).
Payer, C., *The Debt Trap: The IMF and the Third World* (1974).

4. *Miscellaneous:*
See also various issues of *IMF Survey, IMF Financial Statistics, Euromoney, The Banker.*

Problem III

INTERNATIONAL MONETARY REFORM: Ordering the Future

Throughout the period of managed floating, new practices have resulted in an ad hoc reform of the international monetary regime. But there have also been extensive discussions directed toward more deliberate attempts at reform. These discussions return, in large part, to some fundamental issues originally raised at the Bretton Woods Conference, although some proposals for a sweeping reform address new issues.

1. BRETTON WOODS REVISITED

Questions raised at Bretton Woods still have a bearing on future monetary reform, and we might draw lessons from the experience of the Bretton Woods system. A student of the Bretton Woods negotiations has recently asked "How did the intellectual, economic and political forces on both sides of the Atlantic affect the final outcome at Bretton Woods? In what major respects does the Bretton Woods compromise need revision today?" In answering these questions, he focuses on three main points.

THE INADEQUACIES OF BRETTON WOODS*

First, the emphasis on universal organisation on both sides of the Atlantic led to the neglect of regional arrangements, a neglect that had to be corrected later, beginning with the Marshall Plan. We are still struggling with the question of how regional arrangements can be accommodated to the universal design.

Second, there was an underestimate on both sides of the magnitude of the liquidity problem. Neither side foresaw that inflation would double the price of commodities over the pre-war level and that the stock of gold would be inadequate to finance world trade and payments. Nobody foresaw the extent to which new gold production would be discouraged by the concurrence of inflation with a fixed gold price. The liquidity problem was not understood in the same way that we understand it today.

The lack of foresight was particularly striking, of course, on the American side. The U.S. negotiators were worried about Congress; they could not take for granted that even the modest White plan would be accepted. They fought the overdraft concept of the Clearing Union, pressed for a depository scheme in which drawing rights were strictly related to contributions, insisted on conditional rather than unconditional liquidity and smaller quotas for countries like France than those countries wanted. All of these policies worked against U.S. interests and had to be reversed by American negotiators two decades later.

If the U.S. had accepted the Keynes plan in its original form and had undertaken post-war aid to Europe through the Clearing Union rather than through Marshall Aid, the U.S. would have accumulated over $30 billion of overdraft facilities which would have financed nearly all of the U.S. deficits in the 1950s and the 1960s. Admittedly, too much should not be made of that point. The Keynes plan would not have been the right device for post-war reconstruction. Still, it would have served the long-term U.S. interest to have negotiated on the basis of the Keynes plan, adapting it as necessary to remove its inflationary bias and its other defects. Fortunately, this failure has been remedied a quarter of a century later by the activation of the facility for Special Drawing Rights in the I.M.F. At long last we have achieved what Keynes wanted—a quantum of international reserves automatically available to all countries that can be increased in accordance with the needs of

* Richard N. Gardner, "Bretton Woods," in Milo Keynes (ed.), *Essays on Keynes* (1975), pp. 208–211.

> world trade. However, we still have to solve the problem of assuring the orderly coexistence of different reserve assets—gold, dollars, sterling, and SDRs.
>
> Third, the interaction of American and British forces left us with no adequate solution to the adjustment problem. . . .
>
> The Bretton Woods compromise left a good deal of ambiguity about the responsibilities for adjustment of surplus and deficit countries. It ruled out adjustment through freely fluctuating exchange rates or by controls on payments for current transactions—since exchange stability and multilateral trade were two primary Bretton Woods objectives. But it said very little about how adjustment *was* to be achieved. The architects at Bretton Woods apparently hoped that, with the aid of Fund resources, deficit and surplus countries could be relied on to restore a balance within a relatively short time by reasonable domestic policies and by occasional changes in exchange rates to correct a "fundamental disequilibrium." Unfortunately, however, this system just has not worked out. . . .
>
> When "dollar shortage" gave way to "dollar glut" and a U.S.-centred system was replaced by a more balanced distribution of economic power, the shortcomings in the Bretton Woods design became apparent.

On the question of adjustable pegs and exchange rate flexibility, a close colleague of Keynes has recently written:[1]

> Keynes had allowed himself to be completely misled as to the manner in which the Fund was going to operate. *For the first twenty-one years of its existence it operated on the principle that exchange rates were almost, though not entirely, sacrosanct* (this was the fault of central bankers and governments as well as of the authorities of the Fund). Keynes visualized fairly frequent exchange-rate adjustments. But even had this hope been realized, and also his other hope that there *would be immunity from criticism by the Fund*, his *objectives* would not have been attained. Keynes failed to foresee that, of all the advanced industrial countries, Britain would *systematically exhibit the highest excess of the rate of increase of wages over the rate of growth of productivity*, and that, more generally, the ranking order of this excess among

1 Lord Kahn, "Mr. Eltis and the Keynesians," *Lloyds Bank Review* (April 1977), p. 5.

> industrial countries would remain systematically fairly stable over decades. It is one thing to operate a system of changeable exchange rates when the changes are sometimes in one direction, sometimes in the other; it is *quite another thing when they are always in the same direction. Holders, and potential holders, of sterling balances have always known in which direction the cat (the sterling exchange rate) would jump when it did jump.*

Interpreting postwar international monetary history, Professor Richard Cooper has emphasized some major weaknesses in the Bretton Woods system:[2]

> The Bretton Woods Agreement asserted the primacy of domestic economic policy aimed at the maintenance of full employment and at the same time established the responsibility of each nation to the community of nations in the realm of international financial policy—a reaction to the self-serving, defensive, and ultimately destructive free-for-all of the 1930s. Domestic economic policies were to be protected from the strictures of the balance of payments through a double screen: *temporary* imbalances were to be financed, if necessary by drawing on lines of credit at a newly established lending institution, the International Monetary Fund (IMF); and *fundamental* imbalances were to be corrected by an alteration in the country's exchange rate. Responsibility to the community of nations was to be assured through a new set of agreed rules, policed by the IMF, that among other things(1) required each country to establish a fixed value (par value) for its currency, (2) forbade restrictions on payments for goods and services, and (3) required international approval of any change in an exchange rate that ultimately had to be made to correct a fundamental disequilibrium in the balance of payments.
>
> In formulating the above regime, the British and American architects had to reach some balance between liberty to pursue domestic economic objectives and license to run payments deficits at the expense of the rest of the world. The final agreement was an unsatisfactory compromise between an earlier American plan to involve the IMF in closer scrutiny and even direction of each nation's domestic and exchange rate policies and a British plan to permit large-scale borrowing if necessary but which was subject to increas-

2 Richard N. Cooper, "Prolegomena to the Choice of an International Monetary System," *International Organization* (Winter 1975), pp. 85–87.

ing penalties. The resulting IMF had too little authority for the first and too little lending capacity for the second. Thus the Bretton Woods regime could not fulfill its assignment. Moreover, the distinction between temporary and fundamental imbalance proved less sharp in practice than it was in theory, so that countries procrastinated in changing their exchange rates. When changes finally did come, their need was clear, and they were large, providing an opportunity for large profits from private speculation on a change in the exchange rate. As the mobility of capital increased over time, this last feature developed into a fatal flaw in the Bretton Woods conception. To work, the agreement implicitly required effective control of international capital movements, something that cannot be assured.

A second weakness of the system was its failure to provide in any realistic way for steady increases in international reserves, since the mechanism for this implied by the system would have called for steady increases in the price of gold, which involved both political and conceptual difficulties.

The consequence of these two weaknesses was that the regime that actually functioned during the 1950s and 1960s was rather different from the Bretton Woods system, even though the latter was formally in force. After the major devaluations of 1949, changes in exchange rates by major countries were virtually unknown until the late 1960s. This was not because imbalances in payments did not arise. Rather, it was because the alteration of a par value was fraught with both political and economic risks. Thus, alternative mechanisms were found—adjustments in domestic economic policy, and the introduction or removal of restrictions on foreign trade and other foreign transactions—both of which were sharply out of keeping with the origins and the stated objectives of the Bretton Woods Agreement.

Similarly, the problem of augmenting international liquidity was "solved" through a process whereby countries added US dollars, earned through balance-of-payments surpluses, to their international reserves, a development for which there was no real place in the Bretton Woods system. This emergence of a dollar exchange standard was fraught with difficulties of its own, however, and proved to be only modestly more durable than the Bretton Woods system. . . .

Governments perceived the difficulties of the regime regarding international liquidity earlier than they saw the difficulties regarding the adjustment mechanism. After prolonged and laborious negotiation, they propounded a solution to the international liquidity problem involving special drawing rights (SDRs), which were created to relieve both gold and dollar of the burden of providing future international liquidity. The solution was in principle an adequate one, but it did not deal with the other weaknesses in either the Bretton Woods or the dollar exchange regimes.

A final assessment of shortcomings of the international monetary system is offered by Robert Triffin, the Yale economist, who as early as 1959 predicted that the gold-convertible dollar standard would prove unviable and should be reformed.

INTERNATIONAL MONETARY ORDER, OR DISORDER?*

The money which we use in our daily life has long ceased to be fully international, i.e. readily and universally acceptable in payment all over the world. Unlike the former gold and silver coinage, it now consists of paper currency and bank deposits without any intrinsic commodity value whatsoever, normally accepted in payment only within each country's national borders.

Whenever payment has to be made abroad, the national currency of the payer has to be exchanged for the national currency of the payee. This is what the international monetary system is about. To ensure its functioning, each country must be ready to provide its own currency, or to redeem it, against what is called "international reserves," i.e. some kind of asset acceptable to all countries for that purpose.

On the eve of the First World War, the main type of asset universally used for this purpose was gold, but gold has been increasingly supplemented, and ultimately displaced, in this role since then by one or a handful of national, so-called "reserve" currencies, convertible at any time into gold, at the request of the holder, under the "gold-exchange standard."

This system, however, was clearly unviable in the long run. The reserve-currency centre was thereby enabled continually to spend more than it earned, and to settle its mounting deficits by piling up a foreign indebtedness which ultimately exceeded its ability to repay it in gold, at the request of its creditors.

The gold-convertible British pound sterling standard of the late

*Robert Triffin, "Reshaping the International Monetary Order," *International Social Sciences Journal* (1978), pp. 302–305. Extract from an article from the *International Social Sciences Journal,* vol. XXX No. 2. © UNESCO 1978. Reproduced by permission of UNESCO.

1920s collapsed, after only a few years, in September 1931, and the world returned to the pure gold standard, experiencing in the process deflation and recession despite the devaluation of all currencies—including sterling and the dollar—in terms of gold.

The post-Second World War gold-convertible dollar standard lasted for much longer, but ultimately proved equally unviable, as I had predicted to the Joint Economic Committee of the United States Congress in October 1959. The dollar became increasingly inconvertible *de facto* in the following years, and *de jure* on 15 August 1971.

By contrast with 1931, however, no other currency was ready and able to take its place. Despite its inconvertibility, and exchange-rate instability, the dollar has remained the main currency used for international settlements, for the accumulation of reserves by central banks and other monetary authorities, and for the investment of so-called "working balances" by other banks, private enterprises and individuals.

The marathon official debates and negotiations opened, at long last, in October 1963, on the need for international monetary reform, were overtaken by events. They were still going on when the dollar became inconvertible in 1971, just as the debates of the Gold Delegation of the League of Nations had still been going on, forty years earlier, when the pound sterling became inconvertible in 1931.

Yet a wide intellectual consensus had finally been reached by officials, as well as by independent experts, on the major shortcomings of the system, and the broad features of the reforms essential to its reconstruction. The most authoritative expression of this consensus may be found in the latest report of the Committee on Reform of the International Monetary System and Related Issues (Committee of Twenty).

It was agreed, in brief, that: (a) reserve creation should aim at adjusting world reserves to the legitimate—non-inflationary—requirements of potential growth in the world economy (presumably about 4–6 per cent a year on the average); (b) it should apply adequate pressures for the readjustment of excessive, persistent, disequilibria on all countries alike, whether in surplus or deficit; (c) the lending potential inevitably derived from world reserve growth should be used for internationally agreed objectives, such as the financing of temporary, reversible deficits, and of other high-priority goals of the international community including, among others, the feasible acceleration of economic development in the Third World.

> The record of the last seven years amply demonstrates that the present system of reserve creation exhibits exactly the opposite characteristics on all three points.

Historical interpretations of postwar international monetary events and other assessments of the Bretton Woods system will undoubtedly continue to be forthcoming. But for our purposes, the major outline is clear.

2. COMMITTEE OF TWENTY'S AGENDA FOR REFORM

If the world's monetary regime is to cease being characterized as in "suspended animation" or an "evolving status quo," a new Bretton Woods agreement will have to be reached. The future course of international monetary negotiations still entails not only the complexities of technical economic issues, but also the difficult questions of relinquishing some national sovereignty in monetary matters and forgoing some domestic autonomy in economic policy-making—stumbling issues of the past. Among all the political-economic problems requiring collective decision making by many states, the problem of international monetary reform retains high priority.

Against the background of international currency crises and the dollar problem, the Executive Directors of the IMF published a study in 1972 on *Reform of the International Monetary System.* This report identified five main problem areas of the international monetary system that may call for new arrangements through international discussion and negotiation:

(i) The exchange-rate mechanism, including both the indications of when changes in par-values are necessary and the respective responsibilities of the deficit and surplus countries for making par-value changes;

(ii) the re-establishment of convertibility and the arrangements for the settlement of imbalances among countries;

(iii) the position in the system of the various reserve assets and in particular the status and function to be given to foreign exchange reserves, gold, and SDRs;

(iv) the problem of disequilibrating capital movements and what might be done to lessen the intense market pressures that accompany them; and

(v) the possibility of new provisions in the Fund arrangements for the special needs of developing countries.

This is a succinct summary of the agenda for monetary reform. It will be useful to keep it in mind as we now turn to the actual course of international negotiations and consider what progress these negotiations have made in moving toward a new world monetary order.

A major step taken by the IMF's Board of Governors, in light of the events following August 15, 1971, was the agreement to establish a Committee of Twenty (C-20) to advise the Board on issues related to international monetary reform. The Committee consisted of one member appointed by each country or group of countries appointed or electing an Executive Director of the Fund. The Committee's task was to advise and to report to the Board of Governors on all aspects of reform of the international monetary system, including proposals for amendments of the Articles of Agreement of the Fund.

The Committee of Twenty adopted a two-year timetable for reform. But this timetable soon had to be abandoned in the face of OPEC's 1974 action in raising the price of oil. The Committee decided to let a new monetary system evolve gradually out of existing arrangements, completed its work, and published its final report together with an *Outline of Reform.*

OUTLINE OF REFORM*

INTRODUCTION

1. It is agreed that there is need for a reformed world monetary order, based on cooperation and consultation within the framework of a strengthened International Monetary Fund, that will encourage the growth of world trade and employment, promote economic development, and help to avoid both inflation and deflation.

2. The main features of the international monetary reform will include:

(*a*) An effective and symmetrical adjustment process, including better functioning of the exchange rate mechanism, with the exchange rate regime based on stable but adjustable par values and with floating rates recognized as providing a useful technique in particular situations;

*Committee of Twenty, *International Monetary Reform* (1974), pp. 7–22.

(*b*) cooperation in dealing with disequilibrating capital flows;

(*c* the introduction of an appropriate form of convertibility for the settlement of imbalances, with symmetrical obligations on all countries;

(*d*) better international management of global liquidity, with the SDR becoming the principal reserve asset and the role of gold and of reserve currencies being reduced;

(*e*) consistency between arrangements for adjustment, convertibility, and global liquidity; and

(*f*) the promotion of the net flow of real resources to developing countries.

3. It is recognized that the attainment of the purposes of the reform depends also upon arrangements for international trade, capital, investment, and development assistance, including the access of developing countries to markets in developed countries; and it is agreed that the principles which govern the international monetary system and arrangements in these related areas must be consistent.

ADJUSTMENT

4. There will be a better working of the adjustment process in which adequate methods to assure timely and effective balance of payments adjustment by both surplus and deficit countries will be assisted by improved international consultation in the Fund, including the use of objective indicators. To this end:

(*a*) Countries will take such prompt and adequate adjustment action, domestic or external, as may be needed to avoid protracted payments imbalances. In choosing among different forms of adjustment action, countries will take into account repercussions on other countries as well as internal considerations.

(*b*) Countries will aim to keep their official reserves within limits which will be internationally agreed from time to time in the Fund and which will be consistent with the volume of global liquidity. For this purpose reserve indicators will be established on a basis to be agreed in the Fund.

(*c*) Countries will apply adjustment measures in a manner designed to protect the net flow of real resources to developing countries, so as to help to achieve any internationally agreed resource transfer targets that they have adopted. Deficit countries in designing their adjustment measures will seek so far as possible not to reduce the access of developing countries and international development finance institutions to their financial markets, nor to reduce the volume of official development assistance or harden its terms and conditions. Surplus countries, particularly those that are not meeting internationally agreed resource transfer targets that they have adopted, will seek so far as possible to increase aid and relax any restrictions on the access of developing countries and international development finance institutions to their financial markets.

5. Fund consultation and surveillance regarding the adjustment process will take place at two levels, the Executive Board and the Council to be established under paragraph 31 as follows:

(*a*) The Council will oversee the continuing operation of the adjustment process. In this connection the Council will at regular intervals review developments in world payments and liquidity and the aggregate net flow of real resources to developing countries. In addition, it may examine particular cases of imbalance which in the light of their international repercussions are referred to it by the Executive Board or are considered by the Council to be of special significance.

(*b*) The Executive Board will at regular intervals:

(i) Survey the world payments situation in relation both to the general working of the adjustment process and to developments affecting global liquidity, with periodic consideration of balance of payments aims;

(ii) review the aggregate net flow of real resources to developing countries and its financing, and the consistency of countries' balance of payments aims and policies with any internationally agreed resource transfer targets that they have adopted; and

(iii) examine particular cases of imbalance that have significant international repercussions.

The Executive Board will as appropriate report to the Council on these matters.

6. Countries will become subject to examination under paragraph 5(*b*)(iii) if either:

(*a*) There has been a disproportionate movement in their official reserves; or

(*b*) in the judgment of the Managing Director, following informal soundings among Executive Directors, there is prima facie evidence that a country is facing significant imbalance, even though this is not indicated by a disproportionate movement in its reserves.

7. In the process of examination under paragraph 5(*b*)(iii), representatives of the country will be expected to comment on the country's economic prospects, including particularly its basic bal-

ance of payments position and prospects, on its external objectives, and on what domestic or external action, if any, it has taken or intends to take. An assessment by the Executive Board will establish whether there is a need for adjustment. In making its assessment, the Executive Board will take account of all relevant considerations, including the factors mentioned above; it will examine the consistency of the country's reserve and current account aims and policies with those of other countries, and will attach major importance to disproportionate movements of reserves. Account will be taken of the special characteristics of developing countries that make it difficult for them to achieve prompt adjustment without seriously damaging their long-term development programs. Following an assessment the Executive Board will, where appropriate, call upon the country concerned to adopt or reinforce policies to correct its imbalance. A country in choosing between different forms of policy will take account of views expressed in the course of the examination on the form and size of policy action.

8. The Fund will continue to hold its normal consultations with member countries. In the course of these consultations the Executive Board will, inter alia, assess the country's payments performance on the same basis as in paragraph 7 and taking into account the factors mentioned there, and will, where appropriate, call upon the country concerned to adopt or reinforce policies to correct its imbalance if it has not previously been so called under paragraph 7.

9. It is agreed that in the adjustment procedures described above separate arrangements will need to be made for a limited number of countries with large reserves deriving from depletable resources and with a low capacity to absorb imports.

10. Normally the provisions of paragraphs 7 and 8 for assessment supported by reserve indicators would be expected to lead to appropriate adjustment action. If they do not do so the Fund will have available graduated pressures to be applied to countries in large and persistent imbalance, whether surplus or deficit. The possibility of the activation of such pressures could of itself encourage timely and effective adjustment action. In considering the application of pressures the Fund will take into account the factors mentioned in paragraph 7.

The Exchange Rate Mechanism

11. In the reformed system exchange rates will continue to be a matter for international concern and consultation. Competitive de-

preciation or undervaluation will be avoided. The exchange rate mechanism will remain based on stable but adjustable par values, and countries should not make inappropriate par value changes. On the other hand, countries should, whether in surplus or deficit, make appropriate par value changes promptly. Changes in par values will continue to be subject to Fund approval. The Fund may establish simplified procedures for appropriate par value changes promptly. Changes in par values will continue to be subject to Fund approval. The Fund may establish simplified procedures for approving small par value changes under appropriate safeguards.

12. Countries will undertake obligations to maintain specified maximum exchange rate margins for their currencies, except when authorized to adopt floating rates. The Fund will be empowered to vary the specified maximum margins on a qualified majority. It is agreed that it would be desirable that the system of exchange margins and intervention should be more symmetrical than that which existed in practice under the Bretton Woods system.

13. Countries may adopt floating rates in particular situations, subject to Fund authorization, surveillance, and review. Such authorization will relieve a country of its obligations with regard to the maintenance of specified margins mentioned in paragraph 12. Such authorization will be given in accordance with provisions to be agreed, on condition that the country undertakes to conform with agreed guidelines for conduct. Guidelines will also be established for intervention by other countries in a floating currency. Authorization to float may be withdrawn if the country fails to conform with the guidelines for conduct, or if the Fund decides that continued authorization to float would be inconsistent with the international interest.

CONTROLS

14. There will be a strong presumption against the use of controls in current account transactions or payments for balance of payments purposes. In this connection arrangements will be made for continuing close coordination between the Fund and the GATT.

15. Countries will not use controls over capital transactions for the purpose of maintaining inappropriate exchange rates or, more generally, of avoiding appropriate adjustment action. Insofar as countries use capital controls, they should avoid an excessive degree of administrative restriction which could damage trade and beneficial capital flows and should not retain controls longer than needed. Such controls should be applied without discrimination ex-

cept as stated in paragraph 16; in this connection appropriate recognition will be given to the special position of countries that maintain close financial ties or that establish an economic and monetary union among themselves.

16. Wherever possible developing countries will be exempted from controls imposed by other countries, particularly from import controls and controls over outward long-term investment. The special circumstances of developing countries will be taken into account by the Fund in assessing controls which these countries feel it necessary to apply. In addition, developed countries should seek to remove legal, institutional, and administrative obstacles to the access of developing countries to their financial markets. For their part, developing countries should seek to avoid policies which would discourage the flow of private capital to them.

DISEQUILIBRATING CAPITAL FLOWS

17. Countries will cooperate in actions designed to limit disequilibrating capital flows and in arrangements to finance and offset them. Actions that countries might choose to adopt could include a more satisfactory degree of harmonization of monetary policies, subject to the requirements of domestic demand management; prompt adjustment of inappropriate par values, use of wider margins, and the adoption of floating rates in particular situations; and the use of administrative controls, including dual exchange markets and fiscal incentives. There will be improved consultation in the Fund on actions designed to limit disequilibrating capital flows, with the following objectives: first, to increase the effectiveness of such actions and to minimize harmful effects on third countries; and secondly, to avoid unnecessary proliferation and escalation of controls and the additional flows which might be prompted by anticipation thereof.

CONVERTIBILITY, CONSOLIDATION, AND MANAGEMENT OF CURRENCY RESERVES

18. It is agreed that the basic objectives to be accommodated in the reformed convertibility system should be symmetry of obligations on all countries including those whose currencies are held in official reserves; the better management of global liquidity and the avoidance of uncontrolled growth of reserve currency balances; adequate elasticity; and as much freedom for countries to choose the composition of their reserves as is consistent with the overall objectives of the reform.

19. As part of the better international management of global liquidity, the aggregate volume of official currency holdings will be kept under international surveillance and management in the Fund. In this connection the Fund will take account of any necessary increase over time in official currency holdings in relation to the growth of international transactions and also of the special position of a limited number of countries with large reserves deriving from depletable resources and with a low capacity to absorb imports.

20. All countries maintaining par values will settle in reserve assets those official balances of their currencies which are presented to them for conversion. The Fund will establish appropriate arrangements to ensure sufficient control over the aggregate volume of official currency holdings.

21. Elasticity within the settlement system, particularly to finance disequilibrating capital flows, may be provided by credit facilities, including Fund credit and official bilateral or regional short-term credit. The Fund may establish as necessary new credit facilities to assist countries exposed to disequilibrating capital flows, particularly those without sufficient access to bilateral or regional credit. The establishment and use of bilateral and regional credit facilities will be reported to the Fund. The extent to which credit facilities are used would be taken into account by the Managing Director for the purpose of paragraph 6(*b*).

22. The Fund will, as necessary, make provision for the consolidation of reserve currency balances to protect the future convertibility system against net conversion of any overhang of such balances which may exist at the restoration of general convertibility, and to ensure that the issuers of the currencies concerned will be able to acquire reserve assets when in surplus and will not lose reserve assets beyond the amount of any future official settlements deficits. For this purpose, and also to permit countries that wish to do so to exchange official currency holdings for SDRs, the Fund will have authority to establish a Substitution Account. In addition, the Fund may also assist those countries that desire to negotiate bilateral funding of currency balances.

23. Countries will cooperate in the management of their currency reserves so as to avoid disequilibrating movements of official funds. Among the possible provisions for achieving this objective, the following have been suggested but are not agreed:

(*a*) Countries should respect any request from a country whose currency is held in official reserves to limit or convert into other reserve assets further increases in their holdings of its currency.

(*b*) Countries should periodically choose the composition of their currency reserves and should undertake not to change it without prior consultation with the Fund.

(*c*) Countries should not add to their currency reserve placements outside the territory of the country of issue except within limits to be agreed with the Fund.

PRIMARY RESERVE ASSETS

24. The SDR will become the principal reserve asset and the role of gold and of reserve currencies will be reduced. The SDR will also be the numeraire in terms of which par values will be expressed.

25. As part of the better international management of global liquidity, the Fund will allocate and cancel SDRs so as to ensure that the volume of global reserves is adequate and is consistent with the proper functioning of the adjustment and settlement systems. In the assessment of global reserve needs and the decision-making process for SDR allocation and cancellation the Fund will continue to follow the existing principles as set out in the Articles of Agreement.

26. The effective yield on the SDR will be high enough to make it attractive to acquire and hold, but not so high as to make countries reluctant to use the SDR when in deficit. The value of the SDR in transactions against currencies will be determined in such a way as to protect the capital value of the SDR against depreciation. The interest rate on the SDR will be set from time to time by the Executive Board in such a way as to maintain an appropriate effective yield, in the light of changing market interest rates.

27. In the light of the agreed objective that the SDR should become the principal reserve asset, consideration will be given to revising the rules governing its use with a view to relaxing existing constraints. . . . Consideration will be given to other aspects of the SDR, including its name, with a view to promoting public understanding.

28. Appropriate arrangements will be made for gold in the reformed system, in the light of the agreed objectives that the SDR should become the principal reserve asset and that the role of gold should be reduced. At the same time it is also generally recognized that gold reserves are an important component of global liquidity which should be usable to finance balance of payments deficits. It is not yet settled what arrangements for gold would be best in the reformed system, having due regard to the interests of all member countries. Under one approach, monetary authorities, including

the Fund, would be free to sell, but not to buy, gold in the market at the market price; they would not undertake transactions with each other at a price different from the official price, which would be retained and would not be subject to a uniform increase. Under another approach, the official price of gold would be abolished and monetary authorities, including the Fund, would be free to deal in gold with one another on a voluntary basis and at mutually acceptable prices, and to sell gold in the market. A third approach would modify the preceding one by authorizing monetary authorities also to buy gold in the market. Arrangements have also been proposed whereby the Fund would be authorized to purchase gold from monetary authorities in exchange for SDRs at a price between the market and the official price, and to sell gold gradually over time in the market; if arrangements of this kind were introduced, questions would arise concerning both the Fund's policy with respect to its sales in the market and the sharing of any profits or losses accruing to the Fund from its gold transactions.

THE LINK AND CREDIT FACILITIES IN FAVOR OF DEVELOPING COUNTRIES

29. In the light of the agreed objective to promote economic development, the reformed monetary system will contain arrangements to promote an increasing net flow of real resources to developing countries. If these arrangements were to include a link between development assistance and SDR allocation, this could take one of the following forms:

(*a*) A link would be established between development finance and SDR allocation, the total volume of which allocation will be determined exclusviely on the basis of global liquidity needs. This link would take the form of the direct distribution to developing countries of a larger proportion of SDR allocations than they would receive on the basis of their share in Fund quotas. Link resources so allocated would be distributed to all developing countries in such a way as to be relatively favorable to the least developed countries.

(*b*) A link would be established between development finance and SDR allocation, the total volume of which allocation will be determined exclusively on the basis of global liquidity needs. This link would take the form of direct allocation to international and regional development finance institutions of a predetermined share of SDR allocations. Link resources distributed to development finance institutions would be disbursed to developing countries on the basis of development need and in such a way as to be relatively favorable to the least developed countries. The use of link funds by development finance institutions, including their distribution and terms, would reflect the nature and purpose of these resources.

30. It is envisaged that there will be a new facility in the Fund, under which developing countries would receive longer-term balance of payments finance.

The Committee of Twenty agreed in its *Outline of Reform* that the structure of the Fund should include a new organ, the Council, that would be established "as soon as practicable." Meanwhile, an Interim Committee of the Board of Governors would come into existence when the Committee of Twenty finished its work. The Committee's terms of reference were to advise the Board of Governors with respect to its functions in supervising the management and adaptation of the international monetary system, including the continuing operations of the adjustment process and in this connection reviewing developments in global liquidity and the transfer of real resources to developing countries. The terms of reference also included the consideration of proposals by the Executive Board to amend the Articles of Agreement and the response to be made to sudden disturbances that might threaten the international monetary system.

The meeting of the Interim Committee in Kingston, Jamaica in 1976 received special attention as the first stage of reform. By reaching agreement on a wide range of issues, the Jamaica meeting laid the basis for the Second Amendment of the Articles of the IMF that was to come into effect in 1978.

3. JAMAICA AGREEMENT

The Interim Committee meeting in Jamaica in 1976 resulted in agreement on a number of issues—but the "major revision" of the Articles of Agreement of the Fund promised in Jamaica bears little relation to the reforms that had been outlined by the Committee of Twenty. Major features of the Jamaica agreement were the following: floating rates were to be legalized under a new "Second Amendment" to the Fund Agreement; the Fund would exercise surveillance over exchange-rate arrangements; quotas would be increased for Fund members; the Fund would dispose of one-sixth of its gold holdings by auction, and the profits from these sales would be used by a Trust Fund to assist developing countries.

Writing for a Princeton symposium, a number of leading international economists assessed the implications of the Jamaica Agreement. They generally discounted the Agreement as a "major reform" and instead stressed how much remained to be done.

Professor Richard Cooper stated[3]:

> Having legitimized a system of flexible rates, the Jamaica conferees left open all the difficult problems of actually managing a system of flexible rates. I take for granted that governments will intervene from time to time in the foreign-exchange markets. All major governments are now held responsible for managing their economies, and this can hardly encompass total abstention from directly influencing an economic variable as important for most countries as the exchange rate. We therefore need supplementary provisions for coordinating both the objectives of intervention and the actual practice of intervention, so that two countries do not find themselves working at cross-purposes on the same exchange rate.
>
> For most countries formal coordination will not be necessary, since they can rely on their small size relative to the world economy and can frame their intervention policies against some major currency or bundle of currencies. For the sake of overall economic stability, however, there must be some mechanism for calling into account countries that either strongly undervalue or strongly overvalue their currencies, in accordance with the limited structure on exchange-rate regimes noted above.
>
> For major countries, coordination of exchange-rate policies needs to be more explicitly cooperative, since stability of the world economy can be aided by avoiding erratic movements in exchange rates among major currencies. Guidance for intervention should involve two components, in my judgment: (a) avoiding rapid rates of change in exchange rates, except when they are manifestly necessary owing to rapid and unexpected changes in underlying conditions, i.e., assuring orderly markets, as we try to do with money and bond markets and in a more limited way with commodity markets, and (b) linking intervention policies to national levels of international reserves to assure that exchange rates are not allowed to

3 Edward M. Bernstein et al., *Reflections on Jamaica*, Princeton Essays in International Finance, No. 115 (April 1976), pp. 10–11. Copyright © 1976. Reprinted by permission of the International Finance Section of Princeton University.

deviate very far from the rates that would clear the market without intervention over a period of time, i.e., requiring that if reserves are built up or run down relative to desired levels (which would have to be established) as a result of intervention designed to smooth movements in exchange rates, the direction of intervention should be reversed when market conditions permit so as to move reserves back to the desired levels. Reserve management, in other words, should be similar in character to ideal buffer-stock management or to monetary management, which involve short-term price targets and long-term volume targets.

The Jamaica Agreement leaves all these important operating details to be worked out. No doubt they will be worked out on the basis of practical experience in the next few years.

Professor Fritz Machlup asked "What, of all these well-considered provisions [of the C-20's *Outline of Reform*], has been retained in the Jamaica Agreement?" He answers[4]:

Almost nothing. Of course, the agreed amendments to the Articles of the Fund will include the permissibility of floating exchange rates—so that the Fund members need not go on living in sin. That the floating will go on is not questioned: it should be clear to anybody in his senses that under present conditions the world has no other choice. Floating is now the only system that can work without continuously recurrent crises in the exchange markets, and all talk about an early return to a system of fixed par values is just for the birds—for the consolation of traditionalists sick with nostalgia and for the reassurance of exporters weak in the art of multiplication.

To be sure, wildly roller-coasting exchange rates are too disconcerting for all but the bravest souls; hence, managed flexibility is preferred and, even to the purist, quite acceptable, provided the managers do not resist movements dictated by market forces that push in a definite direction for more than a few weeks. But since interventions in exchange markets may lead to mischievous cross-rates if the intervening central banks are not in daily communication with one another, arrangements for concerted interventions are desirable. The Jamaica Agreement provided for this accommodation. The Ministers and Governors of the Group of Ten, in their meeting of December 1975, had given their approval to the proposals (agreed between the United States and France) to "inten-

4 *Ibid*, pp. 33–34, 38.

sify" consultation procedures on exchange-rate movements, and they noted that their central banks were in the process of "deepening and broadening" their consultations. One can only hope that this accommodation will not be misused for the purpose of keeping misaligned exchange rates from getting adjusted.

What about the adjustment mechanism? The Press Communiqué of January 8, 1976, contains not a word about it.

What about the control of official reserves? There is a reference to it as follows:

> The amended Articles of Agreement should include a provision by which the members of the Fund would undertake to collaborate with the Fund and with other members in order to ensure that their policies with respect to reserve assets would be consistent with the objective of promoting better international surveillance of international liquidity and making the special drawing right the principal reserve asset in the international monetary system.

This sounds all right but is in fact only an empty phrase. In order to institute effective control (not merely surveillance) of liquidity, the provision would need "teeth," such as real commitments by the members regarding changes in their reserves and pressures upon members who do not live up to these commitments. None of this was retained in the Jamaica Agreement.

What about the substitution of SDRs for existing currency reserves and gold, the consolidation of these reserve assets "at the outset of the reform?" (The *First Outline of Reform,* of October 1973, had used this phrase.) Nothing of this sort has become part of the Jamaica Agreement, except for lip service to the idea in the form of an exhortation that "the Executive Directors should continue their consideration of the subject of a substitution account," and this weak provision was diluted by an injunction that the work should be done "without delaying the completion of the Comprehensive Draft Amendment." The alleged objective of making the SDR the "principal reserve asset" is shown to be a sham by the absence of any attempt to reduce the role of foreign-exchange reserves and by the main features of the new agreement about gold—to allow an increase in the physical amounts of gold in the members' official reserves, to allow increases in the book value of gold held by the monetary authorities, and to enhance the liquidity of gold reserves by making them more usable in official transactions.

. . . .

The only sound way to make the SDR the principal reserve asset is to give it the role of determining the gradual increase in global liquidity and of ensuring an improved adjustment mechanism. That this is practically impossible if SDRs are such a small part of total reserves seems clear. The language used in the Communiqué of the Interim Committee is rather deceptive on this issue. When the Interim Committee recites its earlier "general undertaking" to "ensure that the role of gold in the international monetary system would be gradually reduced," one must wonder whether the parties to such an agreement are trying to deceive themselves or the public.

Robert V. Roosa (Partner, Brown Brothers Harriman & Co. and former Under Secretary of the Treasury for Monetary Affairs) pointed out some of the remaining questions[5]:

The most significant and promising result of the negotiations culminating in Jamaica is the seemingly genuine consensus that floating should be legitimized, and also that central banks should jointly manage the amplitude of fluctuations as exchange rates respond to changes in basic economic relationships among countries. It is equally encouraging that the Interim Committee agreed to increase IMF quotas by nearly one-third and approved an accompanying pledge that each member country will henceforth permit its own currency to be used, at least by the IMF.

Although the details of these and other agreements had not yet been completed by the IMF Executive Directors as these words were written, their articulation will probably not resolve a number of still perplexing unknowns. Among them are these:

Will the various decisions concerning gold lead to more, or less, monetary stability among nations?

Do the decisions at Jamaica, taken as a whole, support the repeated pledges made there to center the international monetary system on SDRs as the world's principal reserve asset?

Will the undertaking by each country to maintain domestic stability as a basis for international monetary stability be consistent with, or permit, symmetrical patterns of adjustment among countries, among those expanding and those contracting, among those inflating and those deflating? For example, is the structure emerging from Jamaica likely to cause countries deliberately to accelerate or to slow their own domestic expansion in order to maintain or

5 *Ibid*, p. 39.

> restore balance in their payments flows with each other, or to maintain stability in their exchange-rate relationships, or both?
>
> Will the combination of additional compensatory financing with enlarged IMF quotas and the new Trust Fund be able to provide adequate "bridging finance" for the balance-of-payments needs of the developing countries? Or is there a risk that the "new" system at times may only generate more constrictive pressure upon some of them? Or may additional actions be needed in the real sector, over and above these monetary facilities, to improve the prospects of most developing countries for stability and growth?
>
> The answers to these questions are still cloudy.

Professor John Williamson of the University of Warwick observed that the Jamaica Agreement made provision "for legalizing the existing nonsystem governing international monetary relations. In place of the explicitly specified and reasonably coherent sets of rights and obligations that constituted the Bretton Woods system . . . or the comprehensively redesigned successor system sought by the Committee of Twenty, the world is to function on the basis of a set of conventions and practices that have evolved out of a mixture of custom and crisis. . . . All this is a far cry from Bretton Woods or the ambitions of the C-20. But that is not to say that it is worse. A written constitution has the advantage of providing an explicitly endorsed framework of rules within which to resolve disagreements according to agreed procedures. But if the rules themselves are such as to compel inefficiency or provoke disagreements, an unwritten constitution may well prove preferable. An evaluation of the existing nonsystem therefore requires enumeration of particular benefits and costs in comparison with defined alternative sets of arrangements."[6]

Among the benefits, Williamson listed the maintenance of the generalized managed floating exchange-rate regime that replaced the former adjustable peg.[7]

> A central fact of international monetary life is that the development of capital mobility has rendered the continued use of the adjustable peg impracticable. The reason is fundamental: under capital mobility, exchange markets can be in equilibrium only if all existing stocks of the several currencies are willingly held, which requires

6 *Ibid*, pp. 54–55.
7 *Ibid*, p. 55.

either that the stocks themselves be adjusted according to the gold-standard "rules of the game" or that the expected yields of different currencies be adjusted in order to satisfy the conditions of asset-market equilibrium.

Governments show no signs of being willing to play the gold-standard game, for the compelling reason that it disrupts internal stabilization policy. And expected yields, which consist of own interest rates plus expected rates of currency appreciation, cannot always adjust, because acceptable interest-rate differentials cannot offset anticipations of discrete changes in exchange rates, and exchange rates cannot always be allowed to adjust without making a mockery of the very idea of a par-value system. Hence, as capital mobility develops, the adjustable peg is bound to generate a series of ever more disruptive crises—as, indeed, it did from the early 1960s to March 1973. This basic inadequacy of the Bretton Woods system was the principal reason for its collapse.

The first and overwhelming benefit of existing arrangements, in comparison with both the Bretton Woods system and C-20 aspirations, is therefore that they make no attempt to force countries to revert to the adjustable peg and do not envisage any such attempt in the future, unless 85 per cent of the IMF membership are prepared to vote for such a reversion, which is an eventuality that can safely be disregarded.

On the cost side, Williamson emphasized four economic costs that attach to the present nonsystem in comparison with a reformed system of the general character sought by the C-20. The first relates to the degree of volatility that exchange rates have exhibited during the period of floating. The second is the total lack of control over the volume of international liquidity, which arises from the absence of asset settlement, the unconstrained freedom to place reserves in Euromarkets, and possibly also fluctuations in the value of gold reserves that may result from variations in the gold price. The third unsatisfactory economic aspect of the present situation, at least in the eyes of many, is the maldistribution of the seigniorage that results from reserve creation. Finally, there is the continued asymmetry in the position of the U.S. dollar, with other countries conceivably able to manipulate exchange rates so as to contribute to stabilization policy, and the inability of the United States to defend herself against manipulation, thereby intensifying the problem of demand management in the United States.

Williamson concludes that "none of these costs is of comparable importance to the benefit of having a workable exchange-rate regime in place of the adjustable peg. Yet collectively they are important enough to make it worthwhile considering whether it is possible to devise arrangements that might reduce those costs without reintroducing the brittleness of the adjustable peg. In my view, there is reason to suppose that this would be technically feasible. The key need is for an exchange-rate regime that retains the flexibility of managed floating but also embodies an official and agreed view as to what rates ought to be, to provide a fulcrum for international management."[8]

Professor Robert Triffin also offered a critical review of the Jamaica Agreement.

COLLAPSE OF REFORM NEGOTIATIONS*

The proposals for a so-called "major revision" of the Articles of Agreement that emerged from the January 1976 meeting of the IMF Interim Committee in Jamaica are essentially confined to the mere *legalization of the present situation, i.e.* of the widespread and illegal repudiation of the very core of the Bretton Woods commitments—particularly on convertibility and exchange rates—without putting any other binding and operational commitments in their place. The proposed new Article IV on "Obligations Regarding Exchange Arrangements" would—under all three of the types of arrangements envisioned as possible in the future—leave all and every country free to do whatever it wishes: to peg its rate to any denominator whatsoever (such as a foreign currency, the SDR, or any other package of currencies, etc.) except gold, or to have *"any exchange arrangements of their choice."*

Glaringly absent are any specific and operational provisions regarding the problems previously regarded as crucial by the negotiators themselves as well as by outside experts: global *liquidity, adjustment* and *convertibility.*

The agreements on *gold* admittedly go in the direction anticipated in former negotiations and hammer out ingenious compromises between opposite viewpoints and interests, as far as the partial liquidation of IMF gold holdings is concerned. But they

*Robert Triffin, "The International Monetary Order," Introductory Remarks presented at the Club of Rome meeting, Algiers (October 26, 1976), processed, pp. 19–21.

8 *Ibid*, p. 58.

certainly do not even begin to solve in a rational way the major problems raised by the far larger gold holdings of the national monetary authorities, *i.e.:* (a) their ultimate disposal or retention as part of the international reserves and settlements system, and (b) the inflationary implications of a sudden revaluation of current holdings at, or close to, current market prices. The communiqué bears little or no trace of the various suggestions made to meet these inescapable problems.

The Jamaica agreements can only be regarded as the official burial of the core of the Bretton Woods system and the dismal failure of twelve years of efforts to reform the international monetary system.

Specific Recommendations

Our first, long-term recommendation is to seek the reaffirmation and implementation of the consensus that had previously been reached about the essential features of a new international monetary order susceptible of serving the obvious goals of the international community:

a) Reserve creation should aim at adjusting the expansion of world reserves to the requirements of feasible, non-inflationary, real growth in world trade and production. It should take primarily the form of international reserve deposits with the IMF—broadly similar to, but more flexible and attractive than, the present SDRs—whose amounts would be jointly decided by the international community. The interim redefinition of SDRs and the increase in interest earnings on SDR claims are useful first steps in this direction.

b) The lending power derived from the acceptance of such IMF reserve deposits in settlement by the surplus countries should be used for collectively concerted and agreed objectives, including among others the financing of development of the Third World. This should entail an appropriate redistribution of voting power among all IMF members.

c) These two basic reforms obviously imply—to use the official jargon—the "phasing out" of gold and, particularly, of national "reserve currencies" from the international settlement and reserve system, and are essential to the restoration of pressures for balance-of-payments adjustment now frustrated for the reserve-center countries by the acceptance of their *national* currencies as *international* reserves.

d) They should also reduce to a more manageable size, and facilitate, the official "recycling" of the disruptive movements of private capital prompted by exchange-rate speculation and which are largely responsible for the wild, reversible, and excessive fluctuations of exchange rates in recent years and months.

e) The other measures necessary to the reconstruction of a viable world monetary order could hardly be negotiated in the absence of agreement on these basic reforms.

Let us note, particularly, that their earlier adoption and implementation would have prevented the wild world inflation which led to the explosion of oil prices, and would have provided in any case the most appropriate mechanism for the investment and "recycling" of the temporary surpluses of the oil-exporting countries, as well as of those of all other countries. This makes all the more bizarre and regrettable—no matter how understandable in the present context—the decision of the negotiators to postpone, rather than accelerate, the basic monetary reforms which they had repeatedly and rightly proclaimed to be as urgent as imperative, in view of the utter collapse of the Bretton Woods system due to their former procrastination in this respect.

It is generally accepted, however, that political obstacles are likely to block, for months and even years to come, the *worldwide* negotiation of these reforms, indispensable to the creation of a new international monetary order serving all its members in a fair and constructive way, and repeatedly—even though not unanimously—endorsed in principle by the IMF, the Committee of 20, the Group of 24, etc. We should all try to do what we can to develop the political will necessary to change this gloomy forecast.

In the meantime, feasible progress should not be sacrificed to the unanimity rule.

4. SECOND AMENDMENT

The text of the Proposed Second Amendment of the Articles of Agreement was sent to Fund members in 1976. In 1978, the Second Amendment entered into force, having been accepted by three-fifths of the members having four-fifths of the total voting power. The Amendment altered Article IV on the exchange-rate regime and now allowed a member to apply the exchange arrangements of its choice, except that it may not maintain a value for its currency in terms of gold. Countries are allowed to participate in cooperative arrangements that stabilize the exchange rates for a group of currencies relative to each other, or to follow another exchange arrangement of its choice, such as a fluctuating rate for the dollar. Provision was also made for a generalized restoration of par-values by an 85 percent majority of the total voting power of the IMF—a return to "stable but adjustable par values" if international economic conditions permit. Such a high vote would require the approval of the United States and the Common Market.

NEW ARTICLE IV*

In accord with the purposes of the Fund as expressed in Article I of the Articles of Agreement, member countries are at all times subject to general obligations to collaborate with the Fund and with other members in order to assure orderly exchange arrangements and to promote a stable system of exchange rates.

This general obligation, set out in the new Article IV of the Second Amendment of the Articles, requires each member to follow exchange policies compatible with its commitment to

"(i) endeavor to direct its economic and financial policies toward the objective of fostering orderly economic growth with reasonable price stability, with due regard to its circumstances;

"(ii) seek to promote stability by fostering orderly underlying economic and financial conditions and a monetary system that does not tend to produce erratic disruptions;

"(iii) avoid manipulating exchange rates or the international monetary system in order to prevent effective balance of payments adjustment or to gain an unfair competitive advantage over other members."

To oversee the compliance of each member with these obligations, and to assure the effective operation of the international monetary system, the Fund, under the Second Amendment, is required to exercise firm surveillance over the exchange rate policies of members and to adopt specific principles for the guidance of all members with respect to these policies. The principles for the guidance of exchange rate policies were adopted by the Executive Board in a decision on "Surveillance over Exchange Rate Policies."

Three general principles are enunciated:

"A. A member shall avoid manipulating exchange rates or the international monetary system in order to prevent effective balance

**IMF Survey* (September 1979), p. 12.

of payments adjustment or to gain an unfair competitive advantage over other members.

"B. A member should intervene in the exchange market if necessary to counter disorderly conditions which may be characterized inter alia by disruptive short-term movements in the exchange value of its currency.

"C. Members should take into account in their intervention policies the interests of other members, including those of the countries in whose currencies they intervene."

This decision also established the principles of Fund surveillance over exchange rate policies and described developments which might indicate the need for discussion with a member. Examples of such developments are protracted large-scale intervention in one direction in the exchange market; an unsustainable level of official or quasi-official borrowing, or lending, for balance of payments purposes; various kinds of restrictions or incentives affecting current transactions or payments, or capital flows; and exchange rate behavior that appears to be unrelated to underlying economic and financial conditions.

Members are free to adopt the exchange arrangements of their choice, except for a prohibition against the maintenance of the value of a currency in terms of gold.

When the Second Amendment entered into force on April 1, 1978, members were required to notify the Fund of the exchange arrangements they intended to apply in fulfillment of their obligations under Article IV. Each member must also notify the Fund promptly of any changes in its exchange arrangements.

For the future, Article IV provides that 85 per cent of the total voting power of the Fund will be able to take decisions recommending general exchange arrangements that accord with the development of the international system, including a system based upon stable but adjustable par values. Even then, however, members would continue to have the right to choose their own exchange arrangements, and will at all times be subject to the general obligations and specified undertakings of Article IV.

Beyond provisions for exchange rates and surveillance by the Fund, the Second Amendment also reduced the role of gold in the international monetary system. The most important changes were to eliminate gold as the unit of value of the SDR; to specify that gold could not again become a common denominator for par-values of currencies even if at some future time par-values were introduced; to abolish the official price of gold and to allow members to deal in gold in the private market and among themselves without reference to any official price; and to provide for the disposition of part of the Fund's own holdings of gold by sales to the market. Along with the reduced role of gold, the Amendment also sought to promote the SDR as the principal reserve asset.

5. LIQUIDITY PROBLEM

All discussions of international monetary reform have to consider the liquidity problem. Since 1971, the discussions have centered mainly on the future role of SDRs and gold in the system. The possibility of new reserve currencies—the Deutsche mark and the yen—have also been considered. And the explosion of international financing by commercial banks has also complicated the problem of controlling international liquidity. The management of world-reserve creation should be of prime concern to a reformed IMF.

5.1 SDR as Chief Reserve Asset?

The Second Amendment of the Fund's Articles of Agreement—which became effective on April 1, 1978—provided for significant changes in the characteristics and uses of the SDR, and called upon Fund members to collaborate with a view to making the SDR the principal reserve asset in the international monetary system.

Several important decisions concerning the SDR were taken recently by the Fund's Executive Board, as outlined below.

DECISIONS ON SDRs*

ALLOCATIONS OF SDRs

On December 11, 1978, the Board of Governors adopted a resolution approving the proposal of the Managing Director, concurred in by the Executive Board, that allocations of SDRs should be resumed and that SDR 4 billion should be allocated on January 1 in the years 1979, 1980, and 1981. The proposal was made in accordance with the Managing Director's conclusion that there was a long-term global need to supplement existing reserve assets. An-

**IMF Survey* (September 1979), pp. 13–15.

other consideration was that exclusive reliance on the accumulation of reserve currencies to provide the needed increases in reserves would not be compatible with the objective of making the SDR the principal reserve asset in the international monetary system.

The allocation of SDR 4 billion on January 1, 1979 brought the cumulative total of SDR allocations to SDR 13.3 billion, about 5 per cent of world official reserves, excluding gold.

SDR INTEREST RATE.

The interest rate on the SDR was increased on January 1, 1979 from 60 per cent to 80 per cent of the combined market interest rate that is calculated each calendar quarter. The combined market rate is determined on the basis of short-term money market rates in the five countries with the largest Fund quotas (France, the Federal Republic of Germany, Japan, the United Kingdom, and the United States) and rounded to the nearest ¼ of 1 per cent. Taking into account the basket method for valuation of the SDR, which was reviewed and updated in 1978, the yield on the SDR is now more competitive with yields on other international reserve assets.

RECONSTITUTION OF SDR HOLDINGS.

Participants may use all of their SDR holdings, and they are not obliged to reacquire SDRs according to any fixed schedule. However, the rules for reconstitution require participants to maintain a minimum level of SDR holdings over time. With effect from January 1, 1979, the Executive Board reduced from 30 per cent to 15 per cent the minimum average SDR holdings that participants are required to maintain, in relation to the average of their net cumulative allocations, for successive five-year periods ending each calendar quarter. The change helps to emphasize the reserve asset character of the SDR and enables participants to maintain lower levels of SDR holdings from day to day, thus increasing their ability to use SDRs without having to reacquire them to meet the reconstitution requirement. The rules for reconstitution will be reconsidered in the light of experience.

WIDER USES OF SDRS.

One change of major importance in widening the use of SDRs under the Second Amendment of the Articles is the freedom of participants to use SDRs to obtain currency in transactions by agreement with other participants. In these transactions, participants may now use SDRs without any requirement of balance of payments need and without the necessity for further authorization by the Fund. Any currency may be exchanged for SDRs, provided the Fund has established a representative rate for the currency.

A further provision of the amended Articles enables the Fund to "prescribe" (permit) operations in which participants may use SDRs by agreement without exchanging them directly for currency. During the past year, the Executive Board has taken a number of decisions which permit the use of SDRs as follows:

To settle financial obligations.

To make loans of SDRs, at interest rates and maturities agreed between the parties. Repayment of loans and payment of interest may be made with SDRs.

As security for the performance of financial obligations, in either of two ways: (1) participants may pledge SDRs, which can be earmarked for the duration of the pledge by being recorded in a special register kept by the Fund; or (2) participants may agree that SDRs would be transferred as security for the performance of an obligation and that the SDRs would be returned to the transferor when its obligation under the agreement had been fulfilled.

Other Holders of SDRs.

The Fund has the authority to extend the range of official holders of SDRs beyond the participants in the Special Drawing Rights Department and the Fund's General Resources Account. Upon the entry into force of the Second Amendment, a wide range of international organizations, national institutions, and nonmembers of the Fund became eligible to be prescribed by the Fund as "other holders" of SDRs. Although at present only the Bank for International Settlements (BIS) is an other holder, the Interim Committee has endorsed the intention of the Executive Board to consider increasing the number of official institutions that might, as other holders of SDRs, be authorized to acquire, hold, and use SDRs on terms and conditions agreed by the Fund.

The sdr as Unit of Account and Currency Peg.

The SDR is the unit of account for all the purposes of the Fund, and now it is also being adopted increasingly outside the Fund as a unit of account (or as the basis for a unit of account) for private contracts and international treaties, and by other international and regional organizations, such as the African Development Bank, the Arab Monetary Fund, the Asian Clearing Union, the Economic Community of West African States, the Islamic Development Bank, and the Nordic Investment Bank. Although a small private market for SDRs exists, there is little information available about it. SDR-denominated currency deposits are now accepted by the BIS and several of the major commercial banks, and bonds denominated in SDRs have been issued in the capital market.

Some of the Fund's member countries have decided to peg their currency to the SDR. The value of the currency is fixed in terms of the SDR and then set in terms of other currencies by reference to the SDR value of the other currencies as calculated and published by the Fund.

INTEREST, CHARGES, AND ASSESSMENT.

A participant with holdings of SDRs in excess of its allocations earns net interest on the excess holdings, and a participant with holdings below its allocations pays net charges at the same rate on its net use of SDRs. Payments of interest and charges in the SDR Department are, therefore, self-balancing—that is, the net charges paid by net users of SDRs are exactly sufficient for the payment of net interest to those that hold SDRs above their allocations, including the Fund's General Resources Account, which holds SDRs but does not receive allocations.

THE SDR AS AN INTERNATIONAL UNIT OF ACCOUNT*

One important conclusion of the Second Amendment of the Articles of Agreement of the Fund is that the monetary role of gold should be gradually reduced. Gold has been eliminated from its central role in the Fund, including its role as a standard of value and even as a denominator for registering the exchange value of a currency. The removal of gold from a central position in the Fund has far reaching consequences going beyond the confines of the Fund. Indeed, many international conventions that are based on gold are being interpreted, revised, or reformulated; as a rule, the conclusion is that the SDR should take the place of gold. However, while a few contracts might still be denominated in gold, as a private unit of account, gold is long defunct.

*Walter O. Habermeier, "The SDR as an International Unit of Account," *Finance & Development* (March 1979), pp. 11–13.

The second major factor which has enhanced the need for some composite currency unit is the fact that large and often violent fluctuations occur under floating exchange rates. Floating exchange rates have not been an unmitigated blessing, especially when market expectations carry rates too far or move them faster than can be justified by underlying economic conditions or changes in these conditions.

While upward floating rates allow countries to protect themselves better against inflation coming from abroad, downward floating rates can aggravate inflation at home. Floating rates are supposed to prevent maladjustments from arising in the first place, but changes in such rates are difficult to use in the short run as a means of effecting adjustment. The changes in rates under a floating system can and have been occurring at a speed and to an extent that is sometimes in stubborn disregard of the relative prices and costs and interest rate differentials. In addition, they have sometimes induced damaging feedbacks on the domestic economy. For strong currencies, these variations can slow down investment and lead to recession; for weak currencies, they act to speed up inflation, tend to drive up the exchange rates of strong currencies, and further push down the rates of weak currencies.

Major currencies—in particular, the U.S. dollar—seem to be susceptible to such disequilibrating movements. It must be recognized that the gyrations of the U.S. dollar in the exchange markets during much of 1978 were in no small part due to the widespread use of the dollar as a unit of account for international trade, to its large share in the Eurocurrency and other offshore money markets, as well as to its preeminence as a transaction and reserve currency. Once confidence is shaken, there can be large-scale shifts from the reserve currency which can lead to much greater exchange rate depreciation and volatility of exchange rates than would be the case if the U.S. dollar were not performing these international functions. Whatever the reason, this instability has rendered the U.S. dollar less efficient as an international unit of account and as a store of value.

It does not automatically follow, however, that other currencies will be able to fill the gap caused by the instability of the U.S. dollar and play a commensurately greater role as the monetary unit for invoicing foreign trade and for denominating international credit. In the first place, it is possible that the appreciating currencies simply reflect the condition of an unstable dollar. It cannot be assumed that other currencies can or wish to shoulder the responsibilities involved, in part because their money and capital markets are not large enough to undertake the substantial task of financing world trade and international capital movements on the scale that the U.S. dollar has been used.

Of course, changes in yields will gradually produce some shifts in financing. For example, Japanese traders have been shifting to yen financing and German banks have expanded their deutsche mark loans but, in such cases, the debtors can be concerned about such arrangements in that they carry the risk of further appreciation of the currencies of the surplus countries.

At the same time it is doubtful that the authorities of the surplus countries are eager to have their currencies used more and more as international units of account. Often such a shift goes hand in hand with a greater use of these currencies as vehicle and reserve currencies. A larger external use of a currency in this way not only has advantages, but can have substantial drawbacks: both the exchange rate and domestic monetary policy can become more difficult to manage.

From an international point of view, the shifts from one currency unit to another are not very desirable either. A reserve currency system tends to be highly unstable when the reserve center, wherever it is, cannot reconcile reasonably stable internal conditions with its external economic and financial commitments and functions. It is, however, too much to expect that a country will, in all circumstances, subordinate its domestic economic aims to its external role as a reserve center; herein lies the inherent long-run instability of a monetary system based on reserve currencies. This is a part of the unfinished business of international monetary reform. In due course, national reserve currencies will almost certainly be replaced to a growing extent by international reserves such as the SDR, and national currencies will be used less.

When great uncertainty develops about exchange rates, as has recently been the case, and when exchange rate changes gather speed in a one-way movement, a number of tendencies may be observed in the market, which weaken monetary standards based on single currencies and encourage composite currency units. These tendencies are not equally strong or equally lasting and some of them already have appeared when exchange fluctuations have been less large and the outlook was less cloudy.

First, attempts are being made to match to the maximum extent assets and liabilities in the same currency and to avoid currency risks. For example, multinational firms will not borrow in the currency with the lowest interest rate but will finance an expansion of their manufacturing or trading activities, say, in the United States, with U.S. dollar credit, even though the interest cost may be substantially higher than taking up credit in another currency. Such attitudes resemble a voluntary freeze on capital movements and tend to delay international payments adjustments.

Second, currency areas tend to grow, and independently floating currencies seek to coalesce. These are welcome developments, but two elements are essential: (1) in order to stabilize successfully exchange rates in such mini-Bretton Woods systems, the economic and, in particular, the monetary policies of the participants must be closely harmonized; and (2) relations with the rest of the world must continue to be based on free trade and payments and on the other principles and objectives which inspired the Fund charter.

Another important tendency is to seek some way to divide exchange risks fairly between parties that are bearing risks in several floating currencies. A greater urgency to use the SDR unit of account and other composite currency units is being felt. In this way the SDR units may serve as a bridge between the major currencies such as the U.S. dollar, the Deutsche mark, and the yen, and the currencies linked to them.

SDR as Official Unit

It is a major objective of the Fund to put the SDR into the center of the international monetary system. Its members have pledged on the occasion of the last amendment to collaborate with each other and with the Fund to make the SDR the principal reserve asset. Practical steps have been and are being taken to strengthen this evolutionary process.

First, the allocation of SDRs will be resumed by the distribution of SDR 12 billion over the next three years. SDRs are being allocated to lessen the increase in foreign exchange reserves that would otherwise occur through the process of official borrowing on the international markets. If successful, this process should reduce the proportion of reserve currencies in future additions to reserves.

Other steps to improve the SDR are in hand. SDRs can now be exchanged freely among the participants against currency, and such voluntary transfers have already taken place on a large scale. In addition, the interest rate on the SDR will be increased and it will be possible to use SDRs to settle obligations without changing them first into currencies, to lend SDRs, and to pledge them as security for a loan by another central bank or government. Further improvements are high on the agenda. They include forward operations in SDRs and swaps of SDRs and enlarging the number of official institutions that may deal in SDRs. This last point is potentially of great significance for enlarging the volume of SDR-denominated financing in the private markets, since many of the institutions—unlike the Fund—have direct links with the private market. Once such institutions hold SDRs in their books, they are likely to seek to increase their SDR-denominated liabilities by developing transactions in private markets.

Second, the credit mechanism of the Fund, which is denominated in SDRs and guaranteed by Fund members in SDRs, has been substantially expanded over the last few years to cope with large-scale BOP deficits. For much of this expansion, the Fund has issued liquid reserve claims denominated in SDRs. As a result, international reserve assets held in the form of SDR-denominated reserve positions in the Fund have tripled in the last five years from SDR 6 billion to SDR 18 billion. (In comparison, official foreign exchange reserves doubled from about SDR 100 billion to SDR 200 billion in the same five-year period.) In addition, the Fund's capital will be increased from SDR 39 billion to almost SDR 59 billion, and during the next few years the institution will be able to borrow under the so-called Witteveen facility up to about SDR 8.5 billion from the creditor countries.

The low interest loans of the IMF Trust Fund to poor countries are also denominated in SDRs. These loans are financed by a portion of the profits realized in the gold auctions. In the first two years of the gold auctions, the Trust Fund disbursed loans of over SDR 800 million. In addition, since June 1978, the Trust Fund has placed over SDR 300 million as short-term dollar deposits with the Bank for International Settlements (BIS).

In sum, the official market in SDR-denominated credit is no doubt of major and growing importance. While such credit is largely connected with the activities of the Fund, this is no longer exclusively the case.

A few of the smaller Fund members are pegging their currencies to the SDR; many others manage their currencies by pegging them to custom-made baskets of currencies usually composed to reflect the geographical distribution of their foreign trade. In a number of instances, these baskets do not differ much in practice from the SDR basket. Thus, a small "SDR area" exists not by special design, but because pegging to the SDR has helped these Fund members in the developing world to stabilize their external and internal positions and to better protect their economies from the effects of instability elsewhere.

SDR IN PRIVATE MARKETS

SDRs are distributed and used only in the official field. But the Fund has no copyright on the use of the SDR as a unit of account. In fact, developments on the international scene will help to give the SDR a firmer and more permanent footing in the private market.

Usually, the private interest in the SDR is strongest when the U.S. dollar is weak. A few transactions are then arranged, but as soon as the U.S. dollar improves the volume tends to ebb. Preferably, however, the SDR should be viewed as an all-weather instrument and not as a short-run speculative alternative to currencies. The viability of the SDR rests on the proposition that it is more stable than individual currencies and that it helps give a means of exchange stability to those whose business is either in SDRs or who are exposed to exchange risks in several currencies in proportions approximately matching the composition of the SDR.

For the time being, the private market for SDRs is still small but more than a dozen commercial banks are presently actively accepting short-term currency deposits indexed in SDRs and many more are interested in developing this business. The banks accepting SDR deposits usually will try to cover themselves, for example, in the forward markets or make loans in the individual currencies which comprise the SDR. . . .

Since the Fund is committed to make the SDR the principal reserve asset, these conclusions on the role of the SDR as a unit of account in the private market may look rather modest. In my view, however, it would be wrong to conclude that the use of the SDR as a unit of account in the markets is an idea whose time has still not come. The role of the SDR officially and privately can only grow. It is both a symbol and an instrument, like the Fund itself, for the markets and for governments alike to promote stable exchange rates and to maintain free international trade and payments as essential elements of economic growth and well-being.

As of January 1, 1981, the Fund decided to unify and simplify the currency baskets that determine the value of and the interest rate on the SDR. The unified basket was changed from the composite value of 16 currencies to the currencies of the five major trading nations—U.S. dollar, Deutsche mark, French franc, Japanese yen, and pound sterling. The Fund believed this change would enhance the attractiveness of the SDR. One consequence was to reduce the overall weight of the dollar in the currency basket to 42 per cent. Weight given to the Deutsche mark is 19 per cent, with 13 per cent each given to the franc, yen, and pound.

5.2 Substitution Account

To meet the problem of the "dollar overhang," there have been proposals for a substitution account. As administered by the Fund, the substitution account would accept deposits of foreign exchange from members on a voluntary basis in exchange for an equivalent amount of SDR-denominated claims. The Executive Board of the Fund agreed in 1979 on the main features of a substitution account, as follows:

MAIN FEATURES OF A SUBSTITUTION ACCOUNT*

To achieve broad participation on a voluntary basis, the Account has to be devised in such a way that it satisfies the needs of depositing members, both developed and developing, in widely different economic circumstances. It is equally essential that the provisions of the Account reflect the principle that its costs and benefits must be fairly shared between the depositors, on the one hand, and the United States, on the other.

The Account is intended to bring about a long-term change in the composition of reserves; accordingly, the substitution brought about by the Account should in principle be permanent, although this does not obviate the need for liquidation provisions.

The possibility of voluntary amortization by the United States is envisaged for the Account; it was widely felt, however, that mandatory amortization should not be a feature of the Account.

Since the Account is intended to enhance the position of the SDR as a reserve asset in the system, the characteristics and uses of SDR-denominated assets issued through the Account and those of the SDR should be consistent, although not necessarily identical; care would have to be taken to ensure that the SDR-denominated claim would not make the SDR itself an unattractive reserve asset.

*IMF, Report of the Executive Committee to the Interim Committee (August 3, 1979).

> This might over time require some changes in the uses and characteristics of the SDR, although differences in the two instruments justify a degree of flexibility in the determination of their characteristics.
>
> Each participant would deposit with the Account acceptable U.S. dollar instruments and receive in return an SDR-denominated claim on the Account; the instruments deposited would be invested by the Account in some suitable form of interest-bearing U.S. Government obligation, in accordance with arrangements to be agreed in advance.
>
> Depositors would be member countries or institutions in member countries that are holding official reserves, and possibly nonmember countries (and their corresponding institutions) and certain multilateral financial institutions. It is not expected that the Account would necessarily attain its full size on a single occasion. Accordingly, there would be arrangements under which deposits could be made over time, in a framework that would ensure that the Account would operate to further its objectives and not as an intervention mechanism. While participation in the Account would be restricted to official institutions, the Account should provide that claims on the Account could also be transferred to and held by nonofficial holders, either from the start or only in a later phase of the Account.
>
> All of the characteristics of the claims on the Account, taken together, must be such as to attract a broad and substantial participation in the Account on a voluntary basis, as well as to make possible an effective secondary market. The chief characteristics considered in this context are the yield of the claim, its liquidity, and the preservation of its capital value. At the same time, these characteristics must be such that the scheme as a whole is acceptable to the issuer of the deposited currency.
>
> The claims should have a yield that makes them sufficiently attractive in comparison with other major reserve components. The Account will require provisions that will ensure its ability under all circumstances to pay the interest rate to holders of the claims.

After first opposing the IMF plan, the United States finally endorsed the scheme prior to the meeting of the Fund's Interim Committee in Hamburg in 1980. But by the time of the meeting, the selling pressure on the dollar eased, and the balance of payments of Germany and Japan had deteriorated. There was also concern over the liquidity of the SDR and the financial solvency of the substitution account itself. If the SDR were to be held instead of the dollar, its liquidity would obviously be important. But if the SDR is not held and traded in private markets, it cannot be used as an intervention currency by central banks. Some currency balances for intervention would be required in addition to the SDR-denominated substitution account claims.

Other countries also wanted the United States to guarantee the future value of the dollars placed in the substitution account so that the value of the dollars would not fall below that of the SDRs issued against them. This reflects concern over the substitution account's solvency. If the account is sponsored by the IMF, but is not backed by any of the Fund's own resources, then dollar assets must be balanced against SDR-denominated liabilities. If the interest yield on the account's dollar assets falls below the yield the account commits itself to pay on its liabilities for any prolonged period, then the account's solvency could be endangered. If the exchange rate of the dollar falls relative to the SDR, solvency could also be questioned. The United States was unwilling to guarantee the account's financial soundness by paying higher interest rates on U.S. Treasury securities held by the account than to other holders of government securities, or by direct exchange guarantees that would assume the exchange rate risk of foreign central banks. The issue of guarantees backing the account has been a major obstacle to agreement on a substitution account.

At the Hamburg meeting, Assistant Treasury Secretary C. Fred Bergsten said that the United States does not expect "final or firm decisions" to be reached, noting that the time is not "ripe" for such decisions, and that there is "no need for final decisions" at this time. He said there was not any "particular urgency" in completing the agreement "now, in September, or at any other particular time." Thus, action on any proposed substitution account was postponed. United States FRB Chairman Paul Volcker, asked to comment on the failure to make progress, said "I would not say there has been any failure. It depends on your expectations."

A few weeks later Henry Wallich, member of the Board of Governors of the FRB, surveyed the world monetary system:[9]

9 Henry C. Wallich, "The World Monetary System after Postponement of the Substitution Account," *Intereconomics* (July/August 1980), pp. 163–165.

In a sense, the lack of urgency to move ahead with this reform of the international monetary system was a backhand compliment to the dollar. Evidently, the world felt no immediate need to reduce the international rôle of the dollar, particularly not at a time when the rise in oil prices was placing an additional premium on the availability of international liquidity.

Whether the project will be reactivated is uncertain at this time. But if progress is to be made, it would have to rest on a more complete agreement concerning the purposes of a substitution account. There has always been some ambivalence between two views of the account: as a long-term structural improvement in the world monetary system, and as a conceivable means for bailing out the dollar from possible short-run difficulties. In the American way of thinking, the support of the proposal has always rested on its long-term rôle. It is not well designed to serve the purpose of dollar support in the short run, even if that purpose were regarded as desirable.

The substitution account's structural long-term rôle has to do with the choice of moving toward an SDR-based world monetary system in which the dollar would play a diminishing rôle, or a continued drift toward a multi-currency reserve system. A diminishing rôle for the dollar seems to be in line with the diminishing weight of the United States in the world economy. The rôle of reserve currency has shown itself to be burdensome, its benefits rather minor in an age of floating exchange rates and ready access to international reserves through world capital markets. Any change in the rôle of the dollar presumably would be a gradual and slow process. It is a process, however, that is carried by market forces and may, therefore, be only in part, perhaps in small part, subject to the policy discretion of the world's monetary authorities. What matters immediately is the direction. Is the process moving toward a gradual increase in the reserve rôle of the SDR, as provided in the amended statutes of the IMF; or is it moving toward an increasing use of other currencies along with the dollar, such as the Deutsche mark, the Swiss franc and the yen? A decision to activate the substitution account would move the process in the direction of an SDR-based system. Failure to activate the substitution account does not necessarily imply that evolution will be away from the SDR. There are other means, besides a substitution account, of enhancing the rôle of the SDR. But the present trend undoubtedly has been toward a multi-currency reserve system and there are many reasons for believing that this trend will continue.

The main impulse toward a multi-currency reserve system comes from the fact that, in a world of floating exchange rates, diversification of international assets reduces risk. For a central bank, ownership of a diversified portfolio of foreign exchange means less risk than ownership of a dollar portfolio. The measure of risk is variability.

It is important to note that comparisons of investment results in different currencies must be based on the concept of total return. An exact equivalence of appreciation expectations, inflation, and interest rates no doubt will never be attained. But broadly speaking it can be assumed that in the long run exchange rate movements will tend to equal inflation differentials and that interest rates will also equal inflation differentials. Thus, expected appreciation of any currency will tend to be offset, in terms of its total investment return, by a lower interest rate. To point out that historically this has frequently not been the case does not invalidate the principle. The market's foresight is very imperfect.

The precise composition of a diversified portfolio will differ for different central banks and different private holders. In the case of a monetary authority, it will depend on the country's trade relations, and on the currencies in which its foreign debt, if any, is denominated. The SDR, for example, at its present 30%, may be giving the dollar a rather high weight, measured by the US share of world trade. Measured in terms of the world's international debt, that proportion may be quite low. Thus, there is a host of considerations to be taken into account in constituting an optimal portfolio for a country's reserves.

It is this possibility of tailoring foreign exchange portfolios to the needs and preferences of individual countries and other holders that may make such portfolios more attractive than an SDR portfolio. Moreover, ownership of SDR claims may deprive the holder of the opportunity, illusory though it may be, of trying to beat the market by timely switches among currencies.

Nevertheless, it is precisely such switches among currencies that constitute the most serious liability of a multi-currency reserve system. The world has had much experience and much grief from such systems in the past. Shifts between sterling and gold, sterling and dollars, dollars and gold have plagued the international monetary community even while the amounts that could or did move were relatively moderate, and even when fixed exchange rates limited some of the consequences of such shifts. Today, with large international reserves lodged in floating currencies, the potentially destabilising effects of switches from one reserve currency into another could be ever greater. Diversification threatens to be destabilising even while it is still a relatively incipient process. Once a degree of diversification commensurate to countries' preferences has been achieved, potential instability will nevertheless continue to be a threat. We have observed that exchange-rate movements of major currencies, during short periods of time, sometimes have exceeded significantly any correction required by underlying economic factors, only to be reversed in short order. This tendency to overshoot would be enhanced, in all probability, by a multi-currency reserve system.

The development of such a system seems all the more probable today because holders' apparent interest in diversification is being supported by a growing willingness of potential reserve currency candidates to have that rôle forced upon them. Not long ago, some of the major candidates seemed determined to avoid that rôle, recognising the problems for stability both of domestic money and capital markets and of the international value of their currencies. More recently, concern over oil deficits seems to have created a greater willingness to tolerate and even encourage accumulation of assets denominated in certain national currencies, especially Deutsche mark, Swiss franc and yen, in the hands of OPEC holders.

It is quite conceivable, of course, that such balance-of-payments financing directly with OPEC surplus countries could be consumated in SDR instead of in national currencies. There is nothing to prevent central banks, given an appropriate legal framework, from issuing SDR liabilities. This would be an alternative means of moving the SDR to a greater rôle in the international financial system. It would be necessary, in that case, to give the SDR claims in question an interest rate and other features that would make them attractive and competitive with a diversified portfolio of currencies.

The SDR claim to be issued by the substitution account would presumably have the same currency basket and interest rate as its namesake, but somewhat different liquidity and liquidating provisions, reflecting the fact that it is an obligation of a special account in the IMF and not an obligation of the IMF itself. But in its case, too, the lack of complete competitiveness with alternative assets is evidenced by the need for elaborate arrangements for transfer and encashment. None of these difficulties needs to inhibit a privately issued SDR claim or even one that central banks might issue. Such an instrument could document its general competitiveness by being sold in the money market in competition with other securities.

There should be room in the reserves of central banks for three types of SDR—the SDR proper issued by the IMF, the SDR-denominated claim issued by a substitution account, and the SDR obligation issued by suitable official agencies in lieu of obligations in their own currencies. For private holders, SDR claims issued by private parties could also be readily available. Instruments issued by the Fund, the substitution account, and official agencies could presumably be made available to private holders by appropriate legal arrangements. Private ownership of SDRs would be helpful to central banks because they would then be able to dispose of SDR holdings to the market instead of only to other official agencies. Open market operations and foreign exchange market intervention in SDR would become possible. This possibility, although not likely to present itself in the near future, would raise the question of the proportion of exchange reserves that might be constituted in SDRs and the broader question of the total volume of these exchange reserves.

5.3 *Toward a Multi-Currency Reserve System?*

The shift in the relative economic positions of the United States and other major countries during recent years has raised questions about the emergence of a multiple-currency reserve system—a system that would reduce the prominence of the dollar and bring the Deutsche mark and yen into more extensive use as world reserve currencies.

Central banks have been diversifying their currency reserves, with a flow of funds into marks and yen. Among the many causes of this development are the recurrent confidence crises centering on the dollar, the exchange-rate variability of major currencies, the integration of international liquidity, and the lack of a suitable, internationally managed, reserve asset. But although the President of the Deutsche Bundesbank recognizes these causes, there has been a reluctance by Germany to undertake the greater international economic responsibility that a reserve currency status would require.

Ottar Emminger, former President of the Bundesbank, argued that the mark could not become a reserve currency because, unlike the situation in the United States, the German economy was too small to withstand the rigors of capital inflows and outflows. He believed that a system of several reserve currencies would be a highly unstable structure, exposed to the risks of constant exchange-rate unrest.

A more moderate, but still cautious approach was taken by the current President of the Deutsche Bundesbank.

OTHER RESERVE CURRENCIES?*

True enough, the share of the dollar in global exchange reserves has remained fairly stable over the years, at about 75 to 80%—a fact to which reference is sometimes made to support the view that there is not all that great a desire to move away from the dollar. Two things, however, have to be noted here:

First, if the reserves of those countries whose currencies are themselves increasingly performing reserve functions (the United States, Germany, France, the United Kingdom, Switzerland and Japan) are eliminated, then the figures tell a somewhat different story: at the end of 1978, roughly two-thirds of total foreign exchange reserves (i.e. excluding gold, SDRs and IMF reserve positions) of countries other than the six reserve currency countries were in dollars. The continuous decline up to that date seems to have been reversed in 1979, when the dollar was more stable on the foreign exchange than before. In absolute terms, the dollar holdings of the non-reserve currency countries increased from $25 billion at the end of 1969 to $210 billion at the end of 1979, that is, more than eightfold. The dollar reserves of the five secondary reserve currency countries (i.e., excluding the United States) rose over the same 10-year period from $8 billion to $114 billion, that is nearly twice as fast. The tendency to diversify reserve holdings may have resulted in more dollars ending up with the central banks in Germany and other major countries than might otherwise have been the case.

Second, the fact that the inflationary growth of international liquidity in recent years was in large part due to deficits in the US balance of payments, and thus accrued in dollars in the first instance, caused the share of that currency in the total to remain large. The size of OPEC surpluses, which are largely financed and held in dollars, may also have contributed to this result. Perhaps

*Karl Otto Pöhl, "The Multiple-Currency Reserve System," *Euromoney* (October 1980), pp. 43, 45.

diversification at times simply could not keep pace with the rate at which new dollars were created.

There are, of course, many factors that will continue to act in favour of the dollar as an international currency, and avert a full-scale move into other currencies. Many of the functions of international money are still far better served by the dollar than by any other currency: as a means of payments, as a store of value and as a unit of account. The existence of superior facilities for the placement of liquid funds in dollars—in New York or in Eurocurrency centres—has always favoured that currency for private as well as official investment. The ease with which dollar reserves can be placed and mobilized may well outweigh other considerations, such as maximizing return on investment, at least to some extent. Diversification is not cost-free, and the desire to avoid exchange rate risks will vary with changing circumstances and expectations. Moreover, not a few central banks, including those of the larger countries, have adhered faithfully to a dollar-only policy when investing their foreign exchange reserves, simply because the dollar remains their major intervention currency and diversification into other currencies would be impractical and possibly counterproductive. Central banks have, on the whole, shown respect for their mutual desire to avoid conflicting behaviour in a scenario that is complicated enough as it is. This is also apparent from the fact that multicurrency intervention has remained the exception to the rule, and is undertaken only in agreement with the partner banks. The European Monetary System is, of course, the most formalized arrangement among central banks based on multi-currency intervention.

There are no ready-made formulae, or criteria, for determining the optimal composition of a country's reserve holdings, or the appropriate share of any major currency in world reserves. If there were, there might be less reason to fear that a multiple-currency reserve system will be rather unstable and difficult to manage. Once a proper distribution of reserves has been achieved, both by individual countries as well as globally, rather greater stability might prevail than is at present the case. Those who questioned the alleged instability of a multiple-currency reserve system seem to base their arguments on such considerations. Only the future can show to what degree they are right.

It is an open question whether the defensive attitudes adopted by certain central banks, which are responsible for the likely candidates for a reserve currency rôle, have effectively prevented or impeded the greater international use of their currencies. The figures suggest that they have not been fully successful. In absolute, as well as relative terms, the Deutschemark has assumed a major rôle, though compared to the dollar it takes second place by far. At somewhere between 10 and 12% of total foreign exchange reserves, or somewhat more if the Bundesbank's own reserves are excluded from the calculation, the Deutschemark's share corresponds roughly to the part it plays as a transaction currency in world trade. Next in line are the yen, the Swiss franc and sterling.

The reasons for the German authorities' strong reservations about a growing reserve currency rôle for the Deutschemark have been sufficiently discussed elsewhere not to need to be repeated here. The main concern was, of course, that temporary flows into and out of the Deutschemark would be increasingly difficult to cope with as the potential for such flows expanded, and that control over domestic liquidity should not be lost in the wake of such flows. The advent of floating exchange rates, especially in relation to the dollar, has eased the problem considerably compared with earlier periods, when the central bank was legally bound to buy dollars at fixed rates and virtually without limit. But the problem never wholly disappeared: even under floating, domestic monetary autonomy had to be paid its price in terms of excessive upward pressure on the exchange rate whenever funds moved into the Deutschemark. This was the situation in 1976 and 1977, when the dollar was under downward pressure.

More recently, when the relative positions of the Deutschemark and the dollar and their prospects changed in the early months of 1980, this was a sharp reminder of the risks involved in the Deutschemark playing an ever-growing rôle as in internationally held currency. Within as little as two months, the Central Bank lost one fifth of its currency reserves to outflows of funds, adding further to the deficit on current account that had to be financed. The impact on domestic monetary conditions was correspondingly powerful.

Considerations of national monetary control were thus predominant in the formulation of policy regarding the reserve role of the Deutschemark. The wider implications of an increasing usage of national currencies for international purposes have so far received surprisingly little attention in monetary debate. The judgement referred to already, namely that a reserve system involving several currencies is likely to be highly unstable, is usually put forward as a foregone conclusion. Hence the widespread feeling that it would

> be immensely preferable if the dollar were to assume its key role again in full, based on renewed strength and permanent stability; or if an internationally accepted reserve asset such as the IMF's Special Drawing Right (with a more attractive name to it) could be made "the principal reserve asset in the international monetary system."

Japan is also unwilling to assume the responsibilities of a reserve currency country. Some countries do hold the yen as part of their official reserves, and some also partially link the value of their currencies to the yen in "basket formulas." But even in Asia, most of the foreign trade is settled in dollars, to which currencies are closely linked. Japan's own foreign trade is also chiefly conducted in dollars. A strong yen bloc has not yet emerged.

The reluctance of Germany, Japan, and Switzerland to become reserve currency countries stems from the relative narrowness of their financial markets compared with U.S. financial markets, and the fact that large-scale operations in their currencies, both for investment and for intervention, would have significant consequences for their domestic monetary and fiscal policies, as well as foreign-exchange implications. Once a country's currency assumes reserve currency status, exchange rate movements can be unrelated to the country's balance of payments. The reserve currency country assumes the role of the "*n*-th currency," that is, that of a country that must be passive with respect to its exchange rate because that rate is determined by the exchange market interventions of the "*n*-1" other countries. The discipline of restrictive fiscal and monetary policies is also weakened.

5.4 The Future of Gold?

Although the U.S. government has wished to demonetize gold, and the IMF has wanted to enhance the SDR as the principal reserve asset of the future, there persists in some circles a desire to preserve a significant role for gold. Part of this desire stems from a fear that international monetary cooperation cannot be effectively pursued and that the IMF will become unworkable in the future. Many more share fears of future inflation and look to a restored role for gold as a means of limiting monetary expansion.

A Brookings Institution economist, however, observes

> Those who are worshipful of gold (gold bugs, or, more politely, chrysophilites) are usually motivated by one or more of these concerns: particular economic theories now held by a small minority of economists, distrust of government, international political objectives (there is discernible among non-Americans a correlation, far from complete though it is, between attachment to gold and anti-Americanism), and, last but not least, hope of personal or national pecuniary gain.
>
> We are concerned here, of course, with gold's role as an official reserve asset. In its private role, it will understandably continue to be widely used, given its remarkable properties of indestructibility, ductility (an ounce of it can be drawn into a fine wire fifty miles long), beauty, resistance to corrosion, and high conductance of electricity.
>
> Although a few European officials would like to see established what would effectively be a new official price for gold, it seems unlikely that this will come about. As long as the United States does not change its basic approach to gold as an international reserve asset, a European attempt to peg a new price in the market would have to contend not only with the vagaries of private demand and supply of gold but also with the possibility of gold sales in the market by the U.S. Government.
>
> What seems likely is that gold will continue to remain "at the bottom of the pile" of countries' reserves. On occasions when their reserves in other forms become depleted, countries will either sell gold in the market if the price is attractive, or borrow using gold as collateral (as Italy did from Germany in 1974). Gradually gold is likely to seep out of official reserves and into the market, where it will become available to jewelers, dentists, artists, and industrial users for whom substitutes for gold are less readily at hand than for monetary authorities.[10]

In contrast, University of California Professor Roy Jastram argues

> If we now had a monetary system in which compensatory changes in the price level were expected to take place, then a rise in prices would encourage a deferral of spending until prices fell. This deferral would hasten the day when, in fact, prices would fall. Through the means of rational expectations an incipient inflation would carry within it the source of its own negation. A similar effect would hold for deflations.

[10] Robert Solomon, *The International Monetary System 1945–76* (1977), pp. 333–335.

Rational expectations, if they were pervasive enough, would then foreshorten the swings between inflations and deflations and moderate the extent of each. There is no such moderating influence today. The monetarists and those favoring a return to the gold discipline are not so far apart. Both agree that the supply of money and the way it is managed are crucial. Those favoring a return to a gold backing add: You can't trust politics.

With the money supply showing ominous signs of being out of control, serious thought must be given to a new form of monetary discipline, one which might be suggested by age-old experience."[11]

A contrasting interpretation is offered in the next selection.

CAN THE GOLD STANDARD BE RESTORED?*

It is possible to establish a gold standard if a country is willing to accept the restraints it entails and the economic consequences that may ensue. The minimum tests of a gold standard are (1) maintenance of the equal value of the currency and gold by the monetary authorities through the purchase and sale of gold freely at a fixed price, and (2) limitation of the money supply through gold reserve requirements, including the obligation to reduce the money supply when there is a diminution of the gold reserves. As a practical matter, a gold standard can function properly only as part of an international monetary system. Otherwise, sudden changes in the supply of or demand for gold would fall entirely on one country, as they did on the United States after 1934. Purchases and sales of gold by the monetary authorities at a variable free market price do not constitute a gold standard. Such gold transactions are merely another form of intervention in the exchange market and another type of open market operation.

Those who advocate a return to the gold standard assume that it would be possible to select some price of gold that would enable the monetary authorities to maintain the equivalence of gold and currency without being drained of their gold reserves or being swamped by a backflow of gold from hoarders, investors, and speculators. The change in the price of gold since 1973, and particularly its volatility, should make one skeptical of this possibility. It was

* Edward M. Bernstein, "Back to the Gold Standard?," *Brookings Bulletin*, vol. 17, No. 2 (Fall 1980), pp. 10–12.

[11] Roy W. Jastram, "The Gold Standard: You Can't Trust Politics, *Wall Street Journal* (November 11, 1980).

possible to maintain the equivalence of the value of money and gold for generations under the classical gold standard because the allocation of private monetary assets between gold and money had been adapted to the traditional monetary price in the course of centuries. Changes in the preference for gold relative to money were small and took place gradually, but the monetary authorities could keep gold and money equally attractive in the long run by allowing commodity prices to rise or fall with changes in the cost of producing gold and in the short run by changing interest rates, which raised or lowered the opportunity cost of holding gold instead of money.

Since the price of gold has ranged between $226 and $850 an ounce in the past two years, it is not possible to say now at what price the monetary authorities could expect to maintain the equivalence of gold and money under stable monetary conditions. If gold were an ordinary commodity, with production and consumption usually about equal, apart from relatively small changes in stocks, one could estimate what the price would be if supply and demand were at trend levels. In the long run, the price would have to reflect the cost of production and demand would be adjusted to the relative price of gold and other commodities. The supply of and demand for gold does not fit this pattern. Production accounted for about 59 percent of the supply in 1976–79 and consumption in the arts and industry—jewelry, dentistry, electronics, and other industrial and decorative uses—accounted for 70 percent of the private absorption of gold. The price has fluctuated sharply in this period with no apparent relation to changes in production or in the absorption of gold in the arts and industry.

The present price of gold and the fluctuations in the past two years were brought about by the demand of hoarders, investors, and speculators. Their demand is for holding gold as an asset, but the value of gold cannot be determined in the same way as the value of other assets. It is possible to estimate the value of such typical assets as stocks and bonds because they earn income. Their value is determined by discounting the future flow of earnings, and for bonds also the return of principal, at current interest rates. One may err in projecting corporate profits and the security of the principal of a bond, or the appropriate interest rate at which the flows should be discounted, but the method of valuation is clear. As gold is not an income-earning asset, it cannot be valued in that way. Its sole return to the owner is through a rise in price. What makes the price of gold $635 an ounce today is that buyers expect the price to be about $730 an ounce a year from now.

The view that the price of gold will increase at a rate in excess of the interest rate assumes that the present price is justified by economic conditions and that inflation will accelerate. The inflation of itself does not justify the enormous increase in the price of gold to its present level. At $635 an ounce, the purchasing power of gold as measured by the U.S. wholesale price index (290.8 in September 1980 on a 1957–59 base) is more than two and a half times as high as it was at the two previous peaks—in 1896, when the index was 25.4 and the price of gold was $20.67 an ounce, and in 1934, when the index was 41.0 and the price of gold was $35 an ounce.

The recent rise in the price of gold was not in response to the acceleration of inflation but to the political situation in Iran and Afghanistan. Without saying that world peace was an essential element of the classical gold standard, it is a fact that political disorder in the world adds to the difficulty of maintaining the equivalence of gold and currency at a fixed price. If, for example, the monetary authorities were to establish a gold standard price, a deterioration of the political situation could cause an enormous outflow of gold and a sharp contraction of the money supply, even if the economic situation should become more stable.

A Question of Supply

Under a gold standard, the increase of the money supply is limited by the increase in the gold reserves. Assuming that confidence in currencies were restored so that relatively little of the supply would be absorbed by hoarders, investors, and speculators, the growth of the monetary stock of gold would depend on newly mined production, net sales of the communist countries, and the consumption of the arts and industry. The production of gold outside the communist countries reached a peak of 41 million ounces in 1970, fell to 31 million ounces in 1975, and has remained at that level. The decline was almost all in South African production, although the output of other areas also fell slightly.

Sales by the communist countries, principally the Soviet Union, were very large in 1972–79. Such sales are for the purpose of acquiring foreign exchange to finance imports from the West. They are highly volatile, fluctuating directly with the Soviet balance-of-payments deficit and inversely with the price of gold. Because Soviet gold sales are so variable, they cannot be regarded as a reliable source for the regular growth of the monetary stock of gold.

Even if hoarding, investing, and speculation were to fall to the moderate levels of the early 1960s, the supply of gold that could be added to the monetary stock would be very small. The absorption of gold in the arts and industry exceeded newly mined gold by 20 percent in 1976–79, though some of the gold purchased by fabricators may have gone into inventories. This occurred despite a large reduction in such use of gold in 1979 because of the high price and the economic slowdown in some industrial countries. Perhaps, if a gold standard with a fixed price of gold were restored, the gold-producing countries might increase their output. But unless there were an adequate, steady, and assured growth of the monetary stock of gold, it would not be possible for a gold standard system to function effectively.

The existing stock of monetary gold, apart from the holdings of the communist countries, is more than 1.13 billion ounces, including holdings of the international monetary institutions. Most countries carry these reserves at an average market value over a preceding period, although the United States still values its holdings at the old monetary price of $42.22 an ounce. No large country has monetized its gold reserves at the present price. These gold holdings constitute a huge reservoir of assets that would free the international monetary system from dependence on additions to gold reserves for the growth of the monetary base. Countries could monetize their gold holdings at a regular rate to assure the monetary growth they consider necessary. Sales could also be made from these gold holdings without the necessity of deflating the money supply, and purchases of gold could be added to these gold holdings if they were financed by sales of Treasury bills without inflating the money supply. But if the monetary authorities followed such policies, making the money supply independent of the increase or decrease in the gold reserves, it could not be said that the country was on the gold standard.

The bills introduced in the Senate (S. 3181) and the House of Representatives (H.R. 7874) would establish gold convertibility of the dollar or a gold coinage within a few months of enactment. This attitude of urgency in establishing a kind of gold standard is reminiscent of the debate on the resumption of specie payments after the Civil War. Some thought it would be prudent to accumulate a larger gold reserve and to reduce the amount of greenbacks in circulation before undertaking specie payments. Others, among them Chief Justice Chase, who had been secretary of the Treasury during the wartime inflation, believed that no delay was necessary, that "the way to resume is to resume."

Inherent in this approach to restoration of a gold standard is the assumption that if inter-convertibility of gold and dollars were established at some price previously determined in the New York market, purchases of gold from or sales of gold to the Federal Reserve Banks would by themselves adjust the money supply to an amount appropriate to the monetary price of gold. That could entail a large contraction of the money supply through Federal Reserve sales of gold or an excessive expansion of the money supply through Federal Reserve purchases of gold. It would be ironic if restoration of the gold standard were itself to have a seriously destabilizing effect on the money supply. Actually, it is questionable whether the monetary systems contemplated in the bills referred to above would constitute a gold standard in the usual meaning of that term.

The gold standard is not an end in itself but a means of achieving certain objectives. The first is to restore and maintain a reasonably high degree of stability of prices and costs. This cannot be achieved automatically by establishing gold convertibility of the dollar. It requires greater budgetary discipline, a more cautious monetary policy, and limitation of the growth of incomes to the growth of productivity. The second objective is to achieve greater stability of exchange rates. Initially, the target could be to maintain the average foreign exchange value of the dollar within a moderately broad range relative to the other currencies in a unit of Special Drawing Rights—the D-mark, sterling, the French franc, and the yen. Ultimately the dollar would have to be stable in terms of the strongest of these currencies. That would necessitate keeping down the inflation to the same rate as in the most stable industrial country and giving greater consideration to the behavior of the exchange rate in formulating monetary policy.

These are the conditions that would have to be established before the United States could safely return to a gold standard. If the United States could achieve such a degree of price and exchange stability, there would be no need for a gold standard.

5.5 A World Central Bank?

At the polar extreme from the advocacy of a return to the gold standard is the argument that the IMF should be transformed into a world central bank for central banks. This is reminiscent of Keynes's early proposal for an International Clearing Union and of Robert Triffin's argument in favor of an expanded IMF that would have deposit accounts at the IMF displace national currencies as reserve currencies. In the following selection, the President of the Philadelphia National Bank restates the argument.

THE CASE FOR A WORLD CENTRAL BANK*

The case for a world central bank is similar to the case for a central banking system within a nation—to provide a uniform and universally acceptable currency with a stable purchasing power, and to exercise systematic control over the total supply of currency reserves.

A world central bank could be organized similarly to a strengthened version of the International Monetary Fund. The IMF members would constitute the world central bank. No alteration of the current voting rights arrangement would be necessary; a member's IMF quota would determine its proportionate voice in the central bank's management.

The system would separate the reserve currency function from the functions performed by national currencies on the international exchange markets and as media for international business transactions. This would be accomplished by creating a new unit of international money, which I will call the IM, to be used as a reserve currency and as the means for settlement of imbalances of payments among central banks. IMs could not be held by commercial banks and traders, and thus could not be used as a private transaction currency; nor could they be used by central banks as a means to influence exchange rates among national currencies. Ultimately, the IM would become the only reserve currency used to settle imbalances of payments, while the national currencies would continue to be used to finance international transactions and as the denominators of privately held, internationally-traded financial claims. Under such a system, exchange rates would achieve a more nearly pure floating relationship.

The IM would be defined as equal to a basket of currencies, with each currency valued at its exchange rate and weighted in proportion to the country's share of world trade, or according to some other appropriate economic measure. The value of any particular national currency in terms of IMs would change as exchange rates among the national currencies changed in the market.

The broad composition of the currency basket in such a scheme would give the IM a stable value in comparison with the dollar or with any other major reserve currency. Thus it would be an attractive unit for pricing internationally traded goods and services, and it would serve as the international unit of account as well as the official reserve asset.

*Frederick Heldring, "The Case for a World Central Bank," *Euromoney* (September 1979), pp. 60–63.

GRADUAL TRANSITION

How could we accomplish the transition to such a unit? It would have to be done gradually with the IM initially taking its place beside the Deutschemark and other currencies used as reserves. The IM would eventually replace these reserve assets in two ways:

1. Central banks could deposit national currency holdings in a substitution account at the world central bank, receiving IMs in return. This transaction would not change the amount of total world reserves. Such a substitution account was conceived in 1972 by the IMF's Committee of Twenty. It was discussed at an IMF-sponsored meeting two months ago. In that case, the proposed substitution unit would have been the Special Drawing Right or SDR.

2. The world central bank would issue any additional reserves needed for adequate growth of the world economy. The national currencies would constitute a steadily declining portion of the world's monetary reserves.

When national currency reserves had been translated into an internationally managed money supply, all national currencies could be made convertible into IMs. While national currencies would be allowed to fluctuate freely on the market, each nation would be required to convert its own currency into IMs if the foreign government or central bank holding the currency requested such a conversion.

For example, if the US incurred balance of payments deficits and the dollar fell in value, the surplus countries could request settlement in IMs rather than dollars. If the US lacked sufficient IM reserves, it would have to borrow from the world central bank and agree to modify its economic policy. This would have the effect of dampening exchange rate fluctuations and reducing the vulnerability of the international exchange markets to speculation.

The volume of new reserves to be supplied would be left to the judgement of the world central bank's governors, subject perhaps to approval of a substantial proportion of the member countries. Growth could be adapted to the need for orderly expansion of the world economy. Reserves could be supplied to the financial system through loans to participating nations or by purchases of securities denominated in their national currencies. In order to control the supply of reserves, member nations could be given the power to adjust reserve requirements provided they agree to hold a proportion of their international reserves in the form of IMs.

The idea of a world central bank is not new, yet little visible result has come from it. Is this because it poses a threat to national monetary sovereignty? And has the creation of the European Monetary System and its European currency unit meant a step away from the world central bank?

THE ILLUSION OF SOVEREIGNTY

Since John Maynard Keynes proposed a world central bank more than three decades ago, various scholars, notably Robert Triffin of Yale, have pursued the idea and modified it. So have the former IMF managing director H. Johannes Witteveen, the former Federal Reserve Board chairman William McChesney Martin, Jr., the former Lloyds Bank president Oliver Frank and the former British prime minister Harold Macmillan. The idea has been judged impractical because nations fear the loss of sovereignty over their monetary affairs. And yet, national monetary authorities are far from free to act independently, and cost of maintaining the illusion of sovereignty has been a high one. The existing system certainly does not shelter nations from the international consequences of ill-considered domestic economic policies, nor does it protect nations with sounder domestic policies from the effects of the instabilities created by the improvident.

Changes in the last few years in the US have made the traditional rôle of the dollar as the international reserve currency unsatisfactory both for the US and for the rest of the world. The weakening of the dollar has reduced its usefulness as a reserve currency. As nations have diversified their reserves into other currencies, the US has lost much of the former political and economic advantage associated with the dollar standard, without much decrease in the pressure to maintain the dollar's value in the market. The US has little interest in trying to restore the dollar as a reserve currency. Anthony Solomon, undersecretary of the Treasury for monetary affairs, said: "Let me make it clear that the US has no interest in artificially perpetuating a particular international rôle for the dollar."

I would go a step beyond Mr. Solomon's comment to argue that it should be the official policy of the US to seek disengagement from the dollar's rôle as reserve currency and from the burdens associated with that rôle. The most responsible and equitable approach to such a policy is to internationalize this rôle and these burdens through a world central bank.

All this doesn't mean that nations will no longer be apprehensive about the possible loss of monetary sovereignty. However, if the conversion to an international reserve currency unit is done gradually, it may be possible to reduce such fears.

There are signs that national resistance to the world central bank concept can be overcome. When the IMF was founded some doubted that it could survive to exercise discipline over countries that needed assistance, yet it has become accepted as an integral part of the international monetary system.

The establishment of the European Monetary System, far from being a backward step, serves to reinforce my belief that the concept underlying the world central bank is winning acceptance. Each of the EMS members had to consider the benefits of union against the benefits of continued national sovereignty. The EMS and its currency unit serve almost as a prototype for the broader concept of the world central bank. Their creation signals a decision on the part of many nations to co-ordinate monetary policy and to exercise a co-ordinated discipline in the growth of money supply for the nation's mutual benefit. The world central bank adds very little to that basic step. The greater stability provided by the EMS for its members may reduce their incentive to accept a worldwide monetary system, but other effects of the EMS may work in the opposite direction.

The strongest argument in favour of the creation of a world central bank is that no alternative has worked well. Each succeeding system has tended to generate instabilities in the world economy. Unless international unity can be created in money matters, the probability of continued instability will remain high.

6. ADJUSTMENT PROBLEM

All discussions of international monetary reform have had to consider the adjustment problem as well as the liquidity problem. For the less effective the adjustment mechanism, the greater the need for reserves as the final means of international payment. Changes in a country's reserves can also be viewed as indicators of pressure that should be applied to induce a country to adopt adjustment policies.

6.1 Pressure and Reform

After August 15, 1971, the United States' proposals for reform included a memorandum to the C-20 that elaborated how movements in monetary reserves should serve as "objective indicators" to guide the balance-of-payments adjustment process.

THE NEED FOR OBJECTIVE CRITERIA*

The U.S. proposals take as a point of departure that the stability and durability of a new monetary system will be crucially dependent on finding an equitable and effective means of promoting the adjustment of external imbalances.

In approaching that objective, we believe success is dependent upon finding an appropriate blend among three possible approaches, each of which contains some advantages, but none of which is satisfactory by itself. The three approaches are:

a) national discretion—a degree of which is essential in a world of sovereign nations and desirable in allowing maximum practicable freedom of action among individual countries, but which, relied on alone, assures neither equilibrium nor an equitable sharing of adjustment responsibilities;

b) discretionary authority of a central institution—which can bring to bear the influence and collective wisdom of the entire world community on particular adjustment problems, but which can lead to endless debate, indecision, or unbalanced decisions in a potentially politically charged atmosphere, and which requires at least the appearance of ceding more authority to an international body than nations will yield at this stage of international development; c) objective criteria—which can be helpful in establishing measurements for indicating adjustment needs for various nations and various situations on a standardized basis, but which do not unerringly point to appropriate adjustments or permit needed discretion by national authorities.

The U.S. proposal aims at a balance among these approaches—to utilize the advantages of each, while avoiding the disadvantages which might result from excessive or singleminded reliance on any of the three. We propose that objective criteria be established to note and locate the existence of an undesirable degree of balance-of-payments disequilibrium, and to create a strong presumption that effective adjustment policies should be implemented. But we would leave the country concerned substantial discretion in determining the composition of those adjustment policies. And international consultations would be utilized to determine the applicability of the criteria to particular situations and to consider exceptional cases in which the rules might be overridden. . . .

*Memorandum on "The U.S. Proposals for Using Reserves as an Indicator of the Need for Balance-of-Payments Adjustment," submitted to Committee of 20, November 1972; reprinted in *Economic Report of the President* (January 1973), pp. 162–171.

A critical defect of the system in the past was that while it tried to promise unlimited convertibility, and while fundamentally it required a broad measure of balance-of-payments equilibrium for sustained operation, it did not provide the supply of acceptable reserve assets or the discipline on adjustment policies necessary to achieve these objectives. A basic feature of the U.S. proposal is that nations must, through the process of negotiation, reach a collective decision on the appropriate normal stock and rate of increase of reserves, and be prepared to accept the consequences of that decision in terms of their own individual reserve positions and their own freedom of action to run surpluses or deficits.

It would be essential in the proposed system that countries regard their balance-of-payments disequilibria, whether surplus or deficit, as a source of concern before the agreed indicators came into play. In other words, countries would not be expected to ignore imbalances blithely until their disequilibria had become so extreme as to prompt strong *international* concern through the indicator mechanism. Reserve fluctuations would signal emerging disequilibria; movement to outer indicators signalling strong *international* concern would occur only when countries failed to make the appropriate responses as the disequilibria built up.

Convertibility itself cannot promote adequate or equitable adjustment. Convertibility is in that sense an asymmetrical tool, operating only on deficit countries. In the framework of the U.S. proposal, the inherent link of convertibility to reserve fluctuations would result in broadly symmetrical pressures upon surplus and deficit nations.

In short, the logic of the U.S. proposals is that a) better balance-of-payments adjustment is required and is essential to the maintenance of a convertibility system; b) such an adjustment process, in turn, requires recognition by both surplus and deficit countries of their obligations and responsibilities to take action; c) in that context, objective indicators of the need for adjustment are essential; d) a broad equality between the availability of, and demands for, reserves in the system must be satisfied; and e) all of these needs can be brought together, in the context of a system of established exchange rates supported by convertibility, by the use of reserve movements as the main indicator of the need for adjustment.

Description of the Proposed
Adjustment/Reserve/Convertibility System

These principles could be incorporated into several alternative operational frameworks. Such alternative formulations could, for example, (a) emphasize the use of net or gross reserves as the basis for measuring fluctuations in reserves; (b) focus attention largely on changes in reserves from an existing starting level or an appropriate distribution of individual countries' reserves in relation to some "objective" standard; and (c) provide for either relatively narrow or relatively wide ranges of fluctuation in reserves before international disciplines come into play. While the underlying principles and logic of the various approaches would be broadly similar, the particular formulation chosen would determine the speed, force and manner with which the adjustment pressures would operate. For its part, the United States wishes to continue to examine the advantages and disadvantages of the alternatives with care, and would welcome the contribution toward this effort that others can make.

The use of fluctuations in countries' reserves as the main indicator of adjustment need requires a judgment about a "base" level and trend of reserves for each country. Abstracting from transitional problems (noted later), these "base levels" could be established in several different ways. For instance, the distributional pattern of national quotas in the IMF (allowing for any agreed revisions in the future) might represent one approach toward determining a broadly acceptable distribution of reserves in normal circumstances. Another approach would be to give heavy weight to the actual level of reserves at the start of the system for the majority of countries, relying on separate negotiations for those countries whose reserves at the start of the system were judged to be seriously excessive or inadequate. Countries' "base levels," in any case, would be expected to rise over time, consistent with collective decisions about world SDR creation. The manner in which "base levels" should be calculated would clearly be a matter for careful negotiation. What is necessary is that *some* pattern be accepted that is generally satisfactory. . . .

Under a reserve-indicator system, certain points would be established above and below each country's base level to guide the adjustment process and to assure even-handed convertibility disciplines. Such points would be set according to uniform procedures for each country, and could be described as follows, again abstracting from special arrangements that would be appropriate during a transitional period.

(a) A "low point" would be set at some point below the "base level." In concept, this might approximate a level of reserves considered to be close to the minimum level ordinarily necessary to maintain confidence and to guard against extreme emergencies. If a country's reserves fell below its "low point" for a period of time, definite adjustment pressures would be anticipated and acceptable adjustment measures would be expected. In the absence of adequate policies over a specified period, international sanctions—for example, refusal to provide credit, or loss of scheduled SDR allocations—might become effective. Such sanctions would be avoided only if the IMF, through approval of a satisfactory program of adjustment, made a finding that sanctions were not warranted. Negotiated credits to deficit countries would ordinarily be permitted—but excessive or prolonged borrowing to circumvent the indicators would not be allowed.

(b) A "lower warning point" would be set at a point between a country's "base level" and the "low point." Small devaluations would be freely permitted a country at any time its reserves were below its base level. Proposals for larger devaluations would always require IMF approval; such proposals would not ordinarily be looked upon with favor unless a country's reserves had fallen below its "lower warning point."

(c) An "outer point" would be established above a country's "base level." As a country moved toward its "outer point," it would be expected to apply adjustment measures of progressive intensity. If reserves rose to the "outer point," remained at or above that level for a specified period, and an adequate program of adjustment were not in place, international action to induce adjustment would take effect. For example, the IMF might authorize other countries to impose general import taxes or surcharges against the country concerned, there might be a loss of scheduled SDR allocations, or there might be a tax on the country's excess reserve holdings with proceeds to go to development assistance. Such sanctions could be avoided, or postponed, only if the IMF made a positive finding they were not warranted, on the basis of an agreed program of adjustment—involving, for example, major moves toward liberalization of import restrictions, removal of any controls on the outward flow of capital provision of concessional untied aid, or revaluation. Standards should be developed for judging the adequacy of such programs and their consistency with progress toward a liberal world economic order. If reserve gains persisted despite the agreed program, authorization for sanctions would, after a further period, take effect. In any event, the IMF would review the country's position periodically, and make such recommendations and authorizations as it deemed appropriate.

(d) An "upper warning point" would be set between the "base level" and the "outer point," analogous to the lower warning point, representing an international judgment that adjustment is called for. The IMF would be expected to report on the country's balance-of-payments position and prospects, and revaluation or other adjustment measures would be anticipated.

(e) Depending on the volume of total reserves relative to primary reserves in the system, this "upper warning point" might coincide with a "convertibility point" representing the maximum accumulation of *primary* reserves for each country that would be justified, consistent with the level of aggregate primary reserves in the entire system, for the convertibility mechanism to operate equitably with respect to both deficit and surplus countries. Both to provide an incentive for adjustment, and to prevent countries from placing further convertibility pressures on others, a country reaching such a "convertibility point" would be unable to acquire additional primary reserves, through either purchase or SDR allocation.

A reserve-indicator system such as the one sketched above should be supplemented and elaborated by consultative procedures within the IMF concerning adjustment programs and problems. For such procedures to be effective, national policy officials at a politically responsive level should be drawn into the process. Such IMF review could take into account supplementary criteria in considering the nature and magnitude of any need for adjustment.

Countries would not be expected to delay adjustment action until they had reached the indicator points. The purpose of a reserve-indicator system is to provide strong incentives for countries to act in limited steps, using a variety of tools suited to their circumstances before their situation becomes so urgent as to involve international concern and action. Moreover, while countries would at given points be brought under overt international pressure for adjustment, they would still have a range of policy options at their disposal. The range of "acceptable adjustment measures" for the system would, however, be limited to those consistent with market mechanisms and a liberal world trade and payments order. Exchange rate changes are not seen as the only, or necessarily the most desirable, means of adjustment in all cases. . . .

> The United States proposal neither gives special rights to nor imposes special obligations on any country or group of countries. It assumes a monetary system in which all countries are treated equally. All would have the same freedom to use the full exchange rate margins permitted in the system. All would have the same rights to allow their currencies to float, transitionally or indefinitely, under the same internationally agreed rules of behavior and surveillance. All maintaining established values for their currencies would have the same obligation to assure convertibility of their currencies—meaning that officially held balances of foreign currencies could be freely presented to the issuing country for conversion into primary reserve assets, with the choice among SDR's, reserve positions in the IMF and gold to be made by the issuing country.

The C-20 Report also considered various "graduated pressures" that might be applied to induce adjustment policies.

FORMS OF PRESSURE*

It is generally agreed that provision should be made for graduated pressures in the reformed system to be available to the Fund for application to both surplus and deficit countries in cases of large and persistent imbalance. It is not agreed what forms these pressures should take; in particular it is not agreed whether there should be severer forms of pressure, such as trade pressures and the publication of reports. Nor is it agreed how such pressures should be activated, and in particular whether some pressures should be activated presumptively or automatically on the basis of reserve indicators.

Forms of pressure which have been suggested for the reformed system include the following:

PRESSURES THAT COULD BE APPLIED TO COUNTRIES IN SURPLUS

(i) A country could be subjected to a charge on reserve accumulations above a reserve norm or other specified level. The rate of charge could be graduated with respect to the size of the reserve accumulation and the duration of the imbalance.

(ii) Countries could be required to deposit reserves above a specified level with an Excess Reserves Account to be established in the Fund at zero interest. This pressure combined with the pre-

*IMF, *International Monetary Reform,* Documents of Committee of Twenty (1974), pp. 28–29.

ceding one would amount to the payment of negative interest on excess reserve accumulations.

(iii) All or part of future SDR allocations of a country in surplus could be withheld for a specified or an indefinite period.

(iv) A report could be published on the external position and policies of a country in surplus.

(v) Countries could be authorized to apply discriminatory trade and other current account restrictions against countries in persistent large surplus, subject to any necessary modification in the rules or practice of the GATT. This would be the most extreme form of pressure on countries in surplus.

PRESSURES THAT COULD BE APPLIED TO COUNTRIES IN DEFICIT

(vi) A country could be subjected to a charge on reserve deficiencies below a reserve norm or other specified level. The rate of charge could be graduated with respect to the size of the deficiency and the duration of the imbalance.

(vii) The interest rate charged on borrowings from the Fund could be raised above the general schedule of charges.

(viii) A country's access to the resources of the Fund could be restricted.

(ix) All or part of future SDR allocations of a country in deficit could be withheld for a specified or an indefinite period.

(x) A report could be published on the external position and policies of a country in deficit.

6.2 *Fixed versus Flexible Rates—Once Again*

Instead of emphasizing the reserve problem, other proposals have sought to improve the adjustment process by advocating greater flexibility of exchange rates. At the extreme end of the spectrum of flexibility are fully flexible or freely floating rates. A strong statement in favor of this type of exchange-rate regime was made in the early 1960s by Professor Milton Friedman.

PROFESSOR FRIEDMAN'S STATEMENT*

[L]et us consider the national objective with which our payments system is most directly connected: the promotion of a healthy and balanced growth of world trade, carried on, so far as possible, by

*Professor Friedman's 1963 statement before the Joint Economic Committee, 88th Congress, 1st Session, *The United States Balance of Payments,* Part 3 (November 14, 1963), pp. 452–459.

private individuals and private enterprises with minimum intervention by governments. . . .

Suppose that we succeed in negotiating far-reaching reciprocal reductions in tariffs and other trade barriers with the Common Market and other countries. Such reductions will expand trade in general but clearly will have different effects on different industries. The demand for the products of some will expand, for others contract. This is a phenomenon we are familiar with from our internal development. The capacity of our free enterprise system to adapt quickly and efficiently to such shifts, whether produced by changes in technology or tastes, has been a major source of our economic growth. The only additional element introduced by international trade is the fact that different currencies are involved, and this is where the payment mechanism comes in; its function is to keep this fact from being an additional source of disturbance.

An all-around lowering of tariffs would tend to increase both our expenditures and our receipts in foreign currencies. There is no way of knowing in advance which increase would tend to be the greater and hence no way of knowing whether the initial effect would be toward a surplus or deficit in our balance of payments. What is clear is that we cannot hope to succeed in the objective of expanding world trade unless we can readily adjust to either outcome.

Suppose then that the initial effect is to increase our expenditures on imports more than our receipts from exports. How could we adjust to this outcome?

One method of adjustment is to draw on reserves or borrow from abroad to finance the excess increase in imports. The obvious objection to this method is that it is only a temporary device, and hence can be relied on only when the disturbance is temporary. But that is not the major objection. Even if we had very large reserves or could borrow large amounts from abroad, so that we could continue this expedient for many years, it is a most undesirable one. We can see why if we look at physical rather than financial magnitudes.

The physical counterpart to the financial deficit is a reduction of employment in industries competing with imports that is larger than the concurrent expansion of employment in export industries. So long as the financial deficit continues, the assumed tariff reductions create employment problems. But it is no part of the aim of tariff reductions to create unemployment at home or to promote employment abroad. The aim is a balanced expansion of trade, with exports rising along with imports and thereby providing employment opportunities to offset any reduction in employment resulting from increased imports.

Hence, simply drawing on reserves or borrowing abroad is a most unsatisfactory method of adjustment.

Another method of adjustment is to lower U.S. prices relative to foreign prices, since this would stimulate exports and discourage imports. If foreign countries are accommodating enough to engage in inflation, such a change in relative prices might require merely that the United States keep prices stable or even that it simply keep them from rising as fast as foreign prices. But there is no necessity for foreign countries to be so accommodating, and we could hardly count on their being so accommodating. The use of this technique therefore involves a willingness to produce a decline in U.S. prices by tight monetary policy or tight fiscal policy or both. Given time, this method of adjustment would work. But in the interim, it would exact a heavy toll. It would be difficult or impossible to force down prices appreciably without producing a recession and considerable unemployment. To eliminate in the long run the unemployment resulting from the tariff changes, we should in the short run be creating cyclical unemployment. The cure might for a time be far worse than the disease.

This second method is therefore also most unsatisfactory. Yet these two methods—drawing on reserves and forcing down prices—are the only two methods available under our present international payment arrangements, which involve fixed exchange rates between the U.S. dollar and other currencies. Little wonder that we have so far made such disappointing progress toward the reduction of trade barriers, that our practice has differed so much from our preaching.

There is one other way and only one other way to adjust and that is by allowing (or forcing) the price of the U.S. dollar to fall in terms of other currencies. To a foreigner, U.S. goods can become cheaper in either of two ways—either because their prices in the U.S. fall in terms of dollars or because the foreigner has to give up fewer units of his own currency to acquire a dollar, which is to say, the price of the dollar falls. . . . Similarly, foreign goods can become more expensive to an American in either of two ways—either because the price in terms of foreign currency rises or because he has to give up more dollars to acquire a given amount of foreign currency.

Changes in exchange rates can therefore alter the relative price of U.S. and foreign goods in precisely the same way as can changes in internal prices in the United States and in foreign countries. And they can do so without requiring anything like the same internal adjustments. If the initial effect of the tariff reductions would be to create a deficit at the former exchange rate (or enlarge an existing deficit or reduce an existing surplus) and thereby increase unemployment, this effect can be entirely avoided by a change in exchange rates which will produce a balanced expansion in imports and exports without interfering with domestic employment, domestic prices, or domestic monetary and fiscal policy. The pig can be roasted without burning down the barn.

The situation is, of course, entirely symmetrical if the tariff changes should initially happen to expand our exports more than our imports. Under present circumstances, we would welcome such a result, and conceivably, if the matching deficit were experienced by countries currently running a surplus, they might permit it to occur without seeking to offset it. In that case, they and we would be using the first method of adjustment—changes in reserves or borrowing. But again, if we had started off from an even keel, this would be an undesirable method of adjustment. On our side, we should be sending out useful goods and receiving only foreign currencies in return. On the side of our partners, they would be using up reserves and tolerating the creation of unemployment.

The second method of adjusting to a surplus is to permit or force domestic prices to rise—which is of course what we did in part in the early postwar years when we were running large surpluses. Again, we should be forcing maladjustments on the whole economy to solve a problem arising from a small part of it—the 5 percent accounted for by foreign trade.

Again, these two methods are the only ones available under our present international payments arrangements, and neither is satisfactory.

The final method is to permit or force exchange rates to change—in this case, a rise in the price of the dollar in terms of foreign currencies. This solution is again specifically adapted to the specific problem of the balance of payments.

Changes in exchange rates can be produced in either of two general ways. One way is by a change in an official exchange rate: an official devaluation or appreciation from one fixed level which the government is committed to support to another fixed level. . . . But this method has serious disadvantages. It makes a change in rates a matter of major moment, and hence there is a tendency to postpone any change as long as possible. Difficulties cumulate and a larger change is finally needed than would have been required if it could have been made promptly. By the time the change is made, everyone is aware that a change is pending and is certain about the direction of the change. The result is to encourage a flight from a currency, if it is going to be devalued, or to a currency, if it is going to be appreciated.

There is in any event little basis for determining precisely what the new rate should be. Speculative movements increase the difficulty of judging what the new rate should be, and introduce a systematic bias, making the change needed appear larger than it actually is. The result, particularly when devaluation occurs, is generally to lead officials to "play safe" by making an even larger change than the large change needed. The country is then left after the devaluation with a maladjustment precisely the opposite of that with which it started, and is thereby encouraged to follow policies it cannot sustain in the long run.

Even if all these difficulties could be avoided, this method of changing from one fixed rate to another has the disadvantage that it is necessarily discontinuous. Even if the new exchange rates are precisely correct when first established, they will not long remain correct.

A second and much better way in which changes in exchange rates can be produced is by permitting exchange rates to float, by allowing them to be determined from day to day in the market. This is the method which the United States used from 1862 to 1879, and again, in effect, from 1917 or so to about 1925, and again from 1933 to 1934. It is the method which Britain used from 1918 to 1925 and again from 1931 to 1939, and which Canada used for most of the interwar period and again from 1950 to May 1962. Under this method, exchange rates adjust themselves continuously, and market forces determine the magnitude of each change. There is no need for any official to decide by how much the rate should rise or fall. This is the method of the free market, the method that we adopt unquestioningabgly in a private enterprise economy for the bulk of goods and services. It is no less available for the price of one money in terms of another.

With a floating exchange rate, it is possible for governments to intervene and try to affect the rate by buying or selling, as the British Exchange Equalization Fund did rather successfully in the 1930's, or by combining buying and selling with public announcements of intentions, as Canada did so disastrously in early 1962. On the whole, it seems to me undesirable to have government intervene, because there is a strong tendency for government agencies to try to peg the rate rather than to stabilize it, because they have no special advantage over private speculators in stabilizing it, because they can make far bigger mistakes than private speculators risking their own money, and because there is a tendency for them to cover up their mistakes by changing the rules—as the Canadian case so strikingly illustrates—rather than by reversing course. But this is an issue on which there is much difference of opinion among economists who are agreed in favoring floating rates. Clearly, it is possible to have a successful floating rate along with governmental speculation.

The great objective of tearing down trade barriers, of promoting a world-wide expansion of trade, of giving citizens of all countries, and especially the underdeveloped countries, every opportunity to sell their products in open markets under equal terms and thereby every incentive to use their resources efficiently, of giving countries an alternative through free world trade to autarky and central planning—this great objective can, I believe, be achieved best under a regime of floating rates. All countries, and not just the United States, can proceed to liberalize boldly and confidently only if they can have reasonable assurance that the resulting trade expansion will be balanced and will not interfere with major domestic objectives. Floating exchange rates, and so far as I can see, only floating exchange rates, provide this assurance. They do so because they are an automatic mechanism for protecting the domestic economy from the possibility that liberalization will produce a serious imbalance in international payments.

Despite their advantages, floating exchange rates have a bad press. Why is this so?

One reason is because a consequence of our present system that I have been citing as a serious disadvantage is often regarded as an advantage; namely, the extent to which the small foreign trade sector dominates national policy. Those who regard this as an advantage refer to it as the discipline of the gold standard. I would have much sympathy for this view if we had a real gold standard, so the discipline was imposed by impersonal forces which in turn reflected the realities of resources, tastes, and technology. But in fact we have today only a pseudo gold standard and the so-called discipline is imposed by governmental officials of other countries who are determining their own internal monetary policies and are either being forced to dance to our tune or calling the tune for us, depending primarily on accidental political developments. This is a discipline we can well do without.

A possibly more important reason why floating exchange rates have a bad press, I believe, is a mistaken interpretation of experience with floating rates, arising out of a statistical fallacy that can be seen easily in a standard example. Arizona is clearly the worst place in the United States for a person with tuberculosis to go because the death rate from tuberculosis is higher in Arizona than in any other State. The fallacy in this case is obvious. It is less obvious in connection with exchange rates. Countries that have gotten into severe financial difficulties, for whatever reason, have had ultimately to change their exchange rates or let them change. No amount of exchange control and other restrictions on trade have enabled them to peg an exchange rate that was far out of line with economic realities. In consequence, floating rates have frequently been associated with financial and economic instability. It is easy to conclude, as many have, that floating exchange rates produce such instability.

This misreading of experience is reinforced by the general prejudice against speculation, which has led to the frequent assertion, typically on the basis of no evidence whatsoever, that speculation in exchange can be expected to be destabilizing and thereby to increase the instability in rates. Few who make this assertion even recognize that it is equivalent to asserting that speculators generally lose money.

Floating exchange rates need not be unstable exchange rates—any more than the prices of automobiles or of government bonds, of coffee or of meals need gyrate wildly just because they are free to change from day to day. The Canadian exchange rate was free to change during more than a decade, yet it varied within narrow limits. The ultimate objective is a world in which exchange rates, while free to vary, are in fact highly stable because basic economic policies and conditions are stable. Instability of exchange rates is a symptom of instability in the underlying economic structure. Elimination of this symptom by administrative pegging of exchange rates cures none of the underlying difficulties and only makes adjustment to them more painful.

The confusion between stable exchange rates and pegged exchange rates helps to explain the frequent comment that floating exchange rates would introduce an additional element of uncertainty into foreign trade and thereby discourage its expansion. They introduce no additional element of uncertainty. If a floating rate would, for example, decline, then a pegged rate would be subject to pressure that the authorities would have to meet by internal deflation or exchange control in some form. The uncertainty about the rate would simply be replaced by uncertainty about internal prices or about the availability of exchange; and the latter uncertainties, being subject to administrative rather than market control, are likely to be the more erratic and unpredictable. Moreover, the trader can far more readily and cheaply protect himself against the danger of changes in exchange rates, through hedging operations in a forward market, then he can against the danger of changes in internal prices or exchange availability. Floating rates are therefore far more favorable to private international trade than pegged rates.

Though I have discussed the problem of international payments in the context of trade liberalization, the discussion is directly applicable to the more general problem of adapting to any forces that make for balance-of-payments difficulties. Consider our present problem of a deficit in the balance of trade plus long-term capital movement. How can we adjust to it? By one of the three methods outlined: first, drawing on reserves or borrowing; second, keeping U.S. prices from rising as rapidly as foreign prices or forcing them down; third, permitting or forcing exchange rates to alter. And, this time, by one more method: by imposing additional trade barriers or their equivalent, whether in the form of higher tariffs, or smaller import quotas, or extracting from other countries tighter "voluntary" quotas on their exports, or "tieing" foreign aid, or buying higher priced domestic goods or services to meet military needs, or imposing taxes on foreign borrowing, or imposing direct controls on investments by U.S. citizens abroad, or any one of the host of other devices for interfering with the private business of private individuals that have become so familiar to us since Hjalmar Schacht perfected the modern techniques of exchange control in 1934 to strenghten the Nazis for war and to despoil a large class of his fellow citizens.

Fortunately or unfortunately, even Congress cannot repeal the laws of arithmetic. Books must balance. We must use one of these four methods. Because we have been unwilling to select the only one that is currently fully consistent with both economic and political needs—namely, floating exchange rates—we have been driven, as if by an invisible hand, to employ all the others, and even then may not escape the need for explicit changes in exchange rates. . . .

If for some economists the merit of freely floating rates is that the price of foreign exchange would be determined daily in the market for foreign currency by the forces of demand and supply, to others this is its very disadvantage because the exchange rate is considered too strategic to be determined freely.

If the exchange rate is left to market forces, its impact would be general—in effect, the scale changes for all prices, whereas a government may want to alter only some prices of specific exportables and importables. Depreciation, for instance, will have a general effect on all prices in the foreign trade sector, acting as an ad valorem subsidy on all exportables and an ad valorem tax on all importables. The capacity for selective price changes is lost.

Another serious concern for some governments is the domestic price instability that might result from fluctuating rates. Countries with high ratios of foreign trade to domestic production might find that price changes in the foreign sector can dominate their entire domestic economy. And this domination may bear no relation to any need for general price changes. A short-term capital outflow, for example, might cause a depreciation in the exchange rate and have a general inflationary impact on the domestic economy.

Critics also claim that freely floating rates would fluctuate widely, and the uncertainty that this creates would inhibit international transactions. Under some circumstances, exchange markets might degenerate into destabilizing speculation: a massive buying or selling wave fed by capital movements that could force exchange rates to extreme movements.

The counter-argument to this fear is that "speculators who engage in genuinely destabilizing speculation—that is, whose speculations move the exchange rate away from rather than toward its equilibrium level—will consistently lose money, because they will consistently be buying when the rate is 'high' and selling when it is 'low' by comparison with its equilibrium value."[12] This reply is not completely satisfying to critics who still persist in arguing that professional speculators may be able to profit by leading amateur speculators who are the herd-like followers into destabilizing speculation. As long as new groups of amateur speculators can be at-

12 Harry G. Johnson, "The Case for Flexible Exchange Rates, 1969," *Report*, Federal Reserve Bank of St. Louis (June 1969), p. 20.

tracted to the market, the instability can be perpetuated, and the professional speculators can continue to profit.[13]

Even if the exchange-rate fluctuations are not severe, there is nonetheless some uncertainty that increases the risk of doing international business. True, "traders averse to uncertainty would be able to hedge their transactions through forward exchange markets, which would, if necessary, develop in response to demand."[14] But critics reply that "even assuming that forward cover is available, the added cost of buying it will reduce the volume of international trade. . . . Furthermore, forward cover will be very difficult to obtain for transactions with long lead times such as custom designed machinery, jet planes, or ships. Also certain services like insurance involve assuming liabilities well into the future and the absence of forward cover for exchange risks could easily seriously inhibit the supplying of this service on an international basis. Thus some degree of international specialization might have to be sacrificed. Some productive capital movements like bond flotations would also be seriously inhibited."[15]

Another major argument against freely fluctuating rates is that the free market would establish an inappropriate exchange rate that promotes inflation. This is because the discipline against inflationary policies would be lost if the consequence of inflationary policies is only exchange-rate depreciation. Central banks would lose their leverage on governments concerning fiscal matters that would have led to reserve losses in the absence of rate flexibility.[16] Moreover, fluctuations in exchange rates are in themselves inflationary. If effective, depreciation will lead to an increase in exports and a decrease in imports that will be inflationary through the impact on aggregate demand. In addition, there may be a cost-push type of inflation to the extent that imports rise in price, are inputs, and firms have sufficient market power to raise prices. With a rising cost of living, wages will also tend to rise, and another round of price increases will ensue. In contrast, when a currency appreciates, not all cost reductions are translated into price reductions. Wage rates are

13 Lawrence B. Krause, "Fixed, Flexible and Gliding Exchange Rates," *Journal of Money, Credit, and Banking* (May 1971), p. 331.
14 Johnson, "The Case for Flexible Exchange Rates," p. 20.
15 Krause, "Fixed, Flexible and Gliding Exchange Rates," p. 331.
16 *Ibid*, p. 332.

sticky downward, and part of the appreciation gain will simply be absorbed in higher real wages; and instead of reducing their prices, producers may simply raise profit margins when their import costs fall. This asymmetric adjustment to exchange-rate movements—depreciation leading to higher prices and appreciation to higher real factor returns—will, on balance, leave the price level higher than it would be in the absence of exchange-rate fluctuations.[17]

For these reasons—its overly general impact, creation of uncertainty, and fostering of inflation—a freely fluctuating exchange market can be criticized as establishing an inappropriate price. A free market exchange rate will adjust to price and cost disparities—but the price and cost disparities may be fostered by the system itself, and the rate established by the uncontrolled market need not be considered any more appropriate than a rate that is managed in a constrained market. Just because it is not an ordinary, but such a special price, the critics contend that the determination of the exchange rate should not be left to market forces. A domestic analogy is the interest rate structure—again, the price of money—which is determined by national monetary authorities.

Another set of arguments is based on the contention that no change in price—whether determined by market forces or the government—would be appropriate for some sources of balance-of-payments disequilibria. Exchange-rate variations do not fit the situations of inflation coupled with a balance-of-payments deficit or unemployment coupled with a balance-of-payments surplus. In the former situation, disinflationary measures are appropriate—not currency depreciation that would in itself be inflationary. Freely fluctuating rates might set in motion a spiral of depreciating exchanges, subsequent wage increases to meet the rise in cost of living, further price increases, balance of payments deterioration, and further exchange depreciation. In the opposite situation of unemployment and an international surplus, the appropriate policies are domestic reflationary measures and not currency appreciation which would be deflationary.

An alteration of the exchange rate would also be unsuitable for cases of structural disequilibrium. If there is a loss of export markets for nonprice reasons, it is of little avail to reduce the price of exports

17 *Ibid.*

through currency depreciation. When an external deficit is not caused by inappropriate relative prices, a change in the exchange rate is ineffective as a remedial policy. If the source of the deficit is an outflow of capital, it may also be considered inappropriate to place the burden of adjustment in the current account. In a world of volatile short-term capital movements, this consideration carries special force.

One can also argue against exchange-rate changes out of an interest in maintaining the benefits of international money. Thus, Professor Kindleberger has stated that his

> basic regret about [the] second devaluation [of the dollar] is that the world is now left without an international money. Most international economists lack interest in this. Their concern is with the medium-of-exchange function of money only, and this they believe can be discharged effectively by fluctuating exchange rates. Strong believers for the most part in the services of money within national economies, they see little need beyond the exchange function in the international sphere. I believe this is a mistake. We need money internationally not only as a medium of exchange but as a unit of account, store of value, and standard of deferred payment, that is, to calculate world prices in, for holding international liquid balances, for fixing long-term contracts. The devaluation of August 1971 produced upsets in the world markets for oil, coffee, airfares, tanker construction, that is in long-term contracts and commodity agreements which need to fix prices over a considerable period of time. The elasticities economists brush aside this problem by referring airily to forward markets. They do not solve it. And they ignore the need for an international money as a store of value, a vehicle currency which countries can hold to balance temporal excesses against deficiencies. International lending and borrowing will suffer without an international money.[18]

Freely floating rates are also criticized as causing a deficit country to bear excessive costs of adjustment. No mechanism of adjustment is without its costs, but the problem is to minimize the burden and distribute it equitably among deficit and surplus countries. For

18 Statement of C. P. Kindleberger, Hearings before the Subcommittee on International Finance of the Subcommittee on Banking and Currency, House of Representatives, 93rd Congress, 1st Session, p. 313. For elaboration, see also Kindleberger, "The Benefits of International Money," *Journal of International Economics* (September 1972), pp. 425–42.

a deficit country that has to undergo currency depreciation, the costs may be considered unduly burdensome in entailing resource reallocation, deterioration in the country's terms of trade, change in the distribution of income, and reduction in the total amount of resources available for home consumption and investment. For a surplus country, currency appreciation will weaken the country's competitive position in world markets, to the disadvantage of exporters and domestic competitors with imports. The burden of adjustment will be heavier when price elasticities are low, responses are slow, and the economy's capacity to transform is limited.

A regime of freely fluctuating rates may be especially undesirable for the less-developed countries (LDCs). Beyond the previously mentioned disadvantages, there are several other considerations of special concern to LDCs: freely fluctuating rates could inhibit regional integration unless the countries could agree to a joint float or a common currency; the creation of uncertainty for the foreign investor who wants to reconvert funds into the creditor's currency may be a significant deterrent to capital inflow; the increased burden of servicing external debt could be severe; the calculation and management of development plans would be made more complex; and the facilities for a forward market may be extremely thin in a developing country. Exchange-rate depreciation would also be ineffective to the extent, as is often true, that domestic inflation persists; the demand for imports is a function of output and is unresponsive to price changes; the marginal propensity to save is a constant that cannot be readily altered by relative price changes; and exports have a low price elasticity of demand.

In the final analysis, the merits of the case for or against freely floating rates will depend in reality on how gradual the exchange-rate adjustments would be, how predictable, how effective and rapid the adjustment process, and what would be the costs of feasible alternative policies.

Some general assessment of experience since 1971 has been offered in the preceding Problem, pp. 182–206. We there concluded that experience has departed from textbook expectations and that in reality neither the case for nor against flexible rates has been as strong as proponents and critics earlier maintained. What is evident from the post-1971 experience is that countries are reluctant to allow unlimited flexibility. This has been demonstrated by competitive

Table III.1 Rate Flexibility under Alternative Exchange-Rate Systems

	Exchange-rate system		
Characteristic	*Fixed rates*	*Full flexibility*	*Limited flexibility*
Formal parity	Formal	None	Formal
Formal intervention limits	Announced	None	Announced
Conditions for change in parity	"Last resort"	None	"Fundamental disequilibrium" or "objective indicators"
Exchange values in short run	Fixed	Unlimited market flexibility	Limited flexibility within "band"
Desired exchange values in long run	Fixed	Unlimited market flexibility	"Internationally managed flexibility"

SOURCE: Adapted from Samuel I. Katz, *The Case for the Par-Value System, 1972,* Princeton Essays in International Finance, No. 92 (March 1972), p. 3.

nonrevaluations and "dirty floats." In practice, the essential question is what degree of flexibility is feasible—what is the acceptable and desirable range of "managed floating" or limited flexibility short of fully flexible rates?

The discretionary approach that has been practiced reveals substantial variability over time in both the exchange rate and a country's external reserve position. For in managing the rate, the country alters its reserve position. This joint variability may therefore be labeled either "managed fixing" or "managed variations" of external reserves. The label itself has no substantive importance; the key word, in any case, is "managed."[19]

Table III.1 indicates the distinguishing characteristics of different exchange-rate regimes—fixed rates, fully flexible, or limited flexibility. Fully flexible rates are distinguishable from fixed-rate and limited-flexibility systems by the absence of a commitment to a formal parity, to specific intervention points, and to conditions that must be met before a change in parity can be made. The fixed-rate and limited-flexibility systems have in common the commitment to a formal parity and to announced intervention points in the short

19 Ralph C. Bryant, "Financial Interdependence and Variability in Exchange Rates," Brookings Institution Staff Paper (1980), p. 17.

run. But in the long run, a fixed-rate system (such as the pre-1914 international gold standard) would not undergo a change in parity except as a "last resort" measure after reserves and credits had been exhausted. Under limited flexibility, in contrast, a change in parity over the longer run would be more readily possible under conditions of "fundamental disequilibrium" (as in the original IMF agreement) or under other guidelines for adjustment, such as the "objective indicators" suggested in the earlier United States proposals for international monetary reform.

To the extent that countries have been unwilling to revert to a fixed-rate system and have not yet been ready for fully flexible rates, monetary reform has had to focus on the limits of rate flexibility. If there are to be predetermined limits of flexibility in the short run, how are the limits to be set? And in terms of what reserve asset are the support points to be defined—gold, the dollar, or the SDR?

If regional integration is desired, can the member countries maintain a sufficient degree of monetary cooperation and policy harmonization to form an "optimum currency area?" Which exchange rates, if any, should be allowed to fluctuate?

Finally, if there are to be exchange-rate variations in the longer run, how are the changes to be determined? By what presumptive rules of objective indicators? And by what form of collective monitoring or "internationally managed" flexibility?

Some of the major issues of international monetary reform have centered on these questions.

6.3 Managing the Managed Float

The Second Amendment provided that "the Fund shall exercise firm surveillance over the exchange rate policies of members, and shall adopt specific principles for the guidance of all members with respect to these policies." The Executive Board of the Fund has agreed on a surveillance document.

SURVEILLANCE OVER EXCHANGE RATE POLICIES*

The General Principles are derived mainly from the text of Article IV itself. The first paragraph begins by drawing attention to the

*John H. Young, "Surveillance over Exchange Rate Policies," *Finance & Development* (September 1977), pp. 17–19.

Fund's responsibilities to oversee the international monetary system and to exercise firm surveillance over exchange rate policies. The surveillance principles adopted by the Fund are to be consistent with cooperative arrangements by which members maintain the value of their currencies in relation to other currencies, as well as with other exchange arrangements. These principles are also to respect the domestic social and political policies of members, and, in the application of the principles, the Fund is to pay due regard to the circumstances of members. Finally, members are reminded that Article IV, Section 3(b), requires them to provide the Fund with the information necessary for surveillance and, when requested, to consult with the Fund on their exchange rate policies.

The second paragraph of General Principles stresses the point that the principles and procedures are adopted by the Fund in order to perform its functions under Article IV, Section 3(b), that is, to exercise firm surveillance over exchange rate policies.

Thus, the surveillance document is concerned primarily with surveillance over exchange rate policies rather than with surveillance over economic policies as a whole.

The Guidance of Members

The second section on Principles for the Guidance of Members' Exchange Rate Policies is the shortest and the simplest. Principle A is taken directly from Article IV. It provides that "A member shall avoid manipulating exchange rates or the international monetary system in order to prevent effective balance of payments adjustment or to gain an unfair competitive advantage over other members." This is the central paragraph of the surveillance document and in effect says that a country shall not have the "wrong" exchange rate, that is, a rate which overvalues or undervalues its currency. There are, of course, forces at work that make it difficult for a country to persist in having the wrong exchange rate. But while it has such a rate, misleading signals are being given to the domestic price system of the country itself, and to the price systems of its trading partners and competitors. When the inevitable correction comes, the adjustments affecting a number of countries have to be made. The purpose of Fund surveillance is to reduce the economic costs and the international political frictions which result from a country having the wrong exchange rate over a significant period.

Principles B and C are carried over from the guidelines for floating although in a somewhat revised form. Paragraph B provides that "A member should intervene in the exchange market if necessary to counter disorderly conditions which may be characterized inter alia by disruptive short-term movements in the exchange value of its currency." Guideline 1, on the other hand, stated that a member should intervene on the foreign exchange market "as necessary to prevent or moderate sharp and disruptive fluctuations from day to day and from week to week in the exchange value of its currency." The guideline involved a wider commitment to intervention, and Principle B reflects the position that the obligation of members to intervene should be limited to countering disorderly market conditions.

Principle C provides that, in their intervention policies, members "should take into account" the interests of other members including those of the countries in whose currencies they intervene. This is a slightly stronger form of Guideline 6 which reads that members with a floating rate will "bear in mind" the interests of other members.

FUND SURVEILLANCE

The Principles of Fund Surveillance over Exchange Rate Policies are designed to indicate the broad lines which will guide the Fund in exercising surveillance. The section thus begins with a general statement that surveillance will be adapted to the needs of the international adjustment process. This emphasizes the point that the balance of payments positions of countries need to be looked at in a world context. Thus if, as is the case today, some oil exporting countries have large current account surpluses which are likely to persist, equivalent deficits will necessarily persist elsewhere in the world.

Paragraph 2 of this section outlines the developments which the Fund is to consider as among those which might indicate the need for discussion with a member. There is nothing surprising about the first four items on this list. If one were to ask what actions are typically associated with having a wrong exchange rate, one would begin with protracted large-scale intervention in one direction in the exchange market, go on to the closest substitute for this, namely, an unsustainable level of official or quasi-official borrowing, then pass to restrictions on, or incentives for, current and capital transactions, and finally turn to the use of monetary and other financial policies to provide abnormal encouragement or discouragement to capital flows. Since borrowing, restrictions, and monetary policy can all be used for purposes other than influencing the outcome of the balance of payments or the exchange rate, the last three sets of measures include the phrase "for balance of payments purposes." It was often stressed during the debate on the surveillance document that actions of this kind were to be regarded as "pointers" indicating the need for discussions, rather than treated as conclusive evidence of inappropriate exchange rate policies.

The fifth item on the list is not directly connected with action by the country but rather with "behavior of the exchange rate that appears to be unrelated to underlying economic and financial conditions including factors affecting competitiveness and long-term capital movements." The phrase "behavior of the exchange rate" was used rather than a "change in the exchange rate" in order to emphasize that the attention of the Fund should be drawn to situations in which the exchange rate, either because of movement or because of the *absence* of movement, appears to be out of line with developments in the long-run determinants of the exchange rate, for example, relative rates of inflation among countries.

These indicators are intended to suggest the need for discussion with a member. No conclusion is to be drawn, however, until a more detailed appraisal has been made of a member's exchange rate policies. Paragraph 3 of the Principles of Fund Surveillance contains a number of references to the considerations which will have to be taken into account in reaching any conclusions. The appraisal is to be based on an evaluation of the developments in a member's balance of payments against the background of its reserve position and its external indebtedness. This is a very abbreviated statement, partly reflecting the thinking underlying the reserve paragraph in the guidelines for floating which indicated that the Fund would take a member's reserve situation into account in assessing its behavior. . . .

It is clear that difficult judgments will have to be made in the exercise of surveillance. Both members and the Fund will want to avoid too rigid and troublesome a surveillance of exchange rate policies, and there is evidence in the agreed document of an awareness of this danger. At the same time, members and the Fund will want to ensure that the Fund can exercise the "firm surveillance" that is recognized by Article IV as being in the interests of the international community.

7. DEVELOPING COUNTRIES' RECOMMENDATIONS

The future of the international monetary system is as important to Third World countries as it is to the United States, EEC, and Japan.

The developing countries are anxious for monetary reform that will allow a higher rate of growth throughout the world economy, with indirect benefits to the late-developing nations. Even more, these countries have sought direct benefits from some plan that would provide a link between the creation of additional international liquidity and additional development assistance. They are also concerned about reform of the adjustment mechanism and how greater exchange-rate flexibility will affect the course of their development.

7.1 Linking Reserve Creation and Development Assistance

THE "LINK"*

CHAIRMAN REUSS. Good morning.

The Subcommittee on International Exchange and Payments will be in order for a hearing to consider a new facility for increasing financial assistance to developing nations.

While the proposals under discussion today are new in the sense that they are not now in being, the idea of using the multilateral creation of reserves not only to ease the liquidity problem but also to finance real transference to developing countries has been discussed for almost ten years.

Today we hope to consider the arguments for and against the so-called "link," what the form of such a mechanism might be, the advantages and disadvantages of alternative mechanisms, and the benefits that the less-developed countries might potentially get from such a facility.

We have an exceptionally distinguished panel of witnesses to participate in our discussion this morning. . . .

I would like each one of you, starting with Mr. Dell, to give or summarize the points that you wish to make, and then I would hope that we can have some discussion not only among members of the subcommittee but also among members of the panel on this most important question.

Mr. Dell?

STATEMENT OF SIDNEY DELL

Director, New York Office of UNCTAD

MR. DELL. Mr. Chairman, among the indispensable conditions for a healthier world economy is a willingness on the part of the

*Joint Economic Committee, *Hearing Before the Subcommittee on International Exchange and Payments*, 91st Congress, 1st Session, 1969, pp. 1–5, 16–19, 29–30.

industrial countries to assist in the development of the less-developed countries.

It is generally recognized that, as the World Bank has lately reaffirmed, the current flow of capital to the less-developed countries is well below the capacity of these countries to make effective use of it. Among the reasons frequently cited by donor countries for curtailment of aid programs is the fear of losing reserves, and if action is taken to increase the world level of reserves, it is to be presumed that one of the deterrents to an enlargement of aid would be pro tanto removed.

It cannot, however, be taken for granted that restrictions on aid, once imposed, will be readily relaxed. Such limitations on aid have by now acquired a life of their own, and all kinds of reasons have been found to justify them. There is therefore no assurance that an easing of the world's liquidity position will be accompanied by an increase in the flow of resources to the less-developed countries, unless specific steps are taken to insure that this occurs.

This is the basic rationale for a link between liquidity creation and the provision of aid to less-developed countries. Such a link would enable donor countries to respond to the need for more aid, without running the risk of incurring any loss of reserves, and without having to increase taxes for this purpose, although not of course without increasing the transfer of real resources.

One contention commonly advanced against the link is that liquidity creation is not designed to effect a permanent transfer of real resources from one group of countries to another, a contention that would apparently rule out the gold standard as well, since countries acquiring gold for their reserves have always had to transfer real resources to the gold producing countries in exchange. This argument would also rule out the newly established system of SDR's, which allows participating countries to maintain as little as 30 percent of their net cumulative allocation of SDR's, and use the balance to acquire real resources from other participants.

Another objection is that linking liquidity creation with the provision of assistance to less-developed countries may tend to generate pressures for excessively large amounts of SDR creation in relation to world liquidity needs.

It is important to note, however, that throughout the discussion of this matter by both industrial and less-developed countries in UNCTAD, the point has never been questioned that the amount of any new reserve creation should be determined by the monetary requirements of the world economy, and not by the need for development finance.

In any case, there is very little risk of excessive creation of SDR's in circumstances in which a mere 15 percent of the total vote in the International Monetary Fund suffices to prevent a proposed act of liquidity creation.

Finally, it has been suggested that if the industrial countries are not prepared to expand their aid by direct means, that is by direct contributions to bilateral and multilateral aid programs, they are not likely to be willing to do the same thing indirectly, that is through the link.

Now although the real burden of aid is the same, whether the transfer takes place by conventional methods or through such methods as the link, governments may see some advantages in the latter method.

As I have already mentioned, two advantages of this method are that it avoids any risk of reserve losses, and that it makes it possible to expand aid programs without having to increase taxes.

The possibility that introduction of the link would tempt governments to reduce other forms of aid cannot be entirely dismissed. It is, however, unlikely that the opening up of new channels of aid adds nothing at all to the total flow. The net increase in the total level of aid resulting from the link may turn out to be less than the direct allocations of SDR's or their equivalents in national currencies for lending to less-developed countries, but there would probably be some net increase, and my own impression is that the net increase would be considerable.

We come finally to the question of the most suitable form for the link. Although there are important advantages in establishing the link as an integral part of the mechanism through which SDR's are distributed, we have to face the fact that in the immediate future this has been ruled out by the terms of the new amendment to the articles of agreement of the International Monetary Fund, which preclude the holding of SDR's by any such agency as the World Bank group.

There is therefore a strong case for considering a voluntary form of the link, as suggested by Professor Triffin, and by Dr. I. G. Patel, economic adviser to the Ministry of Finance of India and one of the members of the UNCTAD expert group on international monetary issues. . . .

What Dr. Patel suggests is that every act of international liquidity creation should be accompanied by voluntary contributions to IDA (the International Development Association of the World Bank Group) by all the Part One member countries of IDA, the size of the voluntary contribution being a certain uniform proportion of the share of every Part One country in international liquidity creation.

Most of the objections to the link in its organic form do not apply to this alternative version. From a legal standpoint, there is nothing in the amendment to the articles of agreement of the IMF that would preclude such an arrangement, and from the standpoint of economic and banking policy, this alternative version of the link would provide for a clear separation between liquidity creation and development assistance as recommended by the critics of the organic link. . . .

As to the possible ratio of IDA contributions to the newly created reserves, this is a matter for discussion and negotiation just as the obligation to reconstitute 30 percent of cumulative SDR allocations was a matter for discussion and negotiation.

Ideally one would like to see IDA contributions equal to the value of the newly created reserves, but one might have to settle for less than this. . . .

All in all, the link would significantly increase the efficiency of new reserve creation in improving the international economic environment.

Thank you, Mr. Chairman.

STATEMENT OF HARRY G. JOHNSON

Professor of Economics,
University of Chicago, and the London School of Economics and Political Science

MR. JOHNSON. Thank you, Mr. Chairman.

The proposal of the link does have a lot of attraction at the present time for two reasons, one being that the balance of payments deficits for the United Kingdom and the United States have been used as justifications for reducing the flow of aid. The other is that the developing countries have become much more capable of absorbing aid, just at a time when the flow of aid relative at least to the capacity to bear the burden has been falling.

Nevertheless, it seems to me that there are fairly strong arguments against the general proposal to link international reserve creation and development assistance. One which I have advanced in the past is that development assistance and the creation of international reserves are separate issues, each with its own economics and, more important, with its own politics.

One can argue that the linkage of these two problems in policy discussions is really a matter of willingness of governments to link them, and that perhaps at the present time this possibility is greater than it has been in the past, and that is a matter on which I am not competent to pass a judgment.

The more fundamental argument against the proposal, I think, is that contrary to widely held views the creation of international reserves does not need to involve the generation of a pool of resources which have to be allocated somehow and on which the less-developed countries have a moral claim.

Perhaps some years ago this view was more plausible, in the sense that plans for international monetary reform at that time were generally modeled on the concept of a bank, with liabilities which would constitute the reserve assets, being backed by assets in the form of loans and securities, but it has come to be understood in the course of the discussion that what is required of international reserves is acceptability to those who have to hold them, and that the quality of acceptability does not require that there be assets to back the reserve instrument. And that principle is in fact embodied in the SDR scheme which from that point of view constitutes a considerable advance on earlier discussions.

The fact that it is embodied in the SDR scheme makes it much more difficult to disguise the fact that linking reserve creation to development assistance does demand a deliberate choice to transfer real resources from the developed countries which want to hold larger stocks of reserves to the less-developed countries which would benefit either by initially receiving the reserve assets or by receiving the funds paid in exchange for them.

Now the real transfer involved is entirely unnecessary from the standpoint of creating new international reserve assets, and you could only justify it either on the political feasibility argument, which I have already mentioned, or else by creating some sort of fiction to the effect that it is more desirable that countries earn their additional reserves than that they simply create them.

Creating reserves is a costless procedure, at least in economic terms. On the other hand, giving reserves away and then earning them back does involve a very substantial real cost in terms of transferring real resources and it seems to me that countries would be unlikely to accept that unless they already had a strong desire to increase their transfers of resources to the promotion of the economic growth of the less-developed countries, and in that case the question is whether the linkage is the best way of doing this.

Well, the specific proposal before the subcommittee is for the linkage of creation of SDR's in addition to those created under the present agreed scheme to the financing of the development of the less-developed countries.

Now the basic argument for that proposal has to rest on the assumption that under the agreement, the creation of new reserves in the form of SDR's will promote the healthy development of the international economy and that the creation that is prospective will be insufficient to the needs of the international economy. Otherwise the proposal to create additional SDR's is really a proposal for financing economic development by world inflation, and the policy of promoting development by inflation is not usually regarded as a good policy in the context of single nation's policies.

Well, the whole thing has to rest then on the assumption that reserve creation would otherwise be inadequate, and this raises two problems. The first is to establish that in fact it will be inadequate by some kind of economic standard, and this raises difficulties, because in spite of the alleged seriousness of the international liquidity problem, the world economy has been characterized by a mild but marked inflation of prices since World War II. . . .

The second difficulty, while it is a political one, is one which I do feel competent to discuss, and that is that if the developed countries having negotiated the present scheme then negotiate a sizable increase of reserves in the form of SDR's, then even if it is true that those new reserves will be inadequate and will prove to be inadequate, I do not see the countries involved accepting a renegotiation of their decision in the form of extra SDR's. Rather I expect them to insist on seeing what happens with the reserves they create, and if necessary correcting their decision in the event of experience.

Well, these considerations suggest that in the light of the questions posed by the subcommittee for these hearings, that aid-linked SDR's would virtually have to be and should be created as an integral part of the decision to create new international reserves, and that they would not constitute a net addition to the total of SDR's created, only a redistribution of a predetermined quantity of SDR's.

Now in connection with the proposal that creation of extra SDR's should be on a voluntary purchase basis there is I think a real question of how many might be purchased. As reserve assets, SDR's will be significantly inferior to U.S. dollars, and though I am not very confident at the moment, they might even be inferior to sterling, because the SDR's carry a very low rate of interest on accumulations additional to a country's quota.

The development of the use of SDR's as an international reserve asset will depend on the establishment of a central bank preference for them, and it is not altogether clear that such a preference will in fact be established. It is possible that the rest of the world will get used to the present de facto dollar standard, and that the use of dollars as reserve assets rather than being terminated as is assumed in many of these discussions, may in fact revive.

Another consideration is that it would be perfectly possible for countries, if they want to accumulate reserves and also want to have the accumulation of reserves matched by contributions to the less-developed countries, to do that entirely apart from the SDR scheme itself. It is possible, as I suggest in my statement, that this could be done simply by purchasing World Bank bonds, and using them as reserve assets.

They would be less liquid, obviously, than SDR's. On the other hand, they would offer a rate or return substantially superior.

Now, this consideration—and I had not read Mr. Dell's paper before I came this morning—but the proposal that you should couple the creation of SDR's with contributions to IDA, for example, really accepts this point, and I do not see that to say that that is a proper procedure really amounts to accepting any link at all other than some sort of moral obligation to contribute to the developing countries.

If we accept my argument that aid linked SDR's would simply be a redistribution of a predetermined total of SDR's, it is obvious that the benefit of aid linking to the developing countries is going to depend on the total size of the SDR's created and the proportion of them which are linked to aid. This is an answer to another one of the subcommittee's questions which is how much benefit the developing countries would get from this.

Insofar as SDR's are decided on the basis of how much extra money the world needs, then the amount of them created would have to depend among other things on how much use of the dollar as a source of additional reserves is made, and also on the estimate of how many extra reserves the world needs.

Again I would say that it is not all that clear that the dollar is finished as an international reserve asset. Some of my colleagues have argued on the contrary that the dollar is going to be the currency of the future, and in that case, the amount of SDR's required will be rather substantially less than current estimates indicate.

As to the proportion of SDR's to be aid linked, this depends very much on the scheme of linking, but it seems to me very unlikely that the developed countries would really make a major proportion of the SDR subject to the linkage.

STATEMENT OF RAUL PREBISCH

Former Secretary-General of UNCTAD, and Director-General of the United Nations Latin American Institute for Economic and Social Planning

MR. PREBISCH. Thank you, Mr. Chairman.

Undoubtedly, international monetary reform and the transfer of resources to developing countries are two different things, and we should not mix them. However, this does not mean that they cannot be combined. What we are trying to do, therefore, is take advantage of the reform in order to add more resources to developing countries.

But it is obvious that the amount of new monetary resources to be created should be considered quite independently of any consideration as to the external financial needs of developing countries. This is essential in order to avoid monetary inflation in the use of this reform.

I think that, given the voting power of the different countries in the IMF, there is no risk of developing countries exercising a very effective pressure on developed countries. As you know, the latter have the real power to decide the amount of resources to be created. Indeed, I am afraid that if there is any risk of bias, this risk would be in favor of an insufficient rather than an excessive creation of resources.

The question of whether the link should be organic or not, as Mr. Dell already said, has been considered. The amendment of the articles of the Fund has not entailed an organic link, and in order to introduce an organic link, it would be necessary to amend the amendments. This could be a very serious difficulty. But it is perfectly conceivable to make a parallel agreement whereby developed countries receiving additional resources would put part of the equivalent of these resources at the disposal of the World Bank, or IDA, or regional banks, in order to increase the amount of their resource transfers to developing countries.

There is nothing unsound in the transfer of real resources in that way; this was the nature of the transfer of resources during the golden age of the gold standard. There is nothing new in this. Countries willing to capture part of the increment of gold supplies would exercise all their competitive power through their exports of goods and services to obtain a part of the new gold resources. The results of this SDR scheme, if the idea of a link was accepted, would be the same. Instead of gold, countries could capture these new instruments which are representative of gold.

As to the proportion of resources to be transferred to developing countries, Mr. Chairman, I have suggested in my short paper that it be a 50-percent proportion. There is, of course, nothing dogmatic about this. It is a matter of negotiation, as Mr. Dell has said. But the final target should be 100 percent at some future date.

As to conditions of transfer, Mr. Chairman, I consider that it would be unfair to charge a rate of interest to developing countries in this operation, except in exceptional cases. On the contrary, I would like to see this new resource as an element to alleviate the already heavy load of services plaguing developing countries in the form of interest, amortization, and related capital remittances.

It is a well known fact that many developing countries are in a very critical situation in this matter of a substantial and still rising debt-servicing burden. Especially in Latin America. This concerns me very much, not only in regard to the present, but also to the critical situations that would appear in the course of the next few years, if present tendencies continue, and worse yet, if they are aggravated, as seems to be the case.

There is, naturally, the risk that this new transfer of financial resources to developing countries would diminish in a parallel fashion the resources that are presently transferred and which are very scarce indeed. However, I would rather see this as part of the policy commitment accepted by developed countries at the UNCTAD Conference in New Delhi a year ago, whereby in principle they agreed to transfer 1 percent of their gross product to developing countries. I think that this new operation, through the link, can and should help developed countries achieve that target as soon as possible.

7.2 General Aspects of Monetary Reform

After the events of August 15, 1971, the LDCs expressed a strong determination for an active role in international monetary negotiations, as evident in the Lima Action Program and statements of UNCTAD. The following extract conveys some general attitudes on reform of the system.

THE DEVELOPING WORLD AND MONETARY REFORM*

In the establishment of a new monetary system, the following main objectives and criteria should be borne in mind:

(a) The system should permanently guarantee a situation of international liquidity appropriate for the expansion of world trade and for the acceleration of the growth of the exports and economies of the developing countries. This means that from its inception the system—unlike that established at Bretton Woods—should incorporate a body of rules taking due account of the special problems of the developing countries. This call for differential treatment should not be considered in any way unusual, since it simply means extending to the monetary and financial field a principle which has already been accepted in the sphere of trade. Steps should be taken to see that this principle is put into full practical effect. . . .

(b) It is a matter of crucial importance that the developing countries should participate effectively from the outset in the negotiations concerning the reform of the monetary system and, later, in its actual operation. . . . Moreover, the Lima Action Programme notes that it is "entirely unacceptable that vital decisions about the future of the international monetary system which are of concern to the entire world community are sought to be taken by a limited group of countries outside the framework of the International Monetary Fund."

(c) In the Lima Action Programme it was agreed that "the role and authority of the International Monetary Fund should be reestablished and strengthened in all matters that concern the whole international community, as an effective way of safeguarding the interests of all countries especially of the developing countries." It was further agreed that "the voting power of the developing countries in the International Monetary Fund should be increased by introducing provisions in the Articles of Agreement of the International Monetary Fund in order to increase the number of votes allocated to these countries. . . ."

THE ATTITUDE OF THE DEVELOPING COUNTRIES TO A NEW MONETARY SYSTEM

The Lima Action Programme, which stipulates with great precision the main features that should be introduced in the new monetary system, states that: "The following considerations and guide-

**Economic Bulletin for Latin America*, United Nations, vol. XVII, No. 1 (1972).

lines, among others, should be taken into account in the exploration of solutions to the crisis:

"(a) It is indispensable to the restoration of stability and confidence in the world monetary system that a satisfactory structure of exchange rates maintained within narrow margins should be established;

"(b) The new system must provide a mechanism for creating additional international liquidity, through truly collective international action, in line with requirements of an expanding world economy and the special needs of developing countries, and with such safeguards as will ensure that the total supply of international liquidity is not unduly influenced by the balance-of-payments position of any single country or group of countries;

"(c) The creation of a link between SDRs and additional resources for financing development should be made an integral part of the new international monetary system;

"(d) The adherence of the developing countries to a new international monetary system necessarily presupposes the existence of a permanent system of guarantees against exchange losses affecting the reserves of these countries. In any case a mechanism should be worked out to compensate developing countries against involuntary losses they have suffered because of currency speculations in certain currencies of developed countries."

With regard to paragraph (*a*), it is obvious that a system where parities fluctuate within fairly wide margins would have an unfavourable impact on developing countries. This is particularly so because excessive fluctuations introduce a permanent factor of instability in international trade which has a more serious effect on countries which are less prepared and lack the experience to contend with problems of this kind, i.e., precisely the less developed countries.

Bearing in mind that short-term capital movements are the main determining factors in parity fluctuations, it is particularly important that the industrialized countries should attach more importance to the adoption of internal measures to curb such movements. This course was actually envisaged at Bretton Woods but, with few exceptions, the developed countries never put it into practice.

In order to comply with paragraph (*b*) of the excerpt from the Lima Action Programme reproduced above, it would seem necessary to include an additional feature in the new system. As strongly

> maintained by the Latin American spokesman at the last meeting of the International Monetary Fund in Washington, the basic source of international liquidity and the central instrument of reserves should not be identified with national currencies and should increasingly become a fiduciary instrument like SDRs.
>
> Clearly this feature is of particular importance because it would enable the dollar-standard system with all its limitations to be gradually eliminated and the stability and independence of the new monetary system to be progressively enhanced. In this latter respect, the IMF would obviously have a better chance of effectively directing the operation of this system if its base unit is a fiduciary instrument which is created independently of the member countries and is issued and circulated under the supervision and control of the IMF itself.
>
> If a more important role is assigned to Special Drawing Rights it becomes more urgent to adopt procedures whereby the developing nations can have greater access to them. The first step, as already suggested, would be to adopt a different criterion for the distribution of SDRs when they are next allocated, so that developing countries may receive a bigger proportion than that determined by the IMF quotas. The adoption and implementation of this formula is not an alternative to the establishment of a link between the allocation of SDRs and additional development finance, but on the contrary complements such a measure. An important fact to remember is that, in view of the slowing-up of the expansion of international trade, an increase in the purchasing power of developing regions in the near future would be a much-needed stimulus.
>
> The second step would be to establish a link between the allocation of Special Drawing Rights and the provision of additional finance to developing countries, a point which was also included in the Lima Action Programme. . . .

Extremely active in considering how monetary reform might affect the interests of the developing countries has been the Group of 24 (G-24)—a group of Ministers from developing nations. In 1979, the G-24 approved the following outline for a program of action on monetary reform.

TOWARD A FUNDAMENTAL INTERNATIONAL MONETARY REFORM*

1. It will be apparent from the foregoing considerations that the basic tasks of international monetary reform have yet to be accomplished. Developing and developed countries alike have a common interest in a viable international monetary system. Such a system should foster development, employment, and trade, and, in particular, support the development of developing countries in the overall context of the establishment of the New International Economic Order [based on a plan endorsed by the UN General Assembly in May 1974].

2. The principal features of a viable system should include:

(a) An effective, symmetrical, and equitable adjustment process that would be consistent with the maintenance of high levels of employment and rates of growth and the dynamic expansion of world trade. This would require access to official credit facilities on terms and conditions responsive to the nature of balance of payments problems, as well as to the level of development of the countries concerned. It would also require the maintenance of free and secure access for developing countries to the goods and financial markets of developed nations.

(b) An exchange rate regime which, while flexible, is capable of promoting adequate stability.

(c) In exercising its surveillance over exchange rate and balance of payments policies, the IMF should give equitable and symmetrical treatment to surplus and deficit countries with a view to ensuring that surplus developed countries and reserve currency countries accept an equitable share of the burden of adjustment at high levels of economic growth.

(d) Arrangements should be made for the creation of international liquidity through truly collective international action in line with the requirements of an expanding world economy, and the special needs of developing countries, and with such safeguards as would ensure that the total supply and distribution of international liquidity is not unduly influenced by the balance of payments position of any country or group of countries. The SDR should become the principal reserve asset of the system.

*Text of an Outline for a Program of Action on International Monetary Reform prepared by the Group of 24, Belgrade, Sept. 29, 1979, reprinted in *IMF Survey* (October 15, 1979), pp. 321–323.

THE PROGRAM OF IMMEDIATE ACTION

The developing countries require the formulation of a program of action with specific items in which solutions may be found within the framework of a general program of reform. The Ministers of the Group of 77 at the meeting in Arusha, Tanzania, decided upon a substantial number of proposals. These give a sense of direction to our efforts to achieve a New International Economic Order.

The Group of 24 has reassessed and elaborated upon these proposals within the context of the reform of the international monetary and financial system, and considers that the following should be given priority for immediate action.

A. MEASURES RELATED TO THE TRANSFER OF REAL RESOURCES

1. There is an urgent need to accelerate the flow of concessional aid to developing countries. Each developed donor country, particularly those falling behind in meeting the internationally agreed target, should establish its program and make binding commitments for the annual growth rate of ODA disbursement for each of the next three years. This should result in a general increase in real terms and an improvement in the quality of ODA flows to the developing countries; in the context of this general increase, the quantum in real terms of ODA flows to least developed countries, most seriously affected countries, and landlocked and island developing countries should double.

2. The Group of 24 urges the early establishment of a link between SDR allocation and additional development assistance. The creation of such a link is long overdue and a positive decision to establish it should be arrived at without further delay.

3. The Group of 24 calls for an increase in program lending of the multilateral financial institutions to make it equal to at least 25 per cent of total loans, and stresses in this context that the lending programs of the multilateral financial institutions should become increasingly responsive to the overall priorities, and in particular to sectoral priorities, of the recipient developing countries. It also calls for the provision of adequate local cost financing.

4. There is a need for an effective strategy to deal with the official external indebtedness of some developing countries, designed to avert debt servicing difficulties and sustain the development process of these countries. The Group urges early conclusion of the negotiations regarding internationally agreed guidelines for debt reorganization of interested developing countries, in the light of the general principles adopted in UNCTAD Resolution 165 (S-IX).

The Group also stresses the need for immediate and full implementation of Part A of the same resolution regarding the retroactive adjustment of terms on past ODA in favor of the low-income countries, particularly of the least developed and most seriously affected countries.

5. The Sixth Replenishment of IDA [International Development Association] should be effected without delay so as to result in a significant increase in real terms. The contributions to IDA should come from a wider group of countries, provided that the additional contributions from new donors do not prejudice the increase in real terms of the contributions of the traditional donors.

6. All member countries should provide a substantial and effective increase in the capital base of the multilateral financial institutions so as to ensure that their commitments in favor of developing countries increase in real terms at a satisfactory rate consistent with the needs of these countries. In this connection, the Group of 24 urges early approval and acceptance by all member countries of the capital increase of the World Bank of the equivalent of $40 billion and the prompt payment of subscriptions when due.

B. MEASURES RELATED TO THE INCREASE IN TOTAL RESOURCES

7. Taking into account the long-term global liquidity needs, the Group supports:

(a) an increase in the present agreed SDR allocations to meet the current difficult economic conditions;

(b) regular annual allocations of SDRs, in amounts adequate to members' needs for reserve increases.

8. The Group urges early completion of legislative action by the member countries concerned, to make effective the Seventh General Review of Quotas. It also urges the revision of the criteria, both in terms of the variables used and the weights attached to them, for determining the quotas of the membership in the International Monetary Fund, and the advancement of the date for the Eighth General Review of Quotas. In this review, the quota share of no developing country should be reduced. Due regard should be paid to increasing the representation of developing countries in the Executive Boards of both the Fund and the World Bank. In any event, the present geographical representation by developing country regions should be preserved.

C. MEASURES RELATED TO BALANCE OF PAYMENTS SUPPORT

9. The Group of 24 attaches importance to the establishment of a medium-term balance of payments facility to respond to the adjustment needs of the developing countries. The new balance of payments financing facility should add a substantial level of additional resources and must be able to provide support that is significant in relation to present levels of deficits, should carry minimum conditionality, since it is responding to an externally induced balance of payments deficit, and should provide support on longer-term maturity. This facility should have as one of its basic characteristics an interest subsidy account for the low-income developing countries.

10. The existing IMF facilities should be reviewed to enable them to cope more adequately with the deteriorating world economic environment.

In particular, it is necessary to consider:

(**a**) lengthening repayment periods;

(**b**) modifying the quantitative restrictions on the availability of such facilities;

(**c**) setting conditionality with due regard to causes of deficits;

(**d**) reviewing the Fund's compensatory financing facility, including a significant increase and the liberalization of access in order to compensate adequately for shortfalls in export earnings, import fluctuations, and deterioration in the terms of trade of development countries.

At the South-North Conference on the International Monetary System and the New International Order, held in Tanzania in 1980, the "Arusha Initiative" was issued as a call for a new monetary system to be negotiated by the entire community of nations.

THE ARUSHA INITIATIVE*

The post-1945 international monetary system has broken down. The ensuing inflationary and speculative disorders inflict serious damage on the majority of peoples and countries. It is imperative to conceive and negotiate new monetary structures and procedures. The international community has given little attention up to now to this major component of a new international order. This

**Development Dialogue* (1980:2), pp. 11–12, 17–21.

ARUSHA INITIATIVE is a contribution to the development of the necessary debate and action.

MUTUAL INTEREST IN ENDING MONETARY DISARRAY

There is today a common interest, shared alike by the countries of the OECD, Eastern Europe and the Third World, to articulate a new monetary system that would reflect the employment and development needs of people living in different material conditions, social systems and cultural environments. Inflation, protectionist tendencies, competitive deflationary policies, unstable exchange markets, unregulated Eurocurrency transactions, recurrent and growing balance of payments disequilibria, and the "conditionality" of the International Monetary Fund are problems which affect us all, though in different ways. If there is an area in which interdependence has almost immediate effect, it is that of money and finance.

The present monetary disarray does no credit to human rationality and ingenuity. Inaction is increasingly costly and dangerous. Policy initiatives for a new monetary order and public debate on them are needed now. The necessary political decisions must be taken urgently by governments acting in a collective and democratic manner.

THE COLLAPSE OF THE BRETTON WOODS SYSTEM

Money is power. This simple truth is valid for national and international relations. Those who wield power control money. Those who manage and control money wield power. An international monetary system is both a function and an instrument of prevailing power structures.

The monetary system devised at Bretton Woods in 1944 reflected the historical conditions of the time, particularly the domination of the United States of America within the capitalist world and the persistence of colonial empires. The Third World as we know it today did not exist then. Moreover, the Union of Soviet Socialist Republics and other socialist countries refrained or withdrew from participation in the system, which thus came to lack universality. The monetary results of such a structural situation were inevitable: the United States dollar became the *de facto* international currency and the policy prescriptions on international monetary and financial affairs were designed to provide a stable basis for economic relations within the capitalist world. The International Monetary Fund is the institutional expression of these aims and conditions.

The world has been dramatically transformed since the Bretton Woods conference, while the formal monetary framework and the values it expresses remain unchanged. Third World countries have insistently questioned the adequacy and legitimacy of monetary rules and mechanisms in whose design the majority of them did not participate.

A UNITED NATIONS CONFERENCE ON INTERNATIONAL MONEY AND FINANCE

The experience of world development has demonstrated with increasing force that it is impossible to implement a genuine international development strategy without fundamental restructuring of the international monetary system. It is imperative that a new monetary system be constructed with the agreement of the international community. If this is not done, the current non-system will continue to evolve through the *ad hoc* arrangements made in their own interests by a few industrialized countries and the transnational corporations and banks under the constant threat of an international financial catastrophe.

We therefore call for a United Nations Conference on International Money and Finance. This will provide a universal, democratic and legitimate forum for the negotiation of a new monetary system—one, moreover, which can be open to public scrutiny. We also urge that the drafting of a charter for a new system should start now and we call upon the extragovernmental community ("third system") to take the lead in this endeavor, so as to show the way to governments.

CHARACTERISTICS OF A NEW INTERNATIONAL MONETARY SYSTEM

A new international monetary order must serve two fundamental objectives. First, it must be capable of achieving monetary stability, restoring acceptable levels of employment and sustainable growth, and checking the present strong inflationary and stagflationary policies and tendencies in the world economy. Second, it must be supportive of a process of global development, especially for the countries of the Third World, which contain the majority of the world's poor.

The main attributes of a new monetary system must be:

(a) *Democratic management and control.* While it may be inevitable that significant influence will be wielded by economically powerful countries, the interests of the majority of the world must be clearly reflected.

(b) *Universality.* As trade and payments have become increasingly internationalized, global interdependence demands that all countries should participate in the institutional arrangements for international monetary management.

(c) *The establishment of an international currency unit* as the international means of exchange and primary reserve asset. The world cannot continue to afford a situation where one country imposes its own currency to play this role, and uncontrolled international money creation and transnational speculative movements are allowed to occur.

(d) A certain degree of *automaticity in transfers of resources* through reserve asset creation by the international community.

A new international monetary authority would need to be established to manage the monetary system. Universal and democratic, it would be capable of accommodating the needs of different development patterns and economic and social systems. Such an authority would have to control the supply of international money and be capable of redistributing national payment surpluses and existing exchange reserves. To prevent manipulation, firm rules and adequate mechanisms governing the creation and distribution of the international currency would be required. The existence of an international currency unit must serve to reintroduce in the international payments system the principle of asset settlement, the abandonment of which in the late 1960s was both a symptom of past contradictions and a cause of further disorder. Observance of this principle would imply convertibility of national currencies into the international currency unit. However, provision would have to be made by international agreement for the limitation and suspension of convertibility to meet special circumstances, such as those of some Third World countries and socialist countries.

Urgent Transitional Measures

As the process of building a new international monetary order will undoubtedly be long and difficult, there are a number of urgent steps which must be taken in the meantime to deal with the immediate problems, while supporting the transition to a fundamentally new system. Most of these short-term steps have to be taken within the framework of the IMF.

First, the IMF should be equipped and prepared to finance those deficits which are the natural consequence of serious and disciplined efforts at development and structural change. The conditionality of such financing must reflect the sovereign right of states to choose their own social and economic models and development paths. In particular, there must be no penalization of countries which opt for strategies which emphasize national planning, systems of administrative budgeting (of foreign exchange, imports, investment and credit), the reform of traditional institutions, and an active role for the public sector. Rather, assistance needs to be provided to help these countries to overcome the difficulties and obstacles which such a development model necessarily encounters, and to help improve the efficiency of their planning, economic management and allocation of resources. In this context, the use of quarterly performance tests, based on a small number of narrowly defined monetary variables, is highly inappropriate to the conditions of a Third World country.

Secondly, Third World countries' access to the higher credit tranches of the IMF must be guided by an unambiguous recognition that a large part of the deficits they now experience is attributable to factors for which they are in no way responsible. These include high international inflation, weak and fluctuating export prices, low demand for their exports, deterioration of their terms of trade and high interest rates: all symptoms of the present international monetary disorder and more generally of an unjust international system. Financing such deficits by the IMF must be much more flexible and automatic; it must not be guided by present conditionality criteria.

To this end, the Compensatory Financing Facility should be expanded and a new low-conditionality facility established to deal with external shock deficits (like the former Oil Facility). Access to these facilities should be related to the size of externally caused deficits, not tied to quotas. Repayment should be related to recovery of the balance of payments from export deterioration or external shocks, instead of being tied to arbitrary time periods.

Next, further decisions need to be taken to make the Special Drawing Rights the principal reserve asset in international payments and to ensure that the role of national currencies in international settlements is effectively reduced. For that purpose, the SDR should be made more attractive. The allocation of SDRs and proceeds from sales of IMF gold should be made according to criteria separate from the IMF quota structure and should be based on relative need, economic vulnerability and development deficits.

Finally, there is an urgent need for the establishment of a mechanism of appeal and international arbitration, independent of the Fund, to deal with cases of dispute between the Fund and member countries applying for the use of Fund resources. The enormous power wielded by the staff and management of the Fund in negotiations with these countries provides the justification for a mechanism which would ensure the equitable resolution of such disputes.

A leading spokesman for developing countries has also outlined a number of reforms for a new world monetary order:[20]

Overall, the global monetary system is in such bad shape at present that an entirely fresh start may have to be made. No marginal improvisations will suffice in the 1980s. The new premises on which the monetary order should be rebuilt are implied by the foregoing analysis and are worth recapitulating.

National reserve currencies must be phased out of the international payments system and replaced by an international currency (modified Special Drawing Rights), to be created and managed by international jurisdiction.

The creation of international currency should be guided by the real increase in world output and exports so as not to generate inflationary pressures.

The distribution of this international currency should be based on present as well as potential balance-of-payments needs, including a link between international currency and development assistance.

The IMF, or a wholly new institution, should be gradually evolved to perform the role of an International Central Bank (ICB).

For this purpose, the ICB should include all nations (socialist bloc as well) and its management and control should be genuinely international.

The ICB should be empowered to put as much pressure on deficit countries to adjust their balance of payments as on surplus countries, so that the present asymmetry of treatment is removed.

The ICB should also act as the lender of last resort, to refinance short-term debts, provide a "safety net" against unforeseen liquidity crises, and play a decisive role in recycling financial surpluses in collaboration with the private capital market.

These are not minor reforms; this is drastic surgery. The new monetary order can emerge step by step once an overall framework has been accepted. Major economic powers will find this degree of

20 Mahbub ul Haq, "Negotiating the Future," *Foreign Affairs* (Winter 1980), pp. 410–411. Excerpted by permission of *Foreign Affairs,* Winter 1980/81. Copyright 1980 by the Council on Foreign Relations, Inc.

> international discipline irksome to begin with, but they will gain a great deal in the long run from rules which are accepted by all nations. The developing countries, of course, would reap enormous benefits from these reforms. Lord Keynes' vision in the 1940s would finally have been adapted to current realities—after 40 years of drift and indifferent experimentation.

Finally, the widely heralded report by the Brandt Commission on North-South relations argued for a reform of the international monetary order and for a number of changes in the way in which the Fund operates. The Brandt Commission believes that reform is urgent and must encompass the exchange-rate regime, the reserve system, and the adjustment mechanism as it affects countries issuing reserve currencies and countries in payments surplus and deficit. The report argues that any serious reform must aim at greater stability of international currencies. This can only be achieved if the reserve system and adjustment mechanism are reformed simultaneously. The present reserve system is considered unsatisfactory because the expansion of world liquidity is erratic in both its volume and distribution. The report also suggests that the bulk of the Fund's holdings of gold could be used as collateral for IMF borrowings from financial markets that would be lent primarily to middle-income developing countries. Another part could be sold and the profits used to subsidize interest rates on loans to low-income developing countries. The SDR should become the principal means of increasing global liquidity and the system of allocating SDRs should be changed in order to provide liquidity to the countries that need it most. A reformed international monetary system must also ensure that both surplus and deficit countries have the obligation to adjust. The report concludes that the new international monetary system should have a pluralistic basis, offering a broadly based collective leadership, in which developing countries can play a growing role.

8. INTERNATIONAL CAPITAL MOVEMENTS

With the growth of the Eurocurrency market, there has been an intensifying debate over regulating the Eurocurrency markets. Some views follow.

THE REGULATION OF INTERNATIONAL CAPITAL MARKETS*

With the establishment of external convertibility of their currencies by 10 European countries at the end of 1958, the door was opened for the expansion of the international money or capital market which up to then had, for all practical purposes, been centered in the United States. A major element in that expansion was the emergence of the Euro-currency market. . . .

The Euro-currency segment of the international capital market grew rapidly. At the end of 10 years it had acquired resources of about $40 billion. By the end of 1979, its net size (eliminating duplication) was almost $700 billion, denominated in various currencies but with the U.S. dollar comprising roughly 70 percent of the total. It is generally short-term but maturities of credits range upwards to 10 years or more. In 1979, new Euro-currency bank credits to governments and state enterprises averaged almost nine years.

Alongside of the Euro-currency market is the international bond market which handles bonds issued in national markets for non-national borrowers (*e.g.*, foreign bonds issued in the United States), and Euro-bonds floated by international syndicates of commerical banks and investment banks in the Euro-bond market. The bonds are denominated chiefly in U.S. dollars, but there are issues in deutsche marks, French francs, sterling, European units of account, Kuwaiti dinars, etc.

The Euro-currency market has over the years become the subject of extensive analysis and policy scrutiny. It is a volatile market which can and does shift funds from one currency to another on a relatively large scale as does also the much smaller Euro-bond market. This means that Euro-currency transactions affect the exchange rates of major currencies and can reflect speculation rather than market responses to fundamental forces. The market has been characterized as a nonstop liquidity machine which can countermand efforts of central bankers to control their own money stocks. It has also been argued that the huge resources of the market, while enabling it to carry out an indispensable recycling of "petrodollars" in the aftermath of increases in oil prices since 1974, has tempted Euro-bankers into unduly liberal international lending, especially to less-developed countries.

*Atlantic Council, *The International Monetary System in Transition* (May 1980), pp. 34–39.

Those considerations have prompted a renewed review of the pros and cons of bringing the Euro-currency market under more effective regulation by the monetary authorities of the leading countries.

The first question is whether the market has been a source of major speculative assaults on exchange rates, hence contributing to instability and to movements which have not reflected basic or underlying factors.

The Euro-currency market does transmit very large flows of funds from one currency to another. Moreover, although dollars are the principal component of the market, the percentage of dollars in the total has varied—three-quarters in 1973 and 1975, 70 percent in 1977, and two-thirds in 1978. But Governor Wallich's conclusion is persuasive. "The existence of the Euro-currency market as a liquid and efficient mechanism for international dealing has certainly had an important influence on exchange-rate developments in recent years. It would be wrong, however, to view the market itself as having given rise to new stabilizing or destabilizing forces. Rather, it has acted as a conduit and amplifier through which both stabilizing and destabilizing financial flows have been felt in exchange markets with greater speed and intensity." Holders of Euro-dollar deposits can and do shift them into other currencies, if in their judgment the prospect for the dollar is discouraging or back into Euro-dollars if it is encouraging, with consequent downward and upward impact on dollar exchange rates. The B.I.S. concludes that ". . . it is difficult to deny that in the absence of the Euro-currency market dollar borrowing for the financing of hedging or speculative operations in the spot exchange markets would have been somewhat more difficult." But in that event, there would have been (as, indeed, there are today paralleling the Euro-market) ample alternative ways for flows of funds from one currency to another to affect exchange rates.

On balance there is not a strong case for regulating the Euro-currency market as a means of dealing effectively with periodic pressures on exchange rates.

A second argument offered in support of regulating the Euro-market is that it has led to imprudently large international lending, especially to less-developed countries. With the onset of much higher petroleum prices in 1974, the payments position of the less-developed countries worsened dramatically—from a current-account deficit of $11 billion in 1973 to one of $30 billion in 1974. In consequence, they turned to the international money market—and especially to Euro-banks—for financing of their deficits. Large deficits continued, and the total external debt of those countries is now around 30 percent of their gross domestic product, and service charges equal more than 12 percent of their earnings on exports of goods and services. Moreover, with the increase in oil prices in 1979, the current-account deficits of the non-oil LDCs increased from $36 billion in 1978 to an estimated $52 billion in 1979 and, as earlier indicated, may range from $73 to $80 billion in 1980.

Commercial banks (chiefly Euro-banks) have been heavily involved in the financing of those huge deficits. Commercial bank credits amount to some 30 percent of the government and government-guaranteed long-term external debt of non-oil LDCs. Bank credits to the 11 largest borrowing countries increased from $22 billion in 1972 to $126 billion in 1979—12 and 19 percent of gross domestic product, respectively. Over the period, however, they increased their reserves by more than $25 billion.

The issues are whether the Euro-currency market has been imprudently liberal in extending credit, and whether in that event its operations should be brought under regulation by the monetary authorities. Recycling of "petro-dollars" has been essential, and the Euro-banks did that job smoothly and on a large scale. During 1977–78 the plethora of funds available to Euro-banks and the resulting competition probably brought lending rates for some countries unduly close to the London Interbank Offer Rate (LIBOR) and encouraged countries to borrow; and there were undoubtedly instances where banks were slow to cut down lending to countries whose growing external debt burden was exacerbating a worsening payments position.

The commercial banks operating in the Euro-market have become alert to the weakening payments position of the less-developed countries taken as a whole, and it is unlikely that they will finance the very large deficits in the next few years on a scale comparable to that of recent years. Indeed, this caution may in 1980, as earlier indicated, create financing problems for those countries. They will be pushed into greater reliance on public sources of financing, especially the IMF. Moreover, that will increasingly involve the conditional area of IMF resources and will put emphasis on efforts by the developing countries to strengthen their efforts to deal with their payments deficits.

A third issue is whether the international capital market has an impact on world liquidity and hence on domestic money markets which would justify attempting to bring it under more effective regulation by the monetary authorities.

To repeat figures cited above, the gross size of the Euro-currency market was approximately $900 billion at the end of 1979. But after deducting inter-bank liabilities and liabilities to banks and central banks outside the reporting area, it is estimated that the net monetary liabilities to non-bankers may amount to $200 billion, of which possibly one-third is counted in the monetary liabilities of some country. There thus remains possibly $130 billion of what can be called "stateless money" which needs to be taken into account in formulating and executing domestic monetary policy. The Federal Reserve measures introduced on October 6, 1979 included an 8 percent marginal reserve requirement on increases in an aggregate of managed liabilities, above a base amount for each bank. Increases in those liabilities (including net Euro-dollar borrowing) have been an important basis for recent increases in bank credit in the U.S. Also some $40 billion of Euro-dollars are included in the newly-defined U.S. monetary aggregates which brings them within the purview of the monetary authorities.

Most central banks have discriminated in favor of foreign-currency banking—lower reserve requirements and fewer quantitative restrictions. Moreover, in some jurisdictions (Luxembourg, Bahamas, Cayman Islands, Bahrain, Singapore) bank branches and subsidiaries have greater freedom of action than in the countries where the head offices are located. It would be an advantage to have roughly comparable regulatory environments for international and domestic banking activities. It is, of course, evident that for the United States to proceed alone would provoke the shifting of credit operations to banks operating under less restrictive jurisdictions. Indeed, this may to some extent be the result of the reserve requirement mentioned above.

Agreement has by no means been reached among the monetary authorities of the leading countries. Bank of England Governor Richardson concluded that central banks should be responsible for supervising the lending activities of banks of their own nationality, wherever the lending is conducted, using, for this purpose, consolidated accounts for each bank on a world-wide basis. That position, of course, evades the issue of uniform international regulation.

The conclusion reached in a recent study can be accepted: "The Euro-currency market acts . . . primarily as an international transmission mechanism and it is hardly conceivable that, on its own, it could exert major inflationary pressures on a global scale. This is not to deny that, by providing escape routes, the market may tend to blunt the effectiveness of certain domestic monetary policy instruments and that its contribution to international capital mobility may at times exacerbate conflicts between external and domestic requirements." This means that bringing the market under more uniform and effective regulation by the monetary authorities of the countries whose banks are active in that market would not make a major contribution to improving the international monetary system or reducing inflation. As long as wide economic and financial divergences and payments imbalances persist, funds will flow from weak to strong currencies. But the U.S. monetary authorities are justified in continuing their efforts to reach agreement with other leading countries to establish less diverse regulatory rules to be applied to the banks operating in the Euro-currency market. As a minimum, agreement should be sought to apply the same requirements to foreign branches as to home offices. It will not be easy to reach agreement. Some countries do not impose reserve requirements on the domestic operations of their banks, and other jurisdictions, eager to encourage off-shore banking, will undoubtedly be reluctant to impose any regulations which might curb it. Moreover, borrowing countries, especially non-oil developing countries, will not be happy to see any threat to the availability of credit in the Euromarket.

9. EUROPEAN MONETARY SYSTEM

A major innovation in the world monetary system, with implications for international monetary reform, has been the formation of the European Monetary System (EMS). Proponents of the EMS hope that from this form of regional monetary cooperation may emerge a European federation and an arrangement for worldwide monetary cooperation. As Professor Triffin states, "I am convinced that the success of the EMS experiment toward its basic objectives, and of the indispensable cooperation between the EMS and U.S. authorities, might at long last break the deadlock which has paralyzed, since Jamaica, the previous determination to restore a workable world monetary order. I hope I am not entirely a 'loner' and a dreamer in feeling that floating rates and the Second Amendment to the IMF Articles of Agreement should not relegate to the garbage can all the previous proposals for IMF reform, ironed out over ten years of continuous, intensive negotiations. . . . The revolutionary developments of recent years certainly require modification of previous proposals for reform, but to enlarge them—particularly to deal with the fantastic explosion of private international credits—rather than to emasculate them."[21]

The background to the EMS was the European Economic Community "snake" launched in 1972 with its aim of keeping all EEC currencies within ±2.25% of a central rate between each pair—and, originally, each within ±2.25% of a rate against the dollar, the so-called "snake in the tunnel." Rising inflation, the floating of the dollar, and the oil crisis dealt successive blows to the snake, and grand plans for an eventual European Monetary Union had to be abandoned. But an inner bloc of countries—Germany, Belgium, Holland, Luxembourg, and Denmark—carried on inside the snake. Finally, in 1979, the wider EMS was adopted by nine members of the EEC.

The central objective of the EMS is to reduce currency instability among the EEC countries—to create a community exchange-rate regime that will provide a "zone of monetary stability" in Europe. Rather than prolonging the snake, the French insisted that a new European currency unit must be at the center of the system. The acronym of European Currency Unit spells the name of an old French coin, the *écu*. The écu is used as the denominator (*numéraire*) for the exchange-rate mechanism; as the basis for the calculation of the "divergence indicator"; as the denominator for operations under both the intervention and credit mechanisms and for transactions of the European Monetary Cooperation Fund; and as a means of settlement between monetary authorities of the member countries. At the outset the value of the écu was taken equal to the European Unit of Account, which consists of a basket of fixed amounts of the nine currencies of the European Community's members. The weights of the écu can be re-examined periodically.

Each currency participating in the EMS has a central rate in terms of écus. These central rates determine a parity grid of bilateral central rates, around which margins of ±2.25% have been established. Changes in central rates are to be made by "mutual

21 Robert Triffin, "The Future of the International Monetary System," *Banca Nazionale del Lavoro Quarterly Review* (March 1980), pp. 45–46.

agreement." This grid of bilateral central rates and the agreed margins of fluctuation set the limits at which exchange-market intervention is obligatory. With changes in the central rates (the "peg"), the system resembles a "crawling peg" arrangement for altering exchange rates.

In addition to the grid of central rates, there is a "divergence indicator" that serves as an early warning device, signaling when the exchange rate of a currency vis-à-vis the écu reaches a certain figure. A formula determines when a currency crosses its "divergence threshold." Once this occurs, there is a presumption that the authorities will take some policy action. Such action may include market interventions, measures of domestic monetary policy and other economic policies, or changes in its central rates vis-à-vis the écu.

Besides the implementation of an exchange-rate arrangement, the EMS has other functions: the granting of monetary credits on a vastly increased scale; the issue of a new reserve asset, and the pooling by members of part of their monetary reserves. In these basic functions, the EMS is similar to an IMF on a regional basis.

A European Monetary Cooperation Fund has also been created to provide a "very short term facility" for the financing of interventions by central banks in EMS participants' currencies. Countries are also issued écus by the European Fund in return for a deposit with the Fund of 20 per cent of their gold holdings and 20 per cent of their gross reserves in U.S. dollars. This has made gold usable again as a reserve asset. The transactions with the Fund take the form of revolving three-month swaps that are used for settling debts among the members' central banks.

Prospects for the EMS depend on many factors—from whether Britain eventually joins, to whether differential rates of inflation will force frequent currency realignments, to the exchange-rate stability between the dollar and the écu. Especially significant will be future political developments, since European integration is a political undertaking. At a fundamental level, the future depends on whether supranational objectives can be attained without the transfer of sovereign powers to European Community institutions—a transfer in the budgetary and monetary fields that has not yet been effected, even though the Community professes a desire to form eventually an Economic and Monetary Union. Some envisage the European Monetary Fund becoming transformed into the Federal Reserve

System of a full-fledged Monetary Union. Some envisage the écu becoming a fully fledged currency, circulating outside the confines of central banks and becoming a single currency for Europe. Still others regard the EMS as a step toward a system of currency blocs, particularly between those based on a European currency and the dollar, with fixed rates within the bloc and fluctuating rates between the blocs. Or, reminiscent of the attempt in the 1930s to reach a tripartite monetary agreement among key currencies, some envisage a new triparite monetary agreement involving a European Monetary Union, the United States, and Japan.

10. INTO THE 1980s

At the start of the 1980s, many of the persistent issues of international monetary reform continued to plague the IMF, finance ministers, and monetary authorities. At the 35th annual meeting of the IMF in 1980, there was general concern about the Fund being able to play a larger role in the adjustment and financing of prospective payments imbalances. To meet members' needs for resources, the Interim Committee urged that arrangements be made, as soon as possible, for Fund borrowing from various potential sources of financing, "not excluding a possible recourse to the private markets if this were indispensable." But it was still stressed that the Fund should place primary reliance on subscriptions under members' quotas as the source of financing of its operations.

The Interim Committee also supported the decision to unify and to simplify, as of January 1981, the currency baskets that determine the value of and the interest rate on the SDR. The unified basket is now composed of the currencies of the five members having the largest volume of trade: U.S. dollar, deutsche mark, French franc, Japanese yen, and pound sterling.

There follow different views on some of the major issues—by the G-10, the G-24, and the Managing Director of the IMF.

GROUP OF 10 COMMUNIQUE*

The Ministers and Governors noted with concern that the outlook for the world economy has not improved since their last meet-

*IMF Survey, (October 13, 1980), p. 301.

ing in April. The world economy continues to be faced with a high level of inflation, sluggish growth of output, an unstable energy market, and large payments imbalances. They emphasized that these problems call for close co-operation between all members of the international community.

The Ministers and Governors continue to attach great importance to the fight against inflation and to the implementation of effective energy saving policies and oil substitution programs. While the recent slowdown in major industrial countries' rates of inflation is an encouraging development, they consider that at the present time there is little scope for a relaxation of monetary, budgetary and other policies. They also stressed the need to supplement the instruments of demand management with structural policies designed to improve supply conditions. They re-emphasized the importance of avoiding protectionist measures at a time of slow growth of world trade and widening balance of payments disequilibria.

The Ministers and Governors expressed particular concern about the sharp deterioration in the current account balances of many countries. While recognizing that the international banking system and surplus countries will have to play a major role in recycling, they reaffirmed their position that it is desirable for the IMF to assume an enlarged role in the financing and adjustment of payments imbalances. They welcomed the preparatory work accomplished in this context.

In that connection, the Ministers and Governors recognized the need for a larger volume of lending by the Fund and for longer adjustment periods. At the same time, they stressed that the basic character of Fund lending policies that are called for in the present circumstances should be kept under review. The Ministers and Governors also emphasized the importance of a closer cooperation between the Fund and the World Bank which, however, should not alter the respective character of the two institutions.

As regards the financing of enlarged access to the Fund's resources, the Ministers and Governors emphasized that primary reliance should be placed on Fund quotas. At the same time they recognized that in the present situation increased recourse to borrowing is likely to prove necessary. In seeking additional resources the Fund should endeavor to find lenders and to obtain terms which take into account both the special nature of the institution and the needs of the borrowing countries.

The Ministers and Governors agreed that the possibility of further allocations of SDRs should be further considered.

GROUP OF 24 COMMUNIQUE*

The Ministers of the Group of 24 on International Monetary Affairs held their twenty-first meeting in Washington, D.C., on September 27, 1980. The Ministers discussed the international economic situation and the adverse implications for developing countries of the further deceleration in the growth rate of industrial countries, persistence of high inflationary pressures, and the continuing underutilization of resources. They noted with grave concern the widening of the deficits on current account of non-oil developing countries from $56 billion in 1979 to $76 billion in 1980. The prospects for 1981 indicate a further deterioration to $80 billion. The main factors accounting for this deterioration are worsening terms of trade, the weak growth in exports to developed countries induced by slow growth rates, the rising wave of trade protectionism in industrial countries, and higher nominal interest rates. The financing of these deficits is becoming increasingly difficult because of inadequate flows of real resources, particularly those on concessional terms, and increasing resort to financial protectionism by industrial countries. All these will lead to further deterioration in the import capacity and growth prospects of non-oil developing countries, and further aggravate the debt service situation of several developing countries.

The Ministers welcomed the Fund's recognition that the size and structural nature of the imbalances necessitate the provision of larger resources over longer periods than in the past. They were of the view that the bulk of the deficits are exogenously induced and are not amenable to traditional adjustment measures. They urged that adjustment policies should be borne equitably by both developed and developing countries. They reiterated that the developed countries should not shift the burden of their adjustment to developing countries through measures such as reduction of their aid flows and increases in trade and financial barriers.

The Ministers stressed that, particularly in the low-income developing countries, the scope for adjustment without causing severe damage to their already low rates of growth is very limited, and that the mix of financing and adjustment should take into account the special circumstances of individual countries.

Ministers recognized the need for the Fund to increase its resources. They were of the view that the increase should be through

***IMF Survey* (October 13, 1980), pp. 299–302.*

substantial increases in quotas. In this connection they urged the early implementation of the Seventh General Review and advance consideration of the Eighth General Review of Quotas. They observed that the size of quotas in relation to the volume of imports and financing needs has shrunk over the years and urged that this erosion in the relative size of quotas be reversed. Pending such developments Ministers can support the Fund's proposal to supplement its resources through borrowing and urge that the resulting additional resources should be lent with low conditionality.

Ministers noted that most developing countries were facing severe external imbalances. They stressed the need to modify Fund policies to allow this institution to play a greater role than presently in the financing of these imbalances. Furthermore, the Ministers reiterated their support for an expansion to 50 per cent of quota of the first credit tranche to help meet the present situation, and also extended support to the proposed policy of increasing access to IMF funds as presented by the Executive Board.

The Ministers reaffirmed their view that in the present difficult situation additional balance of payments support should be provided with the minimum of conditionality. In this context they emphasized the importance of the establishment of a medium-term balance of payments facility as stated in the Program of Immediate Action of the Group of 24, which would carry minimum conditionality and provide support that is significant in relation to present levels of deficits. The facility should have as one of its basic characteristics an interest subsidy account for low-income developing countries.

Ministers welcomed the initiative of the Fund's management in responding to the request by the Food and Agriculture Organization and the World Food Council for additional financial assistance to low-income food deficit countries with weak balances of payments, when such countries are adversely affected by a crop failure or an increase in the world price of essential food items, especially cereals. They expressed support for an appropriate financing mechanism for this type of assistance by the Fund.

Ministers expressed concern at the proposal to wind up the Trust Fund and to use part of its resources to finance the proposed Subsidy Account aimed at lowering the cost of use of the supplementary financing facility by low-income developing countries. They reiterated their call for the continuation of the Trust Fund and augmentation of its resources. They stressed that the establishment of the Subsidy Account should not lead to the liquidation of the Trust

Fund. They reemphasized that all the resources of the Trust Fund should be used exclusively for the benefit of the low-income developing countries, and should not be linked to drawings under the supplementary financing facility. They observed that the Subsidy Account which the Group of 24 asked for is different from the one now being proposed by the Fund, in that it lacks the essential characteristic of additionality of resources. Any Subsidy Account that is established should lead to additionality of resources to low-income developing countries. It should be financed through voluntary contributions and, if necessary, by other appropriate means.

Ministers noted that decision making in the Fund is determined primarily by the member's voting power, which in turn is derived from the size of the member's quota. In this context, they called for an increase in the share of developing countries in total quotas from approximately 33 per cent to 45 per cent, which will also lead to increasing their weight in the decision-making process. They therefore called for a thorough review of the formula for determining members' quotas and for advancement of work on the Eighth General Review of Quotas. In order to help make the IMF more appreciative of the problems of developing countries, Ministers stressed the need for early recruitment by the Fund of a larger number of middle- and senior-level officials from those countries.

The Ministers welcomed the Fund staff papers on SDR allocations, and they were of the view that unexpected major developments in the world economic situation as contemplated in Article XVIII have taken place since the decision on allocation for the current basic period was taken, and therefore called for a supplementary allocation of SDR 6 billion for the remainder of the present basic period. They also called for allocations of at least SDR 10 billion annually over a five-year period beginning in January 1982. Such allocations, they observed, were justified by the growth in the value of international trade, the increased demand for reserves generated by the current and prospective large external payments imbalances, and the need to make the SDR the principal reserve asset in the system. They further stressed that the role of the SDR as the principal reserve asset in the system could be improved by elimination of the reconstitution requirement, substantially increasing allocations, and an improvement in its characteristics and attractiveness. In this regard, the Ministers noted the decision to make the SDR valuation and interest rate baskets identical.

Ministers observed that the Executive Board had held exploratory discussions on the link between SDR allocations and additional development finance. They noted that the link would provide a means of giving substance to the general agreement on the desirability of promoting the flow of real resources to developing countries and would facilitate the recycling process. It would also correct the maldistribution of international liquidity. They therefore urged the early establishment of the link, which should be direct. They also felt that the link should not be tied to the use of Fund resources.

Ministers noted that the recent liberalizations of the compensatory financial facility have increased the amount of purchases a member can make. However, they requested the IMF to consider further liberalization, including full compensation of the shortfall and longer repayment terms in certain circumstances, taking into account deteriorations in the terms of trade and tying repayments to increases in real exports, and to keep under constant review developments in the area of the stabilization of export earnings, with a view to further improving the benefits to members drawing under the compensatory financing facility. Ministers also urged all concerned to make every effort to bring about the early establishment of a global stabilization scheme on export earnings of developing countries.

Ministers noted that nonconcessional capital flows from the private capital markets and financial institutions are already inadequate to meet the needs of developing countries in 1980, and that the prospects for 1981 and beyond are even more uncertain. They therefore urged the capital market countries to enhance developing countries' access to their markets. They stressed the need to keep these capital markets free from interference and restrictions, by confining regulation to concerns which were truly prudential in nature. This would strengthen the role of private banks in channeling funds to developing countries and enable them to continue to serve as a major international conduit of funds. They called on international organizations to devise means of aiding developing countries in finding access to international capital markets.

Ministers noted the report of the high-level Intergovernmental Group of Experts on the Evolution of the International Monetary System and welcomed the Group's statement that the international monetary system is due for a fundamental and comprehensive reform as an integral part of a restructured system of international economic cooperation. They acknowledged the role of UNCTAD as contributory to further discussion on the broader requirements of the future evolution of the international monetary system. They endorsed the developing country experts' view that an orderly and purposeful evolutionary process for the international monetary system was preferable to alternative methods, and supported their desire to devise a system more favorable to the growth of trade and the prospects of development in cooperation with all countries and all relevant institutions.

ROLE OF THE FUND IN FINANCING AND ADJUSTMENT*

Following is a statement delivered by J. de Larosière, Managing Director of the IMF, in presenting the thirty-fifth Annual Report of the Fund:

At its meeting in April of this year, the Interim Committee endorsed three important guidelines for the life of our institution:

It considered that the Fund should stand ready to play a growing role in the adjustment and financing of payments imbalances.

It reaffirmed that the assistance provided by the Fund should be accompanied by the adoption of adjustment programs appropriate to the needs and problems of members in the present economic situation.

It encouraged me to start discussions with potential lenders on the terms and conditions under which the Fund could borrow funds to increase its resources.

In compliance with these guidelines, a considerable amount of work has been accomplished by this institution, although the Executive Board will still have to work further on some aspects of their implementation.

I will outline the results of this work, the decisions adopted, and the future prospects.

(a) With respect to the *financing* of deficits, the Fund must not engage in financing if there is not a strong effort to adjust on the part of the member or if there is no scope for correcting the balance of payments over a reasonable period. The persistence and nature of the present imbalances make this adjustment effort more imperative than ever. But it is also necessary that the amounts of assistance provided by the Fund be adequate to the situation, so that they encourage members to solve their problems and, where possible, exert a catalytic effect on other sources of financing. In this spirit, the Fund has decided to enlarge its assistance significantly. Countries that are able to adopt adequate adjustment programs can now count on access to the Fund's resources that may,

IMF Survey (October 13, 1980), pp. 313–315.

in certain cases, be several times as large as the traditional amounts. This policy has already been translated into fact. This is reflected in the overall rise in the Fund's new lending commitments; these amounted to SDR 4.3 billion during the calendar year 1979, while in the first nine months of 1980 they already came to SDR 5.9 billion.

(b) As regards the nature of the *adjustment* to be undertaken, I would like to describe the new thrust of our policy. First of all, because of the structural aspects of most of the problems, it must be recognized that correction of disequilibria will often need to be extended over a longer period than that considered normal in the past. Second, our programs need to address the structural aspects. This approach must endeavor to create conditions conducive to the improvement of supply. This will require, of course, supportive measures on the demand side so as to keep the claims on resources in a sustainable relationship with their availability. It is only through the pursuit of such a comprehensive macroeconomic approach that inflation can be reduced, the external situation strengthened, and domestic saving promoted in the context of a sensible plan of investment. The adjustment programs we support will thus be an integral part of a longer-term strategy for fostering investment and economic growth. To this end, we have made the necessary arrangements to collaborate closely with the World Bank and other agencies specializing in long-term investment assistance.

Thus, with flexibility and realism the Fund is endeavoring to make its assistance to members increasingly effective. I am fully aware of the claims by some critics that our policy advice has been too harsh. But this criticism, I believe, is largely misplaced. It is the condition of a country's balance of payments—sometimes in conjunction with the low level of official assistance from abroad—that is the true cause of the harsh adjustment measures that sometimes must be adopted in the attempt to restore its payments equilibrium and to open up prospects of improved future growth.

We have learned from experience how difficult it is to reconcile conflicting claims when countries are forced to cut back on their use of resources. The Fund helps with finance and thereby moderates the severity of the adjustment. But it cannot determine the manner in which the pain of adjustment is distributed within the society. For this extends to the heart of the political process, and there we are vigilant to pay due regard to the domestic social and political objectives, to the economic priorities, and to the individual circumstances of members. There is little that the Fund—or, for that matter, any external agency—can do to help with decisions in this area.

The difficulties associated with many adjustment programs could be eased, or even avoided, if members came to the Fund earlier, before the external situation had become so severe as to require drastic action. It is my hope that the various changes now being introduced into our policies on the use of the Fund's resources will induce members to come to the Fund for assistance whenever needed, and without delay.

(c) As to the *means of financing* this new assistance policy, let me first stress that quotas must remain the fundamental source of the financing provided by the Fund to its members. They are a manifestation of the cooperation among governments that constitutes the very essence of the Fund.

By about the end of this year, the supplementary financing facility will be totally committed, and it will be necessary to have recourse to further borrowing as an interim method of financing. Preparatory work on the Eighth General Review of Quotas is to begin soon in the Executive Board, but completion of the whole process will take time. I have therefore begun examining the possibilities of direct borrowing by the Fund from members that are in a strong external position. The reaction I have had to date shows that these countries have a positive attitude to collaboration with the Fund. The discussion continues. Furthermore, with the strong encouragement of the Executive Board, I am proceeding to explore other sources of financing, including market financing. In the coming months it will be necessary to take decisions on these matters in order to assure the necessary continuity in the financing of our institution to meet the needs of its members.

I am conscious that the Fund's borrowed resources are expensive for its members to use, and this affects particularly members with low per capita incomes. Therefore, the Fund has also undertaken to institute an interest subsidy account designed to decrease the cost of using the supplementary financing facility. Part of the resources of this account will be derived from the expected repayments of loans granted by the Trust Fund. I hope that another portion will come from voluntary contributions or loans, preferably on concessional terms, from countries which are in a position to participate in such operations.

In concluding these remarks on the Fund's policies, I should like to draw attention to one proposal under study in the Executive Board that I believe deserves particular support. This is the suggestion that the Fund should establish a food import facility which could alleviate the problems of countries—especially low-income countries—suffering from crop failures or sharp rises in food import costs. The scheme that has been studied appears workable and fully compatible with the revolving character of the Fund's assistance, and its demand on our resources can be limited. Because of the present serious situation of the developing countries, I consider that an early and positive decision on this matter would be an important manifestation of our concern for human issues.

My remarks so far have been directed to the most urgent problems faced by our member countries in the present economic situation. I have traced a consistent set of policies aimed at securing sustainable growth during this decade. I have explained how the Fund, while retaining its special role, is adapting its policies to the new realities. My concluding remarks concern, more broadly, the future of the international monetary system. This is a fundamental question from which even the most urgent day-to-day concerns must not distract us.

We live in a system that is under strain. There are, nevertheless, important and growing areas of stability and consensus in this system, and I will begin by speaking of these. First, the surge of inflation in the 1970s provoked, or hastened, an increasing awareness of the importance of monetary discipline. By this, I do not mean a naïve and mechanistic faith but a growing recognition that continuous monitoring and restraint of monetary expansion is a necessary, though not sufficient, condition for sustainable growth. Monetary targets and the monitoring of monetary aggregates are widespread in the industrial countries, and increasingly so in the developing world. Second, in close relation to this, there has been, over the last two years, a greater degree of stability in the foreign exchange market than most people would have dared to predict. This market has coped remarkably well with large shifts in deficits and surpluses and with other serious international tensions. The European Monetary System is one example of this stability; and, more generally, the principal world currencies have only in rare cases fluctuated beyond a range conducive to appropriate balance of payments adjustment. Third, despite the regrettable failure to decide on the establishment of a substitution account, the Fund's members have reaffirmed their conviction that a strong SDR should be the centerpiece of the international monetary system. The recent decision to simplify the SDR to a five-currency basket will increase its use both by the private sector and by official holders. Furthermore, the Interim Committee has just requested the Executive Board to give early attention to the question of adjusting the SDR interest rate to the full market rate and of eliminating the remaining reconstitution requirement. Also, the importance of the SDR as a stable and attractive international reserve asset will continue to be enhanced through the Fund's borrowing activities.

I will turn now to those aspects of the system on which a consensus among our members still needs to be built.

The recent special session of the UN General Assembly heard interventions on a wide range of subjects of direct concern to the Fund, including the creation and distribution of international liquidity and the decision-making process in international financial institutions. Indeed, over the past decade the Fund has been engaged in a process of self-examination. This has continued intensively in recent months during the preparation of reports for the Interim Committee on the Group of 24's Program of Immediate Action and for the Development Committee on the Brandt Commission's recommendations. One of the most important areas of study has been the creation and distribution of international liquidity. The allocation of SDRs was resumed in 1979 after a hiatus of seven years. We will soon be actively discussing the question of new allocations in order to achieve a level of SDR holdings commensurate with the growth of world trade, the need for global liquidity, and the objective of reversing the falling share of SDRs in members' reserves. Discussion of the "link" between SDR allocations and development assistance has been resumed in the Fund, and new approaches have been put forward which we are going to study again in greater detail after these Meetings.

The issue of decision-making will be an important element underlying the impending Eighth General Review of Quotas. The elements of the formula used in the calculation of Fund quotas will be reviewed, and we shall have to work for selective increases in quotas that reflect the changing importance of countries and groups of countries in the world economy. In all our discussions, and throughout the range of activities we pursue in the Fund, we must ensure that all our members have a sense of real participation in the Fund's affairs.

These issues are not easy to resolve. The interrelated problems of inflation, slow growth, and energy confront the world economy with profound challenges. They call for a quality of creativity and an intensity of cooperation on the part of the international community that is almost unprecedented. Solutions will need to be worked out in a spirit of patience and day-to-day cooperation. I would emphasize that we are determined to address these issues directly, and to arrive at solutions, within the framework of the Fund's basic objectives.

The Fund is a financial institution which, to survive, must serve its members in a practical and businesslike way. Its operational response must be swift and its financial policies sound. But the Fund is also a collaborative institution, founded to promote cooperation between its member countries. If it is to play its full role at the center of the international monetary system, it must be capable of change; it must adapt itself to new realities; it must respond to the needs and aspirations of its membership. It is only in bringing together and blending these two strands in the Fund's nature that we can successfully respond to the economic challenges of the difficult decade that we now face.

The recycling of petrodollars and debt servicing by developing countries may be the problems commanding most attention at the moment. But although responding to immediate pressing needs, the IMF and the international monetary system are still being challenged by questions of longer-term basic reform. It is unlikely that agreement will come quickly on issues involving SDRs, the link, the price of gold, dollar convertibility, asymmetry in the position of the dollar, volatility of exchange rates, rules for management of flexible rates, and control over the volume of international liquidity. But decisions on these issues will shape the future of any world monetary order.

Although recent years have been the most difficult in the history of the IMF, the Fund appears limited to promoting or responding to an evolutionary process in international monetary relations—in the words of its Managing Director, "a policy of taking one step at a time." The economics of disarray—experienced both domestically and internationally—may require a new Bretton Woods agreement to improve policy management in international monetary affairs. But it is unlikely that a C-20 type of reform can be secured, except under the stimulus of a future crisis. We may conclude that it is more likely that "future writers will look back on the C-20 as a hopelessly over-optimistic exercise in constitution writing. It will be a pity for the world, but not a disaster, if that is the verdict of history."[22] The bold creativity of another Bretton Woods still lies in the future.

QUESTIONS

1. The Executive Directors of the IMF published a study in 1972 on *Reform of the International Monetary System.* This report identified five main problem areas that called for new arrangements through international discussion and negotiation:

(i) The exchange-rate mechanism, including both the indications of when changes in par-values are necessary and the respective responsibilities of the deficit and surplus countries for making par-value changes;

(ii) the re-establishment of convertibility and the arrangements for the settlement of imbalances among countries;

(iii) the position in the system of the various reserve assets and in particular the status and function to be given to foreign-exchange reserves, gold, and SDRs;

(iv) the problem of disequilibrating capital movements and what might be done to lessen the intense market pressures that accompany them; and

(v) the possibility of new provisions in the Fund arrangements for the special needs of developing countries.

Do you think that these five problem areas still require international discussion and negotiation? What policy recommendations would you make regarding each problem area?

2. Consider the debate over objective indicators for adjustment. The financial ministers of the European Economic Community opposed an automatic adjustment mechanism as unworkable and argued that many indicators should be used to decide when exchange-rate changes are needed.

a. What do you consider to be the different implications of mandatory or automatic measures of adjustment as contrasted with presumptive rules that merely request a country to consult with the IMF on possible policy readjustments? How is this problem related to international sanctions?

b. Do you think that a "normal" level of reserves is a sufficient indicator? How should a "normal" level be measured? What other indicators might merit consideration?

c. Does the problem of quantitative or objective indicators involve judgments of fact? or value? or both?

d. Is it a valid criticism that reserve indicators are retrospective and insufficiently refined, pointing to past maladjustments rather than present

22 John Williamson, *The Failure of World Monetary Reform 1971–74* (1977), p. 203.

or future needs and unable to take account of the composition of the balance of payments?

3. Although recognizing that prompter readjustment of clearly undervalued as well as overvalued exchange rates will have to be encouraged in the reconstruction of the international monetary system, Professor Robert Triffin has also stated: "Equally, or more important, will be a system of reserve creation and management, adjusting the total levels of reserves to world needs and making use of them for internationally agreed objectives."

a. Do you think international monetary negotiations have given enough attention to reserve creation—its amount, composition, and distribution?

b. Would you agree with Triffin's proposal that "reserve accounts with the IMF should become the basic instrument for all international settlements and reserve accumulation," whereas "holdings of foreign national currencies should be strictly limited to an agreed ceiling (5 per cent of annual imports or 15 per cent of global reserves) and any currency balances acquired from the market and exceeding this ceiling should be immediately exchanged into the IMF reserve accounts?"

c. Triffin contends that the reformed system would correct the three major shortcomings of the gold-convertible, or gold-inconvertible reserve currency standard: (i) its wild inflationary potential; (ii) the frustration of the adjustment mechanism of balances of payments; and (iii) the financing of the gold market—and increasingly in recent years—of the uncontrolled balance-of-payments deficits of the richest and most adequately capitalized countries, rather than the poorer countries most in need of international capital for their development.

Do you agree with Triffin's diagnosis and reform proposals?

4. Replying to the question "Is monetary reform still desirable?", Professor John Williamson lists five features of the existing arrangements that give cause for concern: (i) the degree of volatility that exchange rates have exhibited during the floating period; (ii) the total lack of control over the volume of international liquidity because of the absence of asset settlement and the unconstrained freedom to place reserves in the Euromarkets and the fluctuations in the gold price; (iii) the maldistribution of seigniorage to reserve centers and possible gold holders; (iv) the continued asymmetry in the position of the U.S. dollar; and (v) the weakness of the defenses against the pursuit of aggressive exchange rate policies.

Do you agree with Williamson's list? Do the weaknesses of the present system constitute a case for moving to a preferable system? If so, how, exactly, would you recommend that the preferable system be established?

5. Would you agree that "the increasing size and mobility of short-term capital and changes in geographical patterns of production by international firms might be the main cause of endemic world monetary instability?" Have international monetary negotiations squarely faced this problem? What controls, if any, would you recommend over international private capital movements?

6. At the time of Bretton Woods, Professor John H. Williams of Harvard argued for a "key currency" approach to international monetary stability. Williams contended that the U.S. dollar and the pound sterling would be the key currencies after the war in the sense that they would play dominant roles in world trade, finance, and foreign-exchange markets. He emphasized that international stability would depend essentially on monetary control within the United States and Britain and cooperation between them. Williams suggested that external monetary stabilization should begin with plans for stabilizing the dollar-sterling rate and for measures on internal policy in the "key currency" countries.

Do you believe that a key currency approach now has any merit—for a new tripartite currency arrangement between the U.S. dollar, Deutsche mark and yen? [*See* Ronald I. McKinnon, *A New Tripartite Monetary Agreement or a Limping Dollar Standard?* Princeton Essays in International Finance, No. 106 (October 1974).]

7. Out of dedication to nondiscrimination, the IMF has applied the doctrine of uniformity in its treatment of member countries. It can be argued, however, that uniform rights and obligations do not have equal effects on members. The argument is that obligations are more onerous and rights more beneficial for some members than for others. The criticism is expressed as the asymmetrical treatment of members, and it is made in favor of a more symmetrical operation of the international monetary system.

Do you think that the Fund should depart from the uniformity doctrine in order to give special treatment to developing countries?

8. "The concept of an international monetary system in which due emphasis is placed on the word 'system' now implies a body of coherent purposes and principles, together with rights and obligations accepted by countries in order to give effect to the purposes and principles, and probably an organization to perform the duties of surveillance and administration." Does such a system now exist?

9. "Because nation-states exist and desire to maintain sovereignty over national monetary policy, it is vain to hope for an integrated worldwide monetary system of which the IMF would be the centralized monetary

authority. The best course would be to ignore the whole question of international liquidity and to encourage countries to remove controls on both capital flows and trade, as well as to permit full flexibility of exchange rates. No rules for managing the exchange rates can be laid down—not even to central banks from acting as exchange-market participants, from holding desired portfolios, and from gambling from time to time on the foreign exchanges." Do you agree?

10. Many who argue for a return to the gold standard maintain that the gold standard is a political and social institution. "It's a special means to achieve a particular end: a stable price level." Do you think that a return to the gold standard that President Roosevelt ended in 1933 would now be an effective way to limit the money supply and hence inflation?

11. The technical substance of the discipline of international economics has improved enormously since the time of the Bretton Woods Conference. But progress toward international monetary reform since 1971 does not compare with what was accomplished in three weeks at Bretton Woods. How do you account for this? Is it due to the inadequacies and shortcomings in the procedure of monetary negotiations, or are there other reasons? Would you have any suggestions for improving the process of collective decision-making in international monetary affairs?

READINGS

1. *On general problems of international monetary reform:*

Acheson, A. L. K. et al., *Bretton Woods Revisited* (1972).

Aliber, Robert Z. (ed.), *The Political Economy of Monetary Reform* (1977).

Artus, Jacques C. and Andrew D. Crockett, *Floating Exchange Rates and the Need for Surveillance*, Princeton Essays in International Finance, No. 127 (May 1978).

Bergsten, C. Fred, *Reforming the Dollar* (1972).

Bhagwati, Jagdish et al., "The International Monetary System: A Symposium," *Journal of International Economics* (September 1972).

Chrystal, K. Alec, *International Money and the Future of the SDR*, Princeton Essays in International Finance, No. 128 (1978).

Cohen, Benjamin J., *Organizing the World's Money* (1977).

de Vries, Tom, "Reforming International Monetary Relations—An Analysis," *Finance & Development* (September 1976).

de Vries, Tom, *On the Meaning and Future of the European Monetary*

System, Princeton Essays in International Finance, No. 138 (1980).
Gold, Sir Joseph, "Substitution in the International Monetary System," *Journal of International Law* (Spring 1980), pp. 265–326.
Hirsch, Fred et al., *Alternatives to Monetary Disorder* (1977).
Katz, Samuel I. (ed.), *United States-European Monetary Relations* (1979).
Mundell, Robert and Jacques J. Polak (eds.), *The New International Monetary System* (1977).
Murphy, J. Carter, *The International Monetary System* (1979).
Trezise, Philip H. (ed.), *The European Monetary System: Its Promise and Prospects* (1980).
Triffin, Robert, *Gold and the Dollar Crisis: Yesterday and Tomorrow,* Princeton Essays in International Finance, No. 132 (1978).
Willett, Thomas D., *Floating Exchange Rates and International Monetary Reform* (1977).

2. *On the role of the IMF and international monetary reform:*
See *IMF Survey, Finance & Development,* various issues since 1972.

3. *On the position of the developing countries:*
Bird, Graham, *The International Monetary System and the Less Developed Countries* (1978).
Cline, William R., *International Monetary Reform and the Developing Countries* (1976).
Diaz-Alejandro, Carlos, *Less Developed Countries and the Post-1971 International Financial System,* Princeton Essays in International Finance, No. 108 (April 1975).
Johnson, Harry G., "International Monetary Reform and the Less Developed Countries," *Malayan Economic Review* (April 1966).
Kafka, Alexandre, "The New Exchange Rate Regime and the Developing Countries," *Journal of Finance* (June 1978).
Lal, Deepak, *A Liberal International Economic Order: The International Monetary System and Economic Development,* Princeton Essays in International Finance, No. 139 (1980).
Leipziger, D. M. (ed.), *The International Monetary System and the Developing Nations* (1976).
Symposium on "The International Monetary System and the New International Order," *Development Dialogue* (1980), No. 2.

APPENDIX

INTERNATIONAL MONETARY CHRONOLOGY

April 1925	Britain returns to the gold-bullion standard at the prewar parity between the U.S. dollar and the pound sterling
September 1931	Bank of England suspends gold payments Britain abandons the gold standard and allows pound to depreciate Other countries follow
April 1933	United States leaves gold standard
January 1934	U.S. Gold Reserve Act of 1934 raises monetary price of gold from $20.67 to $35.00 an ounce of gold
April 1943	British plan for an International Clearing Union was published with American variation on similar theme
July 1–22, 1944	The Articles of Agreement of the International Monetary Fund and those of the World Bank are formulated by 44 nations at the United Nations Monetary and Financial Conference, held at Bretton Woods, New Hampshire
July 31, 1945	Bretton Woods Agreements Act signed by President Truman
March 8–18, 1946	Inaugural Meeting of Board of Governors of IMF, Savannah, Georgia
March 1, 1947	IMF begins operation

May 8, 1947	The first drawing from the Fund takes place
September 18–29, 1949	Exchange rates of European countries devalued in amounts ranging from 30.5 per cent for pound sterling to 12.3 per cent for Belgian franc
August 12, 1957	France devalues the franc by 16.7 per cent
December 29, 1958	France devalues the franc by 14.8 per cent
March 1959	Professor Robert Triffin made the first proposal for an enlarged Fund and for the creation of new type of international reserve asset, proposing that all reserves, except gold holdings, be centralized in the Fund
January 5, 1962	The Executive Directors of IMF approve proposal for IMF to borrow from ten industrial countries—General Arrangements to Borrow (GAB)
February 27, 1963	The Fund's compensatory financing facility is established
November 20, 1964	First use of GAB as the United Kingdom borrows $1 billion from IMF
November 25, 1964	Credits of $3 billion extended to the United Kingdom, the United States and ten other countries
February 5, 1964	President de Gaulle calls for return to gold standard
May 12, 1965	The United Kingdom draws additional $1.4 billion from IMF
September, 1967	Outline of Special Drawing Rights Facility approved at IMF annual meeting in Rio de Janiero
November 17, 1967	Bank of England sells more than $1 billion in foreign-exchange market to support sterling exchange rate
November 18, 1967	Britain announces 14.3 per cent devaluation of pound, from $2.80 to $2.40

March 16–17, 1968	Gold pool members abandon gold pool and establish two-tier gold arrangement
April 30– May 9, 1969	Bundesbank absorbs $4 billion inflow in order to hold exchange rate
June 25, 1969	The buffer stock financing facility is established in the IMF
July 28, 1969	The First Amendment to the Articles of Agreement of the IMF, establishing a facility based on the SDR, goes into effect
August 8, 1969	France devalues the franc by 11.1 per cent
October 24, 1969	Germany establishes new par value, revaluing the mark upward by 9.3 per cent
January 1, 1970	First allocation of SDRs, in the amount of $3.4 billion
January– December, 1970	United States has balance-of-payments deficit of $9.8 billion
January 1, 1971	Second allocation of SDRs in amount of $3 billion
April, 1971	Germany acquires $3 billion of foreign exchange, in holding exchange rate
May 4, 1971	Bundesbank absorbs $1 billion inflow
May 5, 1971	Bundesbank takes in $1 billion in first hour and then suspends official operation in foreign-exchange market
August 12, 1971	President Nixon and economic officials go to Camp David
August 15, 1971	The United States informs the Fund that it will no longer convert dollars into gold and other reserve assets
August 16–20, 1971	Bank of Japan takes in $2 billion in attempt to hold the exchange rate
August 23–27, 1971	Bank of Japan takes in another $2 billion and then decides to let the yen float
December 17–18, 1971	Group of Ten meets at Smithsonian Institution in Washington and agrees on

	a temporary regime and central rates and wider margins, including devaluation of dollar
March 7, 1972	EEC decides to narrow margins for their currencies to 2.25 per cent to form EEC "snake" in the Smithsonian "tunnel"
July 26, 1972	Formation of IMF Committee on Reform of the International System—Committee of Twenty—approved by Board of Governors of the IMF
February 5–9, 1973	Bundesbank purchases $5 billion to hold exchange rate
March, 1973	EEC introduces a joint float of their currencies against the dollar; in effect, a new exchange rate regime with floating rates against the dollar emerged
September 23, 1973	The first Outline of Reform prepared by the Committee of Twenty is published
November 12, 1973	Central bank governors, meeting in Basle, terminate two-tier gold agreement
December 23, 1973	Oil price raised again, quadrupling it from level of early October
January 17–18, 1974	Committee of Twenty decides to adopt evolutionary approach to international monetary reform and abandons timetable for full-scale monetary reform
June 14, 1974	Committee of Twenty issues *Outline of Reform*, and concludes its work
October 3, 1974	New Interim Committee of IMF holds its first meeting
January 7–8, 1976	Interim Committee, meeting in Kingston, Jamaica, completes interim report, with agreement on IMF quota increases, legalization of floating

	rates, treatment of gold, and Trust Fund
April 29, 1977	The Executive Board of the IMF approves a document on "Surveillance Over Exchange Rate Policies"
August 29, 1977	Executive Directors of IMF establish supplementary financing facility
March 30, 1978	Consent by members of IMF to increases in quotas under Sixth General Review of Quotas, raising quotas to SDR 39 billion
April 1, 1978	The Second Amendment enters into force. Members of IMF are given freedom of choice, in their exchange arrangements, but are bound by certain obligations and subject to surveillance by the Fund
April, 1980	Failure of Interim Committee to agree at Hamburg meeting on provisions for a substitution account for dollar
December, 1980	IMF quota increases under Seventh General Review to SDR 60 billion from SDR 39 billion
January, 1981	Allocation of SDR 4 billion. SDR basket reduced from sixteen to five currencies